GLOBAL FINANCIAL MANAGEMENT

GLOBAL FINANCIAL

MANAGEMENT

THOMAS J. O'BRIEN

JOHN WILEY & SONS, INC.

Brisbane • **Toronto** • **New York** • **Singapore** • **Chichester**

ACQUISITIONS EDITOR   Whitney Blake
MARKETING MANAGER   Karen Allman
PRODUCTION EDITOR   Edward Winkleman
INTERIOR DESIGNER   David Levy
MANUFACTURING MANAGER   Mark Cirillo
PHOTO EDITOR   Hilary Newman
FREELANCE ILLUSTRATION COOR.   Gene Aiello
COVER DESIGNER   Dawn L. Stanley
COVER ILLUSTRATION   Chattum Design Group, Inc.

This book was set in ITC Garamond Light by ATLIS Graphics and printed and bound
by R.R. Donnelley, Crawfordsville. The cover was printed by Phoenix.

Recognizing the importance of preserving what has been written, it is a
policy of John Wiley & Sons, Inc., to have books of enduring value pulished
in the United States printed on acid-free paper, and we exert our best
efforts to that end.

This paper in this book was manufactured by a mill whose forest management programs include
sustained yield harvesting of its timberlands. Sustained yield harvesting principles ensure that
the number of trees cut each year does not exceed the amount of new growth.

Library of Congress Cataloging-in-Publication Data

O'Brien, Thomas J.
    Global financial management / Thomas O'Brien.
        p.   cm.
    Includes bibliographical references.
    ISBN 0-471-57854-1 (alk. paper)
        1. International finance.   2. Foreign exchange.   I. Title.
    HG3881.O263   1996
    658.15'99—dc20   95-9585
                                                                  CIP

Printed in the United States of America

10 9 8 7 6 5 4 3 2 1

PREFACE

This text is a result of the development of my own course in international finance. From the outset, I oriented my course to cover corporate financial management with an emphasis on the role played by markets. I wanted a course based on the intellectual content of academic finance but also wanted to stress real-world developments such as financial engineering, currency swaps, and the creative financial structuring of cross-border deals. In addition, I wanted to extend and apply the key concepts of introductory financial management. For example, I wanted to incorporate financial leverage ideas when discussing the use of foreign currency debt financing. It was important also that the topic of capital budgeting build on the CAPM application in an introductory financial management course, by employing global extension of the CAPM that has been developed in the literature. None of the existing international texts at the time used the CAPM in capital budgeting, much less mentioned the advances of the CAPM in a global context. As I developed my course material along these parameters, I came to realize how much my notes diverged from the existing books on the market, and feedback from other professors teaching this course encouraged me to develop my work into a new text for the global financial management course. This text is the result of that effort.

Approach and Objectives

Global Financial Management supports a modern course in global finance by integrating mainstream concepts of finance into a broad global approach. By emphasizing the firm's financial decisions and its interaction with various financial markets, *Global Financial Management* offers a strong basis for real-world concepts and applications by its emphasis on financial engineering and currency, swaps, valuation and financial leverage concepts, and global asset pricing theory. The text covers topics of finance by focusing on financial structuring in global markets, economic currency exposure and capital structure, and international capital budgeting within a global asset pricing framework.

Organization

The book is organized into four parts. Part I, Global Markets, focuses on exchange rates and establishes the framework to enable students to understand and discuss current events as they occur in the real world during the course of the semester and beyond. Forward exchange is discussed in Chapter 4 and serves as a transition to Part II, which covers financial structuring in modern global financial markets. The three chapters in Part II offer students extensive coverage of eurobonds (Chapter 5), currency swaps (Chapter 6), and use of options (Chapter 7). Part III focuses on corporate exposure to foreign exchange risk, especially on economic exposure. Unique to this text is Chapter 9's analysis of foreign currency debt in a firm's capital structure. Chapter 10 compares operating and equity exposures with accounting exposures. Part IV is devoted mostly to capital budgeting and the application of global asset pricing theory. Chapter 12 concentrates on forecasting exchange rates for converting anticipated foreign currency cash flows into forecasted base currency cash flows. The final chapter presents some additional material on multicurrency issues. This chapter and the individual chapter appendices are ideal discussion topics for a more advanced class.

Features

While based on a firm theoretical foundation, *Global Financial Management* stresses application and focuses on real-world firms and examples. This is evident throughout the text, as well as in highlighted boxes. By using a base currency other than the dollar in many examples, the student is often oriented to a non-dollar point of view and is subjected to a broader perspective in the course. To further encourage students to learn and understand these applications, a number of example problems are included within each chapter in addition to the end of chapter problems. All chapters contain a glossary of key terms to review important concepts and definitions. Where appropriate, discussion questions are included and are designed to encourage students to take these ideas further and to allow them to think beyond the obvious. Select chapters are followed by an appendix that includes more advanced material to further satisfy the intellectual appetite and curiosity of the more advanced students. Diagrams throughout the text assist the learning process and provide easy visual reference to important concepts. Photos have been chosen to clarify and highlight important points.

Supplements

An *Instructor's Manual* is available which includes notes to the instructor for each chapter, answers to discussion questions, and solutions to problems. Quizzes for each chapter are also included in the manual. In addition, figures from the text are available in electronic format for use with presentation software such as Powerpoint. A stand-alone software package called *Analytical Application Software for Global Financial Management (AASGFM)* is also available for users of the text. This is a comprehensive software tool to assist students and instructors in global financial management techquines. It is designed to operate on any IBM-compatible, DOS-based personal computer. AASGFM is a collection of flexible applications that can be used for solving a set of similar problems, rather than a set of spreadsheet templates that solve a specific problem. It is a useful tool, not only in class, but also in the students' future careers in global financial management. AASGFM can be used for in-class demonstrations, sensitivity analysis, and general reviews and can save time normally spent on tedious number crunching, which is better devoted to developing theoretical concepts in global financial management.

Acknowledgements

The text was used in my own class throughout the development process and was class tested by several other people teaching the course. I wish to thank Bill Clyde, Quinnipiac College; Mary Cutler, Central Connecticut State University; Qayyum Kahn, University of North Carolina-Charlotte; and especially Ken Nunn, University of Conecticut, for providing invaluable feedback related to their use of the early manuscript drafts. Pre-publication reviews were also supplied by a variety of other professors teaching the global finance course. I am indebted to these people whose feedback and suggestions provided me with invaluable assistance in the development of this work. Their ideas and comments have been incorporated to the best of my ability in the published version. I am especially grateful to the following for their help and input: Michael Palmer, University of Colorado-Boulder; Louis Chan, University of Illinois; P. John Lymberopolous, University of Colorado-Boulder; Craig

Holden, Indiana University; Jack Schnabel, Wilfred Laurier University; Anthony F. Herbst, University of Texas/El Paso; James Owers, Georgia State University; Richard A. DeFusco, University of Nebraska-Lincoln; James O. Desrermaux, Corpus Christi State University, and Haragopal Banerjee, Ball State University.

A number of well-informed and well-respected practitioners have provided me with valuable insights into the practical side of global finance. These include Robert Dubil of Chase Bank, Chris Witsky of United Technologies, Dave Del Ponte of Aetna, Graham Spiers of Travelers, John Fitzpatrick of Union Carbide, and Walter Conklin and Peter Clifford at John Wiley & Sons. I wish also to thank John Nalesnik and Don Quartucci at the currency desk at Shawmut Bank for allowing me to look over their shoulders and ask questions. An accounting colleague at the University of Connecticut, Rob Hoskin, provided me with valuable assistance in developing Chapter 10. My chairman at UConn, Keith B. Johnson, provided strong support for the project in many ways, not the least of which was years of continuously providing me with relevant clippings from business newspapers and periodicals, which helped enormously in my preparing of the real-world examples and problems. Susan Mangiero's help in this same effort was also greatly appreciated. A number of my students, including Carlos Jaramillo, Yansi Eraslan, Ozcan Sezer, and David Biederman, were also of great assistance.

I would like also to thank the Wiley team effort in producing the final published book. Throughout the project, the executive editor, Whitney Blake, and assistant editor, Ellen Ford, supported and guided this project through the development process. The production editor, Ed Winkleman, and copyeditor, Sally Ann Bailey, as well as Hilary Newman (photo research), Gene Aiello and Sigmund Malinowski (illustration department), and Dawn Stanley (designer), all contributed greatly to make the final product the fine book it is. To all, I am truly grateful.

PHOTO CREDITS Page 11: COMSTOCK, Inc. **Page 20:** Bernard Roussel/The Image bank. **Page 35:** David Henstock/Tony Stone Images/New York, Inc. **Page 47:** Tony Stone Images/New York, Inc. **Page 61:** COMSTOCK, Inc. **Page 79:** Michael Simpson/FPG International. **Page 95:** COMSTOCK, Inc. **Page 114:** Burt Glinn/Magnum Photos, Inc. **Page 130:** Bob Thomason/Tony Stone Images/New York, Inc. **Page 145:** COMSTOCK, Inc. **Page 169:** Michael Simpson/FPG International. **Page 178:** COMSTOCK, Inc. **Page 194:** Courtesy United Nations. **Page 205:** Richard Gaul/FPG International. **Page 226:** Ron Lowery/Tony Stone Images/New York, Inc. **Page 241:** Marc Grimberg/The Image Bank. **Page 263:** Courtesy United Nations. **Page 275:** COMSTOCK, Inc. **Page 293:** COMSTOCK, Inc. **Page 303:** Sylvain Grandadam/Tony Stone Images/New York, Inc. **Page 324:** COMSTOCK, Inc. **Page 337:** Ted Horowitz/The Stock Market. **Page 354:** COMSTOCK, INC. **Page 361:** Courtesy Grand Metropolitan. **Page 377:** COMSTOCK, Inc. **Page 389:** COMSTOCK, Inc.

CONTENTS

chapter **12**

EXCHANGE RATE FORECASTING AND GLOBAL CAPITAL BUDGETING 343

appendix

THE CORRELATION ISSUE   367

chapter **13**

MULTICURRENCY EXPOSURE ISSUES   370

part I

GLOBAL

MARKETS

chapter 1

EXCHANGE RATES AND GLOBAL FINANCIAL MANAGEMENT

Currency Exchange and Exchange Rates

The exchange of currencies is fundamental to *global financial management*. The unpredictable fluctuations in the rates of exchange between currencies is a major issue that underlies much of the material in *Global Financial Management*.

CURRENCY EXCHANGE

Let us begin with a simple explanation of a currency exchange in the context of an international business transaction. Assume that Sam's Stores in the United States imports sweaters from Crown Materials Ltd. in England. Naturally, Sam's is ultimately concerned about its financial results in terms of the U.S. dollar. Thus, we'll say that Sam's has a base currency of U.S. dollars. On the other hand, Crown Materials' natural base currency is the British pound sterling. Given these different viewpoints, Sam's and Crown must agree upon the currency in which the payment is to be made.

If Sam's sends payment in pounds, then Sam's must first "buy" the pounds from its bank in exchange for U.S. dollars. If Sam's sends payment in U.S. dollars, then Crown Materials will exchange those funds with its own bank for pounds. Either transaction takes place in the *retail foreign exchange market*, or *retail FX market* for short, which describes the market for transactions that take place between business firms and banks.

The retail exchange of currencies is a fundamental service provided by banks to corporate customers. In either situation in our example, a bank provides its retail customer with British pounds in return for U.S. dollars. To provide this service, the bank needs a place to "buy" pounds and "sell" dollars. A likely candidate for such a transaction would be another bank that happens to be in the process of facilitating a similar import/export transaction, but in the reverse direction. Such a transaction between banks is said to take place in the wholesale *interbank (FX) market.*

The interbank market operates globally, with banks of different nationalities exchanging currencies routinely. In fact, due to the immense need for exchange transactions to support international trade, the interbank exchange market is vast: Roughly 1 trillion U.S. dollars' worth of currency trading occurs daily; of this amount, about 10% is natural retail FX market activity. The rest is mostly interbank trading. The reason for the high volume of interbank trading is that in addition to the direct support of the retail FX market, there is a significant amount of speculation and arbitrage (described later) in the interbank FX market.

The foreign exchange market is unregulated and open 24 hours a day. Concentration of trading follows the business day around the globe, from Tokyo-Singapore-Hong Kong-Sydney to Bahrain, to London-Zurich-Paris, and finally to New York. About 200 banks around the globe operate on a large scale in the interbank foreign exchange market as dealers, or market-makers. These dealers maintain trading positions in various currencies.

The movement of account balances does not necessarily require the paper flow of a physical draft or check. Consider *SWIFT,* the Society for Worldwide Financial Telecommunication, by which the foregoing transactions can be accomplished electronically. SWIFT, begun in 1977, connects over 3000 banks and investment banks in 67 countries. The debits and credits are transmitted from country to country via central, interconnected, operating centers in Brussels, Amsterdam, and Culpeper, Virginia.

If a bank is a small, regional bank without direct trading access to the global interbank market, the bank may obtain the currency from one of the larger interbank participants through one of a number of established foreign exchange brokers. The larger player will "buy" the exporter's currency in the interbank market and, in turn, "sell" the currency, at a markup, to the smaller bank. Large banks also deal in this fashion to their retail customers.

Retail demand for currency exchange originates from other sources in addition to import/export business. One example is *foreign direct investment,* which is the investment of capital into overseas plant and equipment. If a German company wishes to build a plant or buy an existing one in Canada, the German company is likely to need to sell some German marks (abbreviated DM for Deutsche mark) and buy some Canadian dollars (C$) to make the transaction. Figure 1-1 depicts the roles of various players in the retail and interbank FX markets.

Another source of retail demand for foreign exchange is cross-border *port-*

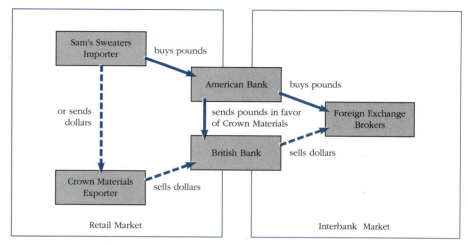

FIGURE 1-1   Relationship Between the Principal Players in the Retail and Interbank Markets

folio investment. Portfolio investment applies to financial securities, as opposed to foreign direct investment into physical capital. (Technically, the purchase of more than 10% of a company's equity by a foreign investor is regarded as a foreign direct investment rather than a portfolio investment.) To see the influence of portfolio investment trades on exchange rates, consider a manager of a portfolio of bonds who wishes to invest in some Japanese bonds, either to take advantage of high interest rates or for diversification. The manager will need to exchange domestic currency into yen to buy the bonds. Upon the liquidation of all or a portion of the foreign holdings, the manager will need to sell the yen for domestic currency. The demand for retail FX services for international portfolio trades is actually larger than the demand by companies engaged in the trade of international goods.

EXCHANGE RATE QUOTES

The convention in the currency market for years has been to quote *most* currencies as the amount of currency per one U.S. dollar. For example, a quote of 5.05 for the French franc (denoted FF) means 5.05 French francs per U.S. dollar, or 5.05 FF/$. A quote of 125 for the Japanese yen means 125 yen per U.S. dollar, or 125 ¥/$. When the exchange rate is quoted this way, it is said to be in *European terms,* even though the currency involved is not necessarily a European currency.

Although most exchange rate quotes are conventionally in European terms, a few are typically quoted by market participants in reciprocal terms, that is, U.S. dollars per unit of other currency, referred to as *American terms.* The most significant currency that is conventionally quoted in American terms is the British pound sterling (£), nicknamed "cable" in the currency market. For example, a quote of 1.75 for the British pound means 1.75 U.S. dollars per British pound, or 1.75 $/£.

The use of the European terms convention for most currencies is reported to have originated when the U.S. dollar became the world's dominant international currency. It was common for those outside of the United States to seek to know the "price of a dollar" in terms of their own currency. European terms exchange rate quotes may be interpreted in this fashion.

The tradition to quote American terms for the British pound is reported to have two sources. One story is that since London is the center of the global currency market, London traders dictated the dollars per pound format for that exchange rate (and for other British Commonwealth currencies). Although the label "American terms" was eventually given to this form of quote by textbooks, this label is contrary to the motivations of the London traders; their choice of "dollars per pound" was for their own convenience and prestige, since the quote could be interpreted as the "price of a pound" (in dollars). Another reason that has been reported is that the custom originated when the British Commonwealth currencies involved were on nondecimal bases, which made them cumbersome to quote in European terms. For example, prior to 1972, a British penny was 1/12th of a shilling, which was itself 1/20th of a pound; a penny has been 1/100th of a pound in England since the early 1970s, but the foreign exchange quotation conventions continue out of tradition.

The *European Currency Unit,* or *ECU,* is also conventionally quoted in American terms, and thus $ per ECU. The ECU is not formally a currency, but a hypothetical basket of major European currencies. Another hypothetical basket is the *Special Drawing Right,* or *SDR,* which is the International Monetary Fund's basket of major currencies. The composition of the SDR is altered from time to time. An end-of-chapter exercise demonstrates the computation of the value of an SDR.

The tradition to quote some exchange rates in European terms and some in American terms contributes to the difficulty in initially understanding changes in currency values. Despite this situation, this text will generally cite exchange rates using the market conventions. The reason is that getting used to the conventions is part of the process of understanding global financial management, and the sooner you get used to these conventions, the sooner you will absorb pertinent items in the news.

Figure 1-2 displays exchange rate quotes for a number of major currencies. The figure is reprinted directly from the January 23, 1995 issue of *The Financial Times,* a daily newspaper originating in London and distributed globally. Note that Figure 1-2 supplies some commonly used currency abbreviations; however, be aware that alternative abbreviations are sometimes used in this text and elsewhere. The first column of numbers in Figure 1-2, labeled "Closing mid-point" may be interpreted as the final exchange rates at the close of London trading, ignoring transaction costs. The legend for Figure 1-2 indicates that the British pound, the Irish punt, and the ECU are quoted in

DOLLAR SPOT FORWARD AGAINST THE DOLLAR

Jan 20		Closing mid-point	Change on day	Bid/offer spread	Day's mid high	low
Europe						
Austria	(Sch)	10.6500	−0.125	475 - 525	10.6700	10.6425
Belgium	(BFr)	31.1150	−0.4175	000 - 300	31.3150	31.0790
Denmark	(DKr)	5.9518	−0.0817	508 - 528	6.0425	5.9508
Finland	(FM)	4.6666	−0.071	627 - 704	4.7193	4.6620
France	(FFr)	5.2230	−0.0703	220 - 240	5.2520	5.2197
Germany	(DM)	1.5087	−0.0216	083 - 090	1.5166	1.5060
Greece	(Dr)	234.900	−3.55	800 - 000	238.850	234.800
Ireland	(I£)	1.5756	+0.0196	748 - 763	1.5779	1.5683
Italy	(L)	1591.50	−20.5	100 - 200	1602.00	1591.00
Luxembourg	(LFr)	31.1150	−0.4175	000 - 300	31.3150	31.0790
Netherlands	(Fl)	1.6919	−0.0237	916 - 921	1.7003	1.6898
Norway	(NKr)	6.6035	−0.089	025 - 045	6.6695	6.5940
Portugal	(Es)	157.770	−0.33	720 - 820	157.820	155.700
Spain	(Pta)	131.230	−2.03	180 - 280	132.150	131.180
Sweden	(SKr)	7.4107	−0.0948	057 - 157	7.4531	7.4028
Switzerland	(SFr)	1.2685	−0.0206	680 - 690	1.2766	1.2655
UK	(£)	1.5901	+0.0203	897 - 904	1.5915	1.5839
Ecu	–	1.2530	+0.0165	525 - 535	1.2535	1.2466
SDR†	–	1.46395	–	-	-	-
Americas						
Argentina	(Peso)	1.0002	-	001 - 003	1.0003	1.0001
Brazil	(Cr)	0.8485	−0.0005	480 - 490	0.8490	0.8470
Canada	(C$)	1.4255	+0.0064	252 - 257	1.4267	1.4205
Mexico	(New Peso)	5.6950	+0.21	700 - 200	5.7200	5.6600
USA	($)	-	-	-	-	-
Pacific/Middle East/Africa						
Australia	(A$)	1.3006	−0.0052	002 - 011	1.3051	1.3002
Hong Kong	(HK$)	7.7330	−0.0067	325 - 335	7.7453	7.7310
India	(Rs)	31.3700	-	675 - 725	31.3725	31.3675
Israel	(Shk)	2.9972	−0.0156	947 - 997	3.0122	2.9947
Japan	(Y)	99.1700	−0.5	400 - 000	99.6500	98.9900
Malaysia	(M$)	2.5515	−0.002	510 - 520	2.5540	2.5440
New Zealand	(NZ$)	1.5576	+0.0009	572 - 584	1.5634	1.5572
Philipines	(Peso)	24.6500	+0.05	500 - 500	24.8500	24.4500
Saudi Arabia	(SR)	3.7506	-	504 - 507	3.7507	3.7504
Singapore	(S$)	1.4455	−0.007	450 - 460	1.4500	1.4450
S Africa (Com.)	(R)	3.5318	−0.0125	310 - 325	3.5375	3.5230
S Africa (Fin.)	(R)	4.1350	−0.03	250 - 450	4.1600	4.1250
South Korea	(Won)	792.650	+0.15	600 - 700	792.900	792.200
Taiwan	(T$)	26.2765	−0.0055	730 - 800	26.2850	26.2630
Thailand	(Bt)	25.0770	+0.0095	720 - 820	25.1300	25.0350

†SDR rate for Jan 19. Bid/offer spreads in the Dollar Spot table show only the last three decimal places. Forward rates are not directly quoted to the market but are implied by current interest rates. UK, Ireland & ECU are quoted in US currency. J.P. Morgan nominal indices Jan 19. Base average 1990=100

FIGURE 1–2   Currency Quotes as Found in the January 23, 1995, *Financial Times*
Source: Financial Times, January 23, 1995. Reprinted with permission.

American terms. The SDR is also quoted in American terms, that is, dollars per one SDR. All the other rates are in European terms. (The part of the legend about forward rates refers to a section of the table that has been omitted here, but will be discussed in Chapter 4.) The currencies of other prior members of the British empire—Australia, Canada, New Zealand, Saudi Arabia, and India—are all quoted in Figure 1-2 in European terms, despite a historical convention for the interbank market to internally quote ex-British empire members' currencies in American terms. *The Wall Street Journal,* for example, quotes the Canadian dollar in American terms in the "Markets Diary" that appears daily on page C1.

TRANSACTION COSTS

Like many securities, exchange rates are quoted by market–making dealers at two rates, a buy rate (the "bid") and a sell rate (the "offer"). The difference between the two rates is the "spread." The spread is the natural profit to the dealer for his service of market-making and is a transaction cost to the other trader. The bid is the exchange rate at which the market-maker will buy the currency whose symbol is in the denominator of the exchange rate quote. For example, using the quotes from Figure 1-2, a market-maker will buy pounds for 1.5897 $/£ and sell pounds for 1.5904 $/£. Of course, we could also say that the market-maker would also be selling dollars (for pounds) at the bid rate of 1.5897 $/£ and buying dollars (for pounds) at 1.5904 $/£. However, thinking this way may be confusing, and it is easier to remember that the bid is the rate at which the market-maker will buy the currency whose symbol is in the denominator. Since the Austrian schilling is quoted in European terms, that is, schillings per dollar, the 10.6475 bid for the Austrian schilling in Figure 1-2 means that the market-maker would buy dollars (and pay Austrian schillings) at 10.6475 Sch/$. The market-maker would sell dollars (for schillings) at the offer rate of 10.6525 Sch/$. Thus, a trader who wishes to buy pounds with dollars is faced with the offer rate, but the same trader would face the bid rate if he or she wishes to buy schillings with dollars. Confused? Do not worry, because this is the last use made of bid/offer spreads in the text, for the following reason.

The spreads in the interbank market are narrow, especially for actively traded currencies. For this reason, transaction costs for interbank trades are relatively small as a percentage of the size of a trade. Interbank traders, of course, will add a markup for their services when trading currency to their retail corporate customers. Thus, retail spreads tend to be a bit wider than interbank wholesale spreads, but are still relatively minor as a percentage of the traded amount of currency.

Of course, as you may know if you have traveled overseas, the spreads to individual tourists, especially at hotels and airports, may be relatively wide. This fact is due in part to the small amounts involved, even though in some places, like Hong Kong, money changers for tourists will negotiate rates on the size of the transaction. This text takes the perspective, however, of a corporate treasurer, for whom dealer spreads and transaction costs are relatively insignificant and are thus ignored.

CROSS-RATES

A *cross-rate* is a rate of exchange between two non-U.S. dollar currencies. In recent times, the high volume of cross-rate transactions has given rise to a viable market in trading directly between major nondollar currencies at market-driven cross-rates. If one wants to change marks into yen, for example, one may do so directly.

Prior to this direct cross market for major nondollar currencies, the dollar served as the *vehicle currency,* meaning that to exchange one nondollar currency for another would involve two trades, first to exchange one currency into dollars and then to exchange the dollars into the other currency. With a vehicle currency system, the cross-rate quote is a *derived* cross-rate. Thus, if the mark trades at 1.50 DM/\$ and the yen trades at 125 ¥/\$, the derived cross-rate would be 125 ¥/\$ divided by 1.50 DM/\$ = 83.33 ¥/DM.

In cases where a viable market for direct cross-rate trading between non-dollar currencies has developed, the quotation conventions follow the following pattern: The currency that dominates, and had the most international vehicle character of its own at the time the particular cross-rate market developed, is generally the denominator currency. Thus, for example, the yen-mark rate is conventionally quoted in ¥/DM, since trading in marks dominated that in yen in the 1980s when that cross-rate market developed. On the other hand, although the yen became a dominant international currency by the late 1980s, the cross-rate market between Hong Kong dollars and yen follows the ¥/HK\$ quotation convention, since that cross-rate market developed prior to the yen's ascendancy to dominance.

The U.S. dollar is still the most commonly used vehicle currency for many currencies for which deep cross-rate markets have not yet developed.

DIRECT TERMS VERSUS INDIRECT TERMS

Often a corporation will wish to view exchange rates from the point of view of the price of, or the value of, a unit of foreign currency using its own base currency as the basis of the value. Thus, a German company dealing in yen may wish to use marks per yen as an exchange rate quote to find the value of a yen in terms of the company's base currency, marks. The expression of an exchange rate as "the base currency value of a foreign currency," which is the number of units of one's base currency per one unit of foreign currency, is referred to as being in *direct terms* from the point of view of the base currency. The expression of an exchange rate in units of foreign currency per one unit of base currency is in *indirect terms* from the point of view of the base currency.

In direct terms rates, the base currency is the currency denoted in the numerator of the ratio. A quote in DM/¥ is in direct terms from the point of view of the mark as the base currency. Thus, one with a German mark base currency would regard 0.012 DM/¥ as a direct terms rate and 83.33 ¥/DM as an indirect terms rate. Conversely, a quote with a Japanese yen base currency would regard 83.33 ¥/DM as the direct terms rate and 0.012 DM/¥ as an indirect terms rate.

EXCHANGE RATE NOTATION

The notation to be used for an exchange rate in this text is the capital letter X. Sometimes, we'll follow X with a double currency subscript. Thus, $X_{FF/SF}$ is the rate of exchange between French francs and Swiss francs, expressed in the number of French francs per Swiss franc, which is in direct terms from the point of view of the French franc as the base currency. $X_{\$/£}$ represents a direct terms rate of exchange between U.S. dollars and British pounds, from the point of view of the U.S. dollar as the base currency (and is also the conventional American terms currency market quote for the pound).

Often, it will be convenient to use the U.S. dollar as a reference currency and exchange rate quotes for a generic nondollar currency (C). The notation for such spot exchange rates is $X_{C/\$}$ for European terms and $X_{\$/C}$ for American terms. Other times, the context will be more general, and either X or $X_{b/C}$ will be used to represent a direct terms exchange rate, given the base currency (b) and a generic foreign currency (C).

CHANGES IN CURRENCY VALUES AND EXCHANGE RATE QUOTES

Now let us return to the earlier example of Sam's importation of sweaters into the United States from Crown Materials in the United Kingdom. Crown Materials' ultimate need for payment in pounds has the result that it increases the demand for pounds and increases the supply of the U.S. dollars. Similarly, in a cross-border investment transaction, the investor's action creates a demand for foreign currency and a supply of the investor's base currency.

Unless there is a source of natural demand elsewhere in the market for the currency being supplied, at the current exchange rate, the imbalance between supply and demand will pressure the exchange rate to change. In the sweater example, dollars are being sold for pounds due to a U.S. import of British products. Thus, the value of the pound, in terms of the U.S. dollar, that is, the price of pounds in dollars, should rise due to the selling pressure on the dollar and the corresponding buying pressure on the pound. Alternatively, we may say that the value of the dollar decreases relative to the pound.

How will this change in value be reflected in the spot exchange rate? The answer is that $X_{\$/£}$ will increase. For example, if the exchange rate prior to the increase in demand for pounds is 1.50 $/£, an increase in the value of the

Exchange rates are affected by the supply and demand for currency for international trade.

pound would mean an increase in $X_{\$/£}$ to a number higher than 1.50 $/£, say, to 1.60 $/£.

From this perspective, we are now ready to interpret Figure 1-3, which shows a time series of the $/£ exchange rate for the years 1922 to 1994. As you can see, the pound generally depreciated in value relative to the dollar (and thus the dollar appreciated relative to the pound) from 1980 until 1985. After that, the pound appreciated in value relative to the dollar until 1992.

For another example, suppose marks are currently being sold for U.S. dollars, other things the same, due to a net German import of U.S. products and/or purchase of U.S. investments. Then the value of the mark, in terms of the U.S. dollar, will drop due to the selling pressure on the mark and the corresponding buying pressure on the dollar. Alternatively, we may say that the value of the dollar increases relative to the mark. How will this change in value be reflected in conventional exchange rate quotes?

Using the same economic logic as the $/£ example earlier, a depreciation in the value of the mark will be reflected in a decline in the American terms exchange rate, $X_{\$/DM}$. A possible source of confusion, however, is that the mark is conventionally quoted in European terms, that is, $X_{DM/\$}$. Since the mark depreciation is reflected in a decline in the American terms quote, the same depreciation must be reflected in a rise in the conventional European terms quote. For example, an exchange rate change from 1.71 DM/$ to 1.85

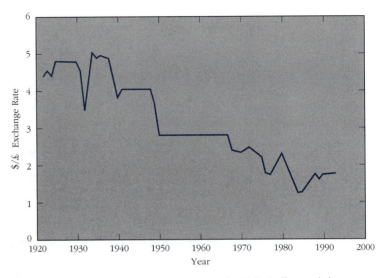

FIGURE 1-3 Exchange Rate Between the U.S. Dollar and the British Pound, 1922–1994

DM/\$ represents an appreciation in the value of the dollar and a depreciation in the value of the mark.

Thus, a rise in the European terms quote for the mark is caused by selling pressure on the mark, and this rise represents a decrease in the value of the mark and a corresponding increase in the value of the dollar. The appreciation of the value of the dollar, relative to the mark, as an increase in the European terms quote, $X_{DM/\$}$, may be better understood in terms of one dollar being able to buy more marks (1.85 marks instead of 1.71 marks) at the higher exchange rate.

Of course, if there is buying pressure on the mark, the value of the mark increases relative to the dollar, and so the value of the dollar decreases relative to the mark. If the value of the nondollar currency increases, then the American terms quote rises and the European terms quote declines. For example, an exchange rate change from 1.71 DM/\$ to 1.59 DM/\$ represents an *appreciation of the mark* relative to the dollar.

The association of a decrease in a European terms quote, $X_{C/\$}$, with an appreciation in the value of the nondollar currency, and vice versa, may require some "processing time" for some students (especially in the United States) just beginning their orientation to global financial management. One approach for such students to keeping things straight is to think of the value of a U.S. stock as rising as its share price (in dollars per share) rises. An American terms quote is an analogous price, expressed in dollars per unit of a "commodity," a nondollar currency; thus, the value of such a unit rises as the American terms quote rises. After using this mental process, one can then reciprocate the American terms view into the conventional European terms.

Figure 1–4 shows the exchange rates for the ¥/$, DM/$, and FF/$ for the years 1960 through 1994. In contrast to the $/£ graph in Figure 1-3, the increases in the exchange rates in Figure 1-4 correspond to depreciation in the value of the currency relative to the dollar and to appreciation of the dollar.

In general, if one identifies one currency as the base currency (b) the other currency as the foreign currency (C), then the direct terms exchange rate, $X_{b/C}$, will decrease if the foreign currency depreciates in value, and vice versa. You may also find it helpful to remember the following device: *A rise in any exchange rate quote is an appreciation of the "denominator" currency.* Perhaps it will be useful to memorize that the exchange rate is the value of the *denominator* currency. For example, if the exchange rate for marks goes from 1.71 DM/$ to 1.85 DM/$, this change represents an increase in the value of the dollar as the dollar is the denominator currency.

Practitioners (and travelers) get used to the exchange rate conventions and value changes by being directly involved in international business and finance. They quickly get to the point where there is no need to go through any mental steps. Much of the challenge of working with exchange rates at first is keeping straight in your head what is going on, especially since exchange rates are quoted in different ways. For beginners, the best way to gain understanding is to practice questions and problems, such as the ones on page 14 and those at the end of the chapter.

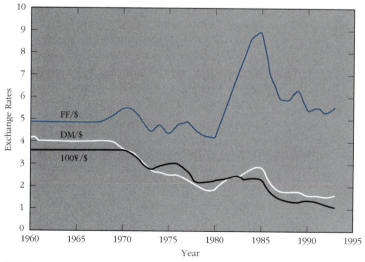

FIGURE 1-4   Exchange Rates Between the U.S. Dollar and Selected Foreign Currencies, 1960–1994, in European Terms

> ### EXAMPLE 1-1
>
> If the exchange rate for Japanese yen decreases from 150 ¥/$ to 120 ¥/$, has the yen depreciated against the dollar?
>
> *Solution 1-1* No; the yen has appreciated. Since the dollar will buy fewer yen at 120 ¥/$, the dollar has depreciated and the yen has appreciated.

> ### EXAMPLE 1-2
>
> If the exchange rate for the British pound decreases from 1.90 $/£ to 1.70 $/£, has the dollar depreciated against the pound?
>
> *Solution 1-2* No; the dollar has appreciated and the pound has depreciated. The value of the pound has depreciated in terms of the dollar, to 1.70 $/£ from 1.90 $/£.

Before proceeding, we note a simple matter in terminology. Some reports will use the term *devaluation* instead of depreciation and *revaluation* instead of appreciation. Technically, this terminology is "loose," even though a devaluation has the same result on an exchange rate as a depreciation, and a revaluation has the same result as an appreciation. The difference is that the devaluation/revaluation terminology refers to an *official* change in an exchange rate by government policy, while the depreciation/appreciation terminology implies a change caused by free market forces. If a central bank, or even several central banks in a coordinated effort, intervene in the currency market and try to influence the value of a currency, then this action does represent an "official policy." In this case, the terms devaluation/revaluation could be interpreted as applicable.[1]

PERCENTAGE CHANGE IN THE VALUE OF A CURRENCY

The percentage change in the value of a currency relative to the another currency is computed using direct terms exchange rates from the point of view of the second currency. For example, the percentage change in the value of

---

[1]A very readable and descriptive book about the currency market, written by a successful currency trader, is Andrew Krieger, *The Money Bazaar* (New York: Times Books, 1992). Further institutional details of the currency market are in J. Orlin Grabbe, *International Financial Markets,* 2nd ed. (New York: Elsevier, 1991), Chap. 3. Some interesting aspects of interbank market dealers' issues are covered in Brian J. Cody, "Reducing the Costs and Risks of Trading Foreign Exchange," Federal Reserve Bank of Philadelphia, *Business Review,* November/December 1990, pp. 13–23.

the pound relative to the dollar is computed using direct terms rates from the dollar point of view ($/£).

Let the notation $\%\Delta X_{b/C}$ represent the percentage change in the value of foreign currency C relative to base currency b. Letting $X^0_{b/C}$ be a beginning, or time 0 exchange rate, and $X^1_{b/C}$ be an ending, or time 1 exchange rate, then the percentage change in the value of currency C is $\%\Delta X_{b/C} = (X^1_{b/C} - X^0_{b/C})/X^0_{b/C} = X^1_{b/C}/X^0_{b/C} - 1$.

In computing a percentage change in the value of the pound relative to the dollar, the American terms exchange rate, $X_{\$/£}$, already has the pound as the denominator currency. Thus, if the exchange rate changes from 2.00 $/£ at time 0 to 1.80 $/£ at time 1, then the value of the pound has changed by $(1.80 \ \$/£)/(2.00 \ \$/£) - 1 = -0.10$, or by minus 10%, relative to the dollar. The pound has thus depreciated by 10% relative to the dollar.

To compute the percentage appreciation/depreciation, relative to the dollar, of currencies that are conventionally quoted in European terms, the exchange rate quote must be reciprocated into American terms.

For example, if the yen/dollar exchange rate changes from 125 ¥/$ at time 0 to 133.33 ¥/$ at time 1, then the American terms rate changes from $X^0_{\$/¥} = 1/(125 \ ¥/\$) = 0.008 \ \$/¥$ to $X^1_{\$/¥} = 1/(133.33 \ ¥/\$) = 0.0075 \ \$/¥$. The yen has changed by $(0.0075 \ \$/¥)/(0.008 \ \$/¥) - 1 = -0.0625$, or by minus 6.25%, relative to the dollar. The yen has depreciated by 6.25% relative to the dollar.

EXAMPLE 1-3

If the French franc, which is quoted in European terms, goes from $X^0_{FF/\$} = 6 \ FF/\$$ to $X^1_{FF/\$} = 5 \ FF/\$$, find the percentage change in the value of the French franc, and state whether an appreciation or a depreciation.

Solution 1-3 Since the quotes are European terms, they must be reciprocated to find the percentage change in the French franc. Performing this reciprocation directly in the percentage change expression, we have $[1/(5 \ FF/\$)]/[1/(6 \ FF/\$)] - 1 = 0.20$, or a 20% appreciation in the French franc relative to the dollar.

SIEGEL'S PARADOX

Reconsider the earlier example where the pound was found to have depreciated by 10%, relative to the dollar, when the exchange rate went from $X^0_{\$/£} = 2.00 \ \$/£$ at time 0 to $X^1_{\$/£} = 1.80 \ \$/£$ at time 1. Can we say that the dollar has, correspondingly, appreciated by 10% relative to the pound? The answer is: "Approximately, but not exactly."

Considering the percentage change in the value of the dollar relative to the pound requires use of direct quotes from the viewpoint of the pound as the base currency (pound as numerator and dollar as denominator). From this

> ## ⬛ EXAMPLE 1-4
>
> Referring to Example 1-3, find the percentage change in the value of the dollar relative to the French franc, and state whether an appreciation or depreciation.
>
> *Solution 1-4*   From the point of view of the French franc as the base currency, the direct rate terms exchange rate has changed from 6 FF/$ to 5 FF/$. The change in the value of the dollar is (5 FF/$)/(6 FF/$) − 1 = − 0.1667, or by minus 16.67%. Thus, the dollar depreciated by 16.67% relative to the French franc, while (as found in Example 1-3), the French franc appreciated by 20% relative to the dollar.

viewpoint, the exchange rate changes from $X^0_{£/\$} = 1/X^0_{\$/£} = 1/(2.00 \text{ } \$/£) = 0.50$ £/$ to $X^1_{£/\$} = 1/(1.80 \text{ } \$/£) = 0.555$ £/$. The percentage change, denoted $\%\Delta X_{£/\$}$, is (0.555 £/$)/(0.50 £/$) − 1 = 0.111, or an appreciation of 11.1% of the dollar relative to the pound. Although the pound depreciates by 10% relative to the dollar, the dollar appreciates by 11.1% relative to the pound. This mathematical oddity is known as *Siegel's paradox*. We'll see Siegel's paradox again in Chapter 12.

*C*URRENCY CONVERSION

If necessary, please review how to treat units of account when performing currency conversions at given exchange rates, since you will be doing a great deal of this as you work the text's problems. Say you want to convert an amount in dollars, $20,000, to yen, given an exchange rate quote of 125 ¥/$. In this case, you should multiply, since the $ symbol in the denominator of the exchange rate will "cancel" with the $ symbol of the currency amount, leaving the "units" for the answer in the numerator currency symbol of the exchange rate, ¥: $20,000(125 ¥/$) = ¥2,500,000.

Now suppose you are given a yen amount of, say, ¥560,000, to convert into dollars at the exchange rate of 125 ¥/$. It would make no sense to multiply ¥560,000 by 125 ¥/$ because there is no cancellation of the ¥ symbol on the currency amount with the denominator currency symbol of the exchange rate, $. To perform the conversion of yen into dollars at an exchange rate expressed in ¥/$, one can take either of two approaches.

One approach is to reciprocate the exchange rate into dollars per yen, which is 1/(125 ¥/$) = 0.008 $/¥, and then multiply ¥560,000 by the reciprocated rate. Thus, you would have ¥560,000(0.008 $/¥) = $4480. Since the currency symbol of the amount, ¥, cancels with the denominator currency symbol, ¥, in the exchange rate, the answer to this multiplication is in dollars. The second approach is a shortcut: Simply divide ¥560,000 by the exchange rate, 125 ¥/$, as in ¥560,000/(125 ¥/$). Now the ¥ symbol in the amount will cancel with the ¥ symbol in the numerator currency of the exchange rate, while the denominator currency symbol, $, as a "denominator of a denominator" goes to the numerator and thus becomes the units for the answer: $4480.

Three Key Topics in Global Financial Management

Beginning with this chapter, Part I of this text provides material on exchange rates and currency valuation, in terms of both goods prices and interest rates. In addition, the chapters in Part I cover some evolutionary aspects of the global monetary, economic, and financial markets. These topics are traditional background material for finance courses with an international orientation.

Following these first four chapters, each of the three remaining parts of the text focuses on a key area of managerial analysis in global financial management—global corporate financial structuring, corporate exposure to foreign exchange risk, and global capital budgeting. Basic financial principles, such as arbitrage, present value, financial leverage, and risk-return theory, are used. Part I serves as an overture to the three key topic areas.

GLOBAL CORPORATE FINANCING TECHNIQUES

In which country (or countries) and in which currency (or currencies) should a company obtain new financing or convert existing financing? Is there a method for structuring a financing package in the global market that results in a lower financing cost than would otherwise be possible in a firm's domestic financial market?

These basic, everyday questions confront financial managers of both large international companies and small domestic ones, given a modern setting of relatively integrated global financial markets. Being able to answer questions such as these may make the difference in a project that gets financed versus one that dies on the planning table.

This topic is the focus of Part II, with particular significance being placed on global financial markets and instruments. The topic relies heavily on a concept known as *financial engineering,* which "involves the design, the development, and the implementation of innovative financial instruments and processes, and the formulation of creative solutions to problems in finance."[2]

Global financial engineering encompasses a variety of corporate motivations, including the reduction of financing costs and taxes and the circumvention of regulations. Although a large portion of global finance is still more "art" than implied by the technical term "engineering," the fact is that technical approaches have become standard practice. Often, financial engineering involves the use of so-called *derivative securities,* which are forward contracts,

---

[2] See John D. Finnerty, "Financial Engineering in Corporate Finance: An Overview," *Financial Management,* Winter 1988, pp. 14–33.

TRIANGULAR ARBITRAGE

Arbitrage is defined as the simultaneous purchase and sale of essentially the same good at different prices. In cases where active cross-rate markets exist, if the actual cross-rate deviates from the derived cross-rate, arbitrage is possible. For example, if the market's cross-rate for yen and marks is 80 ¥/DM at the same time that the yen trades at 125 ¥/$ and the mark trades at 1.50 DM/$, implying a derived cross-rate of 83.33 ¥/DM (as found earlier), then one could make an easy arbitrage profit. The value of the mark, in yen, is lower in the direct cross-rate market than using the dollar as a vehicle. Thus, remembering to "buy low and sell high," you should buy marks with yen at 80 ¥/DM and simultaneously sell marks for dollars and then sell the dollars back into yen. For example, take 80 yen to buy 1 mark directly, sell the 1 mark to get DM1/(1.50 DM/$) = $0.667, and then use $0.667 to buy yen at 125 ¥/$, to get $0.667(125 ¥/$) = ¥83.33. You started with ¥80 and ended up with ¥83.33, for an arbitrage profit of ¥3.33.

The activity of arbitrage will tend to enforce the alignment of actual cross-rates with derived cross-rates. For example, in the arbitrage just outlined, the purchase of marks with yen in the direct cross-rate market will, other things equal, cause the value of the mark (in yen) to appreciate to a value higher than 80 ¥/DM. By the same token, the sale of marks for dollars and the purchase of yen for dollars in the vehicle approach will tend to drive down the value of the mark in dollars and drive up the value of the yen in dollars, resulting in a lower derived cross-rate value of the mark (in yen) than 83.33 ¥/DM. Arbitrage activity is likely to continue until the actual cross-rate and the derived cross-rate have converged, at which point no further arbitrage is possible.

swaps, and options and are described in detail in Part II. Sometimes the term "financial structuring" is used instead of financial engineering.

One underlying concept of financial engineering is arbitrage, the simultaneous purchase and sale of essentially the same financial claim at different prices. A simple example of corporate use of financial arbitrage was Exxon's borrowing of U.S. dollar funds from Japanese investors in the mid-1980s and directly investing the funds into higher-yielding, risk-free U.S. Treasury securities. Some explanation of this financial arbitrage is provided in the next example.

While the exploitation of pure arbitrage opportunities in global markets has been one way that the finance function has contributed to corporate profitability, the practice of *quasi-arbitrage* has been even more significant. Quasi-arbitrage is the exploitation of the most advantageous alternative among equivalent financial strategies. A simple example of quasi-arbitrage would be an opportunity for Exxon to issue U.S. dollar–denominated corporate bonds at a lower interest rate in Japan than in the United States, due possibly to regulatory factors, tax factors, or even a simple demand factor that U.S. investors may already have a substantial amount of Exxon bonds in their portfolios while Japanese investors do not.

Consider another example. Suppose a company wishes for its debt financing to be denominated in U.S. dollars. It could simply issue U.S.

dollar–denominated debt. But suppose the company can issue foreign currency debt and simultaneously perform other transactions in the global derivatives market to "hedge" the foreign currency debt back into U.S. dollars. The company can, in effect, create "synthetic" U.S. dollar debt. If the effective interest cost on the synthetic U.S. dollar debt is lower than that of the actual U.S. dollar debt, the company has found a quasi-arbitrage opportunity. Quasi-arbitrage is also referred to as *one-way arbitrage.*

Competition forces financial managers to find least-cost methods of arranging financing. If a company's competitor makes sophisticated global financing arrangements that result in cheaper financing than can be arranged domestically, then the competitor can use the cost savings to price its product lower and therefore to gain advantage. For a company to remain competitive, the finance function should be competitive, and this involves taking a global perspective.

The material in Part II will build upon Part I as well as your background in the basic financial concepts of compound interest, present value, and bond valuation, obtained in your introductory financial management course.

MEASURING AND MANAGING CORPORATE CURRENCY EXPOSURE

The risk from exposure to fluctuating exchange rates is a primary concern for many companies. When a company has receivables and payables denominated in a foreign currency, the exposure to fluctuating exchange rates is known as *transaction exposure* and may be dealt with in a relatively simple manner, discussed in Chapter 4.

THE EXXON ARBITRAGE

In the early to mid-1980s, Japanese investors were motivated to own U.S. securities but were not permitted (by their own government) to invest in U.S. Treasury securities. However, Japanese regulations did permit investors to hold some U.S. corporate bonds, and Exxon was on the list of approved companies. Exxon was able to exploit this situation for its own profit.

Exxon was able to borrow $199 million from Japanese investors in the form of a 20-year single-payment loan at 11.65%. Thus, Exxon had to repay $199(1.1165)^{20} = $1.8 billion in 20 years. Exxon invested *part* of the loan proceeds into a 20-year single-payment treasury "strip" at 12.20%. The amount Exxon invested was the amount needed to cover the $1.8 billion liability in 20 years, or the *present value* of $1.8 billion at 12.20%, which is ($1.8 billion)/1.1220^{20} = $180 million. Exxon pocketed the difference between the loan proceeds and the invested amount, $199 million −$180 million = $19 million, as arbitrage profit.

The Exxon arbitrage is described in John D. Finnerty, "Zero Coupon Bond Arbitrage: An Illustration of the Regulatory Dialectic at Work," *Financial Management,* Winter 1985, pp. 13–17.

The exchange of currencies is fundamental to global financial management. The percentage appreciation in the value of one currency is not numerically equal to the percentage depreciation in the value of the other currency.

Currency exposure also takes a more sophisticated form, known as *economic exposure,* which is the potential change in a company's equity value and/or in its ongoing cash flows, given a change in exchange rates. One form of economic exposure is the relatively straightforward *conversion exposure,* which relates to repatriating cash flows generated in a foreign currency back into a base currency. Another form of economic exposure is the more subtle *competitive exposure.* An example of competitive exposure for U.S. auto producers is the change in U.S. auto prices and corporate profitability in reaction to a change in Japanese auto prices in the United States. The price changes by the Japanese auto manufacturers are often driven by the desire to compensate for exchange rate changes.

As business becomes more and more global, companies increasingly face situations where competitors have costs/revenues denominated in different currencies, and corporate competitiveness and performance are therefore more and more influenced by changes in exchange rates. The chief problems in the topic of economic exposure are how to determine and measure the exposure, and what, if anything, to do about it.

The basic issues of economic exposure to exchange rate risk are laid out in Part III. Of particular significance is the analysis of the use of foreign currency-denominated debt as a means to manage the exposure. That analysis

XYZ Company Before

Assets	$100 million
Debt	$40 million
Equity	$60 million
Debt + Equity Total	$100 million
Capital structure ratio	$\dfrac{\$40\ \text{million}}{\$100\ \text{million}} = 0.40$

XYZ Company After

Assets	$100 million
Debt	$30 million
Equity	$70 million
Debt + Equity Total	$100 million
Capital structure ratio	$\dfrac{\$30\ \text{million}}{\$100\ \text{million}} = 0.30$

FIGURE 1-5 The Modigliani-Miller Capital Structure Principle

draws upon the fundamental financial concepts of capital structure and financial leverage that you studied in your introductory financial management course. Moreover, we'll use the basic theorem of capital structure developed by Nobel Prize winners Franco Modigliani and Merton Miller: that the total value of a firm is unaffected by the *capital structure ratio,* which is defined to be the ratio of the firm's debt financing to the total value of the firm's assets.[3]

If you have never covered the Modigliani-Miller theorem or do not recall it, don't worry. Here is an example of the basic idea: Suppose that XYZ Company has assets valued at $100 million and debts valued at $40 million, which implies that the equity of the company is valued at $60 million, and that the capital structure ratio is $40 million/$100 million = 0.40. Now suppose that XYZ issues new equity in the amount of $10 million and uses the proceeds from the equity issue to retire $10 million of liabilities. The value of the firm's assets is unchanged, but the firm's debt is now $30 million and represents only 30% of the firm's total asset value. In other words, the firm's total asset value is independent of its capital structure ratio decision. See Figure 1-5.

Of course, you may recall detailed expositions in prior courses on the subject of optimal capital structure. Our use of the Modigliani-Miller principle does not mean that you should forget what you have already learned about capital structure. Instead, the Modigliani-Miller principle is employed here as a simplifying assumption that facilitates a clearer focus on the currency exposure issues in capital structure. The principle that capital structure does not influence asset value will not be needed until Chapter 9, but it is mentioned now as an example of how the topics in *Global Financial Management* are related to basic financial concepts.

Global competition ensures that exchange rate changes have an economic impact even on companies with no international operations. For example, consider a company with purely domestic operations in an *open economy,* that is, an economy where foreign companies are allowed to compete with

[3] Franco Modigliani and Merton Miller, "The Cost of Capital, Corporate Finance, and the Theory of Investment," *American Economic Review,* June 1958, pp. 261–297.

> ### 📄 EXAMPLE 1-5
>
> A Firm with £500,000 worth of assets currently has £300,000 in equity outstanding. The rest of the company's financing is debt. If £100,000 in new debt is issued, and if the proceeds are used to buy back equity, what is the company's new asset value and its new capital structure ratio, given the Modigliani-Miller principle?
>
> *Solution 1-5*   The asset value is still £500,000. The new capital structure ratio is (£200,000 + £100,000)/£500,000 = £300,000/£500,000 = 0.60, since the old debt amount was £500,000 - £300,000 (of equity) = £200,000.

domestic ones on domestic soil. Since the prices that foreign competitors charge may depend upon exchange rate levels, there is a competitive economic exposure to exchange rate fluctuations. Survival may depend on the ability to understand, measure, and manage this type of economic currency exposure.

Overlaid on the economic exposure problem are the accounting rules for reporting the effects of exchange rate changes on financial condition and performance. Sometimes the financial statement effects of exchange rate changes do not correspond with the economic effects. This issue is particularly pronounced for firms with purely domestic operations but with economic exposure to currency fluctuations. The accounting rules and the relationship between accounting and economic exposure are also covered in Part III.

CAPITAL INVESTMENT DECISIONS IN THE GLOBAL CONTEXT

Capital budgeting is the process of evaluating major corporate investment decisions, such as a foreign expansion project. You may recall from your introductory financial management course the two major issues in capital budgeting are (1) the identification of relevant cash flows and (2) the establishment of proper accept/reject criteria.

Traditionally, the focus of multinational financial management courses was on the first problem, cash flow identification, when the proposed investment involves foreign direct investment of corporate capital into overseas plant and subsidiaries. The approach taken in this text, in Part IV, also directs the spotlight onto the second problem, the establishment of proper accept/reject criteria.

Mainly, the approach here applies the fundamental financial concepts of "net present value" and the "capital asset pricing model (CAPM)" that you learned in your introductory financial management course. However, instead of adjusting for risk by using the fundamental "single-country" CAPM, as orig-

Corporate Financing:	Measurement and Management of Corporate Exposure to Currency Risk:	Capital Budgeting Decisions in a Global Economy:
• In which country(ies) and\or which currency(ies) should a company find financing? • Is there an international financial package that minimizes the financing cost?	• What is the company's currency exposure? • What are the methods and problems of managing currency exposure?	• What are the relevant cash flows? • What are the proper accept\reject criteria?

FIGURE 1-6   The Three Major Issues in the Global Financial Management

inally published by Nobel Prize winner William Sharpe,[4] we will use a *global* asset pricing model of risk and return. The global asset pricing model is an extension of the CAPM that has been developed by theorists to describe the situation where capital suppliers face global investment opportunities and multiple currencies. The global asset pricing model is applied in Part IV to two issues in global capital budgeting decisions—risk adjustments and exchange rate forecasting.

Even if a company does not make foreign direct investments, the capital budgeting decisions should be based upon criteria that are global in perspective, since the competing investment opportunities facing the firm's capital suppliers are global ones. For example, a firm evaluating a proposal to build a new domestic plant must consider that the cost of capital is established in a global financial market, not in a segmented domestic financial market. The three key issues in global financial management are diagrammed in Figure 1-6.

Corporate managers are very interested in three related empirical issues that are under debate as part of the development of international asset pricing theory: (1) Do exchange rate fluctuations actually have an influence on the value of firms' equities and, if so, is this influence the same as theory suggests? (2) Do investors care about this exposure? That is, is this exposure a factor for which investors require a risk premium? (3) Assuming that exchange rate changes create a risk that investors are concerned about, do investors want to manage this exposure on their own or have corporate managers try to do something about it?

Global asset pricing theory rests partly on the theory of international investor diversification. The global financial system of markets and institutions involves virtually unrestricted flow of cross-border portfolio investment into

---

[4] William Sharpe, "Capital Asset Prices: A Theory of Market Equilibrium Under Conditions of Risk," *Journal of Finance,* September 1964, pp. 425–442.

financial securities, such as the purchase of a U.S. company's bonds by a Japanese insurance company. Of course, portfolio investment is the mirror image of corporate financing when the assets are corporate securities, such as bonds or equities. More and more investors, large and small, diversify their portfolios internationally. Portfolio diversification itself has a proud academic history, beginning with the original diversification analysis of Nobel Prize winner Harry Markowitz in 1952.[5]

The extension of portfolio theory to international diversification has been relatively straightforward in theory and in practice. However, exposure to currency risk adds a challenging new dimension to the portfolio problem.

GLOBALIZING THE FINANCE FUNCTION

A 1994 report by The Conference Board examines the changing role of the finance function in global firms. The report is based on case studies and on a survey of 251 financial officers and uses instructive comparisons of trends among North American, Asian, and European companies.

The report provides the following major findings:

1. Global firms will in the future follow the trend of Japanese firms to drastically cut the costs of the finance function by reducing staff and reducing the extent of formal financial systems.

2. A detached, control-laden finance function does not facilitate firms' execution of competitive worldwide product and customer strategies. In the future, finance people will have to behave less like "corporate police" and instead will team with and share control with a firm's operating managers. At the same time, operating managers will have to become technically more proficient in the finance area.

3. The finance function will lead the way in the increasingly centralized global strategy process. Particular emphasis will be on foreign acquisitions and analyses of the impact of conditions in the currency and financial markets.

Summary

In this chapter you began to learn about global financial management. This chapter immediately immersed you into the international setting with the key subject of exchange rates and currency markets. This material is designed to prevent the confusion that a novice might have when he or she hears that "the yen has *appreciated* from 110 to 103."

---

[5] H. M. Markowitz, "Portfolio Selection," *Journal of Finance,* March 1952, pp. 77–91.

The three main areas of managerial analysis in global financial management are (1) financing techniques in a global economy with unrestricted cross-border capital flows, including the application of financial engineering; (2) currency exposure measurement and management, including economic exposure; and (3) capital budgeting decisions in a global economy and global financial system. These decision areas apply even to a firm with purely domestic operations.

Glossary

American Terms: An exchange rate quotation convention where the rate is expressed as U.S. dollars per one unit of another currency.

Arbitrage: The simultaneous purchase and sale of essentially the same security at different prices.

Capital Structure Ratio: The ratio of the firm's debt financing to the total value of the firm's assets.

Competitive Exposure: A form of economic exposure to currency fluctuations where corporate competitiveness and performance is influenced by changes in exchange rates.

Conversion Exposure: A form of economic exposure to currency fluctuations where the base currency value, of corporate cash flows generated in a foreign currency, is influenced by changes in exchange rates.

Cross-rate: The exchange rate between two currencies other than the U.S. dollar.

Direct Terms: An exchange rate expressed as the amount of one's base currency price per one unit of a foreign currency.

Economic Exposure: The potential change in a company's equity value and/or in its ongoing cash flows, given changes in exchange rates.

ECU: See *European Currency Unit.*

European Currency Unit: A hypothetical basket of major European currencies.

European Terms: An exchange rate quotation convention where the rate is expressed as the number of units of a currency per one U.S. dollar.

Financial Engineering: The design, the development, and the implementation of innovative financial instruments and processes and the formulation of creative solutions to problems in finance.

Foreign Direct Investment: Corporate capital invested into plant and subsidiaries in a foreign country, as distinct from international portfolio investment into securities.

Indirect Terms: An exchange rate expressed as the amount of foreign currency per one unit of one's base currency price.

Interbank (FX) Market: The wholesale international market for currency trading between major banks and financial institutions around the world.

One-Way Arbitrage: The choice of the most advantageous alternative among equivalent financial strategies. Also referred to as quasi–arbitrage.

Open Economy: An economy that allows foreign trade and competition.

Portfolio Investment: Investments into financial securities such as stocks, bonds, and so forth, as distinct from foreign direct investment into plant and subsidiaries by corporations.

Quasi-arbitrage: The choice of the most advantageous alternative among equivalent financial strategies. Also referred to as one-way arbitrage.

Retail (FX) Market: The market for currency exchange between banks and retail businesses and investment portfolios.

SDR: See Special Drawing Right.

Siegel's Paradox: The mathematical result that the percentage change in the value of currency A relative to currency B is not equal to the negative of the percentage change in the value of currency B relative to currency A.

Special Drawing Right: The International Monetary Fund's basket of major international currencies. See Problem #4 for the computation.

SWIFT: Society for Worldwide Financial Telecommunications, by which international financial flows, including currency exchange, are facilitated electronically through a system of 3000 banks and investment banks in 67 countries.

Transaction Exposure: The exposure of a company's receivables and payables, denominated in a foreign currency, to fluctuating exchange rates.

Vehicle Currency: A currency, usually a major international currency (such as the dollar, the yen, the mark, the pound, and so forth), used as an intermediary to facilitate an exchange between two other currencies.

Discussion Questions

1. Explain why a currency appreciates in value relative to another currency.

2. Explain in your own words the three main issues in *Global Financial Management* and why even a company with purely domestic operations must be concerned with each.

Problems

1. What is the notation for a direct terms exchange rate between U.S. dollars and German marks from the point of view of the mark as the base currency? Is the answer in European terms or American terms?

2. The exchange rate quotation for the French franc increases from 5 FF/$ to 6 FF/$. Has the French franc appreciated or depreciated relative to the dollar?

3. You wish to convert $1000 into British pounds at the exchange rate of 2 $/£. What is the amount in pounds?

4. As of August 26, 1991, one SDR consists of 0.453 German marks, 0.800 French francs, 31.800 Japanese yen, 0.0812 British pounds, and 0.572 U.S. dollars. What is the U.S. dollar value of 1 SDR at the following exchange rates: 1.747 DM/$, 5.935 FF/$, 136.96 ¥/$, and 1.6798 $/£?

5. Assume that the French franc is currently being traded at 5 FF/$, while the Swiss franc (SF) is 1.33 SF/$. What is the derived cross-rate in direct terms from the point of view of the French franc as the base currency?

6. Refer to Problem 5. If the direct cross-rate is 4 FF/SF, explain how to capture arbitrage profits with triangular arbitrage.

7. The time 0 exchange rate between the Belgian franc (BF) and the U.S. dollar is 30 BF/$. The time 1 exchange rate between the Belgian franc and the U.S. dollar is 35 BF/$. What is the percentage change in the value of the Belgian franc relative to the dollar and the percentage change in the value of the dollar relative to the Belgian franc?

8. Exxon borrows $199 million (time 0 loan proceeds) from Japanese investors. The loan is a zero-coupon, or single-payment, instrument with maturity of 20 years and a rate of 11.65%. If Exxon can invest in 20–year U.S. Treasury "strips" (zero-coupon Treasury bonds) at 12%, what would be Exxon's time 0 arbitrage profit?

9. ABC Company has FF5,000,000 in assets, of which FF4,000,000 has been financed with equity. The rest of the financing is debt, denominated in French francs. The company decides to issue FF1,250,000 in new debt and use the proceeds to retire equity. What is the company's new capital structure ratio? Assume the Modigliani-Miller principle.

4. 1.3346 $/SDR.

8. $12.08 million.

9. 0.45.

chapter 2

EXCHANGE RATES, GOODS PRICES, AND THE GLOBAL ECONOMY

The Evolution of Currency Exchange

The international framework for making financial settlements through more than one currency is called the *international monetary system*. The evolution of exchange rate determination in the international monetary system may be examined in three distinct chronological periods: (1) the pre-1944 era, during which gold played a dominant role; (2) the Bretton Woods era of pegged exchange rates, 1944–1973; and (3) the modern era since 1973, during which exchange rates have been flexible, determined more by private market forces and less by government influence.

THE GOLD STANDARD AND EXCHANGE RATES

The gold standard for the exchange of currencies actually began before the time that national currencies existed, when all trade (domestic or cross-border) was conducted by barter. The first widely accepted medium of exchange was gold, when merchants began to judge the value of all other commodities in terms of ounces of gold.

At some point, the volume of business transactions outgrew the supply of gold that was available to serve as a medium of exchange. To solve this problem, those holding large quantities of gold conceived of a profit-making service: banking. A bank with a large quantity of gold would print and circulate paper notes, redeemable for gold. The gold notes became a convenient medium of exchange, and by lending gold to borrowers in the form of paper notes, more in gold notes became circulated than was represented physically by the gold on hand in banks, "in reserve."

Thus, a relatively large volume of business transactions could be supported as if more gold existed than there actually was. The system worked, provided there existed confidence in banks to deliver gold against the notes on demand, and not everyone tried to take physical delivery of gold at once.

Eventually, as paper money systems became nationalized, each country established a *central bank* to control its paper money supply. The system of paper notes expanded to checks and eventually to electronic balances, on the same principle as the gold reserve system: The physical supply of national paper money could be much less than the amount circulated in the form of checks and electronic transfers. A bank, as part of a national financial system, is required to hold paper currency reserves and to provide paper money for deposit balances on demand, but the system is based on the notion that not everyone needs to hold the physical paper money at the same time.

Although now impractical, for some time banks were required to redeem gold for paper money on demand. Banks borrowed paper money from the central bank based upon gold deposits. Under this gold standard system, the price at which a central bank would buy or sell gold to banks for paper money was a federal decision. In other words, the price was not determined by a free market.

The fact that countries' central banks maintained set prices for gold in their national currencies generally dictated exchange rates. For example, the United States might set a rate of $20 per ounce of gold, and the British a rate of £10 per ounce. As long as the two nations maintained these set prices for the redemption of gold, the exchange rate between the national paper currencies (and thus deposit balances) was determined as 2 $/£.

Although national gold standards have disappeared, and thus exchange rates are no longer determined by federally fixed prices for gold, gold still plays a role in settling international trade. If, for example, U.S. businesses import a larger value of goods from the United Kingdom than they export to the United Kingdom, then U.S. merchants need British pounds to pay for the aggregate difference between the imports and exports. The Bank of England ultimately "buys" the supply of dollars from banks with pounds, thus circulating the additional pounds necessary to support the higher volume of English firm business. The Bank of England can then either hold the dollars as official *foreign currency reserves* or redeem the dollars to the U.S. Federal Reserve for gold (or for some of the Fed's official reserves of pounds).

Gold is thus the traditional ultimate means of settling international trade accounts between countries, but gold settlement generally does not have to be requested unless a foreign currency reserve balance grows too large. Many countries have gold reserves stored in the vault at the New York Federal Reserve. As such, gold settlement often simply involves the movement of gold bars from one country's gold cubicle to another's.

Note that the situation where U.S. businesses import a larger value of goods from the United Kingdom than they export to the United Kingdom technically is defined as a *trade deficit* for the United States and a *trade surplus* for the United Kingdom. Thus, unless there are some portfolio investment flows in the opposite direction, countries with trade deficits experience a reduction of gold reserves (and/or official foreign currency reserves). During the era of the gold standard, international trade took place mostly in basic commodities, cross-border portfolio flows were much less extensive than now, and countries' economies were relatively independent. Countries competed with each other to accumulate gold reserves via trade surpluses, a practice known as *mercantilism*.

OFFICIAL DEVALUATION AND THE MODIFIED GOLD STANDARD

Problems with the gold standard began with the start of World War I in 1914. From that point to the end of World War II, the development of international trade was retarded by the chaos of the two world wars and the Great Depression.

International trade arrangements during this time period were largely influenced by national self-interest, characterized by the following scenario: If a government wished to increase the inflow of gold, or decrease the outflow, to settle international trade, it might devalue its currency relative to gold. For example, the British government might decide to value an ounce of gold at £20/oz instead of £10/oz. If the United States maintained a gold price of $20 per ounce, the new exchange rate against the dollar would be 1 $/£. In exchange rate terms, the British pound was devalued relative to the dollar, since 1 $/£ is a lower value of the pound than 2 $/£.

After the devaluation, those in the United Kingdom holding pound balances now would find U.S. products more expensive, import less from the United States, and thus buy more at home.

By the same token, the United States would find British products less expensive and tend to import more from Britain and export less to Britain. If trade were balanced prior to the devaluation, then after the devaluation, the United States would have a trade deficit and the United Kingdom would have a trade surplus. The reason for this disequilibrium situation is that goods market prices would be slow to react to the new price of gold and the new exchange rate.

Figure 2-1 depicts the scenario. The prices for bushels of "wheat" are shown to be representative of domestic prices of nongold commodities. The British devaluation of gold by raising the official price of gold in pounds sterling was not followed quickly by an adjustment in commodity prices. The resulting trade imbalance could be viewed positively by British government officials for two reasons: (1) the ultimate settlement of the exports to the United States would be the accumulation and retention of additional gold in

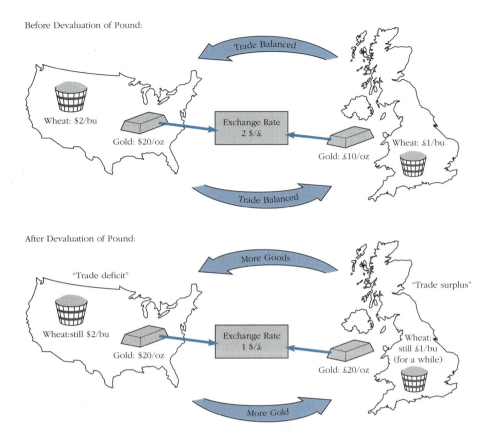

FIGURE 2-1   Devaluation and Resulting Flows in the Gold Standard

the British national treasury, and (2) more jobs would be created in the United Kingdom by the increase in overseas demand for the relatively inexpensive British products.

On the other hand, the devaluation would not be very good news to those outside of Britain holding balances in pounds sterling, nor to those hurt by the loss of British markets. Sometimes, if trade had already become imbalanced, a devaluation of gold could be agreed upon to be in the best interests of all countries involved. But often in the gold standard era, a devaluation of the type described in the scenario was motivated solely by national self-interest, with no regard for the negative effects on trading partners. Such actions tended to damage the international financial system, which ultimately hurt all countries including the one that devalued gold.

The reaction of other countries was often their own devaluations or other protectionist policies, such as trade barriers. Moreover, once there is a belief that a country is willing to devalue its currency, people will not want to hold the currency, but will be inclined to redeem it rapidly to that country's banks for gold. Central banks of other countries would hold less of the currency as official currency reserves if there was some suspicion that a foreign central bank would close its "gold window" or devalue its currency by raising the official price for gold in terms of its own currency. These actions would tend to hasten the devaluation and the chaos.

During the period of the two world wars and the Great Depression, national self-interest caused confidence in the international financial system to be undermined by official devaluations, gold window closings, and protectionist trade barriers. Many countries began allowing the price of gold in their own currency to be determined by market forces. The United States eliminated the national gold standard by discontinuing the redeemability of paper notes for gold by U.S. citizens. The United States continued to maintain a fixed dollar price for gold for the settlement of international trade accounts and for buying gold from U.S. citizens. This era has been called the modified gold standard.

THE BRETTON WOODS SYSTEM OF PEGGED EXCHANGE RATES

As the only major economic system not devastated by World War II, the United States naturally assumed a leadership role in world economic affairs and in helping to rebuild Europe and Japan. This role was formalized at the 1944 international economic summit meeting in the United States at the Bretton Woods resort in New Hampshire.

Led by the legendary British economist, John Maynard Keynes, the Bretton Woods conference established a system of pegged, or set, exchange rates between countries. To implement this plan, central banks would be expected to intervene in the exchange market to stabilize exchange rates by buying and selling currencies with their presumably substantial market power. The stability of the system of pegged exchange rates, it was believed, was a means to promote the international trade that would lead to the economic recovery of the world.

In addition, the Bretton Woods conference established the *International Monetary Fund (IMF)*, an international coordinating organization whose primary functions were originally to oversee the stability of the exchange rate system and to provide assistance to any member country in a short-term international monetary crisis.

For example, suppose that currency traders at banks decided to sell their inventories of a currency back to the central bank that issued the currency, at the pegged exchange rate, and in return receive large quantities of a central bank's gold or foreign currency reserves. If the central bank were to give up too much gold or foreign currency reserves, confidence in that nation's economy and in its currency would decline both inside of that country and out, possibly precipitating a national or international financial crisis. The IMF's role was to lend the beleaguered central bank some funds, in the form of international currencies (often in the form of the SDR basket of currencies), to help the central bank weather the run. The IMF was also established to provide short-term monetary assistance to countries trying to develop modern economies for the first time or to rebuild existing economies after wars or revolutions, including World War II.

Also established at the Bretton Woods conference was the *World Bank,* known more formally as the *International Bank for Reconstruction and Development (IBRD).* The function of the World Bank is to provide long-term capital to countries that are trying to develop or rebuild their economies. Unlike the IMF, the World Bank may issue bonds, in any currency, for purposes of raising capital.[1]

Although the Bretton Woods system of pegged exchange rates may have provided some stability, the system gave way in the early 1970s. At that time, the size of the currency market had grown so large that private traders began to have considerable influence in the market relative to the central banks that were supporting the pegged rates. For reasons that should be understood from the next section, it became necessary for the central banks to abandon the Bretton Woods pegging system and allow exchange rates to be determined by free market forces. One can see where this modern era of floating exchange rates began by referring to Figure 2-2.

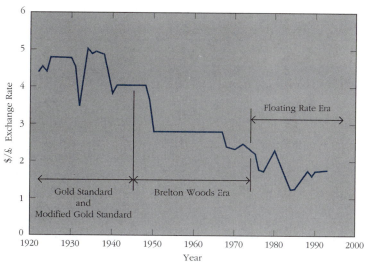

FIGURE 2-2 Chronology of Currency Exchange Evolution

---

[1]For a particularly fascinating account of the Bretton Woods conference, especially the role played by John Maynard Keynes, see Andrew Krieger, *The Money Bazaar* (New York: Times Books, 1992), Chap. 6. Another interesting account of the Bretton Woods conference, and of the evolution of global markets, is in Gregory J. Millman, *The Vandal's Crown* (New York: The Free Press, 1995).

Currency Valuation and Goods Markets

THE INTERNATIONAL LAW OF ONE PRICE

Economists often present a logical argument for why, in a system of *market-determined* exchange rates, the price of a tradable commodity in one country should be equal to the price of the same commodity in another country, after adjusting for the exchange rate between the two currencies and after taking into consideration "frictions" like transportation costs. The argument is that if a country's goods were relatively cheap internationally, global demand for the goods would create pressure on currency values and goods prices, in what might be called "goods market arbitrage," to conform to an approximately uniform international price of a traded commodity. The condition that is theoretically enforced by goods market arbitrage is known as the *international law of one price*.

Consider the exchange rate between the dollar and another currency. Call the price of a bushel of wheat in the United States $p_\$$ and the price of a bushel of wheat in the other currency p_C. Then the international law of one price implies that

$$X_{\$/C} = \frac{p_\$}{p_C} \text{ or } X_{C/\$} = \frac{p_C}{p_\$} \qquad (2\text{-}1)$$

For example, assume a bushel of wheat costs $p_\$$ = $2.00 in the United States and $p_£$ = £1.00 in England. Then the international law of one price says that the exchange rate should be $X_{\$/£}$ = $2.00/£1.00 = 2.00 $/£. At this exchange rate, someone in the United States could either buy a bushel for $2.00 or exchange the $2.00 into £1.00 and purchase a bushel in England for £1.00. Either way, the cost of a bushel of wheat is the same.

EXAMPLE 2-1

Assume that a bushel of corn costs $2.00 in the United States and FF5.00 in France. What does the international law of one price say should be the exchange rate? Express your answer in the form of the accepted quotation convention.

Solution 2-1   Since this exchange rate is conventionally expressed in European terms, we want the answer to be in FF/$. Thus, $p_{FF}/p_\$$ = FF5.00/$2.00 = 2.50 FF/$ is the exchange rate that will make a bushel cost the same in both economies.

In one sense, the international law of one price is the same concept covered earlier in connection with the gold standard. In that case, the traded good was gold. In this discussion, in contrast, the concept is broadened and applied to exchange rates and goods prices that are more free to find equilibrium values than in the gold standard scenario.

According to the international law of one price, the cost of a bushel of wheat should be the same in different countries, after currency conversion at the current exchange rate, assuming that the economies are open to trade. But does the international law of one price hold in reality?

Does the international law of one price hold in reality? Let's look at the Bretton Woods pegged exchange rate system of 1944–1973.

MISVALUATION OF CURRENCIES AND TRADE IMBALANCES

Since exchange rates of the Bretton Woods system were fixed by agreement, the rates could *not* freely adjust to goods price changes according to the international law of one price. This situation eventually caused the demise of the Bretton Woods system of pegged exchange rates. As a preparation for understanding this point, let us now examine the economic ramifications when the international law of one price is violated and goods prices and exchange rates do *not* adjust.

Let us extend the U.S./British wheat example earlier. Assume that the dollar/pound exchange rate is pegged, as it was in the Bretton Woods era, and it therefore cannot respond as it might in a free market. Assume that the exchange rate is pegged at 2.00 $/£ and that England experiences high inflation in goods prices. For instance, assume that the price of a bushel of wheat in England increases from £1.00/bu (as was assumed) to £1.50/bu, but remains at $2.00/bu in the United States. The international law of one price tells us that the new exchange rate should be ($2.00/bu)/(£1.50/bu) = 1.33 $/£, but the actual exchange rate is assumed to be pegged at 2.00 $/£. Thus, the international law of one price is violated once the price of wheat escalates in the United Kingdom.

A wheat buyer in England will now have the incentive to import wheat from the United States. Given the exchange rate of 2.00 $/£, £1.00 will buy a bushel of wheat in the U.S. wheat market, whereas it takes £1.50 to buy a bushel of wheat in the English wheat market. Correspondingly, wheat buyers in the United States will not tend to import any wheat from England, since $2.00 will still buy a bushel in the United States, but $2.00 will only convert to £1.00, which will only buy two-thirds of a bushel in the United Kingdom. In principle, arbitragers could buy wheat in the United States and sell it in the United Kingdom.

At these wheat prices, unless the exchange rate is allowed to change, the pound and the dollar are currencies that are misvalued relative to one another in terms of overseas purchasing power: The pound is an *overvalued currency* (relative to the dollar) in terms of overseas purchasing power; correspondingly, the dollar is an *undervalued currency* (relative to the pound) in terms of overseas purchasing power. An easy way to judge the direction and magnitude of the misvaluation is to compare the actual exchange rate with the hypothetical exchange rate that would prevail under the international law of one price. Since the actual value of the pound (2.00 $/£) is greater than what it should be (1.33 $/£), the pound is overvalued, and thus the dollar is undervalued.

There is less overseas demand for the products of a nation whose currency is overvalued and greater demand for the products of a nation whose currency is undervalued. This in turn implies that a country with an overvalued currency will tend to import more goods than it exports. By definition, a country that imports more than it exports over a period of time has a *trade deficit*. The opposite of a trade deficit is a *trade surplus*, which is the excess of exported goods over imported goods over a period of time. (Trade imbalances can occur for other reasons too, but currency misvaluations have an impact.) Figure 2-3 depicts the scenario of currency misvaluation when the international law of one price is violated.

One might argue that, in theory, with pegged exchange rates there would be pressure on the goods prices to equilibrate in such a way that the international law of one price holds. While pressure for such an equilibration may be present, the frictions and complexity of international goods trade in the real world make such equilibration trends very slow. Thus, trade deficits and surpluses are likely for long periods of time.

We can now understand why the Bretton Woods system of pegged exchange rates was abandoned in the early 1970s. If two countries are experiencing different inflation rates, but exchange rates are held *fixed* by the pegging arrangement, then the country with the higher inflation will lose export markets for its goods due to its overvalued currency. With the loss of export markets, the country's less productive industry will support fewer jobs, and the economy suffers. Trade deficits can thus signal potential problems for a nation's economy.

Under the Bretton Woods system of pegged exchange rates, the participating countries followed dissimilar national policies on inflation, and curren-

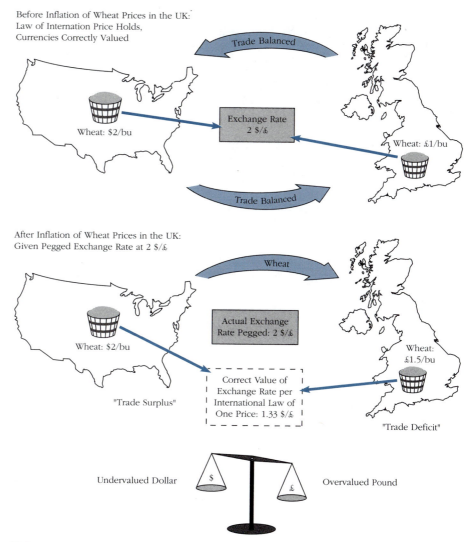

FIGURE 2-3   How Currencies Become Misvalued with Inflation and Pegged Exchange Rates

cies became misvalued as a result. For example, some Western European capitalist countries that tried some socialistic policies experienced high inflation. The high inflation with the pegged exchange rates led to overvalued currencies and trade deficits. At times, these countries had to resort to official devaluation to stimulate their economies and "import jobs."

Such devaluations were contrary to the design of the Bretton Woods system. Realizing that countries were willing to violate the Bretton Woods convention, currency speculators compounded the problem by using a country's

EXAMPLE 2-2

Assume as in Example 2-1 that $X_{FF/\$} = 2.50$ FF/$ and that the prices for a bushel of corn are $p_\$ = \$2.00$ in the United States and $p_{FF} = FF5.00$ in France. Suppose the price of a bushel of corn in France increases by an inflation rate of $i_{FF} = 20\%$ in France. Continue to assume that the price of corn in the United States is $2.00/bushel. Assume that the exchange rate is pegged at 2.50 FF/$. After the French inflation, which currency is overvalued and which is undervalued? Which country is likely to experience a trade deficit and which a trade surplus?

Solution 2-2 After the inflation in French corn prices, a bushel costs $p_{FF} = FF5.00(1.20) = FF6.00$ in France. The price of a bushel in the United States, $p_\$ = \$2.00$, is still convertible into $2.00(2.50 FF/$) = FF5.00. Since this amount will not pay for a bushel in France, the dollar is undervalued relative to the French franc. By the same token, the French franc is overvalued relative to the dollar. One can also see this point by comparing the actual exchange rate (2.50 FF/$) with the hypothetical exchange rate that would hold under the international law of one price [(6 FF/bu)/(2.00 $/bu) = 3 FF/$]; the French franc is more highly valued at the actual exchange rate of 2.50 FF/$ than at the theoretically correct exchange rate of 3 FF/$. Thus, France is likely to be a net importer of U.S. corn and experience a trade deficit, while the United States will be a net exporter and will have a trade surplus.

trade deficit figures to forecast an eventual devaluation, and unload the currency before the devaluation, at the expense of central banks holding reserves of the currency.

At Bretton Woods, the U.S. dollar was pegged at an overvalued rate to both the German mark and the Japanese yen. The purpose was to allow these two most devastated World War II countries help rebuild their economies by making their goods relatively inexpensive in overseas markets. The plan worked so well that the German and Japanese economies became quite powerful by the late 1960s. (Also, these two countries' economic growth was enhanced by the absence of military expenditures.) Moreover, Germany and Japan followed very strict anti-inflation policies to ensure economic recovery and development. So when the United States began to experience more inflation in the 1960s, the dollar became even more overvalued relative to the mark and the yen.

The economic consequences of misvalued currencies led the participants of the Bretton Woods agreement to dispense with the pegging system and allow market-determined, or floating, exchange rates.

FLOATING RATES AND PURCHASING POWER PARITY

The theory behind floating exchange rates is that market forces will cause exchange rates to find their correct valuation, so that the problems incurred under the Bretton Woods system would, it was hoped, be avoided. As demand and supply pressures continuously arise from international trade and investment, floating exchange rates should change to reflect the correct value of the currencies.

A theoretical formulation of the dynamics of floating exchange rate movements and goods prices is the so-called *purchasing power parity (PPP) condition*, which describes the relationship that would hold between exchange rates at two different times and the inflation rates for the two countries involved, assuming that the international law of one price holds at *both* points in time. (Note: The popular press sometimes uses the term "purchasing power parity" to refer to the international law of one price.)

Let us continue the bushel of wheat example to explain. Assume that the international law of one price holds at the beginning point in time, given bushel prices at that time of $p_\$^0$ in the United States and p_C^0 in a nondollar currency. Thus, the time 0 spot exchange rate, $X_{\$/C}^0$, is equal to $p_\$^0/p_C^0$, from an application of equation (2-1).

Denoting inflation in the United States as $i_\$$ and in the non-dollar country as i_C, the new bushel prices are $p_\$^1 = p_\$^0(1 + i_\$)$ and $p_C^1 = p_C^0(1 + i_C)$, respectively. It may help to think of the inflation rates as pertaining to a unit of time, say, a year.

After the year has elapsed, the new (time 1) American terms exchange rate, given that the international law of one price also holds *after* the price changes, is given in equation (2-2), which is the purchasing power parity condition.

PURCHASING POWER PARITY CONDITION[2]

$$X_{\$/C}^1 = X_{\$/C}^0 \left[\frac{(1 + i_\$)}{(1 + i_C)} \right]$$ (2-2)

As an example application of equation (2-2), assume that the $/£ exchange rate is currently at 1.75 $/£. If inflation in the United Kingdom is 20% per year and zero in the United States, the new exchange rate in a year, if purchasing power parity condition holds, will be $X_{\$/£}^1$= (1.75 $/£)(1.00/1.20) = 1.458 $/£.

In this example, the pound depreciates from 1.75 $/£ to 1.458 $/£. This depreciation of the pound offsets the higher inflation in the United Kingdom in international purchasing power terms. Prices went up in the United Kingdom, making goods more expensive, but prices did not change in the United States. The only way for the international law of one price to hold after the goods price changes would be for the dollar to buy more pounds. Thus,

---

[2]To see how equation (2-2) results, note that due to the international law of one price at time 1, $X_{\$/C}^1 = p_\$^1/p_C^1$, which in turn is equivalent to $X_{\$/C}^1 = p_\$^0(1 + i_\$)/p_C^0(1 + i_C)$. Rearranging this last expression, we have that $X_{\$/C}^1 = (p_\$^0/p_C^0)[(1 + i_\$)/(1 + i_C)]$. Given that the original exchange rate, $X_{\$/C}^0$, is equal to $p_\$^0/p_C^0$, equation (2-2) follows.

the exchange rate movement is such that the dollar appreciates and the pound depreciates.

Of course, the purchasing power parity condition may just as easily be expressed in European terms as in the American terms of equation (2-2). Denote the European terms quotes as $X^0_{C/\$}$ and $X^1_{C/\$}$ for the original and new exchange rates, respectively. Then substitution of $X^0_{C/\$} = 1/X^0_{\$/C}$ and $X^1_{C/\$} = 1/X^1_{\$/C}$ into equation (2-2) and rearranging leads to $X^1_{C/\$} = X^0_{C/\$}[(1 + i_C)/(1 + i_\$)]$.

There is an easy way to remember the purchasing power parity relationship, regardless of whether the currency quotation convention is European terms or American terms. Remember to put the *ending* (time 1) exchange rate on the left-hand side. Put the *beginning* (time 0) exchange rate on the right-hand side. Then to remember which inflation rate to put in the numerator and which to put in the denominator on the right-hand side, recall that the numerator inflation rate is the same as the numerator currency in the exchange rate. Thus, if dealing with American terms rates, $\$/C$, the U.S. inflation goes in the numerator. By the same token, when dealing with European terms rates, $C/\$$, country C's inflation rate belongs in the numerator.

In Example 2-3, inflation in U.S. prices was higher than it was in French prices. Thus, the dollar depreciates relative to the French franc for the purchasing power parity condition to hold. The drop in the European terms exchange rate represents an appreciation of the French franc and a depreciation of the dollar.

Despite the appreciation and depreciation of the currencies in Example 2-3, the French franc and the dollar are still correctly valued in overseas purchasing power terms. According to goods market prices, the currencies are correctly valued at the beginning of the period and at the end of the period. If the purchasing power parity condition holds, a currency does not get misvalued in overseas purchasing power terms, even though it may appreciate or depreciate.

DOES THE PURCHASING POWER PARITY CONDITION HOLD IN REALITY?

It is tempting to try to obtain more "mileage" out of the simple purchasing power parity condition than what the condition is able to actually describe in reality. For example, it is tempting to try to generalize the condition to the national rate of

---

EXAMPLE 2-3

Today's quote for the French franc is 6 FF/$. What will be the quote a year from now after 5% inflation in France and 10% inflation in the United States, assuming the purchasing power parity condition holds?

Solution 2-3 $X^1_{C/\$} = (6 \text{ FF/\$})(1.05/1.10) = 5.727 \text{ FF/\$}$.

inflation of a "basket" of goods, and to use this generalization to form *forecasts* of exchange rates based on forecasted national rates of inflation.

In reality, however, such an application may be unwarranted. As has been indicated, the purchasing power parity condition is only a simple description of how exchange rates *should* move in a system of market-determined rates and given the international law of one price of a single goods market. But the international law of one price is not really a law that describes the real world. Rather, it is an economic ideal based on the assumption that it costs nothing to transport and there are no trade barriers (like tariffs, quotas, and language/cultural barriers). In reality, however, there are costs of transporting and other barriers.

Moreover, consider more than one commodity. What happens if the international law of one price says the exchange rate should be 2.00 $/£ given wheat prices but 1.75 $/£ given the U.S. and U.K. steel prices? Violations of the international law of one price for basic commodities have been reported in empirical research.[3]

Furthermore, many consumption goods are unique to a country or at least are not traded across borders in a fashion that would allow goods market arbitrage or quasi-arbitrage. An interesting indicator of the divergence from the international law of one price for a nontraded commodity is *The Economist's* annual Big Mac index. (See Figure 2-4.) Based upon Big Mac prices around the globe and on current exchange rates, the index evaluates the degree of currency misvaluation.

For example, the April 9, 1994, issue of *The Economist* reported that Big Macs cost ¥391 in Japan and $2.30 in the United States (on average). If appropriate, the international law of one price would suggest that the exchange rate be 170 ¥/$. However, the exchange rate was observed to be 104 ¥/$. On a percentage basis, the misvaluation of the yen was reported to be 64%. In other words, the value of the yen was 64% higher than what would be implied by the international law of one price. The range of currency misvaluations in the Big Mac context was from −55% for China and −48% for Hong Kong to 67% for Denmark and 72% for Switzerland.[4]

Given that the international law of one price, upon which the purchasing power parity condition is based, is not a reality, it is hard to justify a belief in the purchasing power parity condition for a single commodity, let alone a version with inflation rates of baskets of goods. Indeed, empirical research on the

---

[3]See Aris Protopapadakis and Hans Stoll, "Spot and Futures Prices and the Law of One Price," *Journal of Finance*, December 1983, pp. 1431–1455.

[4]The percentage by which one observation of the value of a currency differs from another observation must be computed with exchange rates that are in direct terms from the point of view of the base currency. Thus, the value of the yen at 104 ¥/$ differs from the value of the yen at 170 ¥/$ by [1/(104 ¥/$)]/[1/(170 ¥/$)] − 1 = 0.64, or 64%. Note that this answer is not the same as taking the absolute value of the percentage difference in the value of the dollar relative to the yen at 104 ¥/$ from the value of the dollar at 170 ¥/$, which is (104 ¥/$)/(170 ¥/$) − 1 = −0.39, or −39%.

The hamburger standard

	Big Mac prices		Actual $ exchange rate 5/4/94	Implied PPP† of the dollar	Local currency under(-)/over(+) valuation**,%
	In local currency*	In dollars			
UNITED STATES‡	**$2.30**	**2.30**	—	—	—
Argentina	Peso3.60	3.60	1.00	1.57	+57
Australia	A$2.45	1.72	1.42	1.07	-25
Austria	Sch34.00	2.84	12.0	14.8	+23
Belgium	BFr109	3.10	35.2	47.39	+35
Brazil	Cr1,500	1.58	949	652	-31
Britain	£1.81	2.65	1.46‡‡	1.27‡‡	+15
Canada	C$2.86	2.06	1.39	1.24	-10
Chile	Peso948	2.28	414	412	-1
China	Yuan9.00	1.03	8.70	3.91	-55
Czech Rep	CKr50	1.71	29.7	21.7	-27
Denmark	DKr25.75	3.85	6.69	11.2	+67
France	FFr18.5	3.17	5.83	8.04	+38
Germany	DM4.60	2.69	1.71	2.00	+17
Greece	Dr620	2.47	251	270	+8
Holland	Fl5.45	2.85	1.91	2.37	+24
Hong Kong	HK$9.20	1.19	7.73	4.00	-48
Hungary	Forint169	1.66	103	73.48	-29
Italy	Lire4,550	2.77	1,641	1,978	+21
Japan	¥391	3.77	104	170	+64
Malaysia	M$3.77	1.40	2.69	1.64	-39
Mexico	Peso8.10	2.41	3.36	3.52	+5
Poland	Zloty31,000	1.40	22,433	13,478	-40
Portugal	Esc440	2.53	174	191	+10
Russia	Rouble2,900	1.66	1,775	1,261	-29
Singapore	$2.98	1.90	1.57	1.30	-17
S Korea	Won2,300	2.84	810	1,000	+24
Spain	Ptas345	2.50	138	150	+9
Sweden	Skr25.5	3.20	7.97	11.1	+39
Switzerland	SFr5.70	3.96	1.44	2.48	+72
Taiwan	NT$62	2.35	26.4	26.96	+2
Thailand	Baht48	1.90	25.3	20.87	-17

*Prices vary locally   †Purchasing-power parity: local price divided by price in United States   **Against dollar
‡Average of New York, Chicago, San Francisco and Atlanta   ‡‡Dollars per pound
Source: McDonald's

FIGURE 2-4   The Hamburger Standard

Source: The Economist, April 9, 1994, p. 88. ©1994, The Economist Newspaper Group, Inc. Reprinted with permission. Further reproduction prohibited.
The term *purchasing-power parity* here is referred to as the *international law of one price* in the text.

purchasing power parity condition has rejected the condition as a description of reality. Substantial deviations in the short run (over three- to five-year business cycles) have been reported. These deviations are reported to take about three years to be reduced in half.[5]

Thus, although the floating rate exchange market is in theory supposed to prevent currency misvaluations, the reality is that currencies become misvalued, in terms of goods prices, even in the current era of flexible exchange rates.

CENTRAL BANKS AND SPECULATORS IN THE FLOATING RATE MARKET

In addition to the frictions and complexities of goods market arbitrage and quasi-arbitrage, a reason that currencies become misvalued relative to goods prices in the floating rate environment is that the currency market participants often look at factors other than goods prices when trading currencies. Let us examine the roles played by two of the major participants in the market: the central banks and currency speculators.

Central banks cannot regulate the entire global currency market, but instead are market participants, just like businesses and investors. The transactions of central banks are sometimes routine, but other times are intended to further economic policies. For example, a central bank may sell its own currency in the market, thus trying to devalue it. Other times, the central banks may act in a coordinated manner to try to influence exchange rates to achieve some goals reached by negotiation and compromise.

For example, in 1985, when the Federal Reserve believed that the cause of U.S. trade deficits was an overvalued U.S. dollar, the central banks of the *Group of Seven* (*G*-7; the seven major industrialized countries that coordinate economic policies—United States, United Kingdom, Canada, France, Japan, Germany, and Italy) agreed to a coordinated sell-off of their official reserves holdings of dollars. The agreement to do this was called the *Plaza Accord*, so named because the agreement was reached at a meeting at the Plaza Hotel, in New York City. The sell-off has been reported to have caused a depreciation of the dollar relative to other major currencies. Refer to Figures 1-3 and 1-4.

However, some traders in the currency market believe that the dollar was overvalued at the time and already on its way down in value due to other market forces. The central banks' actions were viewed merely as a stamp of approval, not a cause, by these traders. Indeed the traders' view is that the central banks do not carry enough clout to have a lasting impact on market-determined exchange rates with intervention policies.

---

[5]See Niso Abuaf and Phillippe Jorion, "Purchasing Power Parity in the Long Run," *Journal of Finance*, March 1990, pp. 157–174.

For example, in the spring of 1989, the quarter of the greatest market participation by the 11 largest central banks prior to the fall of 1992, the trading volume by those 11 central banks accounted for $47 billion for the *entire quarter*. By contrast, during 1989, the average trading volume in the market was $650 billion *per day*. These statistics support a view that central banks, even in a coordinated effort, do not have enough muscle to determine exchange rates via market intervention. However, central banks are key players in the global economy, and other currency market participants, especially speculators, try to interpret the intervention tactics of central banks for clues about future global economic developments.

Speculators in the currency market are largely interbank traders whose closeness to the market allows them to develop, and to try to profitably exploit, opinions about the future direction of exchange rates. Naturally, speculators are a source of supply and demand pressure on exchange rates, beyond that fundamentally coming from the retail side.

A big question is whether the aggregate trading activity of speculators tends to influence exchange rates or not. Some believe that the actions of speculators tend to cancel out and ultimately be only "noise." In this theory, the aggregate activity of speculators would not influence exchange rates. However, others believe that sometimes many speculators often have the same view, and that their trading therefore influences exchange rates in the aggregate. For example, it has been reported that speculators often try to buy currencies that have been in an appreciation trend. ("The trend is your friend.") If enough currency speculators trade currencies from this perspective, the aggregate trading activity of the speculators would reinforce the original trend.

In general, the trading behavior of central banks and speculators is often thought to be one reason that exchange rates become misvalued in terms of goods prices, even though the floating rate system is in theory supposed to prevent such currency misvaluations from occurring. (Another reason has to do with interest rates and portfolio investors, as will be covered in the next chapter.) Thus, currency misvaluations could be a cause of the trade imbalances, deficits, and surpluses, that have been observed in the era of floating exchange rates.

Despite the arguments and evidence that the purchasing power parity condition is not a literal truth, the condition is not totally useless. Goods prices and their changes *do* play *some* role in determining exchange rates, and violations of the international law of one price can give some indication of how exchange rates may correct in the future. In the real world, the purchasing power parity condition may be relatively more accurate when one of the currencies belongs to a high-inflation country than when neither country of an exchange rate has serious inflation.

In general, in the floating rate environment, nations whose economic policies have promoted economic growth and stability, and controlled inflation, will tend to have currencies that appreciate in value, relative to countries with the opposite policies. The currencies of low-inflation, growth-oriented economies are referred to as *hard currencies*, and the currencies of the weaker, high-inflation economies are referred to as *soft currencies*. The original major hard currencies of the floating rate system were the U.S. dollar, the German mark, the Japanese yen, and the Swiss franc. In the 1980s, following a return to policies oriented toward promoting economic growth and curbing inflation, the British pound and the French franc joined the ranks of the currencies regarded as hard.[6]

Evolution of the Modern Global Economy

GLOBAL TRADE AND BUSINESS ORGANIZATION

The driving force of international business activity is the mutual benefit of trade. Different peoples, endowed with different ideas and resources, produce different products. Exchanging the ideas, resources, and products can be beneficial to both sides of the exchange. If, for example, France has the appropriate natural resources to produce wine while Argentina has the appropriate resources to produce beef, people in both countries can enjoy wine and beef together if France sends some wine to Argentina in exchange for some beef.

Even if it is feasible for both France and Argentina to produce both wine and beef, international trade can leave both countries better off. This point is relatively obvious if France can produce wine more efficiently than Argentina and Argentina can produce beef more efficiently than France (and if transportation costs are not too great.) However, even if one of the two countries can produce *both* commodities more efficiently, both countries may benefit from an arrangement of specialized production and trade. For example, suppose France is significantly more efficient in producing wine but only slightly more efficient in producing beef. In that case, the economic theory of *comparative advantage* suggests that both France and Argentina could be better off by specializing their production and trading with each other.[7]

---

[6]The terms *strong* currency and *weak* currency are also found frequently in the press. Unfortunately, these terms can create confusion. Sometimes "strong currency" is meant to be synonymous with overvalued currency (and "weak currency" means an undervalued currency); other times, "strong currency" is used to describe a currency that is or has been in an appreciation trend. Clearly, a currency that is undervalued could be weak in the first sense, but simultaneously could be in an appreciation trend and thus strong in the second sense.

[7]Further details of the theory of comparative advantage are not included here on the assumption that the topic is covered in economic courses. That international trade is beneficial is viewed as a "given" in this text. An excellent numerical example of the theory of comparative advantage may be found in John F. Marshall and Kenneth R. Kapner, *The Swaps Market* (Miami, FL: Kolb, 1993), pp. 9–14.

Despite the logic of the mutual benefits of trade, the wine producers in Argentina and the beef producers in France would not be very much in favor of such a system of specialized production and international trade. The pressures brought forth by these groups on their governments could lead to trade barriers. Examples of trade barriers are quotas and tariffs on imports and government subsidies to domestic producers. The establishment of these trade barriers demonstrates the concept of *protectionism.*

There exists a spectrum of trade arrangements in between the no-trade and free trade extremes. For example, countries can reduce tariffs and/or increase quotas for trade with specific other countries in mutual preferential trade arrangements.

The basic concept of trade has a very complex structure in the real world of corporations. The simple idea of exporting a product to another country may evolve into the establishment of a factory in the other country. The path of the evolution often follows the steps of (1) licensing in the foreign country, (2) sales offices, (3) service facilities, and (4) foreign direct investment into overseas production facilities. Host country politicians have usually been torn between losing economic control to foreign businesses and gaining the benefits of the inflow of capital and the creation of jobs.

Just as exporting can evolve into foreign direct investment, so can importing. Frequently, the desire to import metals and minerals leads to the importer's investment into facilities to extract the raw materials. Another strategy involving foreign direct investment has been the building of overseas assembly plants. Companies that have evolved to the point of making foreign direct investment are called *multinational corporations (MNCs).*

Some companies have achieved a stage beyond the level of the multinational corporation. There now exist many companies, of many original nationalities, that are capable of competing and coordinating globally, taking raw materials from some countries, producing parts in other countries, assembling in still other countries, and competing to sell final products in markets around the world. The companies' management, employees, and directors are of many nationalities. Nations no longer can claim rights to the discoveries of such companies. As these companies lose their original national identities, they are no longer multinational, but global or *transnational corporations.*[8]

GLOBAL COORDINATION

By the 1980s, the strength of the German and Japanese economies began to have a dramatic effect around the globe. First, in an attempt to regain global economic leadership, the United States took a decided economic turn toward

---

[8]The expanding role of transnational corporations in the global economy is described in "World Investment Report: Transnational Corporations as Engines of Growth," United Nations, 1992. Also see "The Stateless Corporation," *Business Week*, May 14, 1990.

Transnational companies and global economic cooperation have gradually replaced protectionism—and have helped increase worldwide prosperity.

market-based economic policy under the Reagan administration. In Europe, Britain and France led a similar movement away from the socialistic policies that created high inflation and economic stagnation, and toward economic policy aimed at renewing economic growth and wealth. Companies once owned and operated by bureaucratic governments underwent *privatization,* involving sale back to private owners. The European Common Market concept evolved into the detailed *Europe 1992* plan for the elimination of economic trade and investment barriers between participating European countries as of the end of 1992.

In Asia, developing economies began to use Japan's dynamic success as a model. Countries such as South Korea, Taiwan, Hong Kong, Singapore, Malaysia, and others instituted programs aimed at economic growth. The *Asian Development Bank* (ADB) was established to operate in a manner similar to the IMF and the World Bank, but specifically regarding Asian countries.

As the free economies of the Pacific (including Asia, Australia, and New Zealand), Europe, and North America linked toward a common goal of economic prosperity, the global economy grew stronger. The strength of these economies, and the strength of their international economic relationships forged during this period, helped establish the foundation of the modern global economy.

The *Baker plan* of the 1980s initiated a philosophy of economic assistance by the industrially developed countries to those less developed countries (*LDCs*) that want to partake in the global economic prosperity and are willing to participate by making reforms toward sound, free market economic policies. Countries that have dramatically changed their economic direction include Chile, Mexico, Argentina, Venezuela, and Brazil. These Latin American countries and others in other parts of the globe have used the Baker plan to help turn to economic policies designed to reduce inflation, create stable economic growth, and promote free market participation in the global economic effort. The coordinating body for these assistance plans has been the IMF, which has correspondingly taken a leadership role in helping to evolve global economic integration.

ARGENTINA'S CURRENCY BOARD OF THE 1990s

Soft currencies are associated with countries that have chronic inflation, underinvestment, and a weak economy. Often, these currencies are not fully convertible into other currencies. This situation has characterized Latin American and Eastern European countries, including those of the former Soviet Union. A classic example of this situation was Argentina prior to 1991. In one month in 1989, prices in Argentina rose by nearly 2300 percent. This kind of inflation caused currency depreciation and discouraged investment. By January 1992, inflation had been controlled, and Argentina's economy got on track. How did this happen?

In 1991, Argentina adopted a "convertibility plan" patterned after a *currency board*. A currency board is an organizational group with the sole responsibility of defending the value of the nation's currency, and with the power to take the actions necessary to do so. Essentially, the currency board assumes the central bank's monetary control. A currency board has four tenets: (1) To prohibit the central bank from printing money that is not backed by reserves of hard foreign currencies. (2) To permit the country's currency to be freely redeemed on demand for hard foreign currency reserves; this feature is called free convertibility. (3) To peg the currency's value to that of the dominant trading partner, which is the United States in the case of Argentina. (4) To require the government to cut its spending or increase its taxes to eliminate all but the smallest budget deficit, an action that removes the need to print more money, which is inflationary.

Argentina saw its inflation rate drop to single digits in little more than a year following the introduction of the convertibility plan, and foreign investment flowed into the country.

The power of the capitalist economic engine of the cooperating economies eventually proved to be too much for the communist dictatorships in the U.S.S.R. and Eastern Europe, and socialist puppet governments in Latin America and elsewhere. The populations of those countries demanded participation in the global economy as a vastly superior alternative to continuing the "cold war" with the economically integrated "free world." China's free market reforms appear irreversible, as does its willingness to conform to global standards to encourage foreign direct and portfolio investments. In 1992, countries of the former Soviet Union and its former allies in Eastern Europe applied for membership in the IMF. It is hoped that the reform movement in China will lead to eventual membership as well.

The eventual path to a globally integrated economy may follow an evolution through additional regional coordination. Regional plans have evolved following the success of the European example. The United States, Canada, and Mexico have signed the *North American Free Trade Agreement (NAFTA)* to eliminate trade barriers on the North American continent. Similar regional coordination and cooperation is being proposed in Asia, South America, and Eastern Europe. Trade barriers will still exist between regional trading blocks, but regional integration could serve as a step toward fuller global integration.

Despite the global view that has evolved, there are natural problems that arise during the resultant restructuring into global roles. As globalization reduces the number of competing global corporations in a given industry to an efficient number, there have been and will be dislocation costs and losses of jobs. Different kinds of jobs will be available, but for those having to convert from one type of job to another, the shock is dramatic. In countries that must change their systems from communism to market economies, the upheaval is most severe.

These problems, plus the fear of a world where decision makers of other nationalities have control over one's domestic resources, tend to cultivate protectionism. The protectionist strategy is to impose barriers to trade and foreign direct investment to insulate industries from foreign competition and control.

It is fair to say that while much evolution to a global economy has been made, there will continue to be national self-interest and protectionism in foreign trade. However, is protectionism to be a serious challenge to the further evolution of the global economy? The answer is "No," according to Kenichi Ohmae. The reason is that the fate of each nation's economy is already too interdependent with the others. Policies that appear to be in a nation's self-interest may not be. Even "buy American" campaigns in the United States, and "buy European" campaigns in Europe, mean nothing in the "borderless world," where, for example, an automobile's name is no clue as to where the product was manufactured or where the parts were produced. Cars sold by traditional U.S. companies are often produced in Japan (with many U.S.-made parts), while cars sold by traditional Japanese companies are often produced in the United States.[9]

---

[9]A discussion of the global economic concept may be found in Kenichi Ohmae, *The Borderless World* (New York: HarperPerennial, 1990).

TRADE IMBALANCES
IN THE MODERN GLOBAL ECONOMY

In the modern era of a globally integrated economy and transnational companies, concern over trade imbalances (deficits and surpluses), which characterized the mercantilist and Bretton Woods eras, have diminished. One reason is that international business is no longer based on the mercantilist competition between countries to dominate the international trade in basic commodities. Instead, in the integrated global economy, countries are interdependent; for example, the United States exports 747s to Japan, and Japan exports audio/visual equipment to the United States. Trade may become imbalanced at times in this environment, but it seems part of the natural development of the global economy.

Also consider the nature of transnational companies. For example, if a U.S. firm can make more profit by owning a subsidiary in Japan instead of exporting, thereby reducing U.S. exports, are the U.S. owners of the company better or worse off? If the United States imports more products instead of more expensive ones produced domestically, especially if the imports are produced by foreign subsidiaries of U.S. firms and/or with U.S.-exported parts and materials, then are people in the United States better or worse off, even though the higher imports lead to a bigger trade deficit for the United States?

Another reason that concern over trade imbalances has subsided somewhat is the global use of hard currencies. For example, dollars sent to countries outside the United States for imports are not always returned to the United States for gold or official foreign currency reserves. Instead, dollars circulating outside the United States serve as an "international currency." If U.S. officials were to try to depreciate the dollar, confidence in dollars as international currency would drop. While the traditional view of the mercantilist era is that an undervalued currency stimulates a country's export business, this view may not be accurate in the modern global economy. Instead, some now argue that "if a weaker currency promotes exports, Argentina would be the strongest trading nation."[10]

Summary

This chapter has reviewed the evolution of currency exchange in the context of global trade. Some might call this material the *international monetary system*. However, since the collapse of the Bretton Woods arrangements in the early 1970s, the system is not really a system as such, but a market that continues to evolve and develop.

---

[10]The views of this section were drawn from Kenichi Ohmae, "Lies, Damned Lies, and Statistics: Why the Trade Deficit Doesn't Matter in a Borderless World," *Journal of Applied Corporate Finance*, Winter 1991, pp. 98–106. Note that the comment on Argentina referred to the days prior to the establishment of Argentina's convertibility plan discussed on page 48.

The analytical topic of the chapter was the goods market approach to currency valuation. This topic consists of the international law of one price and its corollary, the purchasing power parity condition. While the topic provides some useful theoretical insights, the chapter argued that neither the international law of one price nor the purchasing power parity condition are literal descriptions of reality. In other words, there exist influences on exchange rates other than goods prices, especially in the modern globally integrated economy.

This chapter also introduced the related concept of trade imbalances, that is, trade deficits and surpluses, which are sometimes the subject of emotional discussions in the news and in politics. In this chapter, the subject of trade imbalances was covered as a basic economic concept, without reference to standard balance of payments accounting methods. More aspects of currency valuation and trade imbalances are covered in the next chapter.

Glossary

Asian Development Bank: An international agency established to operate in a manner similar to the IMF and the World Bank, but specifically regarding Asian countries.

Baker Plan: Plan of economic assistance from the core of the global economy to other countries willing to make reforms toward sound, conservative, and free market economic policies.

Bretton Woods Agreement: The post–World War II agreement by many nations to maintain stable, or pegged, exchange rates.

Currency Board: An organizational group with the sole responsibility of defending the value of the nation's currency, and with the power to take the actions necessary to do so.

Europe 1992: A detailed plan for the elimination of economic trade and investment barriers between participating European countries as of the end of 1992.

European Development Bank: An international agency established to operate in a manner similar to the IMF and the World Bank, but specifically regarding European countries.

Floating Exchange Rates: Exchange rates that are determined by free market forces, as opposed to the fixed, or pegged, exchange rates of the Bretton Woods Agreement.

G-7: See Group of Seven.

Group of Seven (G-7): Economic policymakers from seven major industrialized capitalist nations (United States, United Kingdom, Canada, Japan, France, Germany, and Italy) who attempt to coordinate their economic policies.

Hard Currency: A currency that holds its value because the country's economy is strong and growing, and not subject to severe inflation, socialistic policies, and economic deterioration.

International Bank for Reconstruction and Development (IBRD): See World Bank.

International Currency Reserves: Holdings by a central bank, in dollars, yen, marks, pounds, and so forth, to facilitate international trade settlements and to provide backing for its own currency.

International Monetary Fund (IMF): An international organization whose primary goals are to provide assistance to any member country in a short-term international monetary crisis and to provide monetary assistance to countries that are trying to develop modern economies for the first time or to rebuild existing economies after wars or revolutions.

International Monetary System: The organized system for making international financial settlements, given the need to exchange currencies.

LDCs: Less developed countries.

Mercantilism: An economic philosophy of individual countries competing against each other in terms of export levels, with the objective being to accumulate as much gold as possible.

Multinational Corporations (MNCs): Companies that have evolved to the point of making foreign direct investment.

NAFTA: North American Free Trade Agreement, designed to eliminate trade barriers on the North American continent.

Plaza Accord: A 1985 agreement by the central banks of the G-7 countries to sell dollars as a means to reduce the dollar's perceived overvaluation at the time.

Privatization: The return of government-owned and -operated businesses to private owners and operators. Privatization characterized the global trend in the 1980s and 1990s away from socialism and toward market-based economies.

Protectionism: National imposition of barriers of trade and foreign direct investment to keep industries under domestic control and safe from international competition.

Soft Currency: The opposite of hard currency. (See *Hard currency*.)

Theory of Comparative Advantage: An economic theory of organizing global production by relative national efficiency, assuming trade is possible.

Trade Deficit: The amount by which the value of a country's imported goods exceeds the value of its exported goods.

Trade Surplus: The amount by which the value of a country's exported goods exceeds the value of its imported goods.

Transnational Corporation: The name given to a company whose operations are so global that the company appears to be without a national origin or orientation, a "stateless" corporation.

World Bank: Also known as the International Bank for Reconstruction and Development (IBRD), an international agency whose purpose is to provide capital assistance to countries that are trying to develop or rebuild their economies, and for that purpose issues bonds in any currency.

Discussion Questions

1.   Why do you think the global economic concept has maintained its strength despite the strong protectionism that we hear about in the news?

2.   Can a currency that is "strong" in the sense of appreciating also be "weak" in the sense of being undervalued?

3.   Discuss the roles of the following in the exchange market: (a) the need to exchange currencies to conduct international business and for cross-border portfolio investments, (b) policies of national central banks, and (c) speculation.

4.   Explain how a country's overvalued currency can lead to a trade deficit for that country. Which would you prefer: (a) a "strong" currency (in the overvalued sense) and a trade deficit or (b) a "weak" currency (in the undervalued sense) and a trade surplus?

5.   Is a trade deficit bad for a country and a trade surplus (excess of exports over imports) good? Discuss this, first, from the perspective of a country in a world of nations competing for power and, second, from the perspective of a country in a world whose economy is integrated into the "borderless," global economy.

6.   Suppose country A's currency becomes overvalued relative to country B's currency. Explain how natural forces would tend to correct the misvaluation.

7.   Do you think it would ever be possible for the world to adopt a single, global currency and a single monetary authority? What would be the implications?

8.   Explain in your own words the difference between the international law of one price and the purchasing power parity condition.

9.   Do you think that both Japan and the United States would be better off if one country specialized in steel production and one in automobile production? Or would both be better off if each maintained both steel and automobile industries and the countries competed with one another?

Problems

1. If a bushel of wheat costs $2.00 in the United States and ¥350 in Japan, then what does the law of one price say that the exchange rate should be?

2. Let the dollar price of a unit of consumption (thought of as one Big Mac) be $1 at time 0. What would the pound price of a Big Mac have to be so that the time 0 exchange rate of 1.60 $/£ represents a correct valuation of the exchange rate, given the international law of one price?

3. Let the yen price of a bushel of wheat be ¥150 at time 0 and the dollar price of a bushel of wheat be $1 at time 0. Assume that the exchange rate at time 0 is $X^0_{¥/\$} = 150$ ¥/$. Thus, in purchasing power terms, the two currencies are correctly valued against each other at time 0. Now assume that inflation is zero in both countries and that the time 1 exchange rate is $X^1_{¥/\$} = 120$ ¥/$. At time 1, is there (a) an overvalued yen and an undervalued dollar, (b) an overvalued dollar and an undervalued yen, or (c) neither?

4. Assume the same time 0 conditions as in the previous problem. The inflation rate in Japan is 5%, while the inflation rate is 10% in the United States. What would the purchasing power parity condition say that the time 1 exchange rate should be in conventional European terms format?

5. Suppose that, at time 0, the exchange rate of 1.60 $/£ represents a correct valuation in purchasing power terms. Let the inflation in the United Kingdom between time 0 and time 1 be 30%, while in the United States prices drop by 10%. According to the purchasing power parity condition, what should the time 1 exchange rate be in $/£?

6. Suppose that, at time 0, the $/£ exchange rate of 1.60 $/£ represents a correct valuation in purchasing power terms. Let the inflation in the United Kingdom between time 0 and time 1 be 30%, while in the United States prices drop by 10%. If the exchange rate goes from 1.60 $/£ to 1.80 $/£, has the (a) pound become overvalued relative to the dollar, (b) dollar become overvalued relative to the pound, or (c) neither?

7. If the law of one price suggests that the exchange rate between dollars and marks should be 1.60 DM/$ and the actual exchange rate is 1.25 DM/$, what is the percentage misvaluation in the value of the mark relative to the dollar? What is the percentage misvaluation in the value of the dollar relative to the mark? Hint: See footnote 4.

---

4. 143.18 ¥/$.

chapter 3

GLOBAL FINANCE, INTEREST RATES, AND EXCHANGE RATES

Overview of the Global Financial Market

A truly global financial market, one without barriers to cross-border flows of portfolio investments, allows investors to benefit from international diversification and to buy securities that globally offer the highest expected return, given the risk. In such a market, there is nothing in principle to stop a Korean company from issuing German mark–denominated bonds in Switzerland or to prevent Taiwanese investors from buying shares of a Canadian company through a broker in Australia. In a global financial market, capital flows freely across borders to its most productive uses in the most efficient economies.

The world's financial markets have been in a globalization trend. International securities markets (like the eurocurrency market discussed in this chapter and the eurobond market discussed in Chapter 5) have developed and been integrated with national financial markets. In many cases, the international financial markets have found ways to circumvent regulations that otherwise would prevent cross-border flows. In response, many countries have relaxed regulations against cross-border financial flows.

The origins of the modern global financial market lie in the global reach of the British banks that once financed the trade of the far-flung British empire and in the long-standing international banking relationships, often with direct family connections at the top level. Families like the Rothschilds in the eighteenth century managed financial institutions across the borders of Europe. The Morgans in the nineteenth century extended their scope to the new world in the Western Hemisphere. Through this system, the nineteenth-century growth of the United States was financed by Europeans, and the early twentieth-century wars in Asia and Europe were financed by Americans.

The globalization of finance has also been furthered by the role over many years of the secret "numbered accounts" for international capital in Swiss banks. For years, people around the world have relied on the Swiss banks' anonymity policies. Through the Swiss banks, well-heeled investors of many nationalities (the classic "Belgian dentist," as a prototypical wealthy European) have avoided taxes and appropriation. Also, many international rogues, scoundrels, drug lords, and dictators have hidden their stolen wealth behind the secrecy of Swiss accounts. The Swiss banks, in turn, reinvest the capital into significant positions of legitimate internationally issued bonds and equities.

TRADITIONAL TRADE FINANCING

In the early twentieth century, a well-developed international system of *correspondent banking* evolved. Correspondent banking relationships, especially between banks of different nationalities, are based on mutual trust and needs. In the international arena, correspondent banking is necessary to support import/export activity, especially with *trade financing*.

In trade financing, if an exporter of cashmere sweaters is worried about shipping on credit to the importer in a different country, and the importer is equally nervous about sending payment in advance, the two companies can use their respective domestic banks, with an established international correspondent relationship, to guarantee the transaction.

Trade financing begins with a *letter of credit (l/c)*, which is a letter from the importer's bank guaranteeing payment, based on the bank's knowledge of the importer's financial condition.

The exporter knows that the letter of credit means that its bank will guarantee payment, because the exporter's bank can count on collecting from its overseas correspondent bank. (Perhaps there are intermediate correspondents in the chain, as well.) Once the exporter has received the letter of credit, and has documented the shipment of merchandise, these are forwarded to its own bank with an *international draft* for payment to be made at some time in the future, say, 90 days. The exporter's bank forwards these to its correspondent, the importer's bank. The importer's bank accepts the draft by stamping "accepted."

The stamped draft is now a *banker's acceptance* and is a negotiable instrument that may be sold at a discount in the money market, with the face value promised to be paid at maturity time of the draft. Proceeds from the sale of the draft are sent to the exporter's bank, including the detail of currency exchange, and the exporter's bank then credits the exporter's account in the local currency. Meanwhile, the importer receives the shipment, and processes the imports into its products. Later, the importer makes payment for the goods to its own bank, using the cash flows from its sales. At that time, the bank pays the face value of the acceptance to the money market holder. In effect, the money market has been the ultimate source of financing for the international trade. A diagram of this traditional model of trade financing is shown in Figure 3-1.

Trade financing originated in prior times of segmented economies. The use of traditional trade financing and the significance of banker's acceptances have declined somewhat in the modern era of integrated global business, for several reasons. For one, it is more common for an exporter to trust an overseas importer and extend direct credit, as would be done domestically, especially in ongoing global business relationships. For another reason, businesses generally now have global access to short-term working capital financing via the eurocurrency market (covered later in this chapter) and via revolving credit facilities with transnational banks.[1]

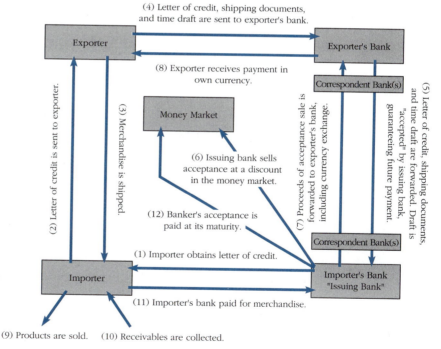

FIGURE 3-1   Flow Diagram for Trade Financing and Banker's Acceptances

---

[1]For a discussion of banker's acceptances, their traditional role in international trade, and their decline in significance as eurocurrency markets have grown, see R. K. LaRoche, "Bankers Acceptances," *Economic Quarterly* (Federal Reserve Bank of Richmond), Winter 1993, pp. 75–85.

INTERNATIONAL BANKING

The development of transnational financial institutions mirrors the evolution of transnational business activity. Banks tend to develop overseas offices, partners, and subsidiaries to service their domestic customers that expand internationally. Services rendered begin with currency exchange and help in the financing of corporate operations in the host country, with either host country or origin country capital, depending on the wishes of local authorities.

Often, overseas banking subsidiaries find ways to avoid local regulation, while at the same time avoiding domestic regulations of the parent office country. For example, a branch of Sumitomo Bank in France is not bound by the same deposit insurance requirements as the domestic branches of French national banks, nor does it have to follow all of the Japanese regulations pertaining to domestic branches of national Japanese banks.

This absence of regulation often permits the subsidiaries to outcompete local financial institutions in providing services to locals. Since the local economy benefits, regulators may tend to leave the situation alone, or even deregulate their domestic financial system to allow it the same freedoms, to be able to compete against the foreign competition. This phenomenon acts as a key counterforce to protectionism.

Globalization of commercial banking services is matched by globalization of investment banking services, including (1) securities underwriting, (2) secondary market brokerage and trading, (3) deal making for mergers and acquisitions, and (4) portfolio management. The internationalization of these services has led to the development of significant cross-border flows of capital investment into bonds and stocks, and of the global bond and equity markets.

A feature of the global financial system is the evolving process of *securitization*, in which corporate borrowing takes the form of negotiable securities rather than commercial bank loans. For example, a company that in earlier times might have simply borrowed on contract with its commercial bank may now find its bank structuring the loan as a *medium-term note (MTN)* that may be resold by the bank into the global capital market and traded there. Given the trend to securitization, the roles of commercial and investment banks are difficult to distinguish in the global financial system, and companies are increasingly shopping around for the financial institution that offers the best financing deal at any given time.

Indeed, many financial institutions on the global scene, particularly European banks, are already *universal banks* in that they do not distinguish between commercial banking and investment banking services. In the United States domestic financial institutions have been required to operate in only one fashion, either as a commercial bank or an investment bank, by the *Glass-Steagall Act*. Prior to this act, banks in the United States were universal banks. The Glass-Steagall Act was passed in 1933 on the assumption that the excessive speculation by U.S. banks into Latin American investments in the 1920s was a source of the financial crisis that led to the Great Depression. The belief in 1933 was that future excessive speculation could be avoided if banks' powers were limited. Following the U.S. model, Japan adopted a similar regulation after World War II.

Currently, there is pressure in the United States for the repeal of the Glass-Steagall Act. For one thing, since domestic regulations do not apply internationally, the foreign subsidiaries of U.S. commercial and investment banks operate as universal banks, performing both investment banking and commercial banking.

In addition, many domestic banks in the United States have already been permitted to conduct business with international companies without the same restrictions that are imposed on business with domestic companies. This situation is due to an amendment to the Federal Reserve Act, passed in 1916, permitting some large U.S. banks to have subsidiaries that operate in the United States like international banks from other countries, subject to an "agreement" with the Federal Reserve. This amendment is called the *Edge Act*, and the banking subsidiaries are called *Edge Act and Agreement companies.*

More recently, after a trend of U.S. banks establishing offshore "shell" branches in the Caribbean to compete more effectively for international deposits without reserve requirements or FDIC insurance payments, the United States further liberalized its regulations by authorizing *international banking facilities (IBFs)*. An IBF is not a physical entity, but a separate set of books at a U.S. bank that is allowed to operate as if it were outside the United States.

Today, international banking is evolving toward fewer and fewer boundaries. It is just as ordinary for a domestic company to obtain financial services from its local office of a foreign bank as from a domestic bank. Each global financial institution has a home office in one of a variety of countries and subsidiaries around the world. These institutions form a network to facilitate the global financial markets and serve international investors and corporations, performing currency exchange, banking, and investment banking services in many currencies.

Often, banks from various national origins will cooperate in a syndicate to assist major multinational firms obtain financing via a large bond or equity issue. The trend, through cross-border mergers and acquisitions of financial institutions, is toward global "megabanks" with no nationally oriented headquarters location. Combinations between such financial giants as Credit Suisse (Switzerland)–First Boston (United States), Deutschebank (Germany)–Morgan Grenfell (United Kingdom), and Sumitomo (Japan)–Goldman Sachs (United States) represent significant events in the trend.

The network of global financial institutions supports the global markets for currencies, loans and deposits, bonds, and equities. This network of markets, with the aid of financial innovation and the global derivative markets in options, futures, forwards, and swaps, increasingly facilitates cross-border financial flows.[2]

GLOBAL FINANCIAL CENTERS

Despite electronic linkage to all markets around the globe and to each other, each of the main global banks maintains an office in one of the major financial centers of the world. For many years, London was the dominant international financial center. After World War II, New York became an important global financial center. In the 1980s, Tokyo would surpass Hong Kong and Singapore to become the leading financial center in Asia. Other important financial centers in the global market are Paris, Zurich (Switzerland), Sidney (Australia), Bahrain, Toronto, and Chicago.[3]

If a country desires a global financial center, the country must deregulate its financial markets, primarily to allow capital to flow freely in and out. Governments have generally acknowledged that the way to remain a viable participant in the global economy is to be a viable participant in the global financial system. The way to do the latter is by having a global financial center, which requires deregulation.

Today, by size and tradition, London may still be regarded as the financial center of the world. The eurocurrency and eurobond markets are centered there. The volume of foreign exchange trading is the largest in the world (roughly $400 billion per day as compared to $200 billion per day in New York).

THE BASEL ACCORD

An important indication of the extent of global coordination and cooperation is the *Basel Accord*, in which central monetary authorities (the U.S. Federal Reserve, Germany's Bundesbank, the Bank of England, the Bank of Japan, and so forth) agreed to international capital standards for global financial institutions. The 1988 agreement was reached in Basel, Switzerland, at the *Bank for International Settlements (BIS)*. The BIS serves as a clearinghouse for transactions between the central banks and serves the role of a "world central bank." The standards established in the Basel Accord are sometimes called the *BIS Standards*.

---

[2]The evolution of the global financial system is lucidly explained in Roy Smith, *The Global Bankers* (New York: E. P. Dutton, 1989). A review of the status of the global financial system as of about 1990 is in Christine Pavel and John N. McElravey, "Globalization in the Financial Services Industry," Federal Reserve Bank of Chicago, *Economic Perspectives*, May/June 1990, pp. 3–18

[3]An interesting survey of financial centers can be found in *The Economist*, June 27, 1992. An excellent review of the trends of the global financial system is in *The Economist*, September 19, 1992, under the title "Fear of Finance."

Deregulation has helped many national financial centers become global financial centers.

The Eurocurrency Market

Not so many years ago, banks generally accepted customers' deposits denominated only in the currency of the country in which the bank was domiciled. The situation is different now. Deposit and loan services in major currencies frequently take place outside the geographical area in which a given currency is legal tender.

The present situation evolved from the *eurodollar* concept, which originated in the 1950s. Reportedly, communist governments needed dollars for international trade, since their own currencies were not acceptable, but feared a potential freeze of any dollar deposits held at U.S. banks or their foreign subsidiaries. Instead, some European banks were asked to hold the dollar deposits. The banks realized that there were no regulations to prevent denominating deposits in dollars, paying interest in dollars, and then relending the dollars elsewhere (outside the United States) at a higher rates of interest.

This idea was soon applied to regular business customers. By the 1960s, it was common for non-U.S. banks to conduct banking services in U.S. dollars. Since this practice originated in Europe, the term eurodollar was coined. Later, when dollar deposits and loans began elsewhere, particularly in Asia, the term eurodollar continued to be used, as well as more limited use of the term "Asian dollars." In general, a eurodollar has come to be a dollar-denominated deposit or loan outside the United States.

Eurodollar deposits are not subject to U.S. Federal Reserve requirements or FDIC insurance payments, since banks outside the United States naturally cannot be made to conform to U.S. regulations. This feature allows banks dealing in eurodollar deposits and loans to offer rates that are more competitive than those available within the United States. The loss of regulatory control has been viewed benignly by the U.S. government, which believes that having the U.S. dollar serve as an "international currency" has benefits in international prestige, influence, and trade.

Gradually, as the economies of Germany, Japan, Britain, France, Switzerland, and others grew strong, the eurodollar concept was extended to include euromarks, euroyen, eurosterling (pounds), euroFrench francs, euroSwiss francs, and so forth. In general, the term *eurocurrency* applies to any currency deposit or loan outside the country that prints the currency. Sovereign governments have accepted the use of deposits and loans denominated in their currency, yet beyond their control, as a necessary and useful aspect of the powerful global economy.

In its current state, the *eurocurrency market* involves *globally traded time deposits and time loans* with market-determined interest rates. The term "eurocurrency market" is misleading, since the deposits/loans are neither European nor exchange transactions between currencies. It is important to comprehend the nature of the eurocurrency instrument as a traded vehicle for which a market is made continuously around the globe, much like the currency market.

Eurocurrency quotes are in simple annualized terms. To find simple annualized interest, one multiplies the actual interest rate by the number of periods in a year. For example, if actual interest is 2% for 3 months, then the simple annualized interest quote is $4(0.02) = 0.08$, or 8%. If one is quoted 6% (an annual rate) on 6-month Dutch guilders, then the actual interest rate paid over 6 months is $0.06/2 = 0.03$, or 3%.

The global eurocurrency market has essentially the same interbank dealer structure as the currency market, with rate quotes continuously reflecting global supply and demand conditions for borrowing and lending for different horizons in the various currencies. Dealing banks will quote their own bid and offer prices in the form of annualized interest rates. For example, a large New Zealand bank might quote 1-year euroyen at 5 15/16 to 6 1/16. This quote means that the bank is willing to pay 5 15/16% interest on 1-year time deposit in Japanese yen and is willing to lend yen for 1 year at 6 1/16% interest. (See Figure 3-2.)

For convenience, we'll ignore the transaction cost of the dealer spread and think in terms of a single eurocurrency interest rate at which both a deposit and a loan may be made. One may wish to think of the midpoint between the dealers' bid and ask rates as *the* eurocurrency interest rate. This

EURO CURRENCY INTEREST RATES

Feb 8	Short term	7 days notice	One month	Three months	Six months	One year
Belgian Franc	$5\frac{1}{8} - 5$	$5\frac{1}{8} - 5$	$5\frac{1}{4} - 5\frac{1}{8}$	$5\frac{7}{16} - 5\frac{5}{16}$	$5\frac{13}{16} - 5\frac{11}{16}$	$6\frac{3}{8} - 6\frac{1}{4}$
Danish Krona	$5\frac{1}{4} - 5$	$5\frac{3}{4} - 5\frac{1}{2}$	$5\frac{7}{8} - 5\frac{5}{8}$	$6\frac{1}{4} - 6$	$6\frac{3}{4} - 6\frac{5}{8}$	$7\frac{7}{16} - 7\frac{5}{16}$
D-Mark	$5 - 4\frac{7}{8}$	$4\frac{15}{16} - 4\frac{13}{16}$	$4\frac{15}{16} - 4\frac{13}{16}$	$5\frac{1}{16} - 4\frac{15}{16}$	$5\frac{1}{4} - 5\frac{1}{8}$	$5\frac{3}{4} - 5\frac{5}{8}$
Dutch Guilder	$5\frac{1}{16} - 4\frac{15}{16}$	$5\frac{1}{16} - 4\frac{15}{16}$	$5\frac{1}{8} - 5\frac{1}{16}$	$5\frac{3}{16} - 5\frac{1}{16}$	$5\frac{3}{8} - 5\frac{5}{16}$	$5\frac{13}{16} - 5\frac{13}{16}$
French Franc	$5\frac{3}{8} - 5\frac{1}{4}$	$5\frac{7}{16} - 5\frac{5}{16}$	$5\frac{1}{2} - 5\frac{3}{8}$	$5\frac{11}{16} - 5\frac{9}{16}$	$6 - 5\frac{7}{8}$	$6\frac{9}{16} - 6\frac{7}{16}$
Portuguese Esc.	$8\frac{3}{4} - 8\frac{1}{2}$	$8\frac{7}{8} - 8\frac{5}{8}$	$9\frac{3}{8} - 7\frac{7}{8}$	$10 - 9\frac{3}{4}$	$10\frac{1}{2} - 10\frac{1}{4}$	$11 - 10\frac{5}{8}$
Spanish Peseta	$8\frac{1}{16} - 7\frac{15}{16}$	$8 - 7\frac{7}{8}$	$8\frac{1}{8} - 8$	$8\frac{5}{8} - 8\frac{1}{2}$	$9 - 8\frac{7}{8}$	$10 - 9\frac{7}{8}$
Sterling	$7 - 6\frac{7}{8}$	$6\frac{1}{2} - 6\frac{3}{8}$	$6\frac{9}{16} - 6\frac{1}{2}$	$6\frac{13}{16} - 6\frac{11}{16}$	$7\frac{1}{8} - 7$	$7\frac{11}{16} - 7\frac{5}{8}$
Swiss Franc	$3\frac{3}{8} - 3\frac{1}{4}$	$3\frac{1}{2} - 3\frac{3}{8}$	$3\frac{11}{16} - 3\frac{9}{16}$	$3\frac{15}{16} - 3\frac{13}{16}$	$4\frac{3}{16} - 4\frac{1}{16}$	$4\frac{1}{2} - 4\frac{3}{8}$
Can. Dollar	$7\frac{11}{16} - 7\frac{7}{16}$	$7\frac{13}{16} - 7\frac{9}{16}$	$7\frac{13}{16} - 7\frac{11}{16}$	$7\frac{15}{16} - 7\frac{13}{16}$	$8\frac{1}{16} - 7\frac{15}{16}$	$8\frac{3}{8} - 8\frac{1}{4}$
US Dollar	$6\frac{1}{16} - 5\frac{15}{16}$	$6\frac{1}{16} - 5\frac{15}{16}$	$6\frac{1}{8} - 6$	$6\frac{5}{16} - 6\frac{3}{16}$	$6\frac{11}{16} - 6\frac{9}{16}$	$7\frac{5}{8} - 7\frac{3}{8}$
Italian Lira	$9 - 7\frac{1}{2}$	$8\frac{5}{16} - 8\frac{3}{16}$	$8\frac{3}{8} - 8\frac{1}{4}$	$8\frac{3}{4} - 8\frac{5}{8}$	$9\frac{1}{4} - 9\frac{1}{8}$	$10 - 9\frac{7}{8}$
Yen	$2\frac{1}{4} - 2\frac{3}{16}$	$2\frac{1}{4} - 2\frac{3}{16}$	$2\frac{1}{4} - 2\frac{3}{16}$	$2\frac{5}{16} - 2\frac{1}{4}$	$2\frac{3}{8} - 2\frac{5}{16}$	$2\frac{9}{16} - 2\frac{1}{2}$
Asian \$Sing	$3\frac{7}{8} - 3\frac{5}{8}$	$4\frac{3}{8} - 4\frac{1}{4}$	$3\frac{5}{8} - 3\frac{1}{2}$	$4\frac{1}{16} - 4\frac{1}{16}$	$4\frac{9}{16} - 4\frac{7}{16}$	$4\frac{3}{4} - 4\frac{5}{8}$

Short term rates are call for the US Dollar and Yen, others: two days' notice.

FIGURE 3-2   Eurocurrency Interest Rates
Source: The Financial Times, February 9, 1995. Reprinted by permission.

simplification allows us to convey basic concepts without the added complexity of transaction costs.

It is important to see that the global nature of the market means that there are *not* different eurocurrency rates in each country; instead, there is only one global eurocurrency rate for each currency (for a given horizon). In other words, at a given bank in any country, a borrower of yen from France would pay the same interest rate as a borrower of yen from Korea.

Consider, as representative of retail activity within the interbank eurocurrency market, a company (in any country) that wants to borrow French francs for a year. If the company already has a sufficient line of credit with its bank, a simple call to its banker and the deal is almost instantaneous. The bank, literally simultaneously, can shop the interbank market on a video monitor. If the best 1-year French franc borrowing rate is quoted by a Japanese bank, the company's bank can instantaneously borrow the French francs from the Japanese bank and then relend the French francs to the customer at a markup.

Just as in the foreign exchange market, eurocurrency deposits and loans are made between banks in the interbank market, and between banks and retail customers in the retail market. And, just as in any national currency market, the total amount of eurocurrency loans and deposits may well exceed the total amount of physical currency in circulation outside of the country issuing the currency.[4]

---

[4]For an introduction to the interbank eurocurrency market and its issues, see Anthony Saunders, "The Eurocurrency Interbank Market: Potential for International Crisis?" Federal Reserve Bank of Philadelphia, *Business Review*, January/February, 1988, pp. 17–27.

LIBOR

Despite the fact that the eurocurrency market is just as global as the currency market, the geographical center of the eurocurrency market is, by size and tradition, London. Hence, London banks' eurocurrency quotes are surveyed as a method for obtaining the representative focus of the market. The average of the borrowing or "offer" rate is the much publicized *LIBOR* (London interbank offer rate), which serves as a daily consensus, or index, of eurocurrency market interest rates.

The offer rates in Figure 3-2 are LIBOR rates for February 8, 1995, as reported in *The Financial Times* on February 9, 1995. From Figure 3-2, we see that LIBOR is not just one interest rate for either the U.S. dollar or the British pound. There exist many LIBORs for different currencies and times to maturity. There is a 3-month yen LIBOR, a 1-year Dutch guilder LIBOR, and so forth. Maturities of 1 week, 3 months, 6 months, 9 months, and 1 year are the most popular in the eurocurrency market. However, markets in some eurocurrencies are active for other maturities, including 2-year, 3-year, 5-year, and higher.

Often interbank interest rate indexes exist in each of the world's financial centers. For example, there is SIBOR for Singapore, PIBOR for Paris, and so forth. However, these rates will not be much different than LIBOR. The global market's eurocurrency interest rate in a given currency will often be called LIBOR in this text.

PROCEEDS AND FACE VALUES

Eurocurrency loans and deposits are zero coupon, or pure discount, instruments. All interest is accrued, and no principal payments are paid or received before maturity. For example, if you borrow ¥100 (= 100 yen) today at 6%, you'll pay back ¥106 in a year, and if you deposit ¥100 at 6% for one year, you'll receive ¥106 in a year. Note that depositing (lending) is the mirror act of borrowing.

If you deposit SF100 (= 100 Swiss francs) for 2 years at a 2-year euroSwiss franc LIBOR rate of 5%, then you'll receive $SF100(1.05)^2 = SF110.25$ two years later; there is no interim interest payment or principal payment. Similarly, if you borrow SF100 for 2 years at the 2-year rate of 5%, the proceeds are SF100, while the payment is SF110.25, to be made two years later.

Sometimes the amount of a eurocurrency deposit/loan is referred to by a face value amount at maturity. Using this convention, for example, a 2-year eurocurrency loan with a face value of ¥100,000,000 at 6% will have proceeds of $¥100,000,000/1.06^2 = ¥88,999,644$. In other words, ¥88,999,644 is borrowed, and ¥100,000,000 (the face value) is repaid 2 years later.

The relationship between the proceeds (PV) and face value (FV) of any *n*-period discount instrument paying an interest rate, or yield to maturity, of *y*, is a simple application of present value/future value of a lump sum, and is given in equation (3-1).

PROCEEDS AND FACE VALUE RELATIONSHIP FOR DISCOUNT INSTRUMENTS

$$PV = \frac{FV}{(1 + y)^n} \quad \text{and} \quad FV = PV\,(1 + y)^n \qquad (3\text{-}1)$$

EXAMPLE 3-1

You make a 4-year eurosterling deposit with face value of £200,000. How much did you deposit if 4-=year sterling LIBOR is 8.5%

Solution 3-1   £200,000/1.085^4 = £144,315.

ARBITRAGE BETWEEN EUROCURRENCY RATES AND NATIONAL RATES

While national monetary authorities do not have direct supervision over the global LIBOR rates, there is a natural link between the eurocurrency rate and those national interest rates that are directly influenced by national monetary authorities. For example, if the U.S. Federal Reserve institutes policies designed to reduce interest rates in the United States, the dollar LIBOR rates will also fall.

The reason for this linkage is the notion of arbitrage. If global banks are offering 3-month eurodollars for 6%, while dollars can be borrowed in local U.S. markets at 5%, then shrewd traders can make arbitrage profits by borrowing at 5% in the local U.S. market and depositing at 6% in the eurocurrency market. Let us look at an example of how the arbitrage profits can be taken immediately, that is, at time 0. This technique will serve as a foundation to more complex arbitrage strategies covered later.

Given that the 3-month interest rate quotes are in simple annualized interest, the 3-month borrowing rate in the *domestic market* is one-fourth the given annualized rate of 5%, or 0.25(0.05) = 0.0125. The 3-month deposit rate in the *eurocurrency market* is one-fourth the given annualized rate of 6%, or 0.25(0.06) = 0.0150.

Assuming $1,000,000 of face value, the proceeds on the borrowing is $1,000,000/1.0125 = $987,654. Only $1,000,000/1.015 = $985,222 needs to be deposited to have a $1,000,000 receipt in 3 months in the eurocurrency market. Thus, at the 3-month horizon, the eurocurrency deposit proceeds may be used to repay the $1,000,000 face value of the local loan. At the same time, the difference between the loan proceeds and the deposit is $987,654 − 985,222 = $2432. This amount is arbitrage profit, available immediately. Similarly, if the domestic rates were higher than the euromarket rates, then the direction of the transaction would be reversed.

If a nation's domestic rate is greater than the euromarket rate (as in Example 3-2), then arbitrage activity will gradually drive the euromarket rate

> ### 📖 EXAMPLE 3-2
>
> Assume that the Hong Kong dollar (HK$) interest rates in the domestic Hong Kong market have risen due to actions of the central monetary authority (which consists of Hong Kong's two large private banks). Assume that the 1-year Hong Kong dollar interest rate in the domestic market has risen to 7.0%, but is 6.5% in the eurocurrency market. Demonstrate how to produce immediate arbitrage profits, and find the amount of the profits for a face value of HK$1,000,000.
>
> *Solution 3-2*   The solution may be demonstrated for any amount, but a face value at maturity of HK$1,000,000 is assumed. Since the rates quoted are for a 1-year horizon, no adjustment for the number of periods per year is necessary, as was the case in the text example. Borrow HK$1,000,000/1.065 = HK$938,967 in the eurocurrency market. Deposit HK$1,000,000/1.07 = HK$934,579 in the domestic market. Keep the difference of HK$938,967 - HK$934,579 = HK$4388 as an immediate arbitrage profit.

up and the domestic rate down to the point where no arbitrage opportunities are available. Alternatively, if the domestic rate is lower than the euromarket rate, then the directions are reversed.

The overnight rate at which national banks may borrow from their central monetary authority is often called the *central bank discount rate*. When a central bank changes its discount rate, interest rates of the domestic banking system are immediately affected. The arbitrage just discussed describes the transmission linkage between domestic interest rates and eurocurrency interest rates in that currency.

Exchange Rates and Asset Markets

Quite often we hear that a central bank has altered its discount rate as a means to influence the value of its currency relative to other currencies. As discussed in the previous section, a change in a central bank's discount rate is transmitted via arbitrage activity into the private global eurocurrency markets.

The reasoning behind such central bank actions to influence currency values via interest rates is related to the theory of *asset market valuation* of exchange rates. The central bank reasoning is as follows: All other things the same, the higher the observed interest rate for a currency, the higher the value of the currency will be. The logic is that if the interest rate in a currency increases, then global investors will tend to reposition their portfolios toward securities denominated in that currency. Since such transactions involve an explicit higher demand for the currency, the value of the currency should appreciate. Similarly, a currency whose interest rate declines, other things equal, should depreciate in value.

The logic is that the asset market dictates what the current currency value should be, given the equality of a global investor's rate of return on eurocurrency deposits, after taking into account the effects of currency conversion, and *given* a predicted future spot exchange rate.

THE INTEREST PARITY CONDITION

For example, ask the following question: Given the predicted (at time 0) future spot exchange rate (for time 1) between the mark and the dollar, $X^{1p}_{DM/\$}$, and given the current euromark and eurodollar interest rates for the same horizon, what is the current exchange rate, $X^{0}_{DM/\$}$, that would make a mark-based investor indifferent between the following two strategies: (1) a direct euromark deposit and (2) a strategy involving the conversion of marks to dollars, depositing the dollars at the eurodollar interest rate and then converting the deposit proceeds back to marks at the assumed predicted future spot exchange rate?

After answering this question, we'll verify that the same spot exchange rate would also make a dollar-based investor indifferent between (1) a direct eurodollar deposit and (2) a strategy involving the conversion of dollars to marks, depositing the marks at the euromark interest rate and then converting the mark deposit proceeds back to dollars in the future at the predicted future spot exchange rate.

Consider the following example. Suppose the 1-year euromark rate is 9.2%, that the 1-year eurodollar rate is 4%, and that global investors predict at time 0 that the DM/$ exchange rate will be $X^{1p}_{DM/\$}$ = 1.50 DM/$ one year from now. Consider a mark-based investor who exchanges the necessary amount of marks into $1000 at the current spot exchange rate (to be determined), deposits the $1000 for a year at 4% to result in $1040, and assumes a conversion at that time of the $1040 into marks at the predicted future spot exchange rate of 1.50 DM/$. The investor predicts an ending amount of marks of $1040(1.50 DM/$) = DM1560. (See Figure 3-3.)

Thus to make the predicted rate of return on this venture equal to the 9.2% that could be had by simply maintaining a deposit in euromarks, we must find the initial amount of marks, x, such that DM1560 represents a 9.2% rate of return on an initial investment of x, or thus that DM1560/x − 1 = 0.092. Thus x = DM1560/1.092 = DM1428.57. Thus, since the mark-based investor would be indifferent between the eurodollar deposit and the euromark deposit if he can turn DM1428.57 into $1000, he would be indifferent if the current spot exchange rate is $X^{0}_{DM/\$}$ = 1.42857 DM/$.

What about a dollar-based investor, who takes $1000, changes that amount at 1.42857 DM/$ into $1000(1.42857 DM/$) = DM1428.57, compounds the marks in a 1-year euromark deposit to DM1428.57(1.092) = DM1560, and then predicts a conversion of the DM1560 back into dollars a year from now at the assumed predicted exchange rate of 1.50 DM/$? The predicted ending dollar amount is DM1560/(1.50 DM/$) = $1040. If the predicted future

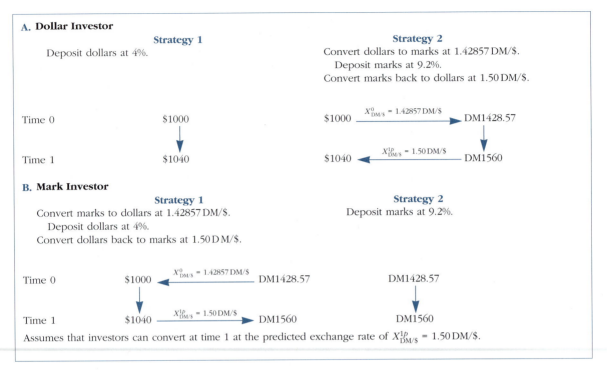

A. Dollar Investor

Strategy 1
Deposit dollars at 4%.

Strategy 2
Convert dollars to marks at 1.42857 DM/$.
 Deposit marks at 9.2%.
Convert marks back to dollars at 1.50 DM/$.

Time 0 $1000 $1000 $\xrightarrow{X^0_{DM/\$} = 1.42857\,DM/\$}$ DM1428.57

Time 1 $1040 $1040 $\xleftarrow{X^{1p}_{DM/\$} = 1.50\,DM/\$}$ DM1560

B. Mark Investor

Strategy 1
Convert marks to dollars at 1.42857 DM/$.
 Deposit dollars at 4%.
Convert dollars back to marks at 1.50 D M/$.

Strategy 2
Deposit marks at 9.2%.

Time 0 $1000 $\xleftarrow{X^0_{DM/\$} = 1.42857\,DM/\$}$ DM1428.57   DM1428.57

Time 1 $1040 $\xrightarrow{X^{1p}_{DM/\$} = 1.50\,DM/\$}$ DM1560   DM1560

Assumes that investors can convert at time 1 at the predicted exchange rate of $X^{1p}_{DM/\$}$ = 1.50 DM/$.

FIGURE 3-3 Equivalence of Asset Strategies for Global Investors

exchange rate actually does occur at time 1, then given the current spot exchange rate of $X^0_{DM/\$}$ = 1.42857 DM/$, the dollar-based investor will have indeed received the 4% rate of return that would make him or her indifferent between the eurodollar deposit and the euromark deposit strategy, after accounting for the currency conversion. The scenario is depicted in Figure 3-3.

If the current exchange rate were different from 1.42857 DM/$, then neither mark-based nor dollar-based investors would be indifferent. If the spot exchange rate were less than 1.42857, the eurodollar alternative would be more attractive than the euromark investment, given the higher predicted dollar appreciation/mark depreciation.

For example, if the spot exchange rate were actually 1.400 DM/$, the mark-based investor should convert DM1400 into $1000, deposit the $1000 at 4% for one year, and predict a conversion of the $1040 proceeds back into $1040(1.50 DM/$) = DM1560 in one year. The mark-based investor's rate of return would be DM1560/DM1400 - 1 = 0.114, or 11.4%. In contrast, if the dollar-based investor converted $1000 to DM1400 and invested the DM1400 at 9.2% for a year, and then converted the proceeds of DM1400(1.092) = DM1528.8 to DM1528.8/(1.50 DM/$) = $1019.20, the dollar-based investor's resulting rate of return would only be $1019.20/$1000 − 1 = 0.0192, or 1.92%.

Now let us put this reasoning into a formula. In the earlier example, we effectively found that a U.S. investor could obtain a 4% dollar rate of return by investing $1 for a year in a eurodollar deposit, or predict to obtain a 4% dollar rate of return by converting $1 into DM1.42857 at the spot exchange rate of $X^0_{DM/\$}$ = 1.42857 DM/$, compounding those marks forward at 9.2%, and then converting the resulting amount back into dollars at $X^{1p}_{DM/\$}$, the time 0 prediction about the future (time 1) exchange rate. Thus, setting $X^0_{DM/\$}(1 + r_{DM})/X^{1p}_{DM/\$}$ equal to $1 + r_\$$ and rearranging, we can generalize the example to equation (3-2) for the equilibrium spot exchange rate in European terms. Equation (3-2) is often called the *interest parity condition* or, to be more precise, the *uncovered (or open) interest parity condition.*

THE INTEREST PARITY CONDITION

$$X^0_{C/\$} = X^{1p}_{C/\$} \left[\frac{(1 + r_\$)}{(1 + r_C)} \right] \tag{3-2}$$

where $X^{1p}_{C/\$}$ is the exchange rate predicted to prevail at time 1 in European terms, $r_\$$ is the eurodollar interest rate, and r_C is the eurorate on the other currency.

Equation (3-2) is presented in its logical form with the spot exchange rate on the left-hand side. Note that equation (3-2) may be rearranged into the form $X^{1p}_{C/\$} = X^0_{C/\$}(1 + r_C)/(1 + r_\$)$. This form allows you to use the same mem-

---

EXAMPLE 3-3

Assume that the 1-year euroyen interest rate is 3%, while the 1-year eurodollar rate is 5%. If global investors' time 0 belief (prediction) about the future spot exchange rate a year from now is $X^{1p}_{¥/\$}$ = 120 ¥/$, what should today's exchange rate be, according to the asset market approach to currency valuation? Demonstrate that, given the current spot exchange rate that is derived, a yen-based investor will be predicted to make the same return on a eurodollar deposit, adjusted for currency exchange, as would be made directly on a euroyen deposit. Also demonstrate that a dollar-based investor will be predicted to make the same return on a euroyen deposit, adjusted for currency exchange, as would be made directly on a eurodollar deposit.

Solution 3-3   From equation (3-2), $X^0_{¥/\$}$ = (120 ¥/$)(1.05/1.03) = 122.33 ¥/$. A yen-based investor can convert ¥122.33 into $1, deposit the $1 for a year at 5% to have $1.05, and then plan to convert the $1.05 back to yen at 120 ¥/$ to get $1.05(120 ¥/$) = ¥126, representing a yen rate of return of ¥126/¥122.33 − 1 = 0.03, or 3%, the same as on a direct euroyen deposit. A dollar-based investor can convert $1 into ¥122.33, deposit the ¥122.33 for a year at 3% to have ¥126, and then plan to convert the ¥126 back to dollars at 120 ¥/$ to get ¥126/(120 ¥/$) = $1.05, representing a dollar rate of return of 5%, the same as on a direct eurodollar deposit.

ory device covered in connection with the purchasing power parity equation of Chapter 2, equation (2-2): With the exchange rate for the future on the left-hand side, the interest rate in the numerator is that of the numerator currency of the exchange rate. If you recall the equation in that form, you can rearrange it into the form of equation (3-2). The reason that equation (3-2) places the spot exchange rate on the left-hand side is to emphasize that the time 0 spot exchange rate is the variable that is determined by the other three variables in the asset market approach to currency valuation.

For an American terms exchange rate, $X_{\$/C}$, the memory device means that $X_{\$/C}^{1p} = X_{\$/C}^0(1 + r_\$)/(1 + r_C)$, which rearranges to the expression for the equilibrium spot exchange rate in American terms: $X_{\$/C}^0 = X_{\$/C}^{1p}(1 + r_C)/(1 + r_\$)$.

Another way to view the basic idea of the asset market valuation of currencies is to start with the predicted rate of currency appreciation/depreciation, given the currently *observed* spot exchange rate. Then in equilibrium, global investors will require higher interest rates on deposits in the currency that they believe will depreciate, so as to be compensated for the depreciation. In the text example just given, if the spot exchange rate is currently $X_{DM/\$}^0 = 1.42857$ DM/$ and the predicted exchange rate is $X_{DM/\$}^{1p} = 1.50$ DM/$, global investors believe that the dollar will appreciate and the mark will depreciate. Thus the interest rate required by global investors on a mark deposit must be higher than the interest rate on the dollar deposit to compensate the investors for the anticipated change in the currency values.

CHANGES IN INTEREST RATES IN ASSET MARKET VALUATION

The view that the currency with the higher interest rate is the one that is *predicted to depreciate*, gradually over time, is sometimes confused with the theory's implication that a positive change in one currency's interest rate leads to an *appreciation* in that currency's spot value.

Recall the original text example where investors believe that the exchange rate a year from now will be $X_{DM/\$}^{1p} = 1.50$ DM/$, the current 1-year eurocurrency deposit rates are 9.2% for the mark and 4% for the dollar, respectively, and the equilibrium spot exchange rate is $X_{DM/\$}^0 = 1.42857$ DM/$.

What would the new equilibrium spot exchange rate be if the interest rate on euromark deposits suddenly jumped to 10.2%? Assuming no change in the predicted exchange rate or the dollar eurorate, the answer, from application of equation (3-2) is $(1.50 \text{ DM/\$})(1.04/1.102) = 1.4156$ DM/$. The notation $X_{DM/\$}^{0+}$ will be used to denote the new equilibrium exchange rate at time 0 "plus" some very small fraction of time. In other words, the exchange rate change is almost instantaneous, as opposed to the gradual change that takes place over a year between time 0 and time 1, and between time 0+ and time 1.

Compared to the original equilibrium spot exchange rate of 1.42857 DM/$, the new equilibrium rate of 1.4156 DM/$ represents a *higher value* for the mark and a corresponding lower value for the dollar. Note that this exchange rate change represents a *virtually immediate* appreciation in the value of the mark relative to the dollar, but the currency with the higher of the two interest rates, the mark, is still the one that is predicted to depreciate over time (to $X_{DM/\$}^{1p}$ = 1.50 DM/$).

This is the point that is sometimes confusing to people who are first learning this material: *The currency with the higher of the two interest rates is the one whose currency is predicted to depreciate over time, but an increase in either currency's interest rate leads to an immediate appreciation of that currency in the spot exchange market.*

Central to the asset market valuation model is the view that (1) there exists a highly mobile pool of global funds that is immediately responsive to

---

EXAMPLE 3-4

Assume that global investors believe that the exchange rate for the British pound will be 2.00 $/£ in one year; that is, the predicted $/£ spot rate for a year from now is $X_{\$/£}^{1p}$ = 2.00 $/£. Assume initially that the 1-year eurodollar rate is 5% and that the 1-year eurosterling rate is 10%. What is the current equilibrium exchange rate? Now let the 1-year eurodollar rate stay at 5% and assume that the 1-year eurosterling rate instantaneously jumps to 12%. What exchange rate changes occur under the theory of asset market valuation of exchange rates?

Solution 3-4   Applying the American terms version of equation (3-2), the original equilibrium exchange rate is $X_{\$/£}^{0}$ = (2.00 $/£)(1.10/1.05) = 2.095 $/£. If the eurosterling rate jumps to 12%, then the new equilibrium exchange rate is $X_{\$/£}^{0+}$ = (2.00 $/£)(1.12/1.05) = 2.133 $/£. This answer means that the equilibrium spot value of the pound is higher (2.133 $/£, compared to 2.095 $/£). This change takes place "instantaneously." However, note that since the predicted future value of the pound 1 year from now is unchanged and is still 2.00 $/£, then over the next year, the pound is still predicted to depreciate to 2.00 $/£. However, at the new spot exchange rate of 2.133 $/£, the pound is now predicted to depreciate by a greater amount between now and time 1. The predicted gradual depreciation of the pound is consistent with the fact that the interest rate on eurosterling deposits is higher than on eurodollar deposits.

---

changes in eurocurrency interest rates, and (2) predictions about future exchange rates do not change with instantaneous time 0 changes in eurocurrency interest rates. The response to an instantaneous time 0 change in eurocurrency interest rate(s) therefore must be an "instantaneous" time 0 change in the current exchange rate.

It is possible, of course, that a change in the interest rate for a currency might cause analysts to rethink their assessment of the nation's future economic outlook and, therefore, to revise their predicted future exchange rate. If this happens, then the entire effect of the interest rate change will *not* be felt in the immediate spot exchange market; some, perhaps all, will be reflected in a change in the *prediction* about the future exchange rate.

In the extreme, it is possible that all of an interest rate change will be reflected in the predicted future exchange rate. In this case, the spot exchange rate would not be affected at all by an interest rate "shock." This situation is described by a theory known as the *international Fisher model*. The international Fisher model employs the same variables and, indeed, even the same relationship as equation (3-2), but the international Fisher model is based on different assumptions and has different implications than the asset market model. The international Fisher model is developed in the appendix to this chapter. The reason for not providing the development in the text is twofold: First, the implications of the asset market model seem to reconcile better with empirical data.[5] Second, the development of the international Fisher model is somewhat lengthy.

For those with the time and the inclination to obtain the best understanding, this would be a good point to tackle the Appendix. Figure 3-4 summarizes the key distinctions between the two theories.

Which of the two models, the asset market model or the international Fisher model, is better? The answer to this question depends upon which assumptions apply the best. While both perspectives can assist in analyzing the effect of interest rate changes, the appropriate application depends on which assumptions are the most relevant in the specific situation.

One quick answer is that the asset market approach may apply more often with relatively hard currencies, while the international Fisher approach may apply more often in soft currency situations. The reason is that interest rate changes are more likely to be a reflection of inflation rate changes in soft currency, high-inflation countries. In support of the asset market perspective when two hard currency nations are involved, it is common to observe central banks' monetary policies influencing spot exchange rates in the fashion suggested by the asset market theory. It will be a rare semester if you do not note this effect in your classroom discussions of current events.

However, events involving hard currencies have not always reconciled with the asset market model. For example, the increases in U.S. interest rates in 1994 were generally coincident with a depreciation of the dollar relative to other currencies, contrary to the implications of the asset market model. According to reports, the reason for the depreciation of the dollar was that foreign investors began to liquidate their U.S. bonds and convert (sell) the result-

---

[5]For evidence supporting the asset market theory over the international Fisher theory, see Jeffrey A. Frankel, "On the Mark: A Theory of Floating Exchange Rates Based on Real Interest Rate Differentials," *American Economic Review*, September 1979, pp. 610–622.

The Asset Market Model	*The International Fisher Model**
Assumptions:	
1. Nominal interest rate differentials reflect the market's predicted change in nominal currency value.	1. The real rate of interest is the same across different countries. 2. An adapted version of the purchasing power parity condition, as a forecasting model, holds.
Implications:	
1. An increase in an interest rate is accompanied by an immediate appreciation in the spot currency value and no change in the predicted currency value.	1. An increase in an interest rate is accompanied by a depreciation in the *predicted* currency value and no immediate change in the spot currency value.
2. A decrease in an interest rate is accompanied by an immediate depreciation in the spot currency value and no change in the predicted currency value.	2. A decrease in an interest rate is accompanied by an appreciation in the *predicted* currency value and no immediate change in the spot currency value.

*The international Fisher model is developed in the appendix to this chapter.

FIGURE 3-4   Comparison of the Asset Market Model and the International Fisher Model. The international Fisher model is developed in the appendix to this chapter.

ing dollars back into their own currencies, as U.S. bond prices fell in connection with the interest rate increases. The behavior of such investors with existing long-term foreign investment positions is not within the scope of either the asset market model or the international Fisher model.

The real world is not necessarily characterized by either the extreme asset market approach, where all of an interest rate change is reflected immediately in the spot exchange rate, nor the international Fisher approach where all of an interest rate change is reflected in a change in the predicted future exchange rate. While many situations can be viewed as an intermediate position that combines elements of both models, there are also many other aspects of exchange rate valuation that neither the asset market model nor the international Fisher model can capture, as is amplified in the next section. The two models discussed above can only provide the basic tools for examining more complex cases.

In this section, the issue of risk has been ignored. Of course, we know that global investors evaluating these alternative strategies are exposing themselves to risk and uncertainty in the exchange-and-eurocurrency strategy. The actual exchange rate that occurs at the horizon time for converting the deposit liquidation amount may be quite different from the original prediction. For this reason, the indifference between the two possible investment strategies is not a condition that is enforceable by a true arbitrage strategy with no risk. While important, the analysis of the influence of risk is quite complicated, and by deferring the issue to a later chapter, we can more easily focus on only those ideas that are important to us at this point. Thus, for now, market participants are simply assumed to believe strongly in identical single-point predictions of the future spot exchange rate, with no uncertainty. The term "predicted" is used in lieu of the term "expected," since the latter term implies the risk (uncertainty) of a probability distribution.

Equilibrium, Disequilibrium, and the Real World

REAL INTEREST RATES, CURRENCY VALUES, AND TRADE IMBALANCES

It may be instructive at this point to note that the asset market approach to currency valuation may *not* lead to an exchange rate that is consistent with the value implied by the goods market approach covered in Chapter 2. To see this point, first assume that the international law of one price and the interest parity condition do both hold initially (at time 0). Subsequently, assume that an instantaneous change in interest rates results in an instantaneous change in the time 0 exchange rate, according to the asset market approach to currency valuation. Given that goods prices have not yet had time to change, the international law of one price will no longer hold under the new spot exchange rate.

Say that the interest rate in currency C increases suddenly. During the time that goods prices are reequilibrating to the new currency value driven by the asset market, currency C is the overvalued currency from the goods market perspective. As we know from the last chapter, country C is likely to experience a trade deficit due to its currency being overvalued in the goods market, although the currencies are correctly valued by asset market standards. Figure 3-5 depicts this scenario.

Moreover, holding predicted inflation the same as it was before the interest rate change, the real rate of interest in currency C is higher, where the real rate of interest is the nominal rate of interest adjusted for predicted inflation. Thus there potentially exists a logical connection between higher *real* rates of interest in a country and a country's trade deficit! Let's explore this conclusion more.

Let us start by assuming that the real interest rate is for some reason higher in country C than in the rest of the world. One potential explanation for this condition is that corporations in country C have discovered new processes that create higher production efficiency and lead to better investment opportunity schedules. Based upon the coverage of capital budgeting in your introductory financial management course, you may envision companies accepting more capital budgeting projects with higher internal rates of return (IRRs), with this increased demand for capital driving up the cost of capital and other interest rates. Holding inflation constant, the real rate of return in country C is higher, and now exceeds the rest of the world.

In this situation, global capital would flow to country C. As this capital competes with country C's own capital, interest rates and real interest rates in country C will be pressured downward. Also, as the global capital is reallo-

I. Initial Scenario: Spot exchange rate = $X^0_{DM/\$}$ = 1.42875 DM/\$
Asset Market and goods market are both in equilibrium.

1. Asset Market Equilibrium

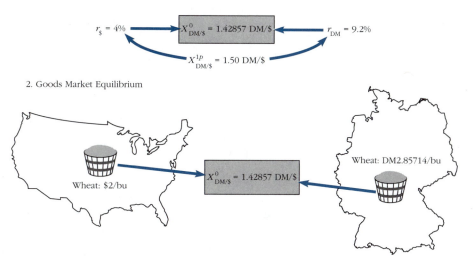

$r_\$ = 4\%$ → $X^0_{DM/\$}$ = 1.42857 DM/\$ ← $r_{DM} = 9.2\%$

$X^{1p}_{DM/\$}$ = 1.50 DM/\$

2. Goods Market Equilibrium

Wheat: DM2.85714/bu
Wheat: \$2/bu
$X^0_{DM/\$}$ = 1.42857 DM/\$

II. New Scenario: Mark interest rate suddenly jumps to r^+_{DM} = 10.2%
New spot exchange rate = $X^{0+}_{DM/\$}$ = 1.4156 DM/\$

1. Asset Market Equilibrium

$r_\$ = 4\%$ → $X^{0+}_{DM/\$}$ = 1.4156 DM/\$ ← r^+_{DM} = 10.2%

$X^{1p}_{DM/\$}$ = 1.50 DM/\$

2. Goods Market Disequilibrium

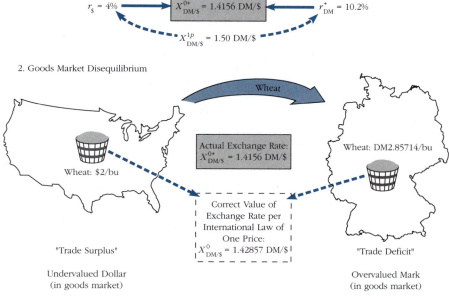

Wheat

Wheat: \$2/bu

Actual Exchange Rate:
$X^{0+}_{DM/\$}$ = 1.4156 DM/\$

Wheat: DM2.85714/bu

Correct Value of
Exchange Rate per
International Law of
One Price:
$X^0_{DM/\$}$ = 1.42857 DM/\$

"Trade Surplus"

Undervalued Dollar
(in goods market)

"Trade Deficit"

Overvalued Mark
(in goods market)

FIGURE 3-5   Equilibrium in the Asset Market and Disequilibrium in the Goods Market
Note: If the purchasing power parity condition held initially, and if inflation rates did not
change when the mark interest rate rose, then the real rate in Germany is higher than the real
rate in the United States.

cated, the lower IRR projects in other countries are forgone, resulting in higher real rates for those countries. These effects continue until a reequilibration in global real interest rates is achieved. This explanation reveals the theoretical economic process for how an equilibrium condition of equal real interest rates across countries would be achieved. Moreover, the explanation reveals how a country that has high real rates of return and rapid growth, and that is attracting capital from overseas, typically will have trade deficits until the reequilibration has occurred. From this perspective, a trade deficit can be indicative of a healthy and strongly growing economy, in contrast to the argument often made in connection with the goods market approach to currency valuation (Chapter 2).[6]

EXAMPLE 3-5

Refer to Example 3-4. Assume that goods prices and rates of inflation remain the same when the sterling interest rate jumps to 12%. Assume that initially trade was balanced and that the real rates were the same in England and the United States. Which currency has the higher real rate of interest after the shock to the nominal British interest rate. Is one of the currencies overvalued by a goods market yardstick? If so, which one? Is trade likely to now be imbalanced and, if so, in which direction?

Solution 3-5 Since the sterling nominal interest rate jumps to 12% from 10%, with no change in inflation rates, England has the higher real rate after the nominal interest rate shock. Since the pound increases in nominal value, from $X^0_{\$/£} = 2.095$ \$/£ to $X^{0\,+}_{\$/£} = 2.133$ \$/£, the pound is now overvalued in the goods market, since goods prices are assumed to have not changed yet. The overvalued pound should theoretically lead to more imports by England, and trade will therefore theoretically be imbalanced in the fashion of a trade deficit for England.

The reality is that significant differences in real interest rates across countries are typical and appear to prevail for long periods, sometimes years. Look at Figure 3-6, which shows (1) the differences over time in long-term real interest rates between the United States and Germany and (2) the changes over time in the value of the dollar against the mark. In Figure 3-6, we see that during periods when the U.S. real rate exceeded that of Germany, the dollar generally appreciated in nominal value relative to the mark, and vice versa.

---

[6]This point is also made in K. Alec Chrystal and Geoffrey E. Wood, "Are Trade Deficits a Problem?" *Federal Reserve Bank of St. Louis Review*, January/February 1988, pp. 3–11, reprinted in Robert Kolb, ed., *The International Financial Reader*, 2nd ed. (Miami, FL: Kolb, 1993), Chap. 4, pp. 49–57.

DYNAMIC SCENARIOS

As we see in Figure 3-6, not only can real interest rates be unequal across countries, the real interest rate differential is generally changing. Thus, the common situation in the real world is not equilibrium, but rather a dynamic state of flux, or disequilibrium.[7]

One can imagine starting from an equilibrium situation and then imposing an immediate increase in the real rate of interest in a currency, as discussed earlier. The higher real interest rate attracts global investment, driving up the currency value. The gradual reequilibration process for goods prices and investment returns could take years, and in the meanwhile, a host of other basic changes could occur, causing more shocks to real interest differentials. These conditions make real-world analysis of exchange rate changes very complex.

In the rest of this section we examine four real-world situations of exchange rates, interest rates, and other economic factors: (1) the U.S. dollar

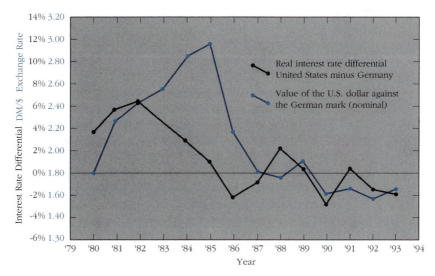

FIGURE 3-6 Comparison of Real Interest Rate Differentials and the Value of the Dollar: The United States and Germany 1980–1993
Source: Adrian W. Throop, "International Financial Market Integration and Linkages of National Interest Rates," *Economic Review Federal Reserve Bank of San Francisco,* No. 3 1994, pp. 3–18.

---

[7]Evidence that real interest rates vary across countries is presented in Adrian W. Throop, "International Financial Market Integration and Linkages of National Interest Rates," *Economic Review Federal Reserve Bank of San Francisco,* No. 3 1994, pp. 3-18, and in Frederic S. Mishkin, "Are Real Interest Rates Equal Across Countries? An Empirical Investigation of International Parity Conditions," *Journal of Finance,* December 1984, pp. 1345–1357.

in the early 1980s, (2) the Canadian dollar in the early 1990s, (3) the British pound in the late 1980s, and (4) the Mexican peso in 1994–1995.

The U.S. Dollar in the Early 1980s

Consider the U.S. situation in the years 1980 to 1985. During that period the real rate in the United States exceeded that in other countries. See Figure 3-6. Assuming that the asset market kept the interest parity condition enforced, the dollar would have been overvalued using a goods market yardstick, and trade deficits would result (as was the case) in the United States.

However, at the same time, the dollar did not depreciate, but instead appreciated, even though it was already overvalued in the global goods market. This dynamic might be explained by the fact that the real rate of interest in the United States was rising relative to the real rate in other countries (Figure 3-6). This trend in the real interest rate differential forced the spot of the dollar higher, thanks to the global asset markets, overriding the pull from the goods market in the other direction.

This scenario has been based on the following reasoning:

1. Differences in real rates of return across countries mean that the exchange rate may not be in equilibrium from both an asset market and a goods market point of view.
2. Actions in the global asset market dominate those in the international goods market in determining spot exchange values.

The second piece of reasoning may be sound, since global financial flows can take place more easily than global goods flows, and since it has been estimated that around 90% of foreign exchange transactions relate to financial transactions and only about 10% to goods transactions.

The Canadian Dollar in the Early 1990s

Moreover, there may be situations where there is more to the story than can be described with the tools just outlined. For example, consider a situation where a central bank believes in the asset market effect on spot exchange rates and is trying to engineer artificially high nominal interest rates to prop up the value of its currency, at a time when the currency would otherwise be naturally depreciating, say due to inflation. If slower economic growth is caused by the higher interest rate and the overvaluation of the currency in the spot exchange market (less demand for the country's export products), the predicted future value of the currency may drop. Shrewd currency traders may begin to sell the currency sooner, rather than later, *despite* the increased (short-term) interest rates. Hence, the central bank's approach may backfire and result, sooner rather than later, in decreased demand for the currency in the spot exchange market. This scenario is one where the interest rate changes

Electronic trading of currencies, deposits, and loans allows portfolio assets to flow across borders more easily than physical goods, enforcing asset market valuation more easily than goods market valuation.

have an influence on the predicted exchange rate that in turn influences the spot exchange rate, overriding the more simplistic prediction of the asset market model. This scenario applied to the Canadian dollar in the early 1990s, according to currency traders at Shawmut Bank.

The British Pound in the Late 1980s

Here is another scenario of a similar nature. In 1987, the Bank of England tried to keep the value of the pound artificially undervalued in purchasing power terms. The strategy was applied by direct intervention, selling pounds in the currency market. The reason for this strategy was presumably to stimulate exports and thus to create domestic jobs, as discussed in Chapter 2. However, the undervalued currency was also undervalued in the asset market and therefore in demand by international investors for purposes of making British investments. Since the global asset market pressure tended to countervail the Bank of England's direct intervention into the exchange market, the Bank of

England also tried to expand the money supply to keep interest rates low in hopes of keeping the spot value of the pound down—in the spirit of the asset market theory of currency valuation. However, the money supply expansion led to high inflation, causing interest rates to surge. High inflation and high interest rates will tend to slow down an economy (i.e., lower the real rate of interest in a country), exactly the opposite result that the undervalued pound was designed to produce. In effect, the Bank of England's tactics affected the predicted future exchange rate, so the implications of the asset market theory did not result.

BALANCE OF PAYMENTS ACCOUNTING

Governments have attempted to measure their countries' international economic and financial activity by means of *balance of payments accounts*. The balance of payments accounts are a record of transactions between domestic residents and the rest of the world over a specific period of time. Like any double entry bookkeeping system, the balance of payments accounts must balance.

The simplest form in which the balance of payments accounts are designed to be expressed is

$$CA + K + F = 0$$

where CA refers to the *current account* balance, K is net nonofficial portfolio flows, and F is official foreign currency reserve financing. Together, K and F constitute the capital account.

The current account has two major components: the *trade balance* and the *services balance* or "invisibles balance." The trade balance is the difference between the value of goods exported and the value of goods imported. The services balance refers to international transactions where there is not a physical product. International tourism counts in the services balance. Nonofficial portfolio flows refer to foreign portfolio investments into domestic government securities, stocks, corporate debt securities, and so forth and to domestic holdings of similar foreign securities. If, on net, either the current account or the nonofficial portfolio account represents an inflow of foreign currency to a country, the account is represented with a "plus" sign, and if, on net, an account represents an outflow of domestic currency to a country, the account is represented with a "minus" sign.

The official foreign currency reserve financing account represents the changes in the official foreign currency reserves of the domestic economy. By design, this account reflects the currency flows of the current and portfolio transactions. If the current account and nonofficial portfolio account add to a positive amount, the change in official foreign currency reserves account should be negative.

For example, suppose that over a period of time, the value of U.S. imports on current account exceeds the value of the exports on current account by $150 million. Then the current account balance would show negative $150 million, a current account deficit. If there are no portfolio flows, then the U.S. official foreign currency reserves should decrease, and/or foreign balances of dollars should increase, by $150 million. This account would show a positive $150 million.

If, instead of zero nonofficial portfolio flows, foreign investors had put $200 million into U.S. securities, the U.S. nonofficial portfolio account would show a "plus" $200 million (since the foreign investment represents an inflow of foreign currency into the United States). Against the negative $150 million on current account, the net inflow of $50 million worth of foreign currency to the United States represents an increase in official foreign currency reserves, and would be shown as a negative $50 million for that account. The U.S. balance of payments accounts would appear as shown below.

Hypothetical U.S. Balance of Payments Accounts

Balance on current account	$−150,000,000
Balance on capital account	
Nonofficial portfolio flows	200,000,000
Changes in U.S. official reserves	
(increase −)	−50,000,000
Balance	$ 0

The Mexican Peso Crisis, 1994–1995

In the late 1980s, Mexico undertook economic reform measures as part of the Baker and Brady plans of assistance from the International Monetary Fund. Subsequently, Mexico experienced economic growth and stabilization, and international investors bought Mexican securities. During the early 1990s, foreigners were drawn to Mexico's 30% short-term interest rates. The foreign investment supported the peso, and Mexico ran a trade deficit, as might be expected from our earlier discussion.

But in early 1994, a political rebellion shook investor confidence. Meanwhile, the U.S. interest rates began to climb, making Mexican rates less attractive by comparison. Foreign investors began to sell Mexican assets, putting pressure on the peso. The Mexican government tried to directly intervene in the currency market, buying pesos in an effort to support the peso's value. By late 1994, renewed political unrest triggered additional flight by foreign investors. By then Mexico had already used most of its reserves of U.S. dollars in its effort to buy pesos, and Mexico had to discontinue the direct support of its currency.

As the value of the peso fell, international investors became apprehensive about their investments in other emerging economies, in Latin America and elsewhere. U.S. officials feared that a global "panic" might result in the form of an avalanche of investment withdrawal from all emerging economies of the world. In early 1995, the United States led an immediate international support effort for Mexico, despite some protectionist opposition. Supporters of the Mexican "bailout" believed that a global investment panic would severely retard the development of the global economy and all of its future benefits.

Summary

This chapter considered some aspects of global finance. First, some of the evolution of the integration of the world's financial markets was discussed. Second, the truly international market for short-term financing in the various currencies of the world, the eurocurrency market, was examined. Eurocurrency deposits and loans are traded in a highly liquid, global market and have prices (the interest rates) that adjust continuously to market supply and demand pressures.

Third, the relationship between exchange rates and interest rates was examined from the viewpoint of the asset market approach, which models the influence of changes in interest rates on spot exchange rates. Some discussion about exchange rate dynamics was also provided, in light of situations where (1) real interest rates differ across countries, (2) the asset market has a more immediate effect in influencing exchange rates than the goods market, and therefore (3) where the exchange rate may reflect misvaluation from a goods market perspective. Some notions of balance of payments accounting were covered in a box.

Glossary

BIS Standards: See Basel Accord.

Balance of Payments Accounts: A record of transactions between domestic residents and the rest of the world over a specific period of time.

Bank for International Settlements (BIS):   An organization in Basel, Switzerland that is the clearinghouse for transactions between the central banks and that has assumed the role of a "global central bank."

Banker's Acceptance: A negotiable money market instrument, representing an accepted international draft, and therefore a promised payment, against a letter of credit issued by a bank.

Basel Accord: The agreement in 1988 that established international capital standards for global financial institutions, established at the Bank for International Settlements (BIS).

Central Bank Discount Rate: The overnight rate at which national banks may borrow from the central monetary authority of a country.

Edge Act and Agreement Companies: Subsidiaries of large U.S. banks operating like international banks from other countries, permitted by the Edge Act, an amendment to the Federal Reserve Act in 1916, and subject to "agreement" by Federal Reserve.

Eurodollar: A U.S. dollar deposit or loan outside of the United States.

Eurocurrency: A time deposit or loan that is traded globally at market-determined interest rates.

Glass-Steagall Act: The law in the United States prohibiting domestic financial institutions from operating both commercial banking and investment banking services.

Interest Parity Condition: A theoretical relationship of equality between the interest rates in different currencies, after adjusting for predicted currency movements.

International Draft: A check drawn against a domestic bank by a foreign exporter, authorized by the bank's letter of credit to the exporter.

International Banking Facility (IBF):   An accounting treatment allowing a U.S. bank to carry on international activity under a separate set of books from the domestic banking operation.

Letter of Credit: A letter from an importer's domestic bank guaranteeing payment, often with conditions for documenting the shipment.

LIBOR: London Interbank Offer Rate: The average of London banks' eurocurrency borrowing or "offer" rate for a currency.

Medium-Term Note (MTN):   A form of bank financing that is securitized and traded in secondary markets.

Securitization: Evolutionary process of the global financial market in which corporate borrowing takes the form of negotiable securities rather than commercial bank loans.

Trade Financing: The use of international correspondent banks to guarantee export/import transactions between corporations with no developed credit arrangement.

Universal Banks: Banks that provide both commercial banking and investment banking services.

Discussion Questions

1.   Assume that the purchasing power parity condition holds for the goods market initially. Also assume that, initially, real rates of return are the same across countries. Given the asset approach, explain why a short-run increase in an interest rate for a currency, other things equal, implies that the real rate of interest for that currency will be higher than the real rate of interest for other countries.

2. Assume that the international law of one price holds initially in the goods market and that the interest parity condition holds. Explain why a short-run increase in the interest rate for a currency, other things equal, implies that the currency will be overvalued in the goods market. Compare your answer to that for Question 1 to demonstrate the reasoning for why countries with high economic growth (high real rates of interest) may have trade deficits.

3. Compare and contrast the implications of an interest rate decrease in the asset market approach and the international Fisher approach. (You may need to read the appendix to answer this question.)

4. This question is intended to enhance your knowledge of global geography. Examine the map below in Figure 3-7. If trading begins in Tokyo at 9:00 A.M., what time is it in London? Hong Kong? Singapore? New York? Hint: You may need to refer to the Photograph 3-1 earlier in the chapter.

Problems

1. You borrow 100 3-year euroFrench francs (proceeds) quoted at 7%. How much do you repay, and when?

2. You make a 2-year euroCanadian dollar deposit with a face value of

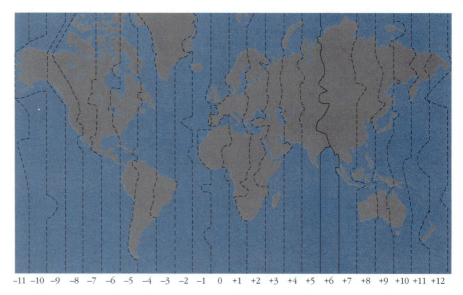

-11 -10 -9 -8 -7 -6 -5 -4 -3 -2 -1 0 +1 +2 +3 +4 +5 +6 +7 +8 +9 +10 +11 +12

FIGURE 3-7 Global Time Zones

C$5,000,000. How much did you deposit if the 2-year Canadian dollar LIBOR is 6.5%?

3. The 1-year German mark interest rate in the domestic German money market has just fallen to 6%, as a result of actions by Germany's central bank, the Bundesbank ("Bubba," as currency traders call it). Assume that the 1-year mark eurocurrency rate is 6.5%. Demonstrate how to produce immediate arbitrage profits (at time 0), and find the amount of the profits for a time 1 face value of DM1,000,000.

4. At time 0, the 1-year euroFrench franc interest rate is r_{FF} = 10%, while the 1-year eurodollar interest rate is $r_\$$ = 6%. If today's prediction for the future spot exchange rate a year from now is 6 FF/$, what should today's spot exchange rate be, according to the asset market approach? Demonstrate that a French franc–based investor will make the same return on a eurodollar deposit, adjusted for currency exchange, as would be made directly on a euroFrench franc deposit, and that a dollar-based investor will make the same return on a euroFrench franc deposit, adjusted for currency exchange, as would be made directly on a eurodollar deposit.

5. The exchange rate for the British pound is predicted to be 1.75 $/£ in 1 year. If the 1-year eurodollar rate is currently 8% and the 1-year eurosterling rate is currently 5%, what is the equilibrium spot exchange rate under the asset market approach?

6. Refer to the previous problem. Assume that the 1-year eurodollar LIBOR rises to 10%, and all else stays the same. By what percentage does the value of the dollar change against the pound, and by what percentage does the value of the pound change against the dollar, in reaction to this interest rate move, according to the asset market approach to currency valuation? At the new exchange rate, what is the predicted percentage change in the value of the dollar and in the value of the pound over the next year?

The following problems and answers relate to material presented in the appendix.

A-1. If the interest rate is 8% and the inflation rate is 2%, find the real rate of interest. Assuming that the real interest rate remains constant, find the new inflation rate implied by a new interest rate of 11%.

3. DM4429 = time 0 arbitrage profit.

5. $X^0_{\$/£}$ = 1.701 $/£.

6. The new exchange rate is 1.67 $/£. The "instantaneous" percentage change in the value of the dollar is 0.0186, or 1.86%. The percentage change in the value of the pound is −0.0180 = −1.80% (or −1.82%, depending on rounding). The new predicted percentage change in the value of the dollar over the next year is minus 4.57%. The new predicted percentage change in the value of the pound over the next year is 4.79%.

A-2. Assume a spot exchange rate of 2.00 $/£, an 8% anticipated rate of inflation in England, and a 5% anticipated rate of inflation in the United States. Assume that the dollar interest rate is 10%. If the dollar interest rate drops to 9%, what will happen to the value of the pound according to the international Fisher approach?

A-3. Assume that the current spot exchange rate for the Swiss franc is 1.35 SF/$. If the 1-year eurodollar rate is currently 5% and the 1-year euroSwiss franc rate is currently 8%, what is the forecasted exchange rate for a year from now under the international Fisher approach?

A-4. Extend the previous problem. If the euroSwiss franc interest rate decreases to 6%, holding the eurodollar rate constant at 5%, what is the result according to the international Fisher approach?

A-2. The new predicted exchange rate is 1.927 $/£.

A-4. The new predicted exchange rate is 1.363 SF/$.

THE INTERNATIONAL FISHER MODEL OF CURRENCY VALUATION

The international Fisher model of currency valuation is based upon (1) the international law of one price, (2) the purchasing power parity condition, and (3) the assumption that differences in interest rates across currencies are always a reflection of differences in *inflation rates* across the respective countries. As the examples that follow will demonstrate, these assumptions imply that an interest rate change will influence the predicted future exchange rate, not the spot exchange rate.

Consider the following example. Let us assume that global investors predict a 4% rate of inflation in marks and a 6% rate of inflation in dollars. Assume further that the investors believe that the purchasing power parity condition, equation (2-2), can be adapted into a forecasting situation. Given a spot exchange rate at time 0 of $X^0_{DM/\$} = 1.40$ DM/\$ and given the inflation rate predictions, the forecasting version of the purchasing power parity condition would imply that the future predicted exchange rate is $X^{1p}_{DM/\$} = (1.40$ DM/\$)$(1.04/1.06) = 1.374$ DM/\$.

Now hold current (time 0) goods prices constant, but assume an immediate rise at time 0 in the assessed inflation rate over the next year for dollar goods, to $i_\$ = 10\%$. Since time 0 goods prices are assumed to be unchanged, the current spot exchange rate cannot change, due to the assumption of the international law of one price. The forecast by the purchasing power parity condition implies that the new predicted exchange rate will be $X^{1p+}_{DM/\$} = (1.40$ DM/\$)$(1.04/1.10) = 1.324$ DM/\$, representing a nominally lower predicted time 1 value for the dollar than the 1.374 DM/\$ originally predicted.

The key link between this purchasing power result and interest rates is that the international Fisher model assumes a direct relationship between anticipated inflation and interest rates. The following example explains that relationship.

If 1 bushel of wheat can be purchased for $1 today or for $1.08 in 1 year (reflecting an 8% inflation rate for the year), and if $1 invested today for a year will earn a 10% interest rate, then one can give up 1 bushel today in return for $1.10/($1.08/bushel) = 1.0185 bushels in the future. The *real interest rate*, which is measured in units of real consumption, is $1.0185 - 1 = 0.0185$, or 1.85%.

Formally, this relationship is known as the *Fisher equation* and is given in equation (3A-1).

FISHER EQUATION

$$(1 + r_{rC}) = \frac{(1 + r_C)}{(1 + i_C)} \tag{3A-1}$$

where r_{rC} is the real interest rate in currency C, r_C is the market or nominal interest rate (henceforth, the "interest rate") in currency C, and i_C is the inflation rate in currency C. The interest rate in currency C is sometimes called the *nominal* interest rate in currency C, when it is necessary to distinguish it from the *real* interest rate. In this text the term "interest rate" implicitly refers to the nominal interest rate.

In the international Fisher model, a time 0 interest rate change is assumed to reflect a change in the predicted inflation rate under the assumption that the *real interest rate is constant.* Thus, if the inflation rate increases, investors raise their required nominal interest rate to compensate for the loss of purchasing power.

For example, if the interest rate in currency C is 11.24% and the inflation rate is 8%, the real interest rate is $r_{rC} = 1.1124/1.08 - 1 = 0.03$, or 3.0%. Given this real rate, and an increase in the inflation rate to 10%, equation (3A-1) may be rearranged to find the new interest rate to be $r_C = (1 + r_{rC})(1 + i_C) - 1 = 1.03(1.10) - 1 = 0.133 = 13.3\%$.

▣ EXAMPLE 3A-1

If the interest rate is 9% and the predicted inflation rate is 4%, find the real interest rate. Assuming the real interest rate remains constant, find the new inflation rate implied by a new interest rate of 7%, given the international Fisher model.

Solution 3A-1 The real rate of interest is $r_{rC} = 1.09/1.04 - 1 = 0.048$, or 4.8%. Given this real rate, and a decrease in the interest rate to 7%, equation (3A-1) may be rearranged to find the new inflation rate to be $i_C = (1 + r_C)/(1 + r_{rC}) - 1 = 1.07/1.048 - 1 = 0.021 = 2.1\%$.

CHANGES IN INTEREST RATES IN THE INTERNATIONAL FISHER MODEL

Now let us apply the Fisher relationship to exchange rates using the purchasing power parity condition. Given a spot exchange rate of $X^0_{\text{DM/\$}} = 1.40$ DM/\$, a predicted rate of inflation in marks of $i_{\text{DM}} = 0.04$, and a predicted inflation rate in dollars of $i_\$ = 0.06$, a predictive application of the purchasing power parity condition (equation 2-2) forecasts the future exchange rate a year from now to be $X^{1p}_{\text{DM/\$}} = (1.40 \text{ DM/\$})(1.04/1.06) = 1.374$ DM/\$. Assume that the interest rate in dollars at time 0 is $r_\$ = 10\%$. If the dollar interest rate suddenly increases to 12% at time 0, what effect does this interest rate change have?

To find the answer, according to the international Fisher approach, one must find the new predicted inflation rate implied by the higher interest rate and then apply the purchasing power parity condition to find the new predicted future exchange rate. The real dollar interest rate, from equation (3A-1) is $r_{r\$} = 1.10/1.06 - 1 = 0.0377$, which is 3.77%. Thus the new predicted dollar inflation rate, consistent with this constant real rate and with the new dollar interest rate of $r_\$ = 12\%$, is $i_\$ = 1.12/1.0377 - 1 = 0.0793 = 7.93\%$. Plugging the new inflation rate prediction into the purchasing power parity condition yields a new predicted exchange rate of $X^{1p+}_{\text{DM/\$}} = (1.40 \text{ DM/\$})(1.04/1.0793) = 1.349$ DM/\$. Thus the higher dollar interest rate, reflecting a higher predicted rate of inflation in the United States, causes an immediate decline in the predicted future value of the dollar relative to the mark for a year from now.

In Example 3A-2, investors still believe that the yen will depreciate over the next year relative to the dollar, from $X^0_{\text{¥/\$}} = 120$ ¥/\$, but now the predicted depreciation is to $X^{1p+}_{\text{¥/\$}} = 123.56$ ¥/\$. The predicted gradual depreciation of the yen from time 0 to time 1 is due to the fact that the Japanese infla-

---

▣ EXAMPLE 3A-2

You are given a current (time 0) spot exchange rate of $X^0_{\text{¥/\$}} = 120$ ¥/\$, an 8% predicted rate of inflation in yen ($i_\text{¥}$), and a 3% predicted rate of inflation rate in dollars ($i_\$$). Assume that the yen interest rate, $r_\text{¥}$, is 11% at time 0. If the yen interest rate instantaneously drops to 9% at time 0, what will happen to the value of the yen, according to the international Fisher model?

Solution 3A-2   Using the purchasing power parity condition, the predicted future exchange rate before the change in the interest rate, is $X^{1p}_{\text{¥/\$}} = (120$ ¥/\$)(1.08/1.03) = 125.83 ¥/\$. At a time 0, a 1-year yen interest rate of 11%, the real yen interest rate is $r_{r\text{¥}} = 1.11/1.08 - 1 = 0.02778, = 2.778\%$. If the yen interest rate instantaneously drops to 9% at time 0, and this change is a reflection of a new inflation rate prediction in conjunction with a constant real rate of interest, then the new yen inflation rate prediction must be $i_\text{¥} = 1.09/1.02778 - 1 = 0.0605$, or 6.05%. The new predicted exchange rate, from the (predictive application of the) purchasing power parity condition, is $X^{1p+}_{\text{¥/\$}} = (120$ ¥/\$)(1.0605/1.03) = 123.56 ¥/\$.

tion exceeds the U.S. inflation, but the new predicted future exchange rate of 123.56 ¥/$ represents a higher yen value than the original predicted future exchange rate of 125.83 ¥/$. By assumption in the international Fisher model, nothing happens to the current spot exchange rate when an interest rate changes; the only change that takes place is in how the spot exchange rate is predicted to gradually change over time.

THE INTERNATIONAL FISHER EQUATION

There exists an interesting special case of the international Fisher model, based on the assumption that the *real* rate of interest in two countries is the same. For convenience in working with conventional international exchange rate quotations, let one of the countries be the United States. Then by setting (one plus) each respective real rate of interest equal and applying Equation (3A-1) to both countries, we have that $(1 + r_C)/(1 + i_C) = (1 + r_\$)/(1 + i_\$)$. When rearranged, this result becomes $(1 + r_C)/(1 + r_\$) = (1 + i_C)/(1 + i_\$)$.

In words, if the *real* rates of interest in two countries are the same, then the ratio of (one plus) each respective interest rate is equal to the ratio of (one plus) each respective inflation rate. By substitution of this result into equation (2-2) for the purchasing power parity condition, we obtain an expression similar to purchasing power parity, but with interest rates rather than inflation rates. This relationship is called the *international Fisher equation* and is given in equation (3A-2).

INTERNATIONAL FISHER EQUATION—EUROPEAN TERMS

$$X_{C/\$}^{1p} = X_{C/\$}^{0} \left[\frac{(1 + r_C)}{(1 + r_\$)} \right] \qquad (3A\text{-}2)$$

The international Fisher equation makes it possible to measure the exchange rate impact of an interest rate change without going through the intermediate steps with inflation rates and a real interest rate. However, the international Fisher equation is a special case that applies only when the real rates of interest are equal in both countries.

For example, assume that the current 1-year eurocurrency deposit rates are r_{DM} = 9.2% for the mark and $r_\$$ = 4% for the dollar, respectively. Assume that the current spot rate of exchange is $X_{DM/\$}^{0}$ = 1.42857 DM/$. Under these assumptions, international Fisher equation predicts that the mark will depreciate to $X_{DM/\$}^{1p}$ = (1.42857 DM/$)(1.092/1.04) = 1.50 DM/$. If the interest rate on euromark deposits instantaneously jumps at time 0 to 10.2%, the predicted future exchange rate would instantaneously become $X_{DM/\$}^{1p+}$ = (1.42857 DM/$)(1.102/1.04) = 1.514 DM/$.

This change in the predicted exchange rate demonstrates the difference between the international Fisher approach and the asset market approach covered in the text: In the international Fisher approach a change in an interest rate, as a reflection of a change in predicted inflation, causes the *predicted future* exchange rate to change. In the asset market approach, a change in an interest rate is reflected in a change in the current *spot* rate of exchange. In both cases, an increase in an interest rate will result in a larger predicted gradual depreciation of the currency, once the new equilibrium is achieved. For American terms exchange rates, the international Fisher equation is $X^{1p}_{\$/C} = X^{0}_{\$/C}(1 + r_\$)/(1 + r_C)$.

EXAMPLE 3A-3

Assume that the spot exchange rate for the British pound is currently 2.095 $/£. If the 1-year eurodollar rate is currently 5% and the 1-year eurosterling rate is currently 10%, what is the predicted future spot exchange rate under the international Fisher equation?

Solution 3A-3   To solve this problem we use the American terms version of equation (3A-2). Thus $X^{1p}_{\$/£} = (2.095 \ \$/£)(1.05/1.10) = 2.00 \ \$/£$. This answer implies that, at a current exchange rate of 2.095 $/£, the pound is predicted to gradually depreciate over time to 2.00 $/£. The direction of the predicted gradual currency movement is consistent with the higher interest rate on eurosterling deposits.

Use the information given in Example 3A-3. Assume that the time 0 eurosterling interest rate suddenly increases to 12%, holding the eurodollar rate constant at 5%. Assume that the real rates of interest rates are the same and constant in both countries. In the international Fisher equation, the current spot exchange rate does not react to the interest rate change. Since the real rates of interest are assumed to be constant and equal for the two countries, $X^{1p+}_{\$/£} = (2.095 \ \$/£)(1.05/1.12) = 1.964 \ \$/£$. After the interest rate change, the pound is still predicted to gradually depreciate over the next year, but by a greater percentage at the higher eurosterling interest rate, since the higher eurosterling interest rate reflects a higher inflation rate in England.

COMPARISON OF THE MODELS

Except for the positioning of the terms, the international Fisher equation is the same as the one derived in the text from the asset market approach to currency valuation and labeled as the interest parity condition (equation 3-2). This fact will make memorization easier. Moreover, the international Fisher equation is sometimes referred to as the interest parity condition, and vice versa, as if the two notions were one and the same thing.

However, the difference in the positioning of the spot exchange rate and predicted future exchange rate in the equations for the two approaches is indicative of the distinction between them in terms of the underlying assumptions and therefore in how the equations are interpreted and applied.

Central to the asset market valuation model is the view that (1) there exists a highly mobile pool of global funds that is immediately responsive to changes in eurocurrency interest rates, and (2) predictions about future exchange rates do not change with instantaneous time 0 changes in eurocurrency interest rates. The response to an instantaneous time 0 change in a eurocurrency interest rate therefore must be an instantaneous time 0 change in the *spot exchange rate*, which is thus the left-hand side variable in equation (3-2).

The assumptions of the international Fisher model, on the other hand, are that (1) instantaneous changes in time 0 eurocurrency interest rates reflect reassessed inflation rate predictions, given constant real interest rates that are equal across countries and (2) both the international law of one price and a predictive adaptation of the purchasing power parity condition hold. In effect, these conditions imply that goods market conditions are the ultimate determinant of exchange rates in the manner discussed in Chapter 2. In the international Fisher approach, interest rate differences simply reflect differences in anticipated rates of inflation, and equation (3A-2) is simply an alternative, equivalent way to express the predictive adaptation of the purchasing power parity condition. Therefore, the only response to instantaneous time 0 changes in a eurocurrency interest rate must be a change in the *predicted future exchange rate*, which is the left-hand side variable in equation (3A-2).

chapter 4

FORWARD EXCHANGE AND INTEREST RATES

Forward Exchange

Suppose that your company's base currency is the U.S. dollar and that a German firm has shipped some products to you in the United States. The terms of the sale call for payment in 3 months in the amount of DM3,000,000. You may be concerned over the uncertainty of how many dollars will be necessary to convert to DM3,000,000 3 months hence. The mark-denominated payable represents a foreign currency *exposure* to your firm.

One means to eliminate the exposure, and thus to resolve your concern, is to simply borrow dollars today in the eurocurrency market, exchange the dollars into marks, and then relend the marks by means of making a euromark deposit. The amounts of the transactions would be geared to have the euromark deposit liquidate for DM3,000,000, so that you'll have the amount necessary to meet your business payable 3 months hence. By means of these currency and eurocurrency market transactions, the uncertainty created by the foreign currency exposure is eliminated, or *hedged*.

This arrangement is called a *money market hedge* of the foreign currency exposure. A future receivable may be similarly hedged via borrowing the foreign currency and converting the borrowed proceeds into the base currency today; later the receivable cash flow can be used to repay the borrowed foreign currency amount. Money market hedges are covered in detail later in the chapter.

Money market hedging, with loans and deposits, tends to inflate corporate balance sheets. However, there exist other techniques available in the financial markets that do not involve the balance sheet implications of money market hedging. One useful method is forward exchange contracting, which is covered in this chapter.

FORWARD EXCHANGE CONTRACTS

The forward exchange market refers to the trading of *forward exchange contracts*, which are contracts by two parties to exchange currencies at a set delivery time in the future at an exchange rate established when the contract is made. The exchange rate in a forward exchange contract is called a *forward exchange rate*.

The forward exchange market is not physically separate from the foreign exchange market for immediate exchange, the "spot" market. Both the spot exchange and forward exchange markets are part of the general currency market. Traders in the currency market routinely conduct retail and interbank transactions in forward exchange contracts, just as they do with spot exchange transactions.

Once a forward exchange contract is established at a given forward exchange rate, that rate is set for that contract. However, the forward exchange rate for originating forward exchange contracts varies continuously with supply and demand conditions, just like the spot exchange rate. At any point in time, the currency market will thus have a market-determined spot exchange rate for immediate delivery as well as a set of market-determined forward exchange rates for various lengths of times until future delivery.

In principle, any two parties may create an informal forward exchange contract for any delivery time in the future. In practice, forward contracts originate for standard periods, with 1-month, 3-month, 6-month, and 1-year contracts being the most common.

The markets for long-dated currency forward exchange contracts are not as well developed as those for near-term forwards. For major currencies, like the U.S. dollar, the British pound, the German mark, the Japanese yen, the Swiss franc, and the French franc, the forward exchange markets are fairly liquid out to at least 3 years or so, and there is sometimes even fair liquidity for long-dated forward exchange contracts. However, sometimes there is little liquidity for the longer-term horizons. This lack of liquidity means wide dealer spreads and thus large transaction fees for retail users.

As usual, this chapter abstracts from dealer spreads and trading costs in numerical examples involving forward exchange contracts. This assumption is tantamount to assuming adequate liquidity and that trading costs are not a significant problem.

The notation we'll use for a forward exchange rate is $F_{C/\$}$. Technically, a superscript could be used to denote the time at which a forward rate is observed. Thus, $F_{C/\$}^0$ should refer to a forward rate at time 0, while $F_{C/\$}^1$ would refer to a forward rate at time 1, and so forth. In this chapter, we will not need to refer to the forward rate at any other time than at the present, that is, at time 0. Thus, the superscript notation is not used and is 0 by implication.

LONG AND SHORT FORWARD EXCHANGE POSITIONS

The party that contracts forward to buy currency A with currency B (at the future delivery time) is said to have a *long forward position* on currency A and a *short forward position* on currency B. The other party in the agreement, with the obligation to buy currency B with currency A (i.e., to sell or "deliver" currency A and receive currency B) has the long position on currency B and the short position on currency A.

Thus, for example, a forward exchange contract to buy marks with dollars at a future time is a long forward position on marks and, more specifically, a dollar-denominated long forward position on marks. Moreover, this same position can be viewed as a contract to sell dollars for marks at the future time, and thus may also be called a short forward position on dollars and, more specifically, a mark-denominated short forward position on dollars.

Companies may use forward exchange contracts to hedge their transaction exposure to changes in exchange rates.

As an example of a forward exchange contract, consider a 1-year dollar-denominated forward exchange contract on marks at the forward exchange rate of $F_{DM/\$}$ = 1.50 DM/\$. To standardize the analysis, we will refer to the *amount of a forward contract* in units of the contract's currency of denomination. Thus, in this example, the amount of the contract should be expressed in dollars. Assume that the amount of the contract is \$1,000,000. The *contract size* of a forward contract is expressed in units of the currency on which the contract is arranged. At the forward exchange rate, the amount of the contract and the contract size can be converted into each other at the forward exchange rate. Thus, in this example, the contract size is \$1,000,000(1.50 DM/\$) = DM1,500,000.

The example contract obligates the long position on marks to pay \$1,000,000 and receive DM1,500,000 a year from the time that the contract is made. (The contract is made at time 0.) At time 1, the short position must deliver DM1,500,000 and will receive \$1,000,000.

No funds are required at time 0 to establish a forward exchange position. Once a forward exchange contract is established, funds are scheduled to change hands only at the delivery time. There are two ways to look at the delivery time funds exchange, (1) the physical delivery view, just discussed, and (2) the cash settlement, difference check view, discussed next.

THE CASH SETTLEMENT, DIFFERENCE CHECK APPROACH

In addition to settling a forward exchange contract with the physical exchange of currencies at the delivery time, an alternative means of settling a forward exchange contract is with cash. This form of settlement is known as a *difference check.*

For example, suppose the spot exchange rate at the delivery time for the forward exchange contract turns out to be $X^1_{DM/\$}$ = 1.25 DM/\$. The long position on marks should deliver \$1,000,000, but the dollar value, at the prevailing spot exchange rate, of the DM1,500,000 that the short position on marks must deliver, is DM1,500,000/(1.25 DM/\$) = \$1,200,000. Thus, the long position on marks is to receive an amount *worth* \$1,200,000 and deliver \$1,000,000. Similarly, the short position on marks is to pay an amount *equivalent* to \$1,200,000 (at the time 1 exchange rate) and receive \$1,000,000.

In effect, the long position on marks has gained \$200,000, while the short position on marks has lost \$200,000. Thus, an equivalent alternative to an actual exchange of currencies at the delivery time is a cash settlement of the net difference in value, given the spot exchange rate that prevails at that time. In this case, the settlement would be \$200,000 (or equivalently \$200,000(1.25 DM/\$) = DM250,000), in the form of a check from the short position on marks to the long position on marks.

If the long position on marks actually wanted the DM1,500,000, but the contract were cash-settled, the \$1,000,000 that would have been exchanged for the marks in a physical delivery situation could instead be combined with the difference check of $200,000 to purchase $1,200,000(1.25 DM/$) = DM1,500,000 in the spot market at the delivery time. Either way, through physical delivery, or through purchase in the spot market at the delivery time with the help of the difference check, the long position on marks ends up with DM1,500,000. However, the key feature in the cash settlement approach is that the cash settlement avoids the necessity for both parties to actually have the full amount of funds in the exchange.

The cash settlement on a forward exchange contract always favors the long position on the currency whose spot exchange value at the delivery time represents a higher currency value than the forward exchange rate. In the example just given, the value of the mark is higher at $X^1_{DM/\$}$ = 1.25 DM/$ than at $F_{DM/\$}$ = 1.50 DM/$, and the long position on marks gained at the expense of the short position on marks.

Had the spot value of the mark at the delivery time instead been lower than the contracted forward exchange value, the short position on marks would have gained at the expense of the long position on marks. For example, if the spot exchange rate had been $X^1_{DM/\$}$ = 2.00 DM/$ at the delivery time, the spot exchange rate at the delivery time would thus have represented a lower currency value for the mark than at the forward exchange rate of 1.50 DM/$. The dollar value of the DM1,500,000 that the short position on marks is obligated to deliver is DM1,500,000/(2.00 DM/$) = $750,000. Thus, the long on marks position has lost $250,000, while the short position on marks has gained this amount. Figure 4-1 lays out the cash settlement scenarios just covered.

In general, the difference check amount in the currency in which the contract is denominated (which is dollars in our example), from the viewpoint of the long position on the other currency (marks in our example), may be calculated as follows: First, convert the exchange rates to direct terms from the point of view of denomination currency of the contract. Next, multiply the contract size (in units of the foreign currency) by the difference between the direct terms spot exchange rate at the delivery time and the direct terms forward exchange rate.

In our example, this calculation indicates the amount of difference check, denominated in dollars, to be received by the long position on marks from the short position on marks; if the calculated amount is *negative*, then the difference check must be sent by the long position on marks to the short position on marks. If $F_{\$/DM}$ = $1/(F_{DM/\$})$ = 1/(1.50 DM/$) = 0.667 $/DM, $X^1_{\$/DM}$ = 1/(1.25 DM/$) = 0.80 $/DM, and the contract size is DM1,500,000, the long position on marks would receive DM1,500,000[(0.80 $/DM) − (0.667 $/DM)] = $200,000. In the second example, where $X^1_{\$/DM}$ = 1/(2.00 DM/$) = 0.50 $/DM, the long position on marks would receive DM1,500,000 [(0.50 $/DM) − (0.667 $/DM)] = −$250,000. The negative amount indicates that the short position on marks would receive $250,000 from the long position on marks.

Assume that the dollar is the denomination of the forward contract on currency *C*. Let *C#* be the forward contract size in units of currency *C*,

Dollar-Denominated Forward Position on Mark
Contract Size: DM1,500,000
Forward Rate: 1.50 DM/$
Contract Amount: $1,000,000
Physical Delivery involves a future exchange of DM 1,500,000 for $1,000,000

I. Cash Settlement for the Long Position on Marks

Spot rate at time 1	1.25 DM/$	1.50 DM/$	2.00 DM/$
Contract value in dollar terms	1,200,000	1,000,000	750,000
Actual amount of dollars obliged to pay	−1,000,000	−1,000,000	−1,000,000
Cash settlement in dollar terms	200,000	0	−250,000

II. Cash Settlement for the Short Position on Marks

Spot rate at time 1	1.25 DM/$	1.50 DM/$	2.00 DM/$
Contract value in dollar terms	−1,200,000	−1,000,000	−750,000
Actual amount of dollars entitled to receive	1,000,000	1,000,000	1,000,000
Cash settlement in dollar terms	−200,000	0	250,000

FIGURE 4-1 The Cash Settlement Approach

$X^1_{\$/C}$ be the delivery time spot exchange rate in American terms, and $F_{\$/C}$ be the forward rate in American terms. Then equation (4-1) states the dollar-denominated gain (loss) from the viewpoint of the long position on currency C.

GAIN ON LONG FORWARD POSITION ON CURRENCY C (IN DOLLARS)

$$\$G_L = C\# \, (X^1_{\$/C} - F_{\$/C}) \tag{4-1}$$

It may seem like an extra step was added in Solution 4-1, using equation (4-1) to first find the cash settlement for the long position in a forward exchange contract and then reverse the sign to find the short position's cash settlement. The reason is to minimize the number of formulas you have to memorize, and to standardize the analysis with only one formula, equation (4-1) for the cash settlement on a *long* position.

FORWARD DISCOUNTS AND PREMIUMS

If a currency's value represented by a forward exchange rate is less than its value represented by the spot exchange rate, the currency is said to be at a *forward discount* (for that forward horizon). Similarly, if a currency's value in

> ### EXAMPLE 4-1
>
> You take a 1-year short position in a dollar-denominated forward contract on the Japanese yen at a forward exchange rate of $F_{¥/\$} = 120$ ¥/\$. The contract amount is \$1,000,000. If the spot exchange rate for the yen at delivery time is $X^1_{¥/\$} = 100$ ¥/\$, what is your dollar gain (loss) on the contract?
>
> **Solution 4-1**   The contract size, C#, is \$1,000,000(120 ¥/\$) = ¥120,000,000. The dollar gain, $\$G_L$ for the long position in the forward exchange contract on yen, using equation (4-1), is ¥120,000,000[1/(100 ¥/\$) − 1/(120 ¥/\$)] = ¥120,000,000 [(0.01 \$/¥) − (0.008333 \$/¥)] = \$200,000. Since the gain to the long position is \$200,000, and you took the short position, your loss is \$200,000.

the forward exchange market is greater than its value in the spot market, the currency is said to be at a *forward premium.*

Of course, for currencies that are conventionally quoted in European terms, higher exchange rate quotes mean lower values for those currencies. For example, suppose the spot exchange rate for the mark is currently $X^0_{DM/\$} = 1.40$ DM/\$ and the 1-year forward exchange rate is $F_{DM/\$} = 1.50$ DM/\$. In this case the forward exchange rate represents a lower value for the mark and a higher value for the dollar. Thus, the 1-year forward mark is at a discount, while the 1-year forward dollar is at a premium.

FORWARD EXCHANGE CONTRACTS AND TRANSACTION EXPOSURE

One basic role of forward exchange contracts is to eliminate the problems caused by the uncertainty about the exchange rate that will apply in future foreign currency transactions. For example, assume that your company's base currency is the dollar and that the firm has shipped some products to Germany. The terms of the sale call for payment in 3 months in the amount of DM3,000,000.

In this situation, your company has a mark receivable that is a *natural long position* in marks. A natural long position in a currency in this context means that an inflow of that currency is expected as part of the company's natural business, rather than as a result of a position in a forward exchange contract. Since you do not know what the DM/\$ exchange rate will be in 3 months, the amount of base currency that the receivable will ultimately bring you is uncertain.

This problem of a natural long exposure may be solved by taking an opposing forward position, which in this case is a *short* position, in a 3-month dollar-denominated forward exchange contract on the mark. The short forward position is said to *hedge* the *transaction exposure* of the natural long position of the receivable.

Assume that the 3-month forward exchange rate is 1.50 DM/$. A short position for a contract amount of $2,000,000 at the forward exchange rate of 1.50 DM/$ would obligate you to deliver a contract size of $2,000,000(1.50 DM/$) = DM3,000,000 and receive $2,000,000 in return at the delivery time. At the delivery time, you simply flow the DM3,000,000 natural receivable through to the party holding the long position in the forward exchange contract on marks, your bank. Your bank, in turn, delivers the $2,000,000 to you at that delivery time. While you do not receive the $2,000,000 until 3 months from now, at least you know now how many dollars you'll be receiving in exchange for the DM3,000,000 that you are owed.

An alternative, but equivalent, view results when we look at the cash settlement. No matter what the spot exchange rate is 3 months from now, if you have a short forward exchange position on marks for a contract amount of $2,000,000, at a contracted forward exchange rate of 1.50 DM/$, the net total of (1) the dollar value of the DM3,000,000 in the spot exchange market at the time the receivable is due, plus (2) the cash settlement on the forward exchange contract position, will be $2,000,000.

For example, if, in 3 months' time, the spot exchange rate is 1.60 DM/$, then the mark receivable will be worth DM3,000,000/(1.60 DM/$) = $1,875,000. Using equation (4-1), a long position in the forward exchange contract would receive DM3,000,000[1/(1.60 DM/$) − 1/(1.50 DM/$)] = −$125,000, implying that your short position would receive $125,000 in cash settlement. Viewing the dollar value of the natural mark receipt combined with the cash settlement on the short forward position, the net result is a receipt of $1,875,000 + $125,000 = $2,000,000.

Regardless of whether you use the cash-settle approach or the physical delivery of the marks (flowed through to physical delivery on the forward contract from the natural receipt), the net result of establishing the short forward exchange position on marks is that the uncertainty about the rate of exchange on the DM3,000,000 receivable has been eliminated.

Companies may also be concerned about the future disbursement or payable of a foreign currency that is owed on services already received or contracted for. The higher the spot value of the foreign currency at the time the payment is to be made, the more base currency it will take to make the payment. This payable is called a *natural short position* in the foreign currency. In a fashion similar to the foregoing analysis, natural short positions are hedged with long positions in base currency-denominated forward exchange contracts on the foreign currency. This analogous scenario is covered in the next example.

Remember the following:

- For a foreign currency receivable (a natural long position in the foreign currency), you hedge with a short forward position on the foreign currency.
- For a foreign currency payable (a natural short position in the foreign currency), you hedge with a long forward position on the foreign currency.

EXAMPLE 4-2

Assume that your company's base currency is the U.S. dollar. You are committed to making a natural yen payment of ¥300,000,000 in 1 year. Assume that the current 1-year forward exchange rate is $F_{¥/\$}$ = 120 ¥/$. Determine from the forward exchange rate the amount of base currency that may be obtained for certain via forward exchange contracting, assuming that you want to eliminate the transaction exposure of your natural short position. Demonstrate that, if the spot exchange rate at the delivery time is $X^1_{¥/\$}$ = 100 ¥/$, the cash-settled forward exchange contract approach hedges the exposure.

Solution 4-2   At the forward exchange rate of $F_{¥/\$}$ = 120 ¥/$, the dollar value of the natural yen liability is ¥300,000,000/(120 ¥/$) = $2,500,000. Thus, the dollar contract amount should be $2,500,000, while the foreign currency contract size is ¥300,000,000. Moreover, $2,500,000 is the dollar amount that can be "locked-in" in lieu of an exposed future natural foreign currency payable. If the spot exchange rate is $X^1_{¥/\$}$ = 100 ¥/$ at the delivery time, the dollar value of the yen payable will be ¥300,000,000/(100 ¥/$) = $3,000,000. If the exposure is hedged with a $2,500,000 long position in a dollar-denominated forward exchange contract on the yen, then the cash settlement to the long position, from equation (4-1), will be ¥300,000,000[1/(100 ¥/$) − 1/(120 ¥/$)] = $500,000. The net dollar payout, combining the dollar value of the natural payment at the time it is made and the gain/loss on the long forward contract position, is the $3,000,000 natural outflow plus the $500,000 inflow on the long forward position, or a $2,500,000 net outflow.

The graph in Figure 4-2 shows the effect of hedging. The future foreign currency amount to be hedged (receivable or payable) is assumed to be DM100,000, and the base currency is assumed to be dollars. As the value of

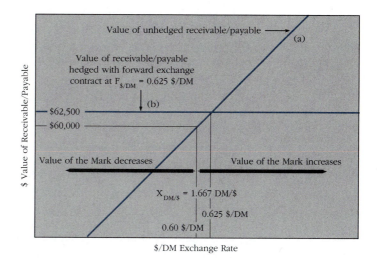

FIGURE 4-2   The Effect of Hedging

the mark (the *x*-axis) increases, the value of the unhedged receivable/payable increases linearly with the direct terms exchange rate, and vice versa. If the forward exchange rate is 0.625 $/DM (= 1.60 DM/$), then the company can hedge the receivable/payable such that the fixed dollar value of the hedged receivable/payable is DM100,000(0.625 $/DM) = $62,000, which is represented by the flat line.

The expression of the exchange rate in direct terms from the base currency point of view, that is, in $/DM, is crucial to the linearity of the relationship in Figure 4-2. The relationship would not be linear if the exchange rate were expressed as DM/$. The linearity property will prove to be convenient later in the text, and is why a company's currency exposure is measured using exchange rates in *direct terms* from the base currency point of view.

HEDGING PHILOSOPHY

If the value of the foreign currency turns out to be greater in the eventual spot market than it was in the forward exchange market, then after the fact you will *wish you had not* taken a short position in a forward exchange contract as a hedge of a natural long exposure. Had you not taken the short forward position, you would have received the benefit of the higher value of the foreign currency. Extending an earlier example, if the spot exchange rate is 1.20 DM/$ when the DM3,000,000 is paid by your German customer, then the dollar value of this receipt would be DM3,000,000/(1.20 DM/$) = $2,500,000 rather than $2,000,000. This higher dollar value is forgone if the short forward position on marks is taken at time 0 to hedge the natural transaction exposure of the receivable. However, to eliminate the uncertainty about one's base currency value of a future natural foreign currency receipt, one must give up the potential for benefiting from a high spot value for the foreign currency at the time the natural receipt arrives and accept the forward exchange rate prevailing in the market at time 0. Thus, you may choose not to eliminate your exposure with a forward contract position if you have a strong belief that the future spot exchange rate will be favorable to your natural position.

Or one may believe the forward exchange rate is not favorable. This situation is often perceived by practitioners with natural long exposures, for example, if the foreign currency is at a forward discount. In this case the base currency forward value of the foreign currency is less than what it is in the current spot market. Thus, many are reluctant to sell a foreign currency short in the forward market at a lower value than the current spot exchange rate, even if the result is a hedge of the natural transaction exposure.

Philosophically, the use of forward exchange contracts for hedging should be to eliminate uncertainty. After a forward exchange position has been taken for purposes of hedging, it really should not matter to the hedger what the spot exchange rate actually turns out to be at the delivery time. Despite this philosophy, many practitioners do observe the eventual spot exchange rate and second-guess the decision to hedge. If there is a natural receipt of foreign currency that has been hedged by a short forward exchange position on that currency, and the foreign currency depreciates, the hedger feels as if he has won the game. On the other hand, if the foreign currency appreciates, the hedger looks at what would have been the gain on the natural inflow, if only he had *not* hedged.

This would-have-been gain is often called the *opportunity cost of hedging with the forward exchange contract.* Observing this would-be gain after having hedged causes some practitioners to feel much regret over having "guessed wrong," even though the second-guessing of the hedging decision is not consistent with the original purpose of eliminating uncertainty. There is a way to pay a set amount to be hedged on the downside only, while capturing upside profits. The procedure involves options, which are covered later in Chapter 7. Buying options makes second-guessing unnecessary and appears to be for those worried about both downside risk and opportunity costs.

FOREIGN EXCHANGE FUTURES CONTRACTS

In basic concept, a foreign exchange *futures contract* is the same as a forward exchange contract. Like a forward exchange contract, a foreign exchange futures contract is an obligation by two parties to exchange currencies at a set delivery time at a set contract-specified rate.

Unlike forward exchange contracts, which are the instruments of the vast interbank currency market, foreign exchange futures contracts are traded on various exchanges in the world. The fact that foreign exchange futures contracts are traded on exchanges requires that they be standardized for ease of secondary market liquidation. Thus, foreign exchange futures contracts have standardized delivery dates, not the standardized horizons of the interbank forward exchange market. For example, a 3-month forward exchange contract may be originated at any time in the interbank market, but available foreign exchange futures contracts have delivery on only certain days of certain months.

The other distinguishing feature of foreign exchange futures contracts is that, unlike forward exchange contracts, futures contracts are cash-settled every day, as the market-determined futures exchange rate fluctuates. This daily settlement is referred to as *marking-to-market.*

Due to their similarity, financial arbitrage between exchange-traded foreign currency futures contracts and interbank forward exchange contracts should keep futures contract rates near to forward exchange rates for the same horizon. Theoretically, volatile daily interest rates and the marking-to-market feature may cause futures exchange rates to differ slightly from the forward exchange rates.

Since foreign exchange futures contract trading accounts for less than 2% of forward exchange contract trading, we will not delve further into the distinctions between futures and forwards. Technically, the text deals with forward exchange contracts, but the reader could substitute "futures" for "forwards," and the general concepts would still apply.

Synthetic Forward Exchange Positions and Covered Interest Arbitrage

SYNTHETIC FORWARD EXCHANGE POSITIONS

Suppose you conduct the following three simultaneous transactions at time 0: (1) borrow $100 (expressed in time 0 proceeds as opposed to time 1 face value) for 1 year at $r_\$$ = 10% in the eurocurrency market, (2) exchange the $100 into marks at an assumed current spot exchange rate of $X^0_{DM/\$}$ = 1.25 DM/$, to have $100(1.25 DM/$) = DM125, and (3) deposit the DM125 into a 1-year euromark deposit yielding r_{DM} = 8%.

Although there are three transactions at time 0, this deal calls for zero *net* time 0 cash flow. A year from now, you will receive DM125(1.08) = DM135 from the liquidation of the euromark deposit, and you will have to repay $100(1.10) = $110 on the eurodollar loan. At time 1, there is an inflow to you of DM135 (proceeds from liquidation of your euromark deposit) and an outflow of $110 (to repay the eurodollar loan). Since at time 1 there is an outflow of $110 and an inflow of DM135, the deal is identical to the cash flows of a long position in 1-year dollar-denominated forward exchange contract on marks, with a contract amount of $110 and a forward exchange rate of DM135/$110 = 1.227 DM/$. (See Figure 4-3.)

In financial markets, a security or instrument that is "manufactured" from other securities and/or instruments is termed a *synthetic*. The deal just detailed is a synthetic long forward exchange position in a dollar-denominated contract on marks. Of course, this synthetic forward position is the same notion as the money market hedge technique introduced at the beginning of the chapter.

▤ EXAMPLE 4-3

At time 0 you borrow $1000 in time 1 face value at a 6% interest rate ($r_\$$), exchange the borrowed proceeds into pounds at the spot rate of $X^0_{\$/£}$ = 1.60 $/£, and place the pounds in a 1-year eurocurrency time deposit at $r_£$ = 8%. How many pounds will you receive from your eurosterling deposit at time 1 and what is the implicit synthetic forward exchange rate?

Solution 4-3 The time 0 proceeds from the eurodollar loan are $1000/1.06 = $943.40, which exchange to $943.40/(1.60 $/£) = £589.62. The time 1 liquidation of the eurosterling deposit is £589.62(1.08) = £636.79. The implied synthetic forward exchange rate is $1000.00/£636.79 = 1.57 $/£.

I. Long Forward Position on a Foreign Currency
  • Used to hedge the foreign exchange risk of a natural payable in the currency.
  • Assume the payable is DM135 at time 1.
  A. Actual long forward position; assume $F_{DM/\$}$ = 1.227 DM/$.

Time 0   Arrange long forward position on DM 135

| Time 1 | From Operations | →$110→ | Forward Contract Counterparty | →DM 135→ | Natural Payable |

B. Synthetic long forward position = money market hedge of payable.
  Assume $r_\$$ = 0.10, r_{DM} = 0.08, $X^0_{DM/\$}$ = 1.25 DM/$.

| Time 0 | Borrow $100 at $r_\$$ = 0.10 in Eurodollar Market | →$100→ | Spot Exchange at 1.25 DM/$ | →DM 125→ | Deposit DM125 at r_{DM} = 0.08 in Euromark Market |

| Time 1 | From Operations (Receivable) | →$110→ | Euro-dollar Market | Synthetic Forward Exchange Rate = 1.227 DM/$ | Euro-mark Market | →DM 135→ | Natural Payable |

II. Short Forward Position on a Foreign Currency
  • Used to hedge the foreign exchange risk of a natural receivable in the currency.
  • Assume the receivable is DM135 at time 1.
  A. Actual short forward position; assume $F_{DM/\$}$ = 1.227 DM/$.

Time 0   Arrange short forward position on DM 135

| Time 1 | From Operations | →DM135→ | Forward Contract Counterparty | →$110→ | Base Currency Revenues |

B. Synthetic short forward position = money market hedge of receivable.
  Assume $r_\$$ = 0.10, r_{DM} = 0.08, $X^0_{DM/\$}$ = 1.25 DM/$.

| Time 0 | Borrow DM125 at r_{DM} = 0.08 in Euromarks | →DM125→ | Spot Exchange at 1.25 DM/$ | →$100→ | Deposit $100 at $r_\$$ = 0.10 in Eurodollar Market |

| Time 1 | From Operations (Receivable) | →DM135→ | Euro-mark Market | Synthetic Forward Exchange Rate = 1.227 DM/$ | Euro-dollar Market | →$110→ | Base Currency Revenues |

FIGURE 4-3 Synthetic Versus Actual Forward Exchange Positions
Note: Synthetic forward positions are the same as money market hedges.

A synthetic short forward position on marks may be created through reversing the three time 0 transactions. First, borrow marks for 1 year in the eurocurrency market at r_{DM} = 8%, with a time 1 face value of DM135 and a time 0 proceeds amount of DM135/1.08 = DM125. Next, change the marks into dollars at the assumed spot exchange rate of $X^0_{DM/\$}$ = 1.25 DM/$ to get $100. Finally, place the $100 at time 0 into a 1-year eurodollar time deposit at the interest rate of $r_\$$ = 10% to end up with $110 at time 1. In effect, you have created a contract that involves no net cash flow at time 0, but requires you to pay DM135 and receive $110 at time 1. Thus, you have manufactured a synthetic short position in a dollar-denominated forward exchange contract on marks. Figure 4-3 compares actual and synthetic forward contracts.

THE SYNTHETIC FORWARD EXCHANGE RATE

Letting r_C denote the eurocurrency interest rate in currency C, while $r_\$$ is the eurodollar interest rate, we can develop a formula for the *synthetic* forward rate, denoted $SF_{C/\$}$. The borrowed proceeds (the present value) of one dollar of time 1 face value is $1/(1 + r_\$$); these proceeds exchanged into the foreign currency at the spot exchange rate yields $X^0_{C/\$}[\$1/(1 + r_\$)]$. Then compound this foreign currency amount forward at the interest rate for currency C to get $X^0_{C/\$}[\$1/(1 + r_\$)](1 + r_C)$. This last amount is the amount of currency C that will be received by the long position on the foreign currency for one dollar owed at the delivery time of the synthetic forward exchange contract, and is thus the synthetic European terms forward rate. Rearranging terms, the final expression is equation (4-2).

THE SYNTHETIC FORWARD EXCHANGE RATE—EUROPEAN TERMS

$$SF_{C/\$} = X^0_{C/\$} \left[\frac{(1 + r_C)}{(1 + r_\$)} \right] \tag{4-2}$$

Note that equation (4-2) is in the same form as the parity conditions in Chapters 2 and 3. With the future exchange rate on the left-hand side, the interest rate in the numerator is the same as the numerator currency in the spot exchange rate. Of course, the interpretation of the equation is different from the interest parity condition, since the future rate of exchange is (synthetically) contracted for today, rather than predicted.

Equation (4-2) can be used to verify the synthetic forward exchange rate in the text example. The text example assumes r_C = 0.08, $r_\$$ = 0.10 and $X^0_{C/\$}$ = 1.25 DM/$. From equation (4-2), the synthetic 1-year forward exchange rate is $SF_{C/\$}$ = (1.25 DM/$)(1.08)/(1.10) = 1.227 DM/$, as found earlier.

Naturally, there is a corresponding American terms version for equation (4-2). Following the same methods as for equations in previous chapters, the American terms formula is $SF_{\$/C} = X^0_{\$/C}[(1 + r_\$)/(1 + r_C)]$.

ONE-WAY ARBITRAGE

Why would anyone want to construct synthetic forward exchange positions? The answer is that if the implied synthetic forward exchange rate were more advantageous than the actual forward exchange rate, then a synthetic forward exchange position would be preferred to an actual forward position, assuming that the user is willing to tolerate the balance sheet implications of the synthetic, or money market, approach. For example, suppose your base currency is dollars and you wish to hedge a DM1,350,000 natural mark liability commitment, due in 1 year, against the uncertainty in the future spot exchange value of the mark. Therefore, you wish to establish a 1-year dollar-denominated long forward exchange position on marks. You call your local banker, and he quotes an actual 1-year forward exchange rate of $F_{DM/\$}$ = 1.20 DM/\$.

Assuming the current spot exchange rate is $X^0_{DM/\$}$ = 1.25 DM/\$, the 1-year euromark interest rate is r_{DM} = 8%, and the 1-year eurodollar interest rate is $r_\$$ = 10%, then we already have established in the preceding example that you can construct a synthetic long position on marks with a 1-year synthetic forward exchange rate of $SF_{DM/\$}$ = 1.227 DM/\$. Which would be more advantageous, the actual forward or the synthetic forward?

The answer is whichever allows you to purchase forward marks at the better rate, that is, with the fewest dollars. Since 1.227 DM/\$ is a better rate than 1.20 DM/\$ for purposes of purchasing marks with dollars, the synthetic forward exchange contract should be the choice for a long forward position on marks. Thus, in lieu of an actual long forward exchange position, you should instruct your banker to take a long forward position on marks synthetically by simultaneously (1) borrowing \$1,100,000 in time 1 face value in the eurodollar market, for proceeds of \$1,100,000/1.10 = \$1,000,000; (2) exchanging these proceeds into marks at the current spot exchange rate of 1.25 DM/\$ to obtain \$1,000,000(1.25 DM/\$) = DM1,250,000; and (3) depositing these marks for a year at r_{DM} = 8% to yield DM1,250,000(1.08) = DM1,350,000. The *synthetic* long forward exchange position for \$1,100,000 yields DM1,350,000 at time 1, while the *actual* long forward exchange position would cost \$1,125,000 to yield \$1,125,000(1.20 DM/\$) = DM1,350,000 at time 1.

The opportunity to obtain a more advantageous forward rate synthetically is an example of a *one-way arbitrage*. One-way arbitrage is the choice of the most advantageous alternative among equivalent financial strategies.

Given these assumptions, if one wanted to hedge a natural mark receivable and therefore to establish a dollar-denominated short position on marks, to pay marks and receive dollars at the delivery time, the choice would be the *actual* forward exchange contract, *not the synthetic* short forward exchange position. The reason is that it is more advantageous to sell marks at 1.20 DM/\$ than at 1.227 DM/\$.

Here is a memory device for recalling the transactions of a synthetic forward exchange position (a money market hedge): The direction of the spot

*E*XAMPLE OF CORPORATE PRACTICE OF COVERED INTEREST ARBITRAGE:

In mid-1993, a U.S. multinational, Northstar, arbitraged the forward market between U.S. dollars and Mexican pesos. The company was borrowing U.S. dollars from its lead commercial bank at the prime interest rate of 6%, exchanging the dollars into pesos at the exchange rate of 3.11 Pe/$, and then investing the proceeds into peso-denominated Mexican government bills yielding about 16%. This strategy represented a dollar-denominated synthetic long forward position on pesos, and based on these interest rates, the synthetic forward exchange rate was (3.11 Pe/$)[1.16/1.06] = 3.40 Pe/$. The synthetic forward exchange rate shows the forward peso to be a discount to the spot peso, since 3.40 Pe/$ is a lower peso value than 3.11 Pe/$.

Northstar's bank was quoting an actual forward contract exchange rate to Northstar at less than the forward discount represented by the synthetic forward exchange rate. Say, for example, that the actual forward exchange rate quote was 3.30 Pe/$. Northstar was covering its long synthetic forward positions on pesos (at 3.40 Pe/$) by going short actual peso forward contracts (at 3.30 Pe/$). Northstar was thus practicing covered interest arbitrage by selling pesos forward at 3.30 Pe/$ while simultaneously buying them forward (synthetically) at 3.40 Pe/$.

This example is adapted from Laurent Jacque and Gabriel Hawawini, "Myths and Realities of the Global Capital Market: Lessons for Financial Managers," *Journal of Applied Corporate Finance*, Fall 1993, pp. 81–90.

exchange in the synthetic transactions is the same as the direction of the forward exchange desired in the actual forward exchange position. Thus, a dollar-denominated synthetic long forward exchange position on a foreign currency involves a spot transaction buying (receiving) the foreign currency with (paying) dollars, since the actual forward involves the same direction of exchange transaction. Once you know this direction of the spot exchange, the loan/deposit transactions fall into place: Since you have to obtain dollars to pay for the foreign currency, you must *borrow* dollars; after the spot exchange, you have foreign currency, so you must deposit the foreign currency. As a mental check, you can think that at the delivery time, you will receive the foreign currency as proceeds from the deposit and pay dollars to repay the loan, the same effective delivery time cash flows involved in an actual long forward exchange position on the foreign currency.

COVERED INTEREST ARBITRAGE

If the forward exchange rate for an actual forward exchange contract differs from that of an equivalent, synthetic forward exchange contract, a pure arbitrage profit can also be obtained. Recall that financial arbitrage involves buying a claim for one price and selling essentially the same claim immediately for a higher price.

> ### EXAMPLE 4-4
>
> Assume that the actual 1-year forward exchange rate for Japanese yen is $F_{¥/\$} = 130$ ¥/$ and that the current spot exchange rate is $X^0_{¥/\$} = 125$ ¥/$. The 1-year euroyen interest rate is $r_¥ = 8\%$, while the 1-year eurodollar interest rate is $r_\$ = 5\%$. You wish to take a short position in a 1-year dollar-denominated forward exchange contract on yen. Decide whether the synthetic or the actual is more advantageous for your purposes, and state the mechanics of constructing the synthetic position.
>
> *Solution 4-4* The synthetic forward exchange rate, from equation (4-2), is $SF_{¥/\$} = (125$ ¥/$)(1.08)/(1.05) = 128.57$ ¥/$. Since you want a short forward position on yen (to deliver yen and receive dollars), you must choose the alternative offering the greater yen value (to receive more dollars for yen). The answer is the synthetic, since 128.57 ¥/$ represents a greater value for the yen than 130 ¥/$. To create the synthetic dollar-denominated short forward exchange position on yen, the spot transaction must involve delivering yen and receiving dollars. To do this, the yen must be borrowed and, after the spot exchange, the dollars time deposited.

If the value of a currency is higher in the actual forward market than implied by the conditions of a synthetic forward exchange contract, then a "buy low-sell high" strategy dictates that the currency should be purchased synthetically (a long synthetic forward position on the currency) and sold via an actual forward exchange contract (a short actual forward position), and vice versa.

For example, assume as in the prior example that the 1-year synthetic forward exchange rate is $SF_{DM/\$} = 1.227$ DM/$, based on a $r_{DM} = 8\%$ mark interest rate, a $r_\$ = 10\%$ dollar interest rate, and a current spot exchange rate of $X^0_{DM/\$} = 1.25$ DM/$. If the actual 1-year forward exchange rate is $F_{DM/\$} = 1.20$ DM/$, then the forward exchange value of the mark is greater in the actual forward exchange market than synthetically, since 1.20 DM/$ represents a higher mark value than 1.227 DM/$.

Thus, when the mark value is higher in the actual forward exchange contract (1.20 DM/$) than in the synthetic (1.227 DM/$), the arbitrage strategy should be to sell marks in the *actual* forward exchange market by taking a short position in an actual dollar-denominated forward exchange contract on marks. Simultaneously one should take an offsetting position to the actual forward sale of marks, in the form of a long position in the *synthetic* forward exchange contract on marks.

Assume a contract size of DM1,200,000. In effect, one arranges an actual contract to sell DM1,200,000 a year from now at 1.20 DM/$ (= 0.833 $/DM) and simultaneously a synthetic contract to buy DM1,200,000 a year from now for 1.227 DM/$ (= 0.815 $/DM). Thus, we see that the arbitrage profit in dollars at time 1 is DM1,200,000(0.833 $/DM − 0.815 $/DM) = DM1,200,000(0.018 $/DM) = $21,600. (Actually, the $21,600 result is due to rounding; the true answer is $22,004.89.)

Let us see how to obtain the arbitrage profit at time 0. The synthetic long forward exchange position on marks should be constructed so that DM1,200,000 will be received at time 1, and these funds can be used for delivery against the actual short forward exchange position on marks. To receive DM1,200,000 a year from now from the synthetic long forward exchange position on marks, you'll need to deposit today DM1,200,000/1.08 = DM1,111,111, and thus you'll need DM1,111,111/(1.25 DM/$) = $888,888 today. If you borrow $1,000,000/1.10 = $909,090, you'll be able to pay off the face value of the loan at time 1 with the proceeds of $1,000,000 from the delivery of the DM1,200,000 against the actual short forward exchange position. Moreover, you may pocket the difference between the time 0 amounts of $909,090 and $888,888, which is $20,202, as the time 0 arbitrage profit. The strategy to capture the time 0 arbitrage profits in the manner just discussed is called *covered interest arbitrage*. Figure 4-4 shows the flows of the example.

EXAMPLE 4-5

Use the information in Example 4-4 to determine the amount of time 0 arbitrage profit that can be made, in dollars, via covered interest arbitrage for a forward exchange contract amount of $1000.

Solution 4-5 The actual 1-year forward exchange rate for Japanese yen is $F_{¥/\$}$ = 130 ¥/$, while the synthetic is $SF_{¥/\$}$ = 128.57 ¥/$. Thus, the synthetic forward exchange rate represents a higher value for the yen than the actual forward exchange rate. Since we want to "buy low-sell high," this situation suggests that arbitrage profits can be made by selling yen forward synthetically and simultaneously buying yen forward via a long position in the actual forward exchange contract on yen.

For a $1000 actual forward exchange contract amount, the long position contracts to receive ¥130,000 (the contract size). To create the offsetting synthetic short position at time 0 to deliver ¥130,000 at time 1, borrow ¥130,000/1.08 = ¥120,370 at time 0 and immediately exchange the yen into dollars at the spot rate of $X^0_{¥/\$}$ = 125 ¥/$ to get ¥120,370/(125 ¥/$) = $962.96. To have $1,000 to deliver against the actual long forward exchange position at time 1, you need only deposit $1000/1.05 = $952.38 at time 0. Thus, $962.96 − $952.38 = $10.58 is the time 0 arbitrage profit.

BANK ACTIVITIES

When a bank makes a retail forward exchange contract with a corporate customer, the customer may be hedging its transaction exposure, but the bank has just created an exposure for itself. If the customer takes a long position in an actual forward exchange contract on a currency, the bank has taken the corresponding short position.

In the Northstar example in the box, the bank was quoting a low discount

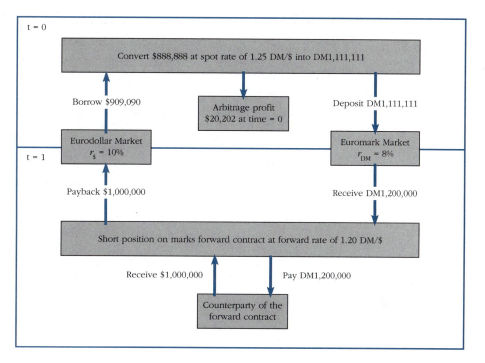

FIGURE 4-4 Covered Interest Arbitrage

forward peso because the bank expected the peso would not depreciate to the extent implicit in the synthetic forward exchange rate and because the bank was not hedging its own exposure created by its long actual forward position on pesos taken against Northstar's actual short forward position.

In other cases, however, before quoting a forward exchange rate, a bank may shop the market of actual and synthetic forward exchange rates for the better one, and then markup that rate when dealing with the retail customer. If the best interbank forward exchange rate, from among all the actual and synthetic alternatives, is 120 ¥/$, and the customer desires a long position in a dollar-denominated forward exchange contract on yen, the bank will quote a retail forward exchange rate to the corporate customer at a higher yen value, like 119.75 ¥/S. If the retail customer wants a short forward position on yen, the retail quote will be at a lower yen value than in the interbank market, say, 120.25 ¥/$.

The bank may be able to offset, or "lay off," this position and its exposure via another actual long forward exchange contract in the interbank market. Alternatively, the bank could construct a synthetic long forward exchange position on the currency in the interbank market to lay off the exposure by simultaneously dealing in the spot currency exchange and eurocurrency markets.

In that sense, a bank that deals in retail forward exchange contracts, and lays off its exposure in the interbank market, is practicing a type of "buy low-sell high" interest arbitrage of its own as a natural means of financial intermediation business.

THE COVERED INTEREST PARITY CONDITION

In theory, the activities of the arbitragers and one-way arbitragers in the market will force the convergence of forward exchange rates and their synthetic counterparts. Thus, in theory, $F_{C/\$} = SF_{C/\$}$. Using this concept, and the definition for the synthetic forward rate in equation (4-2), we have the *covered interest parity condition*, equation (4-3).

THE COVERED INTEREST PARITY CONDITION—EUROPEAN TERMS

$$F_{C/\$} = X_{C/\$}^0 \left[\frac{(1 + r_C)}{(1 + r_\$)} \right] \tag{4-3}$$

Equation (4-3) is a relationship that should hold, in the absence of market arbitrage opportunities, between the actual forward exchange rate, the spot exchange rate, and the interest rates for the two currencies. The equation appears similar to equation (4-2), but the actual forward exchange rate appears on the left-hand side of equation (4-3), not the synthetic forward exchange rate. Equation (4-2) is a definition, whereas equation (4-3) is a "no-arbitrage condition" that holds if arbitrage opportunities have been eliminated from this market.

Empirical testing of equation (4-3), with quotes that would have been observed during the trading day by actual market participants, has provided results that the covered interest parity condition holds fairly well. However, some covered interest arbitrage opportunities, and an even greater number of one-way arbitrage opportunities, were evident.[1] Of course, the Northstar example demonstrates a situation where a corporate treasury was able to exploit an arbitrage opportunity of this nature. Note that the forward exchange rates quoted by *The Financial Times* (Figure 4-5) are the synthetic rates implied by current interest rates, not forward rates directly quoted to the market.

ARE FORWARD EXCHANGE RATES GOOD PREDICTORS OF FUTURE SPOT EXCHANGE RATES?

The covered interest parity condition in equation (4-3) looks very similar to the interest parity condition of equation (3-2). Recall that in the previous inter-

---

[1]See S. Ghon Rhee and Rosita P. Chang, "Intra-day Arbitrage Opportunities in Foreign Exchange and Eurocurrency Markets," *Journal of Finance*, March 1992, pp. 363–379.

DOLLAR SPOT FORWARD AGAINST THE DOLLAR

Feb 8		Closing mid-point	Change on day	Bid/offer spread	Day's mid high	low	One month Rate	%PA	Three months Rate	%PA	One year Rate	%PA	J.P Morgan index
Europe													
Austria	(Sch)	10.7835	–0.0235	810 - 860	10.8030	10.7640	10.7995	0.8	10.7562	1.0	10.6235	1.5	105.2
Belgium	(BFr)	31.5245	–0.0705	155 - 335	31.6000	31.4700	31.502	0.9	31.4495	1.0	31.2295	0.9	106.9
Denmark	(DKr)	6.0245	–0.017	230 - 260	6.0550	6.0191	6.0227	0.3	6.0195	0.3	6.0095	0.2	105.7
Finland	(FM)	4.7238	–0.012	203 - 272	4.7448	4.7198	4.721	0.7	4.7168	0.6	4.7063	0.4	83.2
France	(FFr)	5.2965	–0.0175	955 - 975	5.3196	5.2920	5.2939	0.6	5.2899	0.5	5.269	0.5	106.5
Germany	(DM)	1.5312	–0.0043	309 - 315	1.5374	1.5288	1.5299	1.0	1.5268	1.1	1.5115	1.3	108.3
Greece	(Dr)	239.150	–0.735	100 - 200	239.870	239.000	242.15	–15.1	246.9	–13.0	259.3	–8.4	68.2
Ireland	(I£)	1.5440	+0.0004	435 - 444	1.5471	1.5403	1.5442	–0.1	1.5438	0.1	1.543	0.1	-
Italy	(L)	1615.05	–1.95	455 - 555	1620.65	1613.20	1617.8	–2.0	1624.85	–2.4	1657.05	–2.6	73.3
Luxembourg	(LFr)	31.5245	–0.0705	155 - 335	31.6000	31.4700	31.502	0.9	31.4495	1.0	31.2295	0.9	106.9
Netherlands	(Fl)	1.7167	–0.0041	164 - 169	1.7213	1.7138	1.7152	1.0	1.7116	1.2	1.6929	1.4	106.6
Norway	(NKr)	6.6990	–0.0162	975 - 005	6.7240	6.6915	6.6947	0.8	6.6885	0.6	6.6465	0.8	97.0
Portugal	(Es)	157.860	–0.45	810 - 910	158.400	157.700	158.245	–2.9	159.265	–3.6	163.715	–3.7	95.4
Spain	(Pta)	131.670	–0.695	620 - 720	132.500	131.600	131.9	–2.1	132.49	–2.5	135.265	–2.7	78.7
Sweden	(SKr)	7.4559	–0.0077	513 - 604	7.4863	7.4493	7.4657	–1.6	7.4869	–1.7	7.5749	–1.6	80.4
Switzerland	(SFr)	1.2950	–0.0058	945 - 955	1.3018	1.2935	1.2924	2.4	1.2875	2.3	1.2612	2.6	107.3
UK	(£)	1.5529	–0.0044	525 - 533	1.5601	1.5504	1.5524	0.4	1.5512	0.5	1.5449	0.5	87.3
Ecu	–	1.2329	+0.0033	324 - 334	1.2339	1.2295	1.2331	–0.2	1.2336	–0.2	1.2365	–0.3	-
SDR†	–	1.46484	–	–									
Americas													
Argentina	(Peso)	1.0001	-	000 - 001	1.0000	1.0001	-	-	-	-	-	-	-
Brazil	(Cr)	0.8350	–0.001	340 - 360	0.8360	0.8340	-	-	-	-	-	-	-
Canada	(C$)	1.3965	+0.0014	962 - 968	1.3992	1.3961	1.3984	–1.7	1.4027	–1.8	1.4143	–1.3	81.5
Mexico	(New Peso)	5.3450	+0.005	200 - 700	5.3700	5.3200	5.3458	–0.2	5.3462	–0.1	5.3476	0.0	-
USA	($)	-	-	-									96.9
Pacific/Middle East/Africa													
Australia	(A$)	1.3430	+0.0021	427 - 436	1.3438	1.3373	1.3448	–1.7	1.3494	–1.9	1.3742	–2.3	87.9
Hong Kong	(HK$)	7.7324	+0.0012	307 - 317	7.7320	7.7307	7.7324	–0.2	7.7334	–0.1	7.7382	–0.1	-
India	(Rs)	31.3650	–0.005	625 - 675	31.3725	31.3675	31.445	–3.1	31.69	–4.1			-
Israel	(Shk)	3.0246	+0.0007	221 - 271	3.0300	3.0028	-	-	-	-	-	-	-
Japan	(Y)	98.8250	–0.54	000 - 500	99.4600	98.7500	98.535	3.5	97.835	4.0	94.3	4.6	149.4
Malaysia	(M$)	2.5505	–0.002	500 - 510	2.5532	2.5500	2.5485	0.9	2.544	1.0	2.528	0.9	-
New Zealand	(NZ$)	1.5868	+0.0033	863 - 876	1.5877	1.5802	1.5895	–2.0	1.5971	–2.6	1.6238	–2.3	-
Philipines	(Peso)	24.7000	–0.1	500 - 500	24.8500	24.5500	-	-	-	-	-	-	-
Saudi Arabia	(SR)	3.7503	+0.0001	501 - 504	3.7505	3.7501	3.7529	–0.8	3.7562	–0.6	3.7678	–0.5	-
Singapore	(S$)	1.4557	–0.0063	552 - 562	1.4630	1.4545	1.4507	4.1	1.4454	2.8	1.422	2.3	-
S Africa (Com.)	(R)	3.5523	+0.003	515 - 530	3.5530	3.5485	3.5673	–5.1	3.5983	–5.2	3.7543	–5.7	-
S Africa (Fin.)	(R)	3.9600	–0.025	500 - 700	3.9950	3.9500	3.9875	–8.3	4.0375	–7.8	4.27	–7.8	-
South Korea	(Won)	790.750	+0.6	700 - 800	790.800	790.000	793.75	–4.6	797.25	–3.3	815.75	–3.2	-
Taiwan	(T$)	26.2923	+0.0043	905 - 940	26.3050	26.2905	26.3123	–0.9	26.3523	–0.9			-
Thailand	(Bt)	25.0650	–0.01	600 - 700	25.0850	25.0600	25.0775	–0.6	25.0915	–0.4	25.1175	–0.2	-

†SDR rate for Feb 7. Bid/offer spreads in the Dollar Spot table show only the last three decimal places. Forward rates are not directly quoted to the market but are implied by current interest rates. UK, Ireland & ECU are quoted in US currency. J.P. Morgan nominal indices Feb 7. Base average 1990=100

FIGURE 4-5 Forward Exchange Rates as Shown in *The Financial Times,* February 9, 1995
Source: The Financial Times, February 9, 1995. Reprinted by Permission.

est parity condition the *predicted* future exchange rate is determined by the spot exchange rate and the two interest rates. The distinction between the two versions is that the forward exchange rate, $F_{C/\$}$, appears in the covered version, while the predicted exchange rate, $X_{C/\$}^{1p}$, appears in the original version. Otherwise, the two relationships employ the same variables in the same way.

Some believe that is it reasonable to combine equations (3-2) and (4-3) and to thus draw the conclusion that the forward exchange rate is the best predictor of the future spot exchange rate. However, is it reasonable to assume that the two parity conditions are both valid?

The covered interest parity condition is easy for market participants to enforce with arbitrage. The condition is relatively easy to verify empirically, and as mentioned previously, published tests do support the approximate validity of the covered interest arbitrage condition. Thus, there is no problem believing in the validity of the covered interest parity condition of equation (4-3).

However, the validity of the interest parity condition of Chapter 3 is questionable. The economic enforcement of the uncovered interest parity condition is much more vague than the arbitrage used to enforce the covered version. Recall that the activity of traders with the same predicted future spot exchange rate was the economic mechanism by which uncovered interest parity is theoretically enforced. In reality, traders will find it very difficult to predict future spot exchange rates, and it is extremely doubtful that traders would all arrive at the same predicted future exchange rate. Moreover, risk was ignored in the development of the uncovered interest parity condition. Thus, uncovered inter-

Forward exchange trading takes place in the interbank market with currency and euro-currency trading. The covered interest parity condition is relatively easy for traders to enforce with arbitrage.

est rate parity, and the economic activity that is theorized to enforce it, should be viewed more as useful concepts and less as hard realities.

Moreover, empirical testing is much more difficult and nebulous than with the covered version of interest parity. The empirical examinations of the uncovered version by economists have been numerous and increasingly sophisticated. The results to date suggest that the forward exchange rate is *not* a good predictor of future exchange rates.[2]

Summary

This chapter covered forward exchange contracts and forward exchange rates. The basic mechanics of positions in forward exchange contracts were covered first. Both the physical delivery and cash settlement approaches were discussed. One motivation for corporate use of forward exchange contracts was examined, the hedging of unwanted transaction exposure to fluctuations in foreign currency values.

Next, the creation of synthetic forward exchange positions was treated. A synthetic forward exchange position may be created via eurocurrency loans and deposits, plus a spot foreign exchange transaction. Synthetic forward exchange positions may sometimes offer a one-way arbitrage opportunity, or a lower-cost alternative to an actual forward exchange position.

Synthetic forward positions may also be combined with actual forward exchange positions to exploit potential arbitrage opportunities. The elimination of those opportunities by covered interest arbitrage activity results in the covered interest parity condition.

Whether actual forward exchange rates are useful predictions of future exchange rates is a question that was also discussed. A problem is that the interest parity condition presented in Chapter 3 is not empirically valid.

Glossary

Difference Check: A means of cash settlement on a forward contract that avoids physical delivery.

Forward Exchange Contract: An obligation by two parties to exchange currencies at a set future time at a set exchange rate.

---

[2]A good review of the evidence that the forward exchange rate is not a good predictor is in Bernard Dumas, "Partial- Vs General-Equilibrium Models of the International Capital Markets," NBER Working Paper #4446, September 1993.

Forward Discount: The situation described when the value of a currency is lower in the forward exchange market than in the spot exchange market.

Forward Premium: The situation described when the value of a currency is higher in the forward exchange market than in the spot exchange market.

Forward Exchange Rate: The exchange rate in a forward contract.

Futures Contract: Essentially the same as a forward contract, but with some distinctions, especially the feature of daily settlement, referred to as marking-to-market.

Hedge: The use of a financial instrument to eliminate uncertainty about future base currency cash flows.

Long Position (in a forward exchange contract): The side of a forward contract with the obligation to pay base currency and receive foreign currency.

Marking-to-Market: The daily settlement feature in futures contracts but not in forward contracts.

Natural Long Exposure (to a foreign currency): The uncertainty in base currency value of a foreign currency receivable, due to uncertainty in the future spot exchange rate.

Natural Short Exposure (to a foreign currency): The uncertainty in base currency value of a foreign currency payable (or liability), due to uncertainty in the future spot exchange rate.

One-Way Arbitrage: The choice of the most advantageous alternative among equivalent financial strategies.

Opportunity Cost of Hedging with a Forward Contract: The forgone opportunity of profiting from currency appreciation/depreciation when an exposure is instead hedged with a forward contract.

Short Position (in a forward exchange contract): The side of a forward contract with the obligation to receive base currency and pay foreign currency.

Synthetic: An equivalent to a security that is created, or "manufactured," from other existing securities.

Transaction Exposure: The uncertainty in the base currency value of an already committed foreign currency transaction.

Discussion Questions

1.   Explain why a company might wish to go long a forward exchange contract on a foreign currency.

2.   Assume your company wishes to go long a forward exchange contract on a foreign currency. Explain how its bank might determine the retail forward rate to quote and how the bank might lay off its risk.

3.   Compare and contrast covered interest rate parity with the uncovered interest parity condition of Chapter 3.

Problems

1.   You take a 1-year short position in a dollar-denominated forward contract on the Japanese yen at a forward exchange rate of $F_{¥/\$} = 130$ ¥/$. The contract amount is $500,000. If the spot exchange rate for the yen a year from now is $X^1_{¥/\$} = 120$ ¥/$, what is the dollar gain (loss) on the short position?

2.   You take a long position in a 2-year dollar-denominated forward contract on the British pound at a forward exchange rate of 1.75 $/£. The contract amount is $2,000,000. If the spot exchange rate for the pound two years from now is $X^2_{\$/£} = 2.00$ $/£, what is the dollar gain (loss) on the contract?

3.   Your company's base currency is the U.S. dollar. You are committed to making a natural British pound payment of £9,000,000 in 3 months. Assume that the current 3-month forward exchange rate is 1.75 $/£. Determine from the forward exchange rate the dollar value of the liability that can be locked in by dealing in the forward exchange market. Demonstrate that the cash-settled forward contract approach hedges the exposure for a randomly picked spot exchange rate at the delivery time.

4.   Your base currency is the Japanese yen. Assume that you have a natural long exposure to the U.S. dollar, because you have a receivable in the amount of $6,000,000 due six months from now. The six-month forward rate of exchange is 125 ¥/$. Find the hedged base currency (yen) value of the receivable, and demonstrate how a forward exchange position will cover the exposure, given a randomly picked spot exchange rate six months from now.

5.   At time 0 you borrow C$1000 in time 1 face value at a 7% interest rate $(r_{C\$})$, exchange the borrowed proceeds into U.S. dollars at the spot rate of 1.20 C$/$, and deposit the U.S. dollars at 5% until time 1. How many U.S. dollars

---

1.   The short position on yen incurs a loss of $41,667.

5.   The implied synthetic forward exchange rate is 1.22 C$/$.

will you receive from your deposit at time 1, and what is the implicit forward exchange rate in this synthetic short forward position on Canadian dollars?

6. Apply the appropriate formula to verify the synthetic forward exchange rate from the previous problem.

7. Let the quoted contract exchange rate on an actual dollar-denominated forward contract on Canadian dollars be 1.25 C$/$. You wish to establish a short forward position on Canadian dollars. Given the information in the two previous problems, should you take an actual short forward position on Canadian dollars or a synthetic one?

8. Use the information in the previous 3 problems to determine a covered interest arbitrage strategy, and find the amount of time 0 arbitrage profits, in U.S. dollars, for a forward contract with a contract amount of $1,000.

9. If the 1-year euroFrench franc interest rate is 9%, the 1-year eurodollar interest rate is 3%, and the spot exchange rate is 5.00 FF/$, what should the 1-year forward rate of exchange be if no arbitrage opportunities are possible?

8. $21.14 is the time 0 arbitrage profit.

9. 5.29 FF/$.

part II

CORPORATE

FINANCING IN THE

GLOBAL MARKET

chapter 5

GLOBAL DEBT FINANCING

Many companies have been in the high-growth phase of their business cycle, at least for their international operations, as opportunities for international business have been expanding. Corporations in the high-growth phase will typically have a great need for capital to finance their operations. Obtaining capital financing is a primary function of financial management. Opportunities for obtaining capital have widened and are becoming more sophisticated as the financial markets of the world have globalized and integrated. This chapter introduces aspects of capital financing in an international context.

The chapter emphasizes eurobonds and their valuation, based on the eurocurrency concept and the integration of the eurocurrency and eurobond markets. The bond valuation material paves the way for the mark-to-market valuation of currency swaps in Chapter 6. The chapter also introduces the idea of *financial structuring*, which is the augmentation of traditional financing instruments, like bonds, with innovative "derivatives" features, based on forward contracts, swaps, and options. The ideas of financial structuring continue through Chapters 6 and 7. In all three chapters of Part II, many real-world cases and scenarios are discussed, and many hypothetical examples are constructed to explain the basic ideas in analytical detail.

The chapters of Part II take the view that global capital markets have evolved to the state where it is commonplace for a corporation to consider issuing capital in foreign countries and denominated in any one or more of a number of currencies. The subject of hedging the associated foreign currency exposure with forward exchange contracts is covered in this chapter. This material preludes the next chapter's coverage of swap-driven financing.

Eurobonds

A *eurobond* refers to an international debt obligation offered to investors in countries outside that of the issuer and in a currency, or currencies, other than the natural base currency of the investors to whom the bonds are initially sold. Technically, this definition differs from that of a *foreign bond*, in that a foreign bond is issued in the country and currency of the investor and is traded in the investor's local, and locally regulated, bond market.

For example, the first *eurobond* was a U.S. dollar-denominated bond, issued in the 1960s by the Italian highway authority, Autostrada, and purchased by investors in England, Belgium, Germany, and the Netherlands. Following its issue, the bond was listed on the London Stock Exchange. If Autostrada had issued the bond in the United States, the bond would technically have been a *foreign bond*, and would have had to be registered with the Securities and Exchange Commission (SEC).

EVOLUTION OF THE EUROBOND MARKET

Issuing bonds in a foreign country has been done for some time. However, the practice mostly involved government debt and denomination in the currency of the investor's country. Not too long after the eurodollar market (for trading in short-term deposits and loans) began, investment bankers realized that portfolio investors may have an investment appetite for longer-term securities denominated in currencies other than their own.

During the days of relatively socialistic policies in Europe and Latin America, the denomination of bonds in U.S. dollars appealed to wealthy European and Latin American investors, who believed that their currencies would depreciate in value relative to the dollar. Fearing devaluations and appropriations in their own countries, these investors often kept their wealth outside of their own country, especially in secret "numbered" accounts in Swiss banks. U.S. dollar-denominated eurobonds were an ideal portfolio investment for Swiss banks to purchase for their anonymous clients.[1]

Gradually, investors in a variety of countries became interested in holding bonds denominated in currencies other than dollars or their own base currency. The eurobond concept evolved into a global bond market.

In contrast to foreign bonds, the eurobond market has no regulatory authority. Thus, eurobonds do not have to be registered with authorities like the SEC and are free to take innovative forms that regulatory authorities might not appreciate. Many of the innovations of the eurobond market to avoid regulations have played significant roles in the globalization of the financial mar-

---

[1] A readable and interesting account of the evolution of the eurobond market is in Roy C. Smith, *The Global Bankers* (New York: E. P. Dutton, 1989).

kets. Moreover, eurobonds are *bearer bonds*, which make payments to the bearer on demand, as opposed to *registered bonds*; thus, eurobondholders are anonymous to tax authorities, and eurobonds are therefore frequently favored by investors desiring to evade taxes.

One innovative feature in the evolution of the eurobond market was simply the simultaneous issue of bonds in more than one country by a syndicate of banks from more than one country. Moreover, the banks of the syndicate need not be based in the country of the issuer or the investors. This cross-border organization of issues has been an integral part of the globalization process and has led to some of the largest financing packages in history.

For example, in 1984, Texaco raised $1.5 billion in a convertible bond issue that was lead-managed by Credit Suisse, First Boston (CSFB). The securities were distributed globally, with the Swiss distribution coordinated by Credit Suisse, the German by Deutsche Bank, the Japanese by Nomura Securities, and the rest of the world by Morgan Stanley.[2] Since the Texaco deal, there have been many large global issues of debt (and equities), using international distribution organizations.

Secondary market trading of eurobonds is facilitated by two clearinghouses. *Euroclear*, in Brussels, primarily clears U.S. dollar eurobonds, while *CEDEL*, in Luxembourg, primarily clears eurobonds of other currencies. The clearinghouses are privately owned by member banks. Although unregulated, the eurobond market does have standards that have been set by a voluntary organization called the *Association of International Bond Dealers, or AIBD.*[3]

As with eurocurrencies, none of the features of a eurobond (the currency, the issuer, the buyers, or the underwriters) has to be European, but the "euro" prefix is a tradition that has been held over from the European origins of the market. By the same token, the term "euromarkets" generally refers to the global financial markets that operate without regard to national borders or authorities: the eurocurrency, eurobond, and euroequity markets.

VALUATION OF STRAIGHT EUROBONDS

While some credit, or default, risk is always present in corporate bonds, corporate eurobond issuers often have AAA credit ratings. Other frequent eurobond issuers are governments and supranational organizations (like the World Bank), also with excellent credit ratings. The valuation techniques used

---

[2]A fascinating account of this issue is in Smith, *The Global Bankers.*

[3]A thorough introduction to eurobonds is in Michael Bowe, *Eurobonds* (Homewood, IL: Square Mile Books, Dow Jones-Irwin, 1988). Pioneering empirical research on eurobonds may be found in David S. Kidwell, M. Wayne Marr, and G. Rodney Thompson, "Eurodollar Bonds: Alternative Financing for U.S. Companies," *Financial Management*, Winter 1985, pp. 18–27; and in J. E. Finnerty and K. P. Nunn, Jr., "The Determinants of Yield Spreads on U.S. and Eurobonds," *Management International Review*, 1985/2, pp. 23–33.

*I**SSUANCE OF EUROBONDS***

A corporate eurobond issue involves a number of parties. Internally, a company's senior management may have to approve of the issue and seek authority from the board of directors. The issue must be analyzed by the firm's accountants, who determine the implications for taxes and reporting, from both foreign and domestic points of view. The legal department must assess registration and disclosure requirements. The investor relations, communications, and cash management departments all should be involved in the process. On the external side, such groups as the rating agencies, shareholders, other bondholders, and securities exchanges must be notified and consulted.

A corporate bond issuer will generally engage a bank to manage the issuance by one of two methods. One method is for a bank to fully underwrite the bond, which is called a *competitively priced deal* or a *bought deal*. In a bought deal, a bank buys the bond issue from the company and tries to resell the bonds to investors at a markup. One bank typically becomes the lead underwriter and engages a syndicate of other banks (often from various countries) to assist in the underwriting and/or the distribution. The risk of the bond failing to sell in the market is borne by the underwriters.

The alternative to the bought deal is the negotiated deal, or best efforts deal. In a best efforts deal, a bank simply manages the issue for a fee. If the market does not receive the issue well, the immediate problem is that of the issuing company, not the bank.

in this chapter implicitly assume that the AAA rating applies for all transacting parties and that LIBOR rates are available on eurocurrencies to the same AAA-rated companies. For companies with lower-grade ratings than AAA, the analysis would be similar, but a credit risk premium would have to be added to the LIBOR "flat" rate.

To introduce some of the basic concepts of financial engineering and arbitrage, we value simple, *straight bonds*. A straight bond makes interest and principal payments at a set coupon rate in a single currency and has no call provisions or other innovative features. Sometimes straight bonds are referred to as *bullet bonds*. Often, we'll simply call them coupon bonds. Eurobonds typically make interest payments annually, in contrast to semiannually, as is customary in the U.S. debt markets.

For simplicity, the valuation covered here is for the instant in time after the most recent interest payment. The value might thus be called the ex-interest value of the bond. As with any bond, the value of a straight eurobond may be represented as the present value of the future interest and principal payments, using a market-determined *yield to maturity* as the discount rate. Indeed, the definition of yield to maturity is that interest rate that discounts the promised future bond payments back to the bond's present value.

The yield-to-maturity approach to bond valuation is a technique that you are assumed to have covered in an introductory financial management course. The technique is reviewed in Example 5-1.

> **EXAMPLE 5-1**
>
> Find the value of a straight French franc bond with face value of FF100, 4 years to maturity, and a 5% annual coupon interest rate, assuming the bond's yield to maturity is 7%.
>
> *Solution 5-1*   Since the bond makes annual interest payments at a 5% coupon rate and the face value is FF100, the cash flows for the bond are interest payments of FF5 for each of the next 4 years plus a principal repayment of FF100 4 years from now. The present value of those cash flows, given a yield to maturity of 7%, is
>
> $FF5/1.07 + FF5/1.07^2 + FF5/1.07^3 + FF5/1.07^4 + FF100/1.07^4 = FF93.23.$

In Example 5-1, if the face value had been FF1000, the present value of the bond would be FF932.30, and if the face value had been FF10,000, the present value would be FF9323. Rather than specify a principal amount or face value, one can simply quote, as the bond market does, on the basis of percentage of face value. Thus, the value of a 4-year, 5% coupon, French franc bond with a 7% yield to maturity is simply quoted as 93.23, with the understanding that this value is a percentage of face value.

Figure 5-1 shows some international bond price quotes from *The Financial Times*. The straights reveal the wide variety of currency denominations, including entire sections for bonds in dollars, marks, Swiss francs, and yen. In the section for other straights, we see bonds denominated in Luxembourg francs (LFr), Dutch guilders (Fl, for "florins," an alternative term for the currency of The Netherlands), Canadian dollars, ECUs, Australian dollars, British pounds, New Zealand dollars, and French francs. Take some time to observe that the issuer often corresponds to a different country than represented by the currency denomination of the bond; thus, one may obtain a sense of the global scope of the market. Floating rate notes, also quoted in Figure 5-1, are discussed later in the chapter.

A *par bond* is a coupon bond whose market value is equal to its face value. A bond is a par bond if the yield to maturity is exactly equal to the coupon rate. Many coupon bonds are par bonds, or close to it, when they are issued. If the yield to maturity is greater than the coupon rate, the value of the bond is less than the face value; in this case, the bond is called a *discount bond*. The bond in Example 5-1 is thus a discount bond. If the yield to maturity is less than the coupon rate, the value of the bond is greater than the face value; in this case, the bond is called a *premium bond*.

ZERO-COUPON BONDS

A *zero-coupon bond* makes no interest payments. It only pays off a face value at maturity. Zero-coupon bonds, or "zeros," have become a widely accepted

FT/ISMA INTERNATIONAL BOND SERVICE

Listed are the latest international bonds for which there is an adequate secondary market. **Latest prices at 7:10 pm on February 8**

U.S. DOLLAR STRAIGHTS

	Issued	Bid	Offer	Chg.	Yield
Abbey Natl Treasury 6½ 03	1000	90	90¼		8.21
Alberta Province 7⅝ 98	1000	99¼	99½		7.85
Austria 8½ 00	400	102¾	103		7.81
Bank Ned Gemeenten 7 99	1000	97⅜	97½	+⅛	7.69
Bank of Tokyo 8⅜ 96	100	100¾	101⅛		7.63
Belgium 5½ 03	1000	84¼	84⅜		8.07
BFCE 7¾ 97	150	100¼	100⅞	–⅛	7.60
British Gas 0 21	1500	11⅝	11⅞	–⅛	8.38
Canada 9 96	1000	101⅝	101⅞		7.32
Cheung Kong Fin 5½ 98	500	89⅛	89⅝	+¼	9.12
China 6½ 04	1000	84⅝	85⅜	–⅜	9.23
Council Europe 8 96	100	100⅝	101		7.49
Credit Foncier 9½ 99	300	105½	105⅞		7.86
Denmark 5¾ 98	1000	94⅞	95⅛		7.70
East Japan Railway 6⅝ 04	600	90½	90⅞	–¼	8.14
ECSC 8¼ 96	193	101⅛	101½	+⅛	7.54
EEC 8¼ 96	100	101	101¼	+⅛	7.40
EIB 7¾ 96	250	100½	100¾		7.32
EIB 9¼ 97	1000	103⅞	104⅛		7.62
Elec de France 9 98	200	103⅛	103⅝		7.81
Eurofima 9¼ 96	100	101⅞	102⅛		7.38
Ex-Im Bank Japan 8 02	500	100½	100¾	–⅛	7.90
Export Dev Corp 9½ 98	150	104⅞	105⅛		7.80
Federal Natl Mort 7.40 04	1500	97⅜	97⅝	–⅛	7.95
Finland 6¾ 97	3000	97¾	98	–⅛	7.80
Ford Motor Credit 6¼ 98	1500	95⅝	96		8.05
Gen Elec Capital 9⅜ 96	300	102⅛	102½		7.58
GMAC 9⅛ 96	200	101¼	101¾	–⅛	7.86
Ind Bk Japan Fin 7⅞ 97	200	99¾	100¼		7.98
Inter Amer Dev 7⅝ 96	200	100	100⅜		7.58
Italy 6⅞ 23	3500	79⅞	80¼	–¼	9.00
Japan Dev Bk 8⅜ 01	500	102⅛	102½	–⅛	7.92
Kansai Elec Pwr 10 96	350	102½	102⅞	–⅛	7.59
Korea Elec Power 6⅜ 03	1350	86¼	86¾	–⅛	8.82
LTCB Fin 8 97	200	99⅞	100⅜	–⅛	8.06
Matsushita Elec 7¼ 02	1000	96	96¼	–⅛	8.13
Norway 7¼ 97	1000	99½	99¾		7.49
Ontario 7⅜ 03	3000	95½	95⅞	–⅛	8.32
Oster Kontrollbank 8½ 01	200	102⅞	103⅛	–⅛	7.88
Petro-Canada 7¼ 96	200	99⅝	100⅛		7.53
Portugal 5¾ 03	1000	85½	85¾	–⅛	8.27
Quebec Hydro 9¾ 98	150	104⅝	105⅛		8.20
Quebec Prov 9 98	200	102⅜	102⅞	+⅛	8.10
Sainsbury 9⅛ 96	150	102	102⅜		7.74
SAS 10 99	200	104⅝	105¼	–⅛	8.59
SNCF 9½ 98	150	105	105⅜		7.76
Spain 6½ 99	1500	94¾	95	–⅛	7.88
State Bk NSW 8½ 96	200	101	101¼		7.66
Sweden 6½ 03	2000	90¾	91	–⅛	8.24
Swedish Export 8⅜ 96	700	100⅞	101⅛		7.53
Tokyo Elec Power 6⅛ 03	1000	88¼	88⅝	–⅛	8.08
Tokyo Metropolis 8¼ 96	200	101	101⅜		7.58
Toyota Motor 5⅝ 98	1500	94½	94¾		7.67
United Kingdom 7¼ 02	3000	96¾	97	–⅛	7.81
World Bank 8⅜ 99	1500	103⅛	103¼		7.70
World Bank 8¾ 97	1500	102¾	103		7.42

DEUTSCHE MARK STRAIGHTS

	Issued	Bid	Offer	Chg.	Yield
Austria 6½ 24	2000	84¼	84½	+⅛	7.90
Credit Foncier 7¼ 03	2000	97⅜	97⅞		7.70
Denmark 6⅛ 98	2000	98¼	98½	+⅛	6.74
Depfa Finance 6⅜ 03	1500	91¾	91⅞		7.71
Deutche Bk Fin 7½ 03	2000	98⅝	99	–⅛	7.74
EEC 6½ 00	2900	97⅝	97⅞		7.07
EIB 6¼ 00	1500	96¾	97⅛	+⅛	7.02
Finland 7½ 00	3000	101	101⅜		7.25
Italy 7¼ 98	5000	100⅝	100¾	+⅛	7.01
LKB Baden-Wuertt 6½ 08	2250	89⅛	89¼	+⅛	7.82
Norway 6⅛ 98	1500	98¼	98⅜	+⅛	6.73
Ontario 6¼ 04	1500	90⅛	90¼		7.83
Spain 7¼ 03	4000	97⅝	97¾		7.65
Sweden 8 97	2500	102¾	103	+⅜	6.84

	Issued	Bid	Offer	Chg.	Yield
United Kingdom 7⅛ 97	5500	101½	101⅝	+¼	6.49
Volkswagen Intl Fin 7 03	1000	95¼	95¾	+¼	7.79
World Bank 0 15	2000	23⅛	23½	+¼	7.27
World Bank 5⅞ 03	3000	89½	89⅝	+⅛	7.55
World Bank 8¾ 00	1250	110¼	110¾	–¼	6.36

SWISS FRANC STRAIGHTS

	Issued	Bid	Offer	Chg.	Yield
Asian Dev Bank 6 10	100	102¼	103¼	+¼	5.78
Austria 4½ 00	1000	97¾	98		5.02
Council Europe 4¾ 98	250	99⅝	99⅞		4.89
Denmark 4¼ 99	1000	97¼	97⅜		4.92
EIB 6¾ 04	300	107	107½		5.78
Elec de France 7¼ 06	100	109½	110½		6.04
Finland 7¼ 99	300	107½	107⅝	+¼	5.38
Hyundai Motor Fin 8½ 97	100	106	107½		5.91
Iceland 7⅝ 00	100	109	110	+½	5.66
Kobe 6⅜ 01	240	105	106		5.43
Ontario 6¼ 03	400	102½	103	+½	5.85
Quebec Hydro 5 08	100	85¾	86½		6.66
SNCF 7 04	450	110	110½		5.62
World Bank 5 03	150	97½	98	–¼	5.37
World Bank 7 01	600	108½	109	+⅛	5.32

YEN STRAIGHTS

	Issued	Bid	Offer	Chg.	Yield
Belgium 5 99	75000	104	104¼		4.07
EIB 6⅝ 00	100000	111⅛	111⅜		4.16
Finland 6¾ 96	50000	104⅜	104⅝		2.76
Inter Amer Dev 7¼ 00	30000	113¾	114		4.27
Italy 3½ 01	300000	93¼	93⅜	+⅛	4.80
Japan Dev Bk 5 99	100000	104⅜	104½		3.95
Japan Dev Bk 6½ 01	120000	111¼	111½		4.49
Nippon Tel Tel 5⅞ 96	50000	104⅝	104⅞	+⅛	2.92
Norway 5⅜ 97	150000	104⅜	104⅝		3.10
SNCF 6¾ 00	30000	111½	111¾		4.18
Spain 5¾ 02	125000	106½	106⅝	+⅛	4.65
Sweden 4⅝ 98	150000	102¾	102⅞	+⅛	3.64
World Bank 5¼ 02	250000	104⅜	104⅜	+⅛	4.58

OTHER STRAIGHTS

	Issued	Bid	Offer	Chg.	Yield
Genfinance Lux 9⅛ 99 LFr	1000	104½	105½		7.81
IKB Deut Industbk 8½ 03 LFr	3000	100¼	101¼		8.45
World Bank 8 96 LFr	1000	101⅛	101¾		6.96
ABN Amro 6⅝ 00 Fl	1000	97	97⅜	+⅛	7.34
Bank Ned Gemeenten 7 03 Fl	1500	96	96½		7.68
AlbertaProvince 10⅝ 96 C$	500	101⅞	102¼		8.61
Bell Canada 10⅝ 99 C$	150	103¾	104⅜	+⅛	9.52
British Columbia 10 96 C$	500	101⅜	101¾		8.77
EIB 10⅛ 98 C$	130	103⅞	104⅞	+⅛	8.63
Elec de France 9¾ 99 C$	275	101⅞	102⅜	–⅛	9.20
Gen Elec Capital 10 96 C$	300	101⅜	102	–⅛	8.79
KfW Int Fin 10 01 C$	400	102⅝	103		9.41
Nippon Tel Tel 10¼ 99 C$	200	103⅜	103⅞		9.31
Ontario 8 03 C$	1500	92	92¼	–⅛	9.66
Ontario Hydro 10⅞ 99 C$	500	104⅞	105¼		9.38
Oster Kontrollbank 10¼ 99 C$	150	103⅜	104		9.26
Quebec Prov 10½ 98 C$	200	102¾	103¼		9.58
Belgium 9⅛ 96 Ecu	1250	102⅛	102¼	+⅛	7.04
Council Europe 9 01 Ecu	1100	102⅜	102⅞		8.51
Credit Lyonnais 9 96 Ecu	125	101½	102		7.65
EIB 10 97 Ecu	1125	104¼	104⅜	+⅛	7.64
Ferro del Stat 10⅛ 98 Ecu	500	104⅜	104⅞	+⅛	8.36
Italy 10¾ 00 Ecu	1000	108½	108⅞		8.63
Spain 9 96 Ecu	1000	102	102¼		7.26
United Kingdom 9⅛ 01 Ecu	2750	103⅜	103½	–⅛	8.39
AIDC 10 99 A$	100	98¼	98¾	–⅛	10.48
Comm Bk Australia 13¾ 99 A$	100	111	111½	–⅛	10.57
EIB 7¾ 99 A$	350	93¾	94	+⅜	9.70
NSW Treasury Zero 0 20 A$	1000	8⅞	9¼	+⅛	9.85
R & I Bank 7¾ 03 A$	125	84⅛	84½		10.71
State Bk NSW 9 02 A$	300	91½	92		10.67
Sth Aust Govt Fin 9 02 A$	150	91¼	91⅝		10.72
Unilever Australia 12 98 A$	150	104	104½	–⅛	10.42
Western Aust Treas 7⅝ 98 A$	100	92⅜	92⅞	–¼	10.46
Abbey Natl Treasury 8 03 £	1000	93	93¼	+⅛	9.25
Alliance Leics 11⅜ 97 £	100	105⅜	105¾	+⅛	8.60
British Land 8⅞ 23 £	150	90¼	90⅝		10.15
Denmark 6¾ 98 £	800	94	94¼		8.77
EIB 8 03 £	1000	94⅝	94⅞	+⅛	8.93
Halifax 10⅜ 97 £	100	103⅜	103¾		8.51
Hanson 10⅜ 97 £	500	103¼	103⅝		8.93
HSBC Holdings 11.69 02 £	153	109⅞	110¼		9.74
Italy 10½ 14 £	400	106½	106⅞	–⅛	9.73
Japan Dev Bk 7 00 £	200	92	92¼		8.83
Land Secs 9½ 07 £	200	99¾	100⅛	–⅛	9.52
Ontario 11⅛ 01 £	100	108½	108¾	+⅛	9.22
Powergen 8⅞ 03 £	250	97¾	98	+⅛	9.27
Severn Trent 11½ 99 £	150	108⅜	108¾		9.08
Tokyo Elec Power 11 01 £	150	108⅝	108⅞	+⅛	9.12
Abbey National 0 96 NZ$	100	85⅝	86⅜	–¼	9.83
TCNZ Fin 9¼ 02 NZ$	75	100	101	–¾	9.23
Credit Local 6 01 FFr	7000	89⅞	90⅛		7.99
Elec de France 8¾ 22 FFr	3000	102⅜	102¾	+⅛	8.52
SNCF 9¼ 97 FFr	4000	103¾	104		7.30

FLOATING RATE NOTES

	Issued*	Bid	Offer	C.cpn
Abbey Natl Treasury –1/16 99	1000	99.46	99.55	6.3750
Banco Roma 0 99	200			6.5312
Belgium 1/16 97 DM	500	100.09	100.19	5.1250
BFCE –0.02 96	350	99.81	99.92	6.2300
Britannia 0.10 96 £	150	99.97	100.06	6.8500
Canada –¼ 99	2000	99.23	99.29	6.0000
CCCE 0 06 Ecu	200	99.19	99.39	5.7500
Credit Lyonnais 1/16 00	300	97.36	98.01	6.6875
Denmark –⅛ 96	1000	99.61	99.70	5.0625
Dresdner Finance 1/32 98 DM	1000	99.99	100.07	5.0938
Ferro del Stat 0.10 97	420	99.91	100.07	6.1000
Finland 0 97	1000	99.98	100.06	6.7500
IMI Bank Intl ¼ 99	500	99.96	100.05	6.1875
Italy ¼ 98	2000	100.04	100.10	6.6250
LKB Baden-Wuert Fin –⅛ 98	1000	99.40	99.50	5.8750
Lloyds Bank Perp S 0.10	600	83.25	84.25	5.4125
Malaysia 1/16 05	650	99.19	99.41	5.9375
New Zealand –⅛ 99	1000	99.74	99.83	6.3750
Ontario 0 99	2000	99.45	99.53	5.8125
Renfe 0 98	500	99.40	99.56	6.0000
Societe Generale 0 96	300	99.55	99.66	5.3750
Staatsbank Berlin –0.05 96 DM	6000	99.94	100.00	5.1483
State Bk Victoria 0.05 99	125	99.85	100.02	6.9875
Sweden 0 98	1500	99.83	99.90	6.0625
Sweden –⅛ 01	2000	98.70	98.78	6.1250
United Kingdom –⅛ 96	4000	99.89	99.94	6.2500

CONVERTIBLE BONDS

	Issued	Conv. Price	Bid	Offer	Prem.
Browning-Ferris 6¾ 05	400	52½	94⅛	95	+58.13
Chubb Capital 6 98	250	86	103¼	104¼	+11.69
Gold Kalgoorlie 7½ 00	65	1.0554	92⅜	93⅞	+52.32
Hanson 9½ 06 £	500	2.5875	103¼	104⅛	+13.20
Hanson America 2.39 01	420	30.8756	73	74	+25.22
Hong Kong Land 4 01	410	31.05	74½	75½	-25.30
Land Secs 6¾ 02 £	84	6.72	93⅝	95⅛	+8.85
Lasmo 7¾ 05 £	90	5.64	84⅝	86	
Mitsui Bank 2⅝ 03	200	2332.6	76	78	+11.00
Mount Isa Fin 6½ 97	100	2.283	94⅝	95⅝	+51.00
Natl Power 6¼ 08 £	250	4.33	113¼	114¼	+2.37
Ogden 6 02	85	39.077	81⅞	83⅛	+62.00
Pennzoil 4¾ 03	500	58.8097	89¼	90¼	+13.18
Sumitomo Bank 3⅛ 04	300	3606.9	75⅛	76⅛	+14.76
Sun Alliance 7¼ 08 £	155	3.9	91⅜	92⅜	+17.61
Tesco Capital 9 05 £	200	2.51	115⅛	116⅛	+13.77
Texas Instruments 2¾ 02	300	82⅞	95⅛	96⅜	+7.62

* No information available - previous day's price

‡ Only one market maker supplied a price

STRAIGHT BONDS: The yield is the yield to redemption of the bid-price; the amount issued is in millions of currency units. Chg. day=Change on day.
FLOATING RATE NOTES: Denominated in dollars unless otherwise indicated. Coupon shown is minimum. Spread=Margin above six-month offered rate (‡three-month §above mean rate) for US dollars. C.cpn=The current coupon.
CONVERTIBLE BONDS: Denominated in dollars unless otherwise indicated. Cnv. price=Nominal amount of bond per share expressed in currency of share at conversion rate fixed at issue. Prem=Percentage premium of the current effective price of acquiring shares via the bond over the most recent price of the shares.

FIGURE 5-1 International Bond Prices as Quoted in *The Financial Times* February 9, 1995
Source: The Financial Times, February 9, 1995. Reprinted by permission.

financing instrument of the euromarkets. An early reason for the popularity of zeros related to tax advantages. More generally, zeros have been used as fundamental "building blocks" for financial engineering.

A zero-coupon bond, by definition, is thus a pure discount instrument, just like a eurocurrency deposit. In fact, in principle, there is no distinction between a zero-coupon eurobond and a eurocurrency. If their rates are not equal, then arbitrage activity may occur. For example, assume that the eurobond market's 5-year, zero-coupon yield to maturity on AAA euromark debt is 7% and that the 5-year euromark LIBOR is 6.7%. As long as there is this discrepancy between the two rates, a company needing financing has a one-way arbitrage opportunity, in the sense that it can choose the cheaper of two, essentially equivalent, financing opportunities.

Now note a very important point that will underlie a significant part of the analysis in the rest of this chapter and the next: *A coupon bond is equivalent to a portfolio of zero-coupon instruments.* For example, the 4-year French franc bond in Example 5-1 may be viewed as a portfolio of five zero-coupon bonds: There are four zero-coupon bonds, each with a face value of FF5, maturing at 1-year intervals beginning a year from the time the coupon bond is issued. There is also a 4-year zero with face value of FF100 that matures 4 years from the time the coupon bond is issued. Alternatively, the coupon bond may be viewed as a combination of three zeros with face value of FF5 maturing at 1-year intervals beginning at time 1 and one 4-year zero with face value of FF105. We may say that a portfolio of zeros may be assembled so as to create a *synthetic coupon bond.* Figure 5-2 conveys the concept.

---

1. Question: Ignoring the time 0 cost or proceeds, which of the two alternative future cash flow structures would you prefer, "A" or "B"?

   A. Coupon Bond

   B. Synthetic Coupon Bond
      (Portfolio of Zero-Coupon Bonds)

A. Coupon Bond	B. Synthetic Coupon Bond
FF5 time 1 coupon payment	1-year zero with face value of FF5
FF5 time 2 coupon payment	2-year zero with face value of FF5
FF5 time 3 coupon payment	3-year zero with face value of FF5
FF105 time 4 coupon plus principal payment	4-year zero with face value of FF105

   Answer: With no other information, you should be indifferent.

2. Question: What if the coupon bond would cost FF100 to invest in at time 0, while the portfolio of zeros would cost FF101 to invest in. Which would you prefer?
   Answer: The coupon bond.

3. Question: What if the coupon bond can be issued for FF100 at time 0, while the proceeds from issuing the portfolio of zeros would be FF101. Which would be better to issue by a corporation?
   Answer: The synthetic coupon bond engineered by a portfolio of zeros.

FIGURE 5-2   A Coupon Bond is Equivalent to a Portfolio of Zero-Coupon Instruments

THE DISCOUNT (OR STRIP) YIELD CURVE

Each currency has its own structure of how interest rates vary with the time to maturity. A relationship between the interest rates and time to maturity for a given currency is called a *yield curve* for the currency. A yield curve for pure discount, or zero-coupon, instruments is called a *discount yield curve*, a *zero-coupon yield curve*, or a *strip yield curve*.

If the yield to maturity increases as the time to maturity increases, the yield curve is termed *upward sloping*. A *downward sloping* yield curve shows yields to maturity that decrease as the time to maturity increases. A *flat yield curve* shows the same yield to maturity for all maturities.

From this point on we will assume that a currency's zero-coupon bonds and eurocurrency deposits/loans will have the same yield for a given maturity. In other words we'll assume that market arbitrage activity has already forced the convergence of the market yields on the two types of instruments, so that we can refer interchangeably to eurocurrency loans/deposits and zero-coupon eurobonds.

BOND VALUATION VIA SYNTHETICS AND ONE-WAY ARBITRAGE

This section advances the topic of bond valuation and demonstrates integration of the eurocurrency and zeros market with the coupon bond market. The numerical examples in this chapter assume that one observes the upward-sloping portion of the yen discount yield curve as shown in Figure 5-3.

First, we value a coupon bond given the information of the discount yield curve, making use of the idea that a coupon bond is equivalent to a portfolio of zero-coupon instruments. What we do is create a synthetic coupon bond out of zero-coupon/eurocurrency instruments.

Assume that we wish to value an actual 3-year yen bond with a coupon rate of 6.50%. A bond with face value of ¥100 will pay ¥6.50 at year 1, ¥6.50 at year 2, and ¥106.50 at year 3. Thus, issuing the 3-year coupon bond obligates the issuer to exactly the same liabilities as a simultaneous borrowing of (1) 1-year euroyen with face value of ¥6.50, (2) 2-year euroyen with face value of ¥6.50, and (3) 3-year euroyen with face value of ¥106.50. The proceeds

Time to Maturity	Yen Yield to Maturity
1 year	6.0%
2 years	6.5%
3 years	7.0%

FIGURE 5-3 A Hypothetical Portion of the Discount Yield Curve in Euroyen

from the portfolio of euroyen loans, given the observed discount yield curve in Figure 5-3, would be $¥6.50/1.06 + ¥6.50/1.065^2 + ¥106.50/1.07^3 = ¥98.80$. In essence ¥98.80 is the value that the participants in the eurocurrency market would place on the coupon bond.

Assuming that the actual coupon bond is trading at par, ¥100, then there is a valuation discrepancy between the markets. Given this situation, a company contemplating a yen bond financing would prefer to issue a coupon bond directly rather than one synthetically constructed in the eurocurrency market. Because the 3-year coupon bond can be issued at par for proceeds of ¥100, the direct coupon bond alternative is better, since the eurocurrency portfolio approach provides time 0 proceeds of only ¥98.80 for the same future liability structure. Issuing the coupon bond in lieu of borrowing the euroyen is an example of one-way arbitrage.

In the example just described, as well as many subsequent examples in this section of the text, it is taken as given that the example company needs financing for some "project" to be implemented at time 0. In this example, the need is for roughly ¥100. It is also assumed that the corporate financial management of the company has decided which specific liability structure is best, considering the timing of the future operating cash flows that the company will be generating to service the future liabilities. Some companies might prefer a single liability at some future point in time; other companies may regard a stream of future payments as a more convenient match with anticipated operating cash flows.

EXAMPLE 5-2

You observe eurocurrency yields to maturity of 7% for 1-year French francs and 9% for 2-year French francs. A 2-year French franc coupon bond can be issued at par at a coupon rate of 8.97%. Would it be better to issue the French franc coupon bond or the synthetic equivalent in eurocurrency borrowing?

Solution 5-2 The proceeds from borrowing 1-year euroFrench francs with face value of FF8.97 and 2-year euroFrench francs with face value of FF108.97 would be $FF8.97/1.07 + FF108.97/1.09^2 = FF8.38 + FF91.72 = FF100.10$. Thus, since the proceeds of the par coupon eurobond are FF100, the eurocurrency route is a more effective method of obtaining financing than the 2-year par coupon bond, since more proceeds may be had for the same future liability structure.

The preceding analysis represents an efficient means to compare an actual coupon bond with its synthetic alternative. It may be more intuitive at first to try to either (1) compare the yield to maturity of the direct coupon bond with that of the synthetic alternative or (2) compare the present values of future liability structures for a given amount of time 0 proceeds. These alternative approaches will work, and we use the second one later. However, the approach here, of finding the higher time 0 proceeds for a given liability structure, is analytically more simple to apply in this case. At first, you may have to think carefully about what it is that you are doing, because it may take some getting used to the fact that the liability with the higher "present value" is the one that is preferred, especially since other examples later in the chapter use an approach of minimizing the present value of future liabilities for a given time 0 proceeds amount.

SYNTHETIC ZEROS

Just as it is possible to manufacture a synthetic coupon bond from zeros, or from eurocurrency loans/deposits, it is also possible to manufacture synthetic zero-coupon instruments.

For example, assume that your corporation would like to issue debt in the form of a 4-year, zero-coupon yen bond, for which the market currently requires a yield to maturity of 7.25%. Alternatively, the market would allow you to issue a 4-year, 7% coupon yen bond at par. Although it will not be clear until the end of this example why we are beginning with the following amount, consider a 4-year zero-coupon bond with a time 4 vace value of ¥107. A synthetic 4-year zero with a ¥107 face value may be manufactured by (1)

Companies like Texaco and Exxon have been able to raise capital in more than one currency and "engineer" financing in the euromarkets.

issuing the 4-year coupon bond and (2) simultaneously making 1-year, 2-year, and 3-year euroyen deposits to cover the first three coupon payments.

Let us assume that you face the same example euroyen discount yield curve given in Figure 5-3: 1 year, 6%; 2 year, 6.5%; and 3 year, 7%. Assume that you issue the 7%, 4-year par coupon bond in the face value amount of ¥100. Of these proceeds at time 0, deposit ¥7/1.06 = ¥6.60 into 1-year euroyen, ¥7/1.065^2 = ¥6.17 into 2-year euroyen, and ¥7/1.07^3 = ¥5.71 into 3-year euroyen. The deposits require a total time 0 amount of ¥6.60 + ¥6.17 + ¥5.71 = ¥18.48. Thus, the net proceeds of the entire package at time 0, after making the euroyen deposits, amount to ¥100 − ¥18.48 = ¥81.52.

In effect, the company has synthetically issued 4-year, zero-coupon yen debt with time 4 face value of ¥107 for time 0 proceeds of ¥81.52. Had the company issued an actual 4-year zero with a face value of ¥107 at a 7.25% yield to maturity, the proceeds would have been less, ¥107/1.0725^4 = ¥80.87. Figure 5-4 conveys the concept of a synthetic zero coupon bond.

Of course, if the company desires a different level of zero-coupon liability, say, either ¥100 in time 4 face value or ¥100 in time 0 proceeds, then the synthetic construction with the coupon bond would have to be scaled differently. However, all the yen amounts would turn out to be proportional to the ones in the preceding example, and the same yields would apply. The next example incorporates this idea.

EXAMPLE 5-3

You observe yields to maturity of 7% for 1-year euroFrench francs and 9% for 2-year euroFrench francs. A 3-year French franc coupon bond can be issued at par at a coupon rate of 8.00%. However, you prefer financing via a 3-year zero-coupon liability. Assume that the required market yield to maturity on an actual 3-year French franc zero is 9.50%. You desire for the 3-year zero to have a time 3 face value of FF100. Would you be better off to issue a 3-year zero directly or to issue a synthetic 3-year zero?

Solution 5-3   Consider a coupon bond with a time 3 principal plus interest payment of FF100. This final payment would correspond to a coupon bond with a face value of FF100/1.08 = FF92.59 and interest payments of 0.08(FF92.59) = FF7.407. You can cover the year 1 and year 2 coupon interest payments by depositing FF7.407/1.07 + FF7.407/1.09^2 = FF6.92 + FF6.23 = FF13.15 into eurocurrency deposits. You would be left with net proceeds from the par "covered" bond of FF92.59 − FF13.15 = FF79.44 and with the net year 3 liability of FF100. In effect, you have issued a 3-year French franc zero with time 3 face value of FF100 and time 0 proceeds of FF79.44. Issuing an actual 3-year zero with a face value of FF100 would have only resulted in proceeds of FF100/1.095^3 = FF76.17, less advantageous than issuing the synthetic 3-year zero by issuing the coupon bond and using 1- and 2-year eurocurrency deposits.

1. Question: Ignoring the time 0 proceeds amounts, which of the two alternative future liability structures would a company prefer, "A" or "B"?
   A. Zero-Coupon Bond Issue   B. Synthetic Zero-Coupon Bond Issue
                                               (Coupon Bond Issue Plus Three Eurocurrency Deposits)

Time 4: Redeem 4-year zero for ¥107.	Time 1: Liquidate euroyen deposit for ¥7; make coupon payment of ¥7. Time 2: Liquidate euroyen deposit for ¥7; make coupon payment of ¥7. Time 3: Liquidate euroyen deposit for ¥7; make coupon payment of ¥7. Time 4: Make coupon plus principal payment of ¥107.

   Answer: With no other information, a company should be indifferent to issuing either.

2. Question: If the zero-coupon bond can be sold at time 0 for ¥80.87, while the synthetic zero can be sold for net proceeds of ¥81.52, based on coupon bond proceeds of ¥100 and deposits of ¥18.48 at time 0, then which would a company prefer to issue?
   Answer: The synthetic zero-coupon bond issue.

FIGURE 5-4 Synthetic Zero-Coupon Bond Comparison

Foreign Currency Debt

Take some time to examine the eurobond demographic profile provided in Figure 5-5, which displays eurobond volume (in dollar amounts and number of issues), by currency and issuer type, for the period from 1992 until February 15, 1995. Upon viewing these data and those in Figure 5-1, one must wonder why would any company want to issue debt in a currency other than its base currency? Sometimes the issuance of foreign currency debt is an attempt to speculate on the future depreciation of the currency. Other times, the foreign currency debt can serve to hedge operating income that is exposed to exchange rate changes. (This situation will be covered in later chapters.) Another motivation is the creation of *synthetic base currency* debt via financial engineering and foreign currency debt, to exploit a potentially inexpensive financing alternative, or quasi-arbitrage opportunity.

CURRENCY EXPOSURE OF FOREIGN CURRENCY DEBT

Note, first, that if debt is issued in a foreign currency, the spot foreign exchange market may be used to exchange the issue's proceeds directly into another currency for immediate use. Thus, if a company's base currency is U.S. dollars and the company wants to make a capital investment into a new plant in the United States, it could still issue mark-denominated debt and exchange the proceeds from the issue into dollars in the spot foreign exchange market. For example, if the exchange rate is presently $X^0_{DM/\$} = 1.50$ DM/$, and if the company is planning to invest $50,000,000, then it could issue $50,000,000(1.50 \text{ DM}/\$) = \text{DM75,000,000}$ of mark-denominated debt (proceeds) and then exchange the proceeds into dollars.

	Issuer Type													
	Sov/Govt/Auth		Supranational		Corporates		Banks/Finance		Utilities		Others		Total	
Currency	Amount mm (US$)	Iss.	Amount mm (US$)	Iss.	Amount mm (US$)	Iss.	Amount mm (US$)	Iss.	Amount mm (US$)	Iss.	Amount mm (US$)	Iss.	Amount mm (US$)	Iss.
U.S. dollar	$85,009.75	160	$26,593.50	82	$78,701.48	579	$238,815.50	1418	$19,815.00	81	$10.00	1	$448,945.20	2321
Deutsche mark	44,310.63	68	17,585.79	55	7,472.87	140	57,589.43	245	3,382.54	18	0.00	0	130,341.30	526
European currency unit	8,727.81	53	12,542.05	40	1,406.58	9	15,743.95	83	1,152.85	4	0.00	0	39,573.23	189
Japanese yen	32,073.69	71	20,535.14	44	46,510.57	425	54,051.82	621	1,637.60	17	232.49	1	155,041.10	1179
Australian dollar	1,585.60	21	840.15	7	730.24	11	13,704.05	171	471.32	6	0.00	0	17,331.36	216
Canadian dollar	4,370.17	62	6,130.17	34	1,987.47	17	26,961.61	238	10,253.29	27	44.79	2	59,747.44	380
Sterling	9,657.31	24	8,183.53	34	11,364.88	63	66,219.85	360	9,440.15	48	3.00	0	104,865.60	529
Luxembourg franc	1,033.33	15	1,746.70	27	967.62	25	17,611.75	456	484.75	9	30.45	1	21,874.61	533
Austrian schilling	90.40	1	0.00	0	0.00	0	81.21	1	0.00	0	0.00	0	171.61	2
Belgian franc	0.00	0	0.00	0	0.00	0	0.00	0	31.87	1	0.00	0	31.87	1
Danish krone	201.98	2	235.55	5	483.55	5	1,214.64	25	73.79	1	0.00	0	2,209.51	38
French franc	14,607.51	30	6,702.61	25	10,295.97	49	50,834.07	230	9,499.22	31	0.00	0	91,939.34	365
Dutch guilder	3,357.48	12	3,462.24	14	2,735.24	20	24,828.65	141	958.92	6	0.00	0	35,342.54	193
Hong Kong dollar	0.00	0	0.00	0	0.00	0	129.42	1	0.00	0	0.00	0	129.42	1
Italian lire	1,599.69	12	11,215.02	52	1,420.42	12	22,280.58	186	2,697.32	9	0.00	0	39,213.01	271
Portuguese escudo	0.00	0	0.00	0	0.00	0	358.70	4	0.00	0	0.00	0	358.70	4
Swedish krona	38.14	1	965.40	11	0.00	0	2,164.89	26	61.86	1	0.00	0	3,230.28	39
Finnish markka	22.97	1	0.00	0	238.71	3	417.82	3	0.00	0	0.00	0	679.50	7
Greek drachma	0.00	0	0.00	0	0.00	0	79.57	2	0.00	0	0.00	0	79.57	2
Irish pound	0.00	0	192.96	3	0.00	0	64.11	1	0.00	0	0.00	0	257.07	4
New Zealand dollar	0.00	0	0.00	0	31.85	1	354.18	10	0.00	0	0.00	0	386.04	11
Philippine peso	0.00	0	0.00	0	44.41	1	0.00	0	0.00	0	0.00	0	44.41	1
Total	$216,636.40	533	$116,930.80	433	$164,391.90	1360	$593,504.60	4222	$59,960.54	259	$317.73	5	$1,151,789.00	6812

FIGURE 5-5 Volume Table for Eurobonds by Currency/Issuer Type—1992 to February 15, 1995

Source: Euromoney Bondware, Euromoney Publications plc (data), Computasoft Ltd. (software), 1983–1994.

However, issuing debt in a foreign currency creates a risk exposure that if the foreign currency appreciates relative to the firm's base currency, the payment of interest and principal on the debt will require more base currency to convert to the foreign currency. Continuing the example, assume that the company's debt is issued in the form of a 5-year, 5% coupon mark bond, issued at par. Since the bond is issued in the amount of DM75,000,000, the company is obligated to make payments of DM3,750,000 in interest each year for the next 5 years, and of DM75,000,000 in principal repayment at the fifth year. To meet these obligations, the company will have to exchange its base currency of dollars into marks at those points in time.

PRICING A NEW BOND ISSUE

When a company issues bonds, it might *appear* that it would want to choose a lead manager that offers the best price for the bond in a bought deal, or says it can issue the bond at the lowest yield to maturity in a best efforts deal. However, the issuer really wants the bond to be issued at a fair price that will not drastically change, in one direction or the other, soon after secondary market trading begins.

If the issue is a bought deal and is underwritten with the company receiving too high a price, the underwriter will lose money selling the bonds to investors (the market). While this is the underwriter's fault and not the issuer's, the bad taste in the underwriter's mouth may result in reluctance to issue the company's securities again. The company has thus lost a valuable financing venue, even though the proceeds of the bond deal were higher than they otherwise might have been for this one time.

In a best efforts deal, it is also in both the issuer's and bank's interest for the bond to be priced correctly. That is, the bank will try to issue the bond at par value with a coupon rate that reflects what the market's required yield to maturity will be. If the market ends up requiring a lower yield to maturity than the rate implied by the issue price, then the bond will quickly trade at a higher price than it was issued. Stockholders could get incensed by this mispricing, and possibly file suit, since the gain to the new bondholders is a loss to the shareholders.

On the other hand, if the market ends up having a higher required yield to maturity than the rate implied by the issue price, then the bond will quickly trade at a discount (a lower price) relative to the issue price. Buyers of the bond will be unhappy and not be inclined to buy the company's bonds in the next financing, even though it may have been the intermediary that misjudged the issue's appropriate price/yield to maturity.

In some circumstances, if the bids by banks vary over a wide range, it may be in the issuer's best interests to avoid issuing the bonds at all, at least until a better consensus can be achieved. The wide range of bids implies uncertainty over the correct price for the to-be-issued bond, and thus a greater chance of mispricing.

If the exchange rate were to *stay* at 1.50 DM/$, then the amount of base currency it takes to make each interest payment is $2,500,000, and the principal may be repaid by converting $50,000,000 into DM75,000,000. In effect, the company has raised $50,000,000 in capital and paid a 5% coupon interest rate in dollars.

However, what if the mark appreciates from $X^0_{DM/\$}$ = 1.50 DM/$ to $X^1_{DM/\$}$ = 1 DM/$? We can make a useful analysis of the economic impact of this exchange rate change by taking the perspective of a bond's *market value*, in base currency terms, after the exchange rate changes. Although an exchange rate change is sometimes related to a change in interest rates, we examine the valuation consequences of exchange rate changes, assuming interest rates do not change.

Consider the 5-year, 5% coupon, mark-denominated par bond issued in the earlier example. For simplicity, assume that the 5% par coupon interest rate is a result of a 5% flat discount yield curve. If interest rates do not change, then the value of the bond after each interest payment will always be DM75,000,000. If, just after the first interest payment, the exchange rate is still $X^1_{DM/\$}$ = 1.50 DM/$, then the bond could be paid off, or repurchased in the market, with $50,000,000.

However, if, on the other hand, the mark appreciates to $X^1_{DM/\$}$ = 1 DM/$ at time 1, the time just after the first interest payment, then it would take $75,000,000 to retire the DM75,000,000 market value of the bond. In base currency market value terms, there is a loss to the company of $25,000,000 if the mark appreciates from 1.50 DM/$ to 1 DM/$. The market value in dollars to the bondholders has *increased* from $50 million to $75 million; since the corporation *owes* this bond value to the bondholders, the corporation's economic liability increases from $50 million to $75 million, which is a capital loss to the company. (See Figure 5-6.)

Similarly, if the mark were to depreciate to $X^1_{DM/\$}$ = 2 DM/$, then it would take only DM75,000,000/(2 DM/$) = $37,500,000 to retire the bond in the market. The company's windfall economic gain from the exchange rate change, relative to the time 0 exchange rate at the time of the issue, $X^0_{DM/\$}$ = 1.50 DM/$, is $50,000,000 − $37,500,000 = $12,500,000. Figure 5-6 lays out the alternative possibilities of the example.

Thus, an increase in the base currency market value of the debt is a loss, and a decrease is a gain, from the issuing company's viewpoint. This economic gain/loss is real, and base currency stock investors should be aware of the gains and losses. If they are, then the gains and losses should be reflected in the market value of the company's shares. The accounting treatment of the gain or loss on the base currency market value of foreign currency debt is discussed in Chapter 10.

HEDGED FOREIGN CURRENCY DEBT AS A FINANCING ALTERNATIVE

As the foregoing treatment indicates, the decision to use foreign currency debt is not as simple as choosing to issue debt in a foreign currency when the inter-

> ### ■ EXAMPLE 5-4
>
> Your company issues debt denominated in Japanese yen in the amount of ¥500,000,000, at a time when the yen is at $X^0_{¥/\$}$ = 125 ¥/$. Assume that the dollar is your company's base currency. Assume that interest rates do not change. What is the gain or loss on the market value of the debt, in base currency terms, if the yen goes to $X^1_{¥/\$}$ = 100 ¥/$?
>
> **Solution 5-4** In going from $X^0_{¥/\$}$ = 125 ¥/$ to $X^1_{¥/\$}$ = 100 ¥/$, the yen appreciates relative to the dollar. The appreciation of the yen means an increase in the base currency market value of the yen debt, that is, an economic loss for your company. The base currency market value of the debt, which is ¥500,000,000/(125 ¥/$) = $4,000,000 at $X^0_{¥/\$}$ = 125 ¥/$, increases to ¥500,000,000/(100 ¥/$) = $5,000,000. The loss to the issuer is $1,000,000 in market value terms.

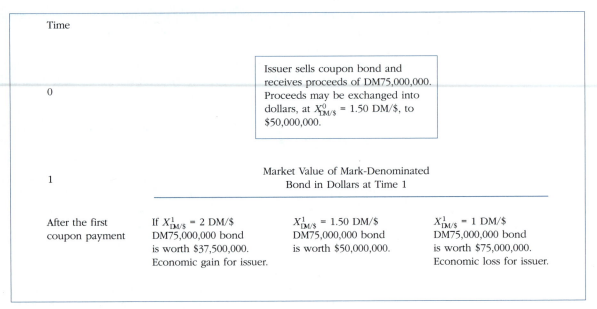

FIGURE 5-6 Currency Exposure to Changes in the Market Value of a Foreign Currency Bond

est rate is lower than that of the base currency. The reason is that the company becomes exposed to exchange risk. If the company has a strong belief that the foreign currency will depreciate, then the risk may be worth taking from its perspective. However, this choice is a matter of judgment. This section considers a less nebulous choice between base currency debt and *synthetic* base currency debt, which is foreign currency debt with the liabilities hedged back into the base currency. Here, this financial engineering is accomplished via forward exchange contracts.

For example, let us assume that a company's base currency is the U.S. dollar. The company needs to raise $17,500,000 for capital expansion and has decided to issue straight eurobonds. The going market yield to maturity on 3-year eurodollar coupon bonds is 8% if issued at par. Thus, the $17,500,000 of time 0 capital can be raised by committing to liabilities of 0.08($17,500,000) = $1,400,000 for 2 years and $1,400,000 (interest) + $17,500,000 (principal) = $18,900,000 for the third year.

As an alternative, consider issuing 3-year eurosterling bonds, for which we'll assume that the market currently requires a coupon interest rate for a par bond of 10%. Assume that the spot exchange rate is $X^0_{\$/\pounds} = 1.75$ $/£. We'll also need to observe the forward exchange rates for 1-, 2-, and 3-year horizons. Assume that your investment banker quotes that the 1-year forward exchange rate is 1.70 $/£, the 2-year forward exchange rate is 1.65 $/£, and the 3-year forward exchange rate is 1.60 $/£.

The question is, Which of the two alternatives do you, or should you, prefer? To answer this question, we must first determine the eurosterling bond's pound obligations. At the current exchange rate of $X^0_{\$/\pounds} = 1.75$ $/£, the face value of the eurosterling issue would be $17,500,000/(1.75 $/£) = £10,000,000. Thus, at the 10% coupon rate, the future pound liabilities would be coupon payments of £1,000,000 in years 1 and 2 and principal-plus-coupon payment at year 3 of £11,000,000.

Since the pound payments are natural short positions in the foreign currency, they may be hedged with *long* positions in dollar-denominated forward exchange contracts on pounds. Long forward positions on pounds imply the future receipt of pounds, which may be used to cover the natural pound liability payments of the coupon bond. The dollar payments made against the forward exchange contract positions thus become the effective liabilities.

Suppose you issue the eurosterling bond at time 0 and simultaneously take a 1-year long forward position on £1,000,000, a 2-year long forward position on £1,000,000, and a 3-year long forward position on £11,000,000. At time 0, you thus effectively commit to a liability structure of dollars in the amounts of £1,000,000(1.70 $/£) = $1,700,000 at time 1, £1,000,000(1.65 $/£) = $1,650,000 at time 2, and £11,000,000(1.60 $/£) = $17,600,000 at time 3.

Now the two financing alternatives boil down to comparing dollar payments of the actual dollar coupon bond—$1,400,000 at time 1, $1,400,000 at time 2, and $18,900,000 at time 3—with the alternative dollar payments of the synthetic dollar bond—$1,700,000 at time 1, $1,650,000 at time 2, and $17,600,000 at time 3. The answer to which is better is not exactly obvious, since the synthetic dollar bond requires more dollars to make the first two payments, but less to make the final payment. In this case, we are going to determine which of the two alternative liability structures has the lower present value, given that both alternatives provide the same time 0 proceeds of $1,000,000.

Finding the final answer requires the time 0 dollar discount yield curve out to three years. Assume for simplicity that the dollar discount yield curve is a flat 8%. Thus, the present value of the dollar liabilities of the synthetic dollar liability is $1,700,000/1.08 + $1,650,000/1.08^2 + $17,600,000/1.08^3 = $16,960,130.

The comparison of the alternatives may be accomplished by looking at which has the lower present value of future liabilities. In this case, the present value of the eurodollar bond's liabilities is $17,500,000, since the bond would be issued at par. Thus, the synthetic dollar liability is the better alternative, since the present value of its dollar liabilities is $16,960,130. In effect, the hedged sterling bond alternative saves $17,500,000 – $16,960,130 = $539,870 in present value of the base currency. Figure 5-7 depicts the synthetic dollar liability engineered from the sterling liability and the long forward exchange positions on pounds.

Another way to look at the final result, and to actually obtain the savings in cash, is to use eurocurrency deposits and loans to make the synthetic dollar bond's liabilities equal to those of the eurodollar bond. For example, your company would take out a 3-year eurodollar loan with face value of ($18.9 million – $17.6 million) = $1,300,000 and use a portion of the proceeds to make a 1-year eurodollar deposit with face value of $300,000 and a 2-year eurodollar deposit with face value of $250,000.

These cash flows, when combined with the dollar obligations of the hedged pound-denominated bonds, would net to liability cash flows of (1) $1,700,000 – $300,000 = $1,400,000, (2) $1,650,000 – $250,000 = $1,400,000, and (3) $17,600,000 + $1,300,000 = $18,900,000. In effect, you have used

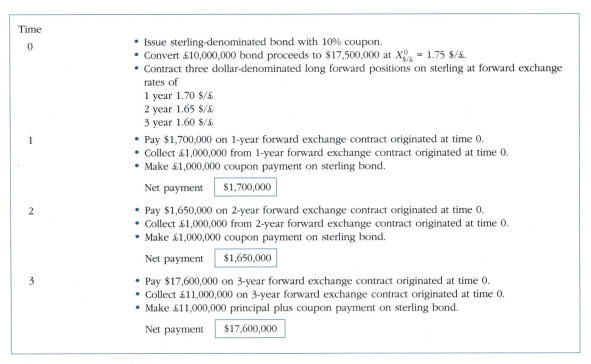

Time	
0	• Issue sterling-denominated bond with 10% coupon.
	• Convert £10,000,000 bond proceeds to $17,500,000 at $X^0_{\$/£}$ = 1.75 $/£.
	• Contract three dollar-denominated long forward positions on sterling at forward exchange rates of
	1 year 1.70 $/£
	2 year 1.65 $/£
	3 year 1.60 $/£
1	• Pay $1,700,000 on 1-year forward exchange contract originated at time 0.
	• Collect £1,000,000 from 1-year forward exchange contract originated at time 0.
	• Make £1,000,000 coupon payment on sterling bond.
	Net payment $1,700,000
2	• Pay $1,650,000 on 2-year forward exchange contract originated at time 0.
	• Collect £1,000,000 from 2-year forward exchange contract originated at time 0.
	• Make £1,000,000 coupon payment on sterling bond.
	Net payment $1,650,000
3	• Pay $17,600,000 on 3-year forward exchange contract originated at time 0.
	• Collect £11,000,000 on 3-year forward exchange contract originated at time 0.
	• Make £11,000,000 principal plus coupon payment on sterling bond.
	Net payment $17,600,000

FIGURE 5-7 Synthetic Base Currency Debt Engineered Via Foreign Currency Debt and Forward Exchange Positions

eurocurrency deposits/loans (or zeros) to recreate the liability pattern of the actual eurodollar bond.

The time 0 proceeds from the 3-year eurodollar loan is $1,300,000/$1.08^3 = $1,031,982$, while the time 0 outflow for the two dollar eurocurrency deposits totals $300,000/1.08 + $250,000/1.08^2 = $492,112$. The net proceeds from these three transactions is $1,031,982 - $492,112 = $539,870$.

The choice is now between two financing alternatives that will require the same future liabilities of $1,400,000, $1,400,000, and $18,900,000. The actual eurodollar bond alternative provides proceeds of $17,500,000, while the synthetic dollar bond alternative (augmented with the eurocurrency loan deposits) provides proceeds of $17,500,000 plus $539,870, which makes the synthetically engineered strategy the better one.

Conditions in the global debt and forward exchange markets will not always favor issuing synthetic base currency debt via hedged foreign currency debt over issuing base currency debt directly. However, each situation needs to be examined on its own merits using the current market conditions. Our example demonstrates a financial manager who saved $539,870 on a $17,500,000 bond issue by simply using a different, but equivalent, method. This manager has identified a one-way arbitrage opportunity in the form of a lower-cost, but equivalent, financing alternative.

EXAMPLE 5-5

You are quoted the following forward exchange rates for the Swiss franc: 1 year, 1.91 SF/\$; 2 year, 1.82 SF/\$; and 3 year, 1.74 SF/\$. The spot exchange rate, $X^0_{SF/\$}$, is 2 SF/\$. Your base currency is dollars and you prefer your liabilities to be in dollars to avoid currency exposure. You can issue a 10% coupon, 3-year eurodollar bond at par, with principal of $1,000,000. Alternatively, you can issue a 6% coupon, 3-year Swiss franc bond at par. Assume a flat term structure of 10%, out to 3 years, for dollars. Which of the two financing alternatives is better: issuing the eurodollar bond or issuing the Swiss franc bond and hedging the liabilities into dollars via forward exchange contracts?

Solution 5-5 If a Swiss franc bond is issued, the principal amount should be SF2,000,000, exchanged into proceeds of $1,000,000, given the time-of-issue spot exchange rate of $X^0_{SF/\$} = 2$ SF/\$. The unhedged Swiss franc liabilities would be $0.06(SF2,000,000) = SF120,000$ in interest for the first two years, plus SF2,120,000 in principal and interest at the third year. Hedging these payments into dollars via long positions in dollar-denominated forward exchange contracts on Swiss francs means promising to pay SF120,000/(1.91 SF/\$) = $62,827 in year 1, SF120,000/(1.82 SF/\$) = $65,934 in year 2, and SF2,120,000/(1.74 SF/\$) = $1,218,390 in year 3. The present value of these dollar obligations, given the discount yield curve, is $62,827/1.10 + $65,934/1.10^2 + $1,218,390/1.10^3 = $1,027,001$. Since the time 0 present value of the dollar liabilities on the hedged Swiss franc bond exceeds that of the eurodollar bond, $1,000,000, the actual eurodollar coupon bond should be issued instead of the synthetic one.

Innovations of the Eurobond Markets

Eurobond investors often have needs or desires for extra features beyond the basic structure of a straight bond. For example, many eurobonds that are issued are convertible bonds, as eurobond investors are often intrigued by the equity participation potential offered by convertible bonds. Figure 5-1 has revealed some actively traded convertible issues. Figure 5-8 displays a eurobond volume breakdown, by major category, for all eurobonds issued from 1992 to February 15, 1995.

In addition to the convertibility feature, the eurobond market has fostered a large number of other innovative features in debt issues. Debt with innovative features is often called *hybrid debt* or *structured debt*. Some of the innovative features of hybrid/structured debt, and the issuers' motivations to provide them, are discussed in the rest of this chapter and in the next two chapters.[4]

FLOATING RATE NOTES

A *floating rate note* (*FRN*) pays interest each period on the basis of a short-term, market-determined interest rate. A common short-term rate used is LIBOR, to which is often added some additional yield to compensate for the credit risk of the issuer. For example, an FRN may pay LIBOR plus 50 basis points (0.50 of 1%). If no additional basis points are added, as might be the case with an FRN with a AAA rating, the payment rate is referred to as *LIBOR flat*.

	Amount in U.S. Dollars (mm)	Number of Issues
Fixed rate coupon	$ 828,498.73	4583
Fixed rate zero coupon	17,303.67	275
Convertible	42,490.91	278
Floating rate note	230,510.90	1467
With equity warrants	32,985.57	209
Total	$1,151,789.00	6812

FIGURE 5-8 Volume Table of Eurobonds by Issue Type—1992 to February 15, 1995
Source: Euromoney Bondware, Euromoney Publications plc (data), Computasoft Ltd. (software), 1983–1994.

---

[4]Additional details on the various types of hybrid/structure debt innovations, including the corporate motivations, may be found in Charles W. Smithson and Donald H. Chew, "The Uses of Hybrid Debt in Managing Corporate Risk," *Journal of Applied Corporate Finance*, Winter 1992, pp. 79–89; and in Christopher L. Culp, Dean Furbush, and Barbara T. Kavanagh, "Structured Debt and Corporate Risk Management," *Journal of Applied Corporate Finance*, Fall 1994, pp. 73–84.

In Figure 5-1 we see how FRN prices are quoted. For example, the government of Belgium issued mark-denominated FRNs due in 1997 at (mark) LIBOR plus 1/16 (of 1%). Many of the FRNs listed in Figure 5-1 are notes whose floating rate is reset semiannually. However, the example that follows assumes an annual reset for simplicity.

Consider a 5-year, annual coupon, Dutch guilder (Fl) FRN that makes payments at LIBOR flat. If the 1-year guilder LIBOR at the time the FRN is issued is 6%, then the first annual interest payment will be Fl6 per face value of Fl100. If the 1-year guilder LIBOR prevailing at the end of the *first* year is 8%, then the *second* annual interest payment will be Fl8.

The valuation of a "plain vanilla" FRN, which is an FRN with no additional features or twists, is surprisingly easy. *Immediately after each interest payment is made, the value of an FRN is par.* To see this point, consider a 5-year FRN with par value of Fl100. Think of time 4, 1 year before the final interest payment and principal repayment, and immediately after the second-to-last interest payment. Assume that the 1-year euroguilder LIBOR at time 4 is 7%. Thus, a year later, at time 5 (the maturity), the holder will receive the final interest payment of Fl7 plus the principal repayment of Fl100, for a total of Fl107. The market value of the bond at time 4, when the 7% 1-year euroguilder LIBOR is observed, should be the present value of Fl107. Since the 1-year interest rate at that time is 7%, the present value must be Fl107/1.07 = Fl100, or else there would be an arbitrage opportunity between the eurocurrency market and this bond with one year remaining to maturity.

Working backward, year by year, yields similar results. At time 3, the new 1-period interest rate sets the interest payment for time 4. Suppose the 1-year euroguilder rate happened to be 5% at time 3, for example. Then the time 4 interest payment will be Fl5. Since we've already established that the FRN will have a market value, after the time 4 interest payment, of Fl100, the FRN's value one year prior is Fl105/1.05 = Fl100.

Continuing to work backward, we can see that, in general, since each interest payment is based directly on the prevailing 1-year discount rate, the value of an FRN is always par immediately after an interest payment. This result should not be too surprising, since a floating rate note is intended to relieve a debtholder from bearing interest rate risk, in the form of fluctuating values of fixed coupon bonds in the face of fluctuating market yields to maturity. Floating rate notes have no such interest rate risk, and have a stable market value. In reality, the actual prices of FRNs (as shown in Figure 5-1) will deviate from par, due to the noise inherent in changing market conditions, and/or if the note has other features associated with it.

DUAL CURRENCY BONDS AND PERLS

A bond that makes interest payments in one currency and principal payment in another currency is called a *dual currency bond*. The par value of the bond is stated in one currency, but is converted to the other currency for purposes of determining the interest payments. The conversion rate is a set contract exchange rate that is generally the spot exchange rate between the currencies at the time the bond is issued.

For example, consider a 3-year dual currency bond, whose principal is denominated in yen, but that pays annual interest at a coupon interest rate of 5% in U.S. dollars. Assume that the par value of the bond is ¥125,000,000 and the contract exchange rate for determining the dollar interest payments is 125 ¥/$. Then the equivalent "shadow" par value of the bond in dollars, necessary for computing the interest payments, is ¥125,000,000/(125 ¥/$) = $1,000,000, and the annual interest payment is 0.05($1,000,000) = $50,000.

Dual currency bonds originated in the eurobond market as a method of circumventing regulations. For example, suppose a country's domestic institutional portfolios are not allowed to own as many foreign currency bonds as the portfolio managers have an appetite to hold. By denominating the principal in the local currency, the bond issuer may claim to have issued a bond in that currency. It is up to the regulatory authorities to prove otherwise or make new rules; in the meanwhile, the portfolio managers may be happy to have a stream of interest receipts in a foreign currency.

The valuation of a dual currency bond is straightforward, given one knows the spot exchange rate and the relevant portion of the discount yield curve in both currencies. The idea is to view the bond as being composed of one synthetic zero in the principal currency and as many synthetic zeros as there are remaining payments in the interest currency. After finding the present values in the respective currencies, these values can be expressed in the same currency using the current spot exchange rate.

What is the market value, for example, of a 3-year dual currency bond that makes interest payments in yen at a 6% coupon rate and principal repayment in dollars, assuming that the par value is $100,000,000 and the exchange rate upon which the interest payments are based is 125 ¥/$? Assume that the yen discount yield curve is the same as that in Figure 5-3 and that the market yield to maturity on a 3-year dollar zero is 8%. Assume that the current spot exchange rate is 110 ¥/$. The spot exchange rate might be different from the contract exchange rate if some time has elapsed since the bond was issued. For example, this bond may be a 3-year bond now, but may have been issued 3 years ago as a 6-year bond.

The answer is found as follows. Since the par value of the bond is $100,000,000, the interest payments are based upon a "shadow" par value in yen of $100,000,000(125 ¥/$) = ¥12,500,000,000. Thus, the interest pay-ment is 0.06(¥12,500,000,000) = ¥750,000,000. Given the yen discount yield curve in Figure 5-3, the present value of the interest payments, in yen, is ¥750,000,000/1.06 + ¥750,000,000/1.065^2 + ¥750,000,000/1.07^3 = ¥1,981,000,000, which converts to ¥1,981,000,000/(110 ¥/$) = $18,000,000 at the current spot exchange rate. Since the present value of the principal is $100,000,000/1.08^3 = $79,383,000, the entire bond is worth $18,000,000 (interest) + $79,383,000 (principal) = $97,383,000. The bond price would be quoted as 97.383 per 100 of par.

Had the current exchange rate been assumed to be 100 ¥/$, all else equal, the yen interest payments would be more valuable in dollar terms, and the bond would be worth more. Specifically, the value of the interest payments would be ¥1,981,000,000/(100 ¥/$) = $19,810,000, and the dollar value of the entire bond would be $19,810,000 + 79,383,000 = $99,193,000.

If the bond did not trade for this value, then an arbitrage strategy could be constructed using zero-coupon instruments. The description of the arbitrage is one of the end-of-chapter discussion questions.

EXAMPLE 5-6

Assume a dual currency bond with a par value of $1,000,000 that makes interest payments in Japanese yen and principal payment in U.S. dollars. The bond has 3 years left until maturity. Assume that the coupon interest rate is 7% and is based upon an exchange rate of 120 ¥/$, which was the spot exchange rate when the bond was originally issued. Assume that the current discount yield curve for the yen is the same as the one in Figure 5-3 (1 year, 6%; 2 year, 6.5%; and 3 years, 7%) and that the 3-year yield to maturity on a dollar zero-coupon bond is 9%. Assume that the current spot exchange rate is $X^0_{¥/\$}$ = 115 ¥/$. What is the time 0 value of the bond in dollars?

Solution 5-6   The shadow principal value in yen is $1,000,000(120 ¥/$) = ¥120,000,000. Thus, the interest payments are 0.07(¥120,000,000) = ¥8,400,000 per year. The present value of the three yen interest payments is ¥8,400,000/1.06 + ¥8,400,000/1.065^2 + ¥8,400,000/1.07^3 = ¥22,187,000. Since the present value of the principal is $1,000,000/1.09^3 = $772,183, the dollar value of the bond, at the current spot exchange rate of 115 ¥/$, is ¥22,187,000/(115 ¥/$) + $772,183 = $965,113.

Some variants of the dual currency idea in the eurobond markets have been more broadly marketed under the name *PERLS*, an acronym for *principal exchange rate linked securities*. Pioneered by the U.S. investment bank Morgan Stanley, around $8 billion in PERLS were distributed between 1987 and 1992 by the investment banks Morgan Stanley, J. P. Morgan, Bankers Trust, and First Boston. The PERLS pay interest in U.S. dollars and principal linked to the value of another currency, or in a complex manner employing other currencies.

For example, one issue of PERLS in 1990 by the Student Loan Marketing Association (known as Sallie Mae) raised a principal amount of $135 million. The principal repayment scheduled for 1995 called for repayment based on the dollar value of an amount of British pounds minus the dollar value of an amount of German marks, at the exchange rates at the time of repayment. Had the time-of-maturity exchange rates been the same as those of the time of the issue, the principal payoff would have called for $270 million in pounds minus $135 million in marks.

PERLS were designed to allow some savings banks and insurance companies that could not play the currency market because of regulatory restrictions to participate in these "global opportunities." PERLS were eventually sold to a wide array of institutions and wealthy individuals.

CURRENCY-INDEXED BONDS

A *currency-indexed bond* is a bond that is legally denominated in one currency, but makes principal and/or interest payments based on the value of an exchange rate. The most basic form of a currency-indexed bond is one where both the interest payments and the principal payment are *proportionately indexed* to an exchange rate, in which case the bond is economically equivalent to straight bond denominated in the foreign currency.

To see this point, consider a bond that is legally denominated in U.S. dollars and stipulates a 5-year, 5% coupon (applied to the dollar principal), with interest and principal payments proportionately indexed to the dollar-mark exchange rate in direct terms from the dollar point of view. Assume that the principal is $1,000,000. If the exchange rate at the time of a payment is the same as the base exchange rate, that is, the spot exchange rate prevailing at the time the bond is issued, the payment would be the base amount in dollars ($50,000 for an interest payment and $1,000,000 for the principal repayment.)

However, if the spot exchange rate at the time of a payment is $x\%$ higher than the base exchange rate, then the payment will be $x\%$ higher than the base amount. Thus, for example, assume an exchange rate of 1.25 DM/$ at the time the bond is issued and an appreciation of the mark to 1 DM/$ at the time of the first interest payment. Thus (in direct terms), $X^0_{\$/DM}$ = 1/(1.25 DM/$) = 0.80 $/DM, and $X^1_{\$/DM}$ = 1/(1 DM/$) = 1 $/DM. Since 1 $/DM is 25% higher than 0.80 $/DM (i.e., the mark has appreciated by 25% relative to the bond's base exchange rate), the interest payment of the proportionately indexed bond should be 25% higher than $50,000, which is 1.25($50,000) = $62,500.

To see that the proportionately indexed bond in the example is econom-

---

▣ EXAMPLE 5-7

Find the interest payment made by the bond in the preceding example at time 2 if the spot exchange rate at that time is 1.333 DM/$.

Solution 5-7 $X^2_{\$/DM}$ = 1/(1.333 DM/$) = 0.75 $/DM. This represents a change in the dollar value of the mark by (0.75 $/DM)/(0.80 $/DM) – 1 = – 0.0625, or a 6.25% depreciation of the mark, relative to the base exchange rate of 1.25 DM/$. Thus, the second interest payment of the bond would be 0.9375($50,000) = $46,875.

Currency-indexed bonds are bonds whose payments are denominated in one currency, but the amount paid is based upon how an exchange rate moves. Economically, currency-indexed bonds should fluctuate in value like a bond denominated in the foreign currency.

ically the same instrument as a fixed coupon bond denominated in marks, note that the interest payments of $62,500 at time 1 and $46,875 at time 2 (in Example 5-7) represent payments that are each equivalent to DM62,500 at the spot exchange rates. Clearly, the first payment of $62,500 is equivalent to DM62,500 at the exchange rate of 1 DM/$. The mark equivalent of $46,875 at the exchange rate of 0.75 $/DM is also $46,875/(0.75 $/DM) = DM62,500. Thus, the proportionately indexed bond is essentially the same security as, and economically equivalent to, a 5% fixed coupon German mark bond with

Time	Mark-Denominated Bond	U.S. Dollar-Denominated Bond Proportionately Indexed to the \$/DM Exchange Rate
0	• Issue 5% mark bond for proceeds of DM1,250,000. • Exchange at $X_{DM/\$}^0$ = 1.25 DM/\$ to \$1,000,000.	• Issue 5% U.S. dollar bond for proceeds of \$1,000,000.
1	Pay DM62,500 interest.	Pay \$50,000 $\left(\dfrac{1 \ \$/DM}{0.80 \ \$/DM} \right)$ = DM62,500.
2	Pay DM62,500 interest.	Pay \$50,000 $\left(\dfrac{0.75 \ \$/DM}{0.80 \ \$/DM} \right)$ = DM62,500.
	And so on.	And so on.

FIGURE 5-9 Equivalence of Mark-Denominated Bond and U.S. Dollar-Denominated Bond, with Payments Proportionately Indexed to the \$/DM Exchange Rate

a principal amount of DM1,250,000. Figure 5-9 demonstrates the economic equivalence of a foreign currency bond and a proportionately indexed bond.

Note that, at the spot exchange rate at the time of issue, 1.25 DM/\$, the principal of an actual mark bond (DM1,250,000) and that of the currency-indexed bond (\$1,000,000) are equivalent. Thus, it would not matter to the issuing company whether the proceeds of the bond issue were ultimately to be used to fund a project in dollars or marks. The dollar proceeds of the currency-indexed bond could easily be exchanged at time 0 for DM1,250,000, or the mark proceeds of the mark-denominated bond could be exchanged at time 0 for \$1,000,000.

Given that a company wants to issue a bond that is economically a foreign currency bond, there may be several reasons for preferring that the bond be legally denominated in a different currency, that is, for preferring the currency-indexed structure to an actual foreign currency bond. One reason could be that the targeted investors are prohibited by regulation from positioning foreign currency bonds per se, but not from investing in currency-indexed bonds. In other words, although economically similar, foreign currency bonds and currency-indexed bonds could be viewed as technically different by regulators. This situation may be significant in accounting interpretation and treatment, as taken up in Chapter 10.

This chapter has described some basic features found in eurobonds. These innovations are meant to serve as examples of the creativity of the global bond market. However, the innovativeness carries much further. Some other important innovations involving options are covered in Chapter 7, but there are even more innovations for which space in the book does not permit coverage. For example, bonds are issued that pay a fixed coupon in one currency over a period of time and then convert to a floating rate note in another currency.[5]

Summary

This chapter covers some concepts in capital financing, valuation, and market integration in the context of modern global markets for eurobonds and zero-coupon instruments. This material was used to advance the framework for the financial engineering of synthetic securities and for the comparison of financial alternatives.

The chapter also introduced the concept of the currency exposure that is induced onto a company by issuing bonds denominated in a currency other than the base currency, other things equal. Moreover, the chapter explored the exploitation of global financing opportunities by the issuing foreign currency debt, exchanging the proceeds into the relevant currency for time 0 use, and hedging the future liabilities into the base currency. The discovery of one-way arbitrage opportunities in this fashion is an important means by which a company can lower its financing costs.

Some innovations of the eurobond market, particularly floating rate notes, dual currency bonds, and currency indexed bonds, were introduced and valued. A technical point concerning yield-to-maturity quotation conventions is explained in the appendix. Figure 5-10 shows the profile of eurobond issues by nationality from 1992 to February 15, 1995.

---

[5]An informative source on the innovative variety of eurobonds is *The CSFB (Credit Suisse First Boston) Guide to Innovations, Structures and Terms of the Eurobond Markets* (Chicago: Probus, 1988).

FIGURE 5-10   Volume Table of Eurobonds by Borrower Nationality 1992 to February 15, 1995

Source: Euromoney Bondware, Euromoney Publications plc (data), Computasoft Ltd. (software) 1983–1994.

Issuer Nationality		Total Amount mm (US$)	Iss.
Supranational		$116,635.80	430
	Supranational	116,635.80	430
Canada		59,623.43	198
United States		141,227.20	718
	United States and Canada	200,850.50	916
Austria		22,906.29	123
Belgium		9,136.87	41
Czech Republic		625.00	2
Czechoslovakia		15.24	1
Denmark		18,411.59	103
Ireland		4,900.85	33
Finland		29,739.45	94
France		91,300.70	526
Germany		28,370.60	277
Greece		3,632.69	11
Hungary		3,951.73	15
Iceland		874.06	10
Italy		29,931.94	87
Luxembourg		15,618,35	237
Malta		205.00	1
Netherlands		100,467.10	669
Norway		8,713.72	31
Portugal		5,163.17	7
Slovakia		261.45	3
Spain		14,798.09	23
Sweden		52,179.17	207
Switzerland		417.63	4
United Kingdom		105,913.30	672
	Europe	543,533.50	3177
Argentina		11,098.19	95
Bolivia		10.00	1
Brazil		12,185.31	176
Chile		321.85	3
Colombia		1,022.00	9
Mexico		12,999.30	84
Panama		1,247.79	2
Peru		60.00	2
Costa Rica		50.00	1
Uruguay		340.00	4
Venezuela		2,161.98	17
Guatemala		60.00	1
	Latin America	41,556.42	395
Australia		24,026.50	245
New Zealand		2,012.68	14
	Australasia	26,039.17	260
Lebanon		400.00	1
Turkey		2,853.73	13
	Middle East	3,253.73	14

FIGURE 5-10 (Continued)

Issuer Nationality		Total	
		Amount mm (US$)	Iss.
China		3,962.17	21
Hong Kong		5,796.23	50
India		1,365.50	13
Indonesia		1,058.00	11
Japan		101,086.00	701
Korea		9,737.74	95
Malaysia		1,845.00	11
Pakistan		195.00	2
Philippines		1,975.43	19
Singapore		340.06	5
Taiwan		1,705.70	16
Thailand		3,160.60	36
	Asia	132,227.40	980
Netherlands Antilles		31,590.47	220
Cayman Islands		36,435.09	315
Bahamas		2,224.26	14
Barbados		50.00	2
Bermuda		2,334.14	13
Trinidad and Tobago		375.00	3
Aruba		2,193.76	8
British Virgin Islands		2,286.78	23
Congo		492.00	1
South Africa		1,548.95	7
	Others	79,531.47	606
		3,194.55	34
		3,194.55	34
Total		$1,151,791.00	6812

Glossary

AIBD: Association of International Bond Dealers; the voluntary organization that sets standards for the eurobond market. AIBD yield-to-maturity quotes do not apply the simple-interest annualization of semiannual yields, as in the USBE approach. See the appendix to this chapter.

Best Efforts Deal: Term for a security issue whereby a bank manages the issue for a fee. Also see *Negotiated Deal.*

Bought Deal: Term for a security issue where an underwriting bank buys the security from the issuer and resells the security to investors. See *Competitively Priced Deal.*

Bullet Bonds: Bonds that pay only interest prior to maturity, with all principal repaid at maturity; also referred to here as straight bonds or coupon bonds.

CEDEL: One of two eurobond clearinghouses; CEDEL is located in Luxembourg and primarily clears non-U.S. dollar eurobonds.

Competitively Priced Deal: Term for a security issue where an underwriting bank buys the security from the issuer and resells the security to investors. See *Bought Deal*.

Currency-Indexed Bond: A bond making interest and principal payments denominated in one currency the amount of which is indexed to the value of another currency.

Discount Bond: A coupon bond whose market value is less than its face value and whose yield to maturity is thus greater than the coupon rate.

Discount Yield Curve: Sometimes called the zero-coupon yield curve or strip yield curve. The observed schedule of available yields to maturity on pure discount instruments of various maturities, in a given currency.

Downward-Sloping Yield Curve: A yield curve in which yield to maturity decreases as time to maturity increases.

Dual Currency Bond: A bond that makes interest payments in one currency and principal payment in another currency.

Euroclear: One of two eurobond clearinghouses; Euroclear is located in Brussels and primarily clears U.S. dollar eurobonds.

Eurobond: An international debt obligation offered to investors in countries outside that of the issuer and in a currency, or currencies, other than the natural base currency of the investor.

Flat Yield Curve: A yield curve in which yield to maturity is the same for all maturities.

Floating Rate Note (FRN): A financial instrument that pays interest each period on the basis of a short-term market interest rate.

Foreign Bond: A bond that is issued in the country and currency of the investor and is traded in a local, and locally regulated, bond market.

Hybrid Debt: Debt that combines a conventional debt issue with one or more derivatives features. Also called structured debt.

Negotiated Deal: Term for a security issue whereby a bank manages the issue for a fee. Also see *Best Efforts Deal*.

Par Bond: A coupon bond whose market value is equal to its face value, and whose yield to maturity is thus exactly equal to the coupon rate.

Premium Bond: A coupon bond whose market value is greater than its face value, and whose yield to maturity is thus less than the coupon rate.

Principal Exchange Rate Linked Securities (PERLS):   Securities whose principal repayment is based on the value of a foreign currency, or the complex combination of the values of more than one foreign currency.

Straight Bonds: Bonds that make interest and principal payments at a set coupon rate in a single currency and have no call provisions or other innovative features. Also called bullet bonds or coupon bonds.

Strip: A synthetic zero created from a coupon bond.

Strip Yield Curve: See *Discount Yield Curve.*

Structured Debt: Debt that combines a conventional debt issue with one or more derivatives features. Also called hybrid debt.

USBE: The system for quoting bond yields to maturity on a comparable U.S. bond equivalent basis to simple annualized interest on semiannual pay bonds. See the appendix to this chapter.

Upward-Sloping Yield Curve: A yield curve in which yield to maturity increases as time to maturity increases.

Yield Curve: A relationship between yields to maturity and time to maturity for a given currency.

Zero-Coupon Bond: A bond that makes no interest payments and that pays off only a face value at maturity.

Zero-Coupon Yield Curve: See *Discount Yield Curve.*

Discussion Questions

1.   Discuss how dual currency bonds helped the global integration of financial markets.

2.   Describe the arbitrage steps one would take if the actual market price of a dual currency bond was greater than the amount it would take to construct a synthetic dual currency bond.

3.   If the discount yield curve is a flat $x\%$, explain why the yield to maturity on a par coupon bond is also $x\%$.

Problems

1. Find the value of a straight Italian lira (L) bond with 3 years to maturity and a 6% annual coupon, assuming that the bond's yield to maturity is 5%. Express your answer as a percentage of face value. Is the bond a premium, discount, or par bond?

2. You observe eurocurrency yields to maturity of 5% for 1-year Australian dollars and 7% for 2-year Australian dollars. A 2-year Australian dollar coupon bond can be issued at par at a coupon rate of 6.80%. Would it be better to issue the coupon bond or the equivalent in eurocurrency borrowing?

3. You observe eurocurrency yields to maturity of 5% for 1-year Australian dollars and 7% for 2-year Australian dollars. A 3-year Australian dollar coupon bond can be issued at par at a coupon rate of 7.00%. However, you desire a 3-year Australian dollar zero-coupon liability, for which the required market yield to maturity is 7.25%. Would you be better off to issue the zero directly or to issue a synthetic zero?

4. Your company is based in Australia and the base currency is Australian dollars. The company issues 5-year, 6% annual coupon U.S. dollar debt at par with face value of $100,000,000 when the spot exchange rate is 1.25 A$/$. If market interest rates do not change, what is the company's gain/loss on the market value of the debt, in base currency terms, if the exchange rate is $X^1_{A\$/\$}$ = 1.50 A$/$ immediately after making the first interest payment?

5. You are quoted the following forward exchange rates for the Swiss franc: 1 year, 1.91 SF/$; 2 year, 1.82 SF/$; and 3 year, 1.74 SF/$. The spot exchange rate is 2 SF/$. Your base currency is Swiss francs, you need to raise SF2,000,000, and you prefer your liabilities to be in Swiss francs to avoid currency exposure. You can issue a 6% coupon, 3-year Swiss franc bond at par, with principal of SF2,000,000. Alternatively, you can issue a 10% coupon, 3-year eurodollar bond at par, with principal of $1,000,000, and turn the time 0 proceeds into Swiss francs. Assume a flat term structure of 6%, out to 3 years, for Swiss francs. Which of the two financing alternatives is better: (a) issuing the Swiss franc bond or (b) issuing the eurodollar bond and hedging the liabilities into Swiss francs via forward contracts?

6. Find the U.S. dollar value of a 2-year dual currency bond with a par value of $1,000,000 that makes interest payments in Australian dollars and principal

---

2. Your calculation should show that the eurocurrency route is less effective.

3. Your calculations should favor the synthetic.

4. The loss to the company is A$25,000,000 in market value terms.

5. Issue the synthetic; it is better by SF50,801.

6. $999,575.

payment in U.S. dollars. Assume that the coupon interest rate is 6% and is based upon an exchange rate of 1.20 A$/$. You observe discount yields to maturity of 5% for 1-year Australian dollars and 7% for 2-year Australian dollars. You observe discount yields to maturity of 6% for 1-year U.S. dollars and 5.5% for 2-year U.S. dollars. Assume that the current spot exchange rate is 1.30 A$/$.

7. Your company issues a 5-year, 5% coupon bond that is legally denominated in U.S. dollars, but stipulates that the amount of the dollar payment of interest and principal is indexed to the spot $/£ exchange rate, expressed in terms of the dollar value of the pound, in a directly proportional manner. The principal amount of the bond is $1,625,000. Assume that the spot exchange rate is 1.625 $/£ at the time the bond is issued. What is the time 1 interest payment on the proportionately indexed bond if the time 1 spot exchange rate is 1.90 $/£? Demonstrate that the actual amount of the time 1 interest would represent a 5% coupon payment in pounds if the same amount of financing had been obtained directly with a pound-denominated coupon bond.

8. (Note: This problem does not have a counterpart in the text and is relatively difficult.) You need $1,000,000 for capital financing at the present time. Consider a 4-year dual currency yen-dollar bond with par value of ¥100,000,000, interest payments in dollars, and principal payment in yen. The coupon interest rate is 7%, based upon an exchange rate of 100 ¥/$, which is also the current spot exchange rate. As an alternative you could issue a eurodollar coupon bond at par at a coupon rate of 6.5%. Assume that the 4-year yen eurocurrency interest rate is 7.5% and that the dollar eurocurrency yield curve is a flat 6.5% out to 4 years. Your company's base currency is the U.S. dollar. Which is the lower-cost financing alternative, the hedged dual currency bond or the dollar bond? (Hint: Think about a synthetic 4-year forward contract to hedge the exposure of the foreign currency liability.)

The following problems and answers relate to material presented in the appendix.

A-1. Find the equivalent AIBD yield-to-maturity quote for a bond quoted to yield 10.5% (annually) under the USBE system.

A-2. The AIBD yield to maturity on a bond is 7.2%. Find the USBE yield-to-maturity quote.

---

8. The conditions in the market favor the dual currency bond alternative by $11,394 in present value.

A-1. 10.78%.

A-2. 7.075%.

a p p e n d i x   t o   c h a p t e r   5

AIBD VERSUS USBE
YIELD QUOTATIONS

If you look at representative information on international government bonds as reported in *The Wall Street Journal* (Figure 5A-1), the yield column is a yield to maturity, but you'll notice the asterisk and the note "equivalent to semiannual compounded yields to maturity." This note might be considered strange since these international bonds make only annual interest payments.

The traditional yield-to-maturity quotation in the United States has been the simple (noncompounded) annual rate on a semiannual pay bond. Thus, if a semiannual coupon bond has a semiannual yield to maturity of 4%, the quoted annualized yield to maturity is simply $2(0.04) = 0.08$, or 8%.

However, consider the following problem. What is the value of a 3-year, *zero-coupon* bond with a traditional U.S. yield-to-maturity *quote* of 8%? Since the quote actually represents a 4% *semiannual* yield to maturity, the correct value of the zero is $100/1.04^6 = 79.03$. But if you try to find the value of the zero directly with the quoted yield to maturity as an annual rate, $100/1.08^3$, you will not get the bond's correct value but instead will get 79.38. Thus, 8% cannot be the true annual yield to maturity.

The same problem also occurs with annual coupon bonds. Since almost all eurobonds are annual coupon bonds or zeros, the AIBD decided that confusion would reign if the yields for these bonds were quoted internationally according to the U.S. custom, which is now called the *U.S. bond equivalent (USBE)* basis. Instead, the AIBD prefers to quote yields at the true annualized rate.

For example, for the 3-year zero with current value of 79.03, the rate that correctly discounts 100 back to 79.03 over 3 years is 8.16%, since $100/1.0816^3$ equals 79.03. Thus, the zero-coupon bond in our example would be quoted at a yield of 8.16% by the AIBD method, despite the 8% USBE quotation.

INTERNATIONAL GOVERNMENT BONDS
Prices in local currencies, provided by Salomon Brothers Inc.

	COUPON	MATURITY (Mo./yr.)	PRICE	CHANGE	YIELD*		COUPON	MATURITY (Mo./yr.)	PRICE	CHANGE	YIELD*
JAPAN (3 p.m. Tokyo)						**GERMANY** (5 p.m. London)					
#119	4.80%	6/99	104.891	+ 0.390	3.57%		7.25%	10/97	101.684	+ 0.376	6.41%
#145	5.50	3/02	107.295	+ 0.725	4.30		8.25	9/01	104.900	+ 0.620	7.14
#164	4.10	12/03	98.004	+ 0.617	4.38		7.00	10/99	100.598	+ 0.409	6.72
#89	5.10	6/96	103.308	+ 0.097	2.53		6.25	1/24	82.836	+ 0.836	7.61
#105	5.00	12/97	105.012	+ 0.216	3.13		7.50	11/04	100.799	+ 0.689	7.24
UNITED KINGDOM (5 p.m. London)						**CANADA** (3 p.m. EDT)					
	10.00%	11/96	103.594	+ 0.156	7.72%		8.00%	6/23	90.800	+ 0.050	8.89%
	8.75	8/17	103.375	+ 1.062	8.41		7.75	9/96	99.800	+ 0.310	7.88
	6.75	11/04	88.219	+ 0.719	8.55		9.00	12/04	101.450	+ 0.300	8.77
	7.25	3/98	97.125	+ 0.312	8.32		8.50	3/00	100.250	+ 0.500	8.44
	8.00	12/00	97.875	+ 0.500	8.45		9.00	6/25	101.050	+ 0.050	8.90

*Equivalent to semi-annual compounded yields to maturity

FIGURE 5A-1   International Government Bonds

Source: The Wall Street Journal, February 24, 1995, p. C20. Reprinted by permission of *Wall Street Journal*, ©1995 Dow Jones & Company, Inc. All Rights Reserved Worldwide.

The AIBD yield can be easily converted to USBE equivalent, and vice versa, since the AIBD yield is the *compounded* annualization of the semi-annual yield from the USBE quote. Thus, for example, since 4% is the semiannual yield to maturity implicit in the USBE 8% quote, the equivalent AIBD annual yield to maturity can be found as $1.04^2 - 1 = 0.0816$, or 8.16%.

The message conveyed by the footnote in *The Wall Street Journal* makes the point that the quotes are consistent with the AIBD method, rather than the USBE method. The examples that follow demonstrate the method of converting from one yield quotation convention to the other.

EXAMPLE 5A-1

Find the equivalent AIBD yield-to-maturity quote for a bond quoted to yield 9% to maturity (annually) under the USBE system.

Solution 5A-1   The bond quoted to yield 9% to maturity under the USBE system actually yields 4.5% semiannually, which is equivalent to $1.045^2 - 1 = 0.092025$, or 9.2025% annually.

(Examples continued on next page.)

EXAMPLE 5A-2

The AIBD yield to maturity on a bond is 6%. What the USBE quoted yield to maturity?

Solution 5A-2   With semiannual compounding, 6% annually is equivalent to $1.06^{1/2} - 1 = 0.0296$, or 2.96%. The USBE equivalent is $2(0.0296) = 0.05912$, or 5.912%.

CURRENCY SWAPS

The advent of swaps, as much as anything else, helped transform the world's segmented capital markets into a single, truly-integrated, international capital market.

John F. Marshall and Kenneth R. Kapner,*

An Introduction to Currency Swaps

The term currency swap is used in more than one way in global financial management. Historically, the term "currency swap" has described a transaction in which a party simultaneously agrees to buy a currency on a near date and sell it on a later date. Such a transaction is known as an *exchange market swap* or a foreign exchange swap.

Recently, the term currency swap has been applied to a new structure developed in the capital markets. A capital market currency swap generally has a much longer time horizon than an exchange market currency swap and is a contract between two parties to make periodic payments based upon exchange rates. This chapter focuses on the capital market currency swaps, which are the swaps that Marshall and Kapner are referring to in the introductory quote to the chapter, and which have been so significant in global financial management and in integrating the world's capital markets.

A capital market currency swap is an exchange of two streams of cash flows in different currencies, or alternatively, the periodic cash settlement based on the notional concept of an exchange of two streams of cash flows in different currencies. Thus, capital market currency swaps are often cash-settled by difference checks, in the same manner described in Chapter 4 for

---

*The Swaps Market, 2nd ed. (Miami, FL: Kolb, 1993).

forward exchange contracts.

Sometimes the streams of (or underlying) capital market currency swaps are fixed amounts per period and other times the streams are based on some floating interest rate or index. A capital market currency swap does not *necessarily* involve any exchange of currencies at time 0, but a time 0 exchange is often part of a currency swap deal. The optional time 0 exchange is not included in many of the examples of this chapter. Since capital market currency swaps are the focus of the chapter, we'll economize on words and simply refer to a currency swap. Exchange market currency swaps are covered in the appendix to this chapter.

FIXED-FOR-FIXED CURRENCY SWAPS

The basic "plain vanilla" currency swap is the *fixed-for-fixed currency swap*. In such a swap, the cash flows of the swap are based upon the future cash flows of two fixed coupon bullet bonds of different currencies. A fixed-for-fixed swap may be best explained by an example. In the example and all examples in the chapter (and usually in the entire text), periodic settlements are assumed to be made annually. This assumption takes a bit of liberty, since settlements are often semiannual. However, as usual, the annual payment assumption is made to allow an easier focus on the concepts.

Assume that 5-year U.S. dollar AAA eurobonds currently pay a coupon interest rate of 6% for the bonds to sell at par in the market. Consider such a eurobond with principal of $1,000,000. Given the assumptions, this bond makes fixed coupon interest payments in the amount of 0.06($1,000,000) = $60,000 per year. At maturity, at the same time as the final interest payment, the $1,000,000 in principal payment must also be paid by the bond issuer to the bondholder.

Next consider a 5-year French franc par AAA eurobond with a principal of FF5,000,000. Assume that the market yield to maturity on such a bond is 9%. Thus, the French franc bond makes coupon interest payments of 0.09(FF5,000,000) = FF450,000 per year and then repays the principal of FF5,000,000 at the same time as the last interest payment. If the spot exchange rate at present were $X_{FF/\$}^0 = 5$ FF/$, then the FF5,000,000 par bond would be equivalent in value to the $1,000,000 par bond.

Now if investor A is holding the U.S. dollar bond and investor B is holding the French franc bond, the two could agree, if they wanted to, to simply exchange, or swap, all the future cash flows of their investments. Investor A would agree to receive the French franc cash flows of FF450,000 annually for 5 years, plus FF5,000,000 at maturity. Investor B would agree to receive the U.S. dollar cash flows of $60,000 annually for 5 years, plus $1,000,000 at maturity. In terms of present value at time 0, the two parties are simply exchanging FF5,000,000 for $1,000,000, which is fair at the assumed current spot exchange rate of 5 FF/$. This agreement to exchange *future* cash flows can take place by contract between investor A and investor B, *without* an exchange of the bonds they hold.

Even if two parties do *not* own the bonds that conceptually underlie the currency swap, they could still agree to exchange the same cash flow streams discussed earlier. The agreement would be to exchange streams of future payments that have equal time 0 present values, at the time 0 spot exchange rate. There would be no time 0 exchange, as long as the present values of the scheduled future flows to be exchanged are equal at time 0. The flows are calculated on the basis of a fictional amount of bond principal, referred to as the *notional principal.* There is only one underlying principal amount in a currency swap; given a principal amount in one currency, the equivalent principal amount in the other currency is found using the spot exchange rate at the time the swap is contracted. Panel A of Figure 6-1 depicts the 5-year fixed-for-fixed currency swap on a notional principal of $1,000,000 of 6% dollars for 9% French francs. The dashed lines pertaining to the bonds indicate that ownership of the underlying bonds may be the case, but is not necessary.

Although currency swaps are often contracted without a time 0 exchange (of principal amounts), a currency swap between two bond *issuers will* often involve a time 0 exchange of principals. For example, if the U.S. firm, Midwest Manufacturing, issues a French franc bond, and the French firm, LeTrec Industries, issues a dollar bond, the two companies may wish to enter a currency swap. The swap would first involve Midwest delivering the time 0 French franc bond proceeds to LeTrec in exchange for LeTrec's time 0 U.S. dollar bond proceeds. In addition, Midwest would make periodic dollar payments to LeTrec, which would use these payments to make the dollar coupon interest and principal payments to its investors. LeTrec would correspondingly send periodic French franc payments to Midwest, which would use those payments to meet its French franc liabilities.

Midwest issues a French franc bond, but swaps effectively into a dollar liability, while LeTrec issues a dollar bond and swaps effectively into a French franc liability. This sounds crazy at first, because one wonders why Midwest and LeTrec did not simply issue dollar and French franc bonds, respectively, in the first place. The motivations of the two companies are discussed later.

In practice, many currency swaps are arranged with a global bank as the counterparty. The bank may "pay French francs to and receive dollars from" a retail user like Midwest and "pay dollars to and receive French francs from" another retail user like LeTrec, or even another swap-dealing bank, often in another country. Banks make intermediation profits by charging a fee and/or a spread for dealer services. The intermediated approach reduces the default risk and lowers the search costs that would be present if two corporations, generally of different nationalities, tried to structure a currency swap directly between themselves. The intermediation of currency swaps by global bankers has played a crucial role in the globalization of the world's financial marketplace. Panel B of Figure 6-1 depicts the scenario of Midwest and LeTrec, where bonds are issued and the swap also includes the proceeds exchange.

An *at-market currency swap* is one where the present values of the underlying notional bonds are equal. The currency swap in the preceding example is an at-market swap, since the present value of the dollar stream ($1,000,000) balances with the present value of the French franc stream (FF5,000,000), given the assumed spot exchange rate of 5 FF/$. Thus, in an at-market swap, no time 0 payment is necessary. In practice, many currency swaps originate as at-market swaps.

CROSS-CURRENCY SWAPS

While the most fundamental type of currency swap is the fixed-for-fixed, another common form of currency swap is the *fixed-for-floating currency swap*, in which, as the term indicates, one of the payment streams is based on a fixed coupon bond in one currency, while the other payment stream is based on a floating rate note in another currency. This type of currency swap is also called a *cross-currency swap*.

Quotation conventions in the swap market have made it convenient to

FIGURE 6-1 Capital Market Currency Swap Scenarios

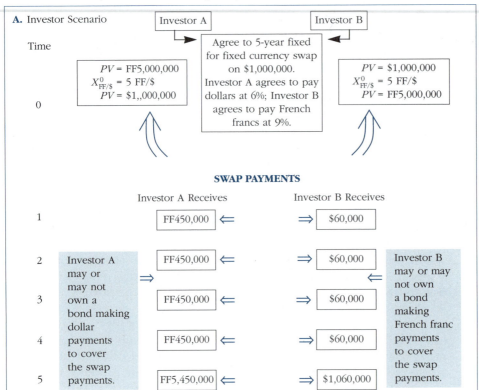

FIGURE 6-1 (Continued)

B. Midwest Manufacturing/LeTrec Industries Corporate Scenario

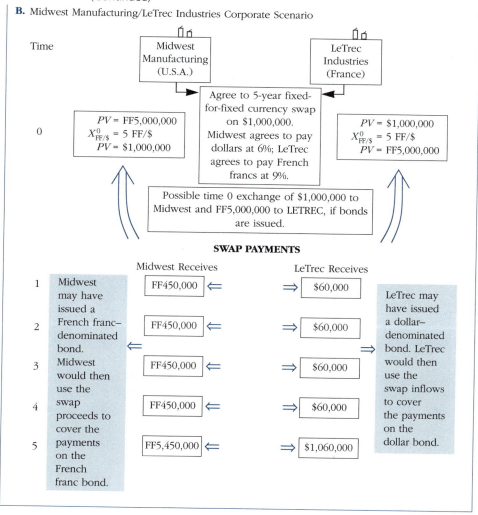

quote capital market swap rates, for at-market swaps, as fixed coupon bond rates against U.S. dollar LIBOR flat. An example of the quotations is shown in Figure 6-2.

In Figure 6-2, the bid for a 5-year yen swap of 5.10% means that you can enter into an at-market swap agreement to receive yen at the coupon rate of 5.10% and pay dollars at a floating rate of LIBOR flat. By the same token if you wanted to take a position to pay fixed yen, you could agree to pay yen at the rate of 5.16% and receive dollars at the floating rate of LIBOR flat. The spread between the bid and ask rates is, of course, the dealer's market-making compensation.

EXAMPLE 6-1

You wish to enter into a 5-year fixed-for-fixed currency swap, such that the cash flow stream you are receiving is in British pounds and the cash flow stream you are paying is in U.S. dollars. There is no time 0 exchange of cash. The swap is to be based on a notional principal of $1,000,000. What are the cash flows upon which the currency swap is based, if the swap is an at-market swap and if the 5-year par coupon rates are 5.5% for dollars and 9% for pounds, and if the spot exchange rate is currently $X^0_{\$/\pounds} = 1.50$ $/£?

Solution 6-1   The cash flow stream you would be paying is 0.055($1,000,000) = $55,000 per year for 5 years, plus a final principal payment of $1,000,000. The cash flow stream you would be receiving must be based on a sterling-denominated bond with a time 0 dollar value of $1,000,000, given the spot exchange rate of 1.50 $/£. Thus, the principal on the sterling bond is $1,000,000/(1.50 $/£) = £666,667. At a coupon interest rate of 9%, the sterling cash flow receipts are £60,000 per year for 5 years and a principal receipt of £666,667 at year 5. The cash flow streams for this solution may be laid out as follows:

	U.S. DOLLAR PAYMENTS	*POUND STERLING RECEIPTS*
Year 1	$ 55,000	£ 60,000
Year 2	55,000	60,000
Year 3	55,000	60,000
Year 4	55,000	60,000
Year 5	55,000	60,000
Principal	$1,000,000	£666,667

The coupon rates for an at-market, fixed-for-fixed currency swap are found by viewing a fixed-for-fixed swap as a combination of two fixed-for-floating swaps. Upon combining a position to receive fixed yen and pay floating dollar LIBOR with a position to receive floating dollar LIBOR and pay fixed dollars, the dollar LIBOR streams net out, and one is left with the fixed-for-fixed swap. Note that a swap of fixed payments for floating payments in the same currency is called an *interest rate swap*, which is covered in more detail in Chapter 7. Because of the "roundabout" construction approach taken in the market, fixed-for-fixed currency swaps are sometimes called *circus* swaps. (Circus also is an adapted acronym for "combined interest rate and currency swap.")

An example interpretation from Figure 6-2 is that if you wanted to enter into an at-market, 5-year, fixed-for-fixed currency swap to pay yen and receive dollars, you would pay yen at the rate of 5.16% of the notional principal and receive dollars at the rate of 9.20%.

Currency		Swap Maturity				
		2 Years	3 Years	5 Years	7 Years	10 Years
Yen	Bid	4.78%	4.85%	5.10%	5.25%	5.36%
	Ask	4.84	4.92	5.16	5.32	5.42
Sterling	Bid	9.65	9.83	9.85	9.98	10.02
	Ask	9.75	9.93	9.95	10.08	10.12
Swiss franc	Bid	3.48	3.79	4.33	4.50	4.78
	Ask	3.52	3.85	4.38	4.55	4.85
Deutsche mark	Bid	4.68	4.98	5.65	6.18	6.60
	Ask	4.78	5.08	5.75	6.28	6.70
U.S. dollar	Bid	8.65	8.89	9.20	9.46	9.67
	Ask	8.72	8.93	9.26	9.52	9.73

FIGURE 6-2 Sample Currency Quotations in the Swap Market

Source: Keith C. Brown and Donald J. Smith, "Currency Swaps: Quotation Conventions, Market Structures, and Credit Risk," in Carl Biedleman, ed., *Cross Currency Swaps* (Homewood, IL: Business One-Irwin, 1992). Reprinted by permission.

OFF-MARKET SWAPS

Of course, any two parties can, if they want to, agree to exchange cash flow streams that do *not* have the same present value, given the spot exchange rate. In that case, the recipient of the cash flow stream with the larger present value should have to make some time 0 balancing payment to the party receiving the cash flow stream with the smaller present value. The time 0 balancing payment would equalize the present value of the exchange. An *off-market swap* is one that requires a time 0 payment to balance the present values. Example 6-2 illustrates.

SETTLEMENT OF CURRENCY SWAPS WITH DIFFERENCE CHECKS

Despite the relative simplicity of the concept of "exchanging" cash flow streams, the settlement of modern swaps at the specific times of cash flow exchange does not necessarily have to take place with an actual two-way exchange. Instead, at each of the settlement times there will be only a single net cash flow, called a *difference check*.[1]

The difference check in a currency swap exchange works the same way as the cash settlement on a forward contract. This feature permits us to see that a fixed-for-fixed currency swap can be interpreted as a portfolio of for-

[1]The concept is introduced in Lee M. Wakeman, "The Portfolio Approach to Swaps Management," in Carl R. Biedleman, ed., *Interest Rate Swaps* (Homewood, IL: Business One-Irwin, 1991).

> ### ▦ EXAMPLE 6-2
>
> Extend Example 6-1, continuing to assume that the time 0 spot exchange rate is 1.50 $/£. Suppose you still want to make the future payments on a 5-year, 5.5% coupon U.S. dollar par bond, but instead of receiving payments based on a 5-year, 9% coupon sterling par bond, you wish to receive payments on a 5-year, 10% coupon sterling bond. Assume that the market-required yield to maturity on 5-year, 10% coupon sterling bonds is 9%. Would you have to pay or receive a time 0 payment and how much?
>
> *Solution 6-2* The sterling notional principal is still £666,667, because the time 0 spot exchange rate is still assumed to be 1.50 $/£. The 10% sterling coupon rate means that you'll receive 0.10(£666,667) = £66,667 per year for 5 years and £666,667 at year 5. Thus, the present value of the underlying sterling bond payments is £66,667/1.09 + £66,667/1.09^2 + £66,667/1.09^3 + £66,667/1.09^4 + £66,667/1.09^5 + £666,667/1.09^5 = £692,600, which is equivalent to a dollar value of £692,600(1.50 $/£) = $1,038,899. Thus, the present value of what you'd be paying is $1,000,000, while the present value of what you'd be receiving is $1,038,899. Thus, you should make a time 0 payment of $1,038,899 − $1,000,000 = $38,899, or equivalently in pounds, $38,899/(1.50 $/£) = £25,932.

ward foreign exchange contracts. However, the forward exchange rates on the contracts are not necessarily the same as the market's forward exchange rates for the individual horizons.[2] The forward exchange rate for an underlying payment of a currency swap is referred to as the *contract exchange rate* for that payment.

Generally, the contract exchange rate for a currency swap's principal payment cash flow, at the swap's maturity, is different from the contract exchange rate on the interest flows. The contract exchange rate for the principal cash flow is usually set equal to the spot exchange rate at the time the swap is originated. As shown later, the contract exchange rate for the interest cash flows is determined directly from the two coupon interest rates involved in the legs of the swap.

The position descriptions in currency swaps are also related to those for forward foreign exchange contracts. A party that receives currency *A* and pays currency *B* has a long swap position on currency *A* and a short swap position on currency *B*. The other party has a short swap position on currency *A* and a long swap position on currency *B*.

---

[2]The insight that a currency swap replicates a portfolio of forward exchange contracts is found in Clifford W. Smith and Charles W. Smithson, "Financial Engineering: An Overview," in *Handbook of Financial Engineering* (New York: Harper & Row, 1990). The insight helps in the understanding of how synthetic debt may be alternatively engineered via swaps and via forward exchange contracts, as covered in Chapter 5.

Consider a 5-year fixed-for-fixed currency swap of 6% U.S. dollars for 9% French francs for a notional principal of $1,000,000. Assume that the time 0 spot exchange rate is 5 FF/$, and thus the notional principal may also be expressed as FF5,000,000. Thus, the currency swap is effectively an exchange of $60,000 for FF450,000 each year for 5 years, and then an exchange of $1,000,000 for FF5,000,000 at year 5. In this case, the contract exchange rate for the interest payments is FF450,000/$60,000 = 7.5 FF/$, while the contract exchange rate for the principal component is 5 FF/$.

The long swap position on French francs may be viewed as effectively "receiving" the French franc cash flow stream and "paying" the dollar cash flow stream, while the short position on French francs effectively "pays" the French franc cash flow stream and "receives" the dollars.

Thus, the long position in the swap on French francs, in effect, has contracted to pay $60,000, and receive FF450,000, each year for 5 years and at year 5 must pay $1,000,000 and receive FF5,000,000. The actual settlement of the swap cash flows takes place with a difference check, based on the contract exchange rates and the respective actual spot exchange rate at the time of each settlement.

What if the spot exchange rate moves to $X^1_{FF/\$}$ = 6 FF/$ at time 1, representing a depreciation of the French franc relative to the dollar? In this case, the FF450,000 notional coupon interest payment at time 1 would be worth $75,000. The long position on French francs is scheduled to pay $60,000, but the value of what is scheduled to be received is $75,000. This situation suggests that the scheduled payments could be settled simply by a difference payment of $75,000 − $60,000 = $15,000, or equivalently $15,000(6 FF/$) = FF90,000, from the party that is short on French francs to the party that is long on French francs.

The settlement of the exchange with a difference check actually implies that the time 1 exchange is simply a forward contract that has a forward exchange rate equal to the contract exchange rate, which is the ratio of the interest payments. Indeed, computation of the periodic settlement is accomplished just as with forward exchange contracts. For a contract size of FF450,000 at a forward exchange rate of 7.5 FF/$, equation (4-1) indicates that the long position on French francs should receive a settlement of FF450,000[1/(6 FF/$) − 1/(7.5 FF/$)] = FF450,000[0.1667 $/FF − 0.1333 $/FF] = $15,000. (See Figure 6-3.)

Remember: If you want to use the forward exchange contract formula to find the difference check settlement on one of the *interest components* of a currency swap where the coupon interest rates are different, you must compute the contract exchange rate by the ratio of the scheduled interest payments. This contract exchange rate then plays the role of the forward exchange rate. Note that the contract exchange rate for the *principal component* is different, since it is the spot exchange rate when the swap originated.

If the spot exchange rate of 6 FF/$ prevails at each of the remaining four settlement dates, then the long position on French francs would continue to

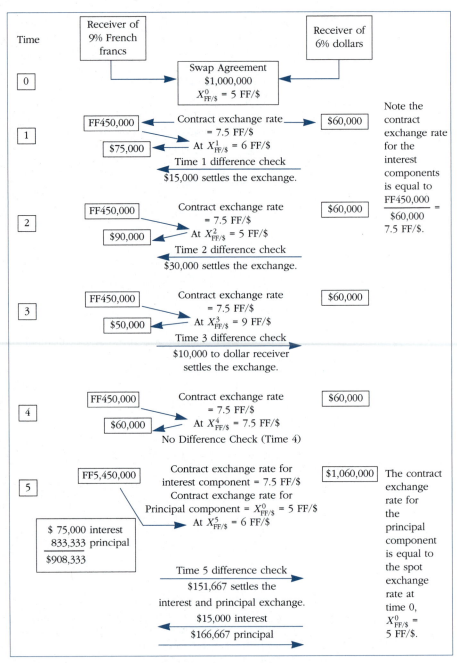

FIGURE 6-3 Cash Settlement of Swap Payments with Difference Checks

receive $15,000 difference payments to settle the interest components, but the final settlement on the principal is different. The short position on French francs effectively owes FF5,000,000, which is equivalent to FF5,000,000/(6 FF/$) = $833,333.33 at the spot exchange rate of $X_{FF/\$}^5$ = 6 FF/$. Since the long position on French francs owes a notional principal of $1,000,000, the long position on French francs must send a difference check for $166,666.67, or equivalently, $166,666.67(6FF/$) = FF1,000,000 to settle the principal exchange at maturity. Since the settlement of the interest component at time 5 is $15,000 *to* the long position on French francs, the net time 5 difference check goes to the short position on French francs in the amount of $151,667 to settle the interest and principal with one difference check.

Thus, if the French franc depreciates from $X_{FF/\$}^0$ = 5 FF/$ to $X_{FF/\$}^1$ = 6 FF/$ and remains at 6 FF/$ thereafter, the difference settlements on the notional interest payment go from the short position on French francs to the long position on French francs, while the maturity settlement on principal must be paid by the long position on French francs to the short position on French francs.

If the exchange rate at year 1 instead is $X_{FF/\$}^1$ = 5 FF/$, coincidentally exactly equal to the current spot exchange rate when the swap originates, then the long position on French francs notionally owes $60,000 and is due FF450,000, or the dollar equivalent of FF450,000, which is FF450,000/(5 FF/$) = $90,000. Thus, the long position on French francs is due a difference pay-

---

☰ EXAMPLE 6-3

Consider a 6-year fixed-for-fixed currency swap of 5% U.S. dollars for 7% Japanese yen on notional principal of $1,000,000. The spot exchange rate when the swap originates is $X_{¥/\$}^0$ = 140 ¥/$. Find the difference check settlements on the swap if the yen depreciates to 160 ¥/$ at time 1, the time of the first payment, and remains at that level through the maturity of the swap.

Solution 6-3   The notional principal in yen is $1,000,000(140 ¥/$) = ¥140,000,000. The notional dollar interest is 0.05($1,000,000) = $50,000, while the notional yen interest is 0.07(¥140,000,000) = ¥9,800,000. The cash flow exchange for the notional coupon interest components is thus at a contract exchange rate of ¥9,800,000/$50,000 = 196 ¥/$. At 160 ¥/$, the interest components settle (from the viewpoint of the long position on yen) at ¥9,800,000[1/(160 ¥/$) – 1/(196 ¥/$)] = $11,250. The settlement of the principal component (from the viewpoint of the long position on yen) is ¥140,000,000[1/(160 ¥/$) – 1/(140 ¥/$)] = –$125,000. Thus, the long position on yen would receive 6 payments of $11,250 from the short position on yen to settle the notional interest payments, while the short position on yen would receive $125,000 (or equivalently $125,000(160 ¥/$) = ¥20,000,000) from the long position on yen to settle the notional principal. Alternatively, we can say that the long position would receive five difference checks of $11,250 and the short position would receive one check for $113,750 at the swap's maturity.

ment of $30,000$, or equivalently, at $X_{FF/\$}^1 = 5$ FF/$, $30,000(5 \text{ FF}/\$) =$ FF150,000. This difference payment is made, even though the spot exchange rate did *not* change from the exchange rate that prevailed when the swap originated. Indeed, if the spot exchange rate were to be 5 FF/$ at the time of *each* of the next 4 years' settlements, the swap would be settled each period with the short position on French francs making a $30,000, or FF150,000, payment each period to the long position on French francs. The settlement on the principal, however, would be nil, since at maturity $1,000,000 and FF5,000,000 negate each other at a spot exchange rate of $X_{FF/\$}^5 = 5$ FF/$. Thus, in this case, the long swap position on French francs has come out ahead, since the French franc interest rate was greater than the U.S. dollar interest rate, but the spot exchange rate did not change.

Figure 6-3 depicts the cash settlements that would be made using some assumptions from the foregoing example.

From Parallel Loans to Global Markets

PARALLEL LOANS AND BACK-TO-BACK LOANS

Currency swaps evolved from the *parallel loan* concept, which was devised by the global private sector for purposes of circumventing cross-border capital controls. To see how a parallel loan arrangement worked, suppose that a British company wanted to establish a subsidiary in the United States in 1975. At that time, it was illegal by British law for the company to raise debt capital in England in the form of British pounds for purposes of overseas investment. The British government's rationale for the control was the belief that stopping overseas investment was a way to require that British capital be used for domestic investment and thus to help create jobs for British citizens.

However, there was no law to prevent a British company from raising British pounds in England and lending them to a British subsidiary of an American firm. In return, on the other side of the Atlantic Ocean, the parent of the American subsidiary could raise the equivalent amount in dollars by issuing debt in the United States and then lend the dollars to the U.S. subsidiary of the British parent.

For the British parent, its U.S. subsidiary could receive the financing it needed. Britain's capital export controls would be circumvented. While the British subsidiary of the U.S. firm made future pound-denominated interest and principal payments to the British parent, the British firm's subsidiary would make dollar interest and principal payments to the U.S. parent. Thus, in addition to the British circumvention of their capital controls, the U.S. parent would be effectively repatriating the earnings of its overseas subsidiary to the United States without any repatriation taxes levied by the host government. Thus, many firms gravitated to the parallel loan concept, not only as a way of circumventing laws preventing domestic capital from leaving its own

Currency swaps paved the way to global financial integration.

country, but also as a way of repatriating returns on overseas investments, without foreign taxes, back into a country.

Figure 6-4 shows the balance sheet configuration idea for a parallel loan arrangement between Uncle Sam's, Inc. (the U.S. firm), and Nigel's English Muffins Plc (the British firm). Note that these two firms need have no trade or other business connection, just mutually compatible financial needs. Both parent's show assets other than the respective investment/ownership of their foreign subsidiaries.

The assumed exchange rate for the example is 2.00 $/£. Assume that Nigel's New York subsidiary needs total capital of $4,000,000 (of which it already has $1,000,000 accumulated, which is also the parent Nigel's asset of £500,000). Uncle Sam's London subsidiary needs total capital of £2,500,000, which could be provided in entirety by the parent firm as an investment of $5,000,000. Instead, Uncle Sam's supplies only $2,000,000 (£1,000,000) of the capital for Sam's-London, which becomes the parent Sam's ownership of the subsidiary and the subsidiary's equity financing, and the parent Nigel lends Sam's-London the other £1,500,000. The parent Uncle Sam's, in turn, lends Nigel's-New York $3,000,000.

Even if two companies in different countries had no need for capital, they

Uncle Sam's (U.S.)		Nigel's English Muffins Ltd.	
Assets	*Debt & Equity*	*Assets*	*Debt & Equity*
Sam's-London $2,000,000		Nigel's-N.Y. £500,000	
Loan-Nigel's N.Y. $3,000,000	$13,000,000	Loan-Sam's London £1,500,000	£7,000,000
Other $8,000,000		Other £5,000,000	
Totals $13,000,000	$13,000,000	Totals £7,000,000	£7,000,000

Sam's-London		Nigel's-N.Y.	
Assets	*Debt & Equity*	*Assets*	*Debt & Equity*
£2,500,000	Debt-Nigel's £1,500,000	$4,000,000	Debt-Uncle Sam's $3,000,000
	Equity-Uncle Sam's £1,000,000		Equity-Nigel's $1,000,000
Totals £2,500,000	£2,500,000	Totals $4,000,000	$4,000,000

FIGURE 6-4 Balance Sheets for U.S. and British Parents and Their Foreign Subsidiaries

could still book mutual hypothetical loans to each other's subsidiaries, for purposes of exchanging future cash flow streams. For example, suppose the U.S. subsidiary of a Japanese parent is generating dollars and the Japanese subsidiary of a U.S. parent is generating yen. The Japanese firm's U.S. subsidiary books a fictional dollar loan amount, payable to the U.S. parent onto its balance sheet, and then makes dollar interest and principal payments to the U.S. parent, while the U.S. parent's Japanese subsidiary books a fictional yen loan to the Japanese parent onto its balance sheet and makes periodic yen interest and principal payments to the Japanese parent. No principal amounts were actually exchanged when the loans were put on the books. This type of an arrangement was called a *back-to-back loan*. The balance sheet configuration in Figure 6-4 could also represent the result of back-to-back loans.

While parallel loans and back-to-back loans served to help circumvent cross-border capital controls and repatriation frictions, there were some drawbacks that could be alleviated with the currency swap structure. First, parallel and back-to-back loans are shown on reported balance sheets, whereas currency swap positions are "off-balance-sheet" items. Parallel and back-to-back loans would thus cause debt ratios to be higher, a key factor in credit ratings. Second, different legal provisions in different countries made it very difficult to tie the loans together. If one party defaulted on its loan, the laws in the other country would still require the other party to pay off the loan on its side of the agreement.

It was natural for global financial intermediaries to enter the picture. Global bankers were naturally suited to serve as brokers for deals so that operating companies would not have to search for suitable partners. At the same time as providing a "clearinghouse" for companies interested in deals, the global banks and their lawyers were able to take a key step by conceiving the deals as exchanges of cash flows (or swaps) instead of exchanges of loans.

This concept solved two problems: (1) swap positions did not have to be booked onto balance sheets, and (2) the cash flows could legally be viewed as "offsetting" legs of a single transaction. As part of this process, global banks began to serve in a dealer capacity for the swaps, meaning that each side viewed its deal only with the intermediary. A bankruptcy by one company would be the bank's problem, not the other company's problem.[3]

By structuring currency swaps as instruments whose periodic exchanges can be settled with one-way difference checks, like forward exchange contracts, the need for the counterparties to have the full amounts of funds at each exchange time is alleviated. This feature, in turn, reduces the counterparty risk of a default on a swap deal. This approach to settlement was endorsed by the International Swap Dealers Association (ISDA) in 1985 in its first standardized swap document, the Master Agreement. The ISDA uses the term *bilateral closeout netting*.[4]

THE IBM–WORLD BANK SWAP

The first actual currency swap transaction is often attributed to a 1981 transaction between the World Bank and IBM.[5] The World Bank had actually wanted to raise capital by borrowing Swiss francs. However, the World Bank had already saturated the Swiss market for its bonds, and the U.S. market regarded World Bank bonds with much less credit risk than did the Swiss investors. IBM had previously financed with some Swiss franc debt, but had developed the view that the Swiss franc was going to appreciate in the future, relative to the dollar. Therefore, IBM wanted to replace its Swiss franc debt with dollar debt.

---

[3]An interesting article on the development of currency swaps is Michael Wood, "The Development of the Cross Currency Swap Market," in C. Biedleman, ed., *Cross Currency Swaps*, (Homewood, IL: Business One Irwin, 1992).

[4]For a useful discussion of counterparty risk and credit risk in swaps, see Ludger Hentschel and Clifford W. Smith, "Risk and Regulation in Derivatives Markets," *Journal of Applied Corporate Finance*, Fall 1994, pp. 8–21.

[5]The IBM/World Bank deal is described in Y. S. Park, "Currency Swaps as a Long-Term International Financing Technique," *Journal of International Business Studies*," Winter 1984, pp. 47–54.

A major global bank, Salomon Brothers, noted that a currency swap might serve both parties; in the swap, IBM received periodic cash flows of Swiss francs from the World Bank, while the World Bank received dollars from IBM. The World Bank could then borrow from U.S. investors and, in effect, use its dollar receipts from the currency swap to make payments on its dollar bonds. In this manner, the Swiss francs that the World Bank paid to IBM represented the ultimate liability for the World Bank. Similarly, IBM could use the Swiss francs received from the World bank to meet its existing Swiss franc debt obligations, while its dollar payments to the World Bank represented its new de facto liability. See Figure 6-5.

The IBM–World Bank currency swap demonstrates a typical application of a basic, fixed-for-fixed currency swap. IBM's motivation was clear—it had issued Swiss franc bonds but, subsequently, wanted to change that liability into a dollar liability, since it predicted an appreciation of the Swiss franc relative to the dollar. In this case, IBM used the currency swap as a more expedient way to effectively convert Swiss franc debt into dollar debt, without actually retiring the existing Swiss franc debt and reissuing new U.S. dollar debt.

The World Bank, on the other hand, used the currency swap as part of its initial financing strategy. Why didn't the World Bank simply issue Swiss franc bonds in the first place? The answer is that the World Bank was able to obtain a lower effective interest rate by issuing U.S. dollar bonds and swapping the dollar liabilities into effective Swiss franc liabilities via the fixed-for-fixed currency swap. This strategy is similar to the one discussed in Chapter 5 for a company that is able to lower its debt financing cost by issuing debt in the currency of receptive investors and then hedging the liabilities with a sequence of forward exchange contracts. The currency swap performs the

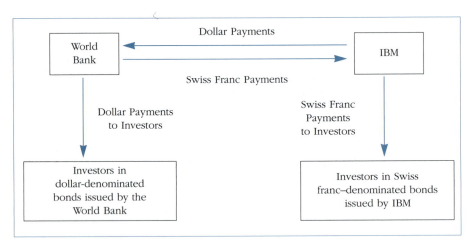

FIGURE 6-5   World Bank/IBM Currency Swap

same hedging service as a package of forward exchange contracts, but in a convenient, already packaged form. The swap is also particularly advantageous in situations where longer-dated forward exchange markets are relatively illiquid.

CREDIT RISK PERCEPTIONS

The World Bank took advantage of an idiosyncratic difference in the perceptions of U.S. investors versus European investors. Europeans view a strong international company, like General Electric, for example, as having lower credit risk than a supranational agency, like the World Bank. U.S. investors, on the other hand, have the opposite perception. Thus, a company like General Electric might be required to pay a higher dollar coupon interest rate than the World Bank by U.S. investors, while the World Bank might be required to pay a higher Swiss franc coupon interest rate than General Electric to Swiss investors. However, given that the two parties each have liabilities, if the World Bank naturally prefers a Swiss franc liability while General Electric naturally prefers a dollar liability, exchange exposure considerations would make both organizations reluctant to take advantage of the asymmetric market perceptions, unless of course a currency swap can be arranged.

Consider the following hypothetical numerical example. Assume General Electric would have to pay an 8% coupon interest rate on dollar bonds while the World Bank would only have to pay 7%, because of a perceived better credit rating for the World Bank by dollar-based investors. Assume that the World Bank would have to pay a 6% coupon interest rate on Swiss franc par bonds while General Electric would only have to pay 5%, because of a perceived better credit rating for General Electric by Swiss franc–based investors.

To finance in their preferred currencies without a currency swap, General Electric would pay an 8% coupon interest rate on dollar bonds, while the World Bank would pay a 6% coupon interest rate on Swiss franc bonds. However, if General Electric issues the Swiss franc bonds at a 5% coupon interest rate, the World Bank issues the dollar bonds at a 7% coupon interest rate, and the two organizations engage in a fixed-for-fixed currency swap of 7% dollars for 5% Swiss francs, both would have lower effective financing costs in their preferred currencies. General Electric's actual 5% Swiss franc liability would be covered by the 5% incoming Swiss francs from the currency swap, and General Electric would ultimately be paying dollar interest at the coupon interest rate of 7%. The World Bank's 7% dollar liability would be covered by its currency swap receipts, and the World Bank would ultimately be paying a 5% Swiss franc liability.

Cross-currency swaps are prevalent because of the preferences of various segments of the global marketplace. In particular, European investors often prefer to own floating rate notes rather than fixed coupon bonds. Thus, given their credit risk perceptions, European investors are good targets for placements of FRN's issued by multinational companies. U.S. dollar–based multinationals, on the other hand, often prefer to make fixed coupon interest payments. Thus, U.S. firms issuing floating rate debt denominated in European currencies would like to be able to take positions in currency swaps to receive the European currency in floating rate payments and pay a fixed coupon in U.S. dollars.

SWAP-DRIVEN FINANCING

When an organization issues securities to raise capital and simultaneously originates a swap as part of the deal, the term *swap-driven financing* applies. In swap-driven financing, the swap is an integral part of the financing package by design. General Electric's synthetic issue of dollar bonds via an actual issue of Swiss franc bonds and a long position on Swiss francs in a currency swap is a hypothetical example of swap-driven financing. See panel A of Figure 6-6.

Swap-driven financing occurs in the global capital markets for reasons other than differences in perceptions of credit quality and differences in concerns/forecasts of future exchange rates, both inherent reasons in the preceding examples. Another reason could be to circumvent legal restrictions on capital mobility. Indeed, as has been pointed out, currency swaps evolved from this motivation originally.[6]

Recently, the traditional use of long swap positions on foreign currency to create synthetic base currency debt has also been reversed. Companies that desire foreign currency debt (and we'll see reasons why in Chapter 9) have often found it cheaper to issue base currency debt and swap to create the foreign currency debt synthetically. See panel B of Figure 6-6. For example, companies whose base currency is the U.S. dollar have found nondollar investors increasingly reluctant to accept the "event risk" of corporate takeovers inherent in foreign currency debt issues by U.S. corporations. Note that this technique is the second method introduced in the text for creating synthetic foreign currency debt; the first was the currency-indexed bond approach covered in the last chapter.

The role played by the intermediaries as central conduits for the cash flows between issuers accelerated global interest in swaps. The evolution of the currency swap is the primary example of how the private markets were able to globalize, despite capital controls in place by governments. This sentiment is reflected in the lead quote to the chapter. The excitement of this process was so great that swaps were called "the vortex of finance."[7]

---

[6]A good example of using currency swaps to arbitrage credit risk perceptions may be found in George Handjinicolaou, "The Place of Currency Swaps in Financial Markets," in Biedleman, *Cross Currency Swaps.*

[7]See J. G. Powers, "The Vortex of Finance," *Intermarket Magazine,* February 1986, pp. 27–38. Further discussion of the role of currency swaps in integrating the global capital markets (and other important aspects of currency swaps) may be found in George Handjinicolaou, "The Place of Currency Swaps in Financial Markets," in Biedleman, *Cross Currency Swaps.*

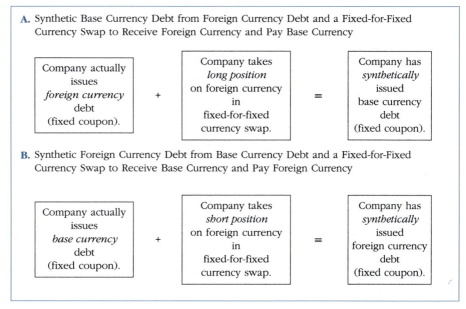

A. Synthetic Base Currency Debt from Foreign Currency Debt and a Fixed-for-Fixed Currency Swap to Receive Foreign Currency and Pay Base Currency

| Company actually issues *foreign currency* debt (fixed coupon). | + | Company takes *long position* on foreign currency in fixed-for-fixed currency swap. | ≡ | Company has *synthetically* issued base currency debt (fixed coupon). |

B. Synthetic Foreign Currency Debt from Base Currency Debt and a Fixed-for-Fixed Currency Swap to Receive Base Currency and Pay Foreign Currency

| Company actually issues *base currency* debt (fixed coupon). | + | Company takes *short position* on foreign currency in fixed-for-fixed currency swap. | ≡ | Company has *synthetically* issued foreign currency debt (fixed coupon). |

FIGURE 6-6 Swap-Driven Financing

It is worth noting that since Britain's overseas capital controls could be circumvented by the private global capital markets anyway, the British government eventually eliminated its regulation. This is an example of how the financial deregulation era of the 1980s was preceded by de facto deregulation by the private sector. Many other governments saw the futility of many financial regulations.

CURRENCY SWAPS AND TAX ARBITRAGE

Here's an example of currency swaps and tax arbitrage. In 1985 New Zealand dollar (NZ$) investments were actively sought by global investors because of that currency's stability compared with the U.S. dollar and the high coupon rates available on New Zealand dollar debt. However, two withholding taxes discouraged foreign investors: (1) a 15% tax on interest paid to resident holders of domestic New Zealand bonds and a 15% withholding tax on interest disbursements to foreign holders of domestic New Zealand bonds and (2) a withholding tax paid by issuing corporations from New Zealand on interest paid to offshore eurobond borrowers in New Zealand dollars, but not in other currencies.

The first tax meant that both domestic and foreign holders of domestically issued New Zealand dollar bonds would require a higher coupon interest rate than on NZ$ eurobonds issued by non New Zealand organizations, which could not be subject to the withholding tax. The second tax meant that New Zealand borrowers would have to pay a higher effective interest rate on New Zealand dollar eurobonds than non New Zealand borrowers.

Suppose that the New Zealand Roadworks Authority (NZRA) sought New Zealand dollar debt financing. If NZRA issued New Zealand dollar bonds in the domestic New Zealand market, but to nonresident investors, a high coupon would have to be paid to compensate the investors for the first tax; if the agency issued New Zealand dollar eurobonds, it would have to pay the second tax. However, consider Nipon Products, Inc., which actually desires U.S. dollar debt financing for a subsidiary in the United States. If Nipon Products issued New Zealand dollar eurobonds to non New Zealand residents, taxes 1 and 2 are avoided.

Assume that NZRA would have to pay 12% on domestic New Zealand dollar bonds and an even higher effective interest rate on offshore New Zealand dollar eurobonds, after accounting for taxes. Assume that Nipon Products would only have to pay a 10% interest rate on New Zealand dollar eurobonds. Assume that either organization could tap the eurodollar bond market at an interest rate of 8%. Rather than NZRA paying 12% on New Zealand dollar debt and Nipon Products paying 8% on U.S. dollar debt, NZRA could issue the U.S. dollar debt at 8%, while Nipon Products issued the New Zealand dollar eurobonds at 10%.

Now assume that NZRA and Nipon Products worked out an 8% U.S. dollar/11% New Zealand dollar currency swap, with NZRA receiving U.S. dollars and Nipon Products receiving the New Zealand dollars. NZRA would pay 8% on its actual U.S. dollar debt, then receive 8% dollars from the swap to offset the dollar liability, and then pay 11% in New Zealand dollars on the swap. Thus, NZRA has effectively lowered its cost of New Zealand dollar financing from 12% to 11%.

Nipon Products pays 10% on its actual New Zealand dollar eurobonds, but receives New Zealand dollars at 11% from the swap to more than offset the actual liability. Since Nipon Products pays 8% U.S. dollars on the currency swap, it comes out better than if it paid 8% on actual eurodollar bonds, since it has the excess New Zealand dollars, which it can exchange into yen, U.S. dollars, or whatever. Both organizations have been able to lower their financing costs relative to what the costs would be without the swap. The currency swap has resulted in swap-driven financing by both organizations as a means of global tax arbitrage.

This scenario is adapted from Michael Bowe, Eurobonds (Homewood, IL: Dow Jones-Irwin, 1988).

SWAP INNOVATIONS

The global marketplace has developed a number of variations on the plain vanilla swap structure. For example, it is possible to engage in a *coupon-only swap*, which is also called an *annuity swap*. As implied by its names, this kind of swap has no principal exchange at the maturity. The coupon-only swap may be useful in hedging amortizing liabilities or the interest portion of dual currency bonds.

It is also possible to execute a *zero-coupon swap*, which is just an exchange of a single cash flow at a date in the future, usually a number of years after the time the swap is arranged. In effect, a zero-coupon swap is the same as a long-dated forward exchange contract. Zero-coupon swaps can be used to hedge zero-coupon bond liabilities or the principal payment in a dual currency bond.

A *forward swap* is one in which there is a delay between the date on which the swap is contracted and the date of the first settlement. Suppose Midwest Co., a manufacturing company, is planning to raise dollar funds three months in the future. The company has determined that, given current conditions, issuing yen bonds and swapping into fixed coupon dollars is the most effective method. However, the company does not want to take on a swap position yet because of the mismatch of the timing of future cash flows on the swap and the yen bond, creating some foreign exchange risk. Midwest can eliminate the currency risk by entering into a forward currency swap that becomes effective three months from now.[8]

The marketplace also offers options to originate swaps and to terminate swaps. Such options are referred to as *swaptions*. Swaptions are very important in managing debt that can be called by corporate management. A significant amount of corporate bonds are callable, but the analysis of such features is beyond the scope of this text.[9]

Mark-to-Market Valuation of Currency Swaps

It is conventional to refer to the value of a security or financial instrument as the amount that the long position must pay to undertake the position. Thus, the value of a currency swap is the payment that must be made by the long position to assume the swap position at that time. The value of a swap is a negative number if a payment is necessary to initiate a short position in the swap.

The value at origination of an at-market swap is zero, since the swap is constructed to avoid any time 0 payment in either direction. The valuation of off-market swaps at origination has already been covered. The value of the swap in Example 6-2 was $38,899.

We now demonstrate the valuation of fixed-for-fixed currency swaps after origination. The principle behind this valuation is the same as that for the valuation of off-market swaps at origination. This valuation is sometimes referred to as mark-to-market, or MTM, valuation.[10]

---

[8]This scenario is adapted from Raj E. S. Venkatesh, Vijaya E. Venkatesh, and Ravi E. Dattatreya, "Structural Variations in Currency Swaps," in Biedleman, *Cross Currency Swaps*.

[9]For a useful presentation on forward swaps and swaptions, see Keith C. Brown and Donald J. Smith, "Forward Swaps, Swap Options, and the Management of Callable Debt," *Journal of Applied Corporate Finance*, Winter 1990, pp. 59–71.

[10]A discussion of MTM valuation of currency swaps is in Daniela Giberti, Marcello Mentini, and Pietro Scabellone, "The Valuation of Credit Risk in Swaps: Methodological Issues and Empirical Results," *Journal of Fixed Income*, March 1993, pp. 24–36. For another, brief example of the valuation of fixed-for-fixed currency swaps, see Keith C. Brown and Donald J. Smith, "Currency Swaps: Quotation Conventions, Market Structures, and Credit Risk," in Biedleman, *Cross Currency Swaps*.

The analysis of currency swap positions is a critical function of global financial management.

Once a currency swap originates, it will change in economic value as the spot exchange rate changes. What would be the value, for example, just after the second interest settlement, of the 5-year, $1,000,000, 6% dollar for 9% French franc currency swap, introduced earlier, assuming that the swap originates as an at-market swap when the exchange rate was $X_{FF/\$}^0 = 5$ FF/\$?

To answer this question, we would need to know (1) the spot exchange rate at that future time and (2) the discount yield curves at that time of the two currencies, for a horizon equal to the remaining life of the swap. In this case, the swap has three settlement times left, since it was given that the second settlement has just been made.

To focus only on the influence of the exchange rate change, let us assume that after the second settlement, the discount yield curves show a flat 6% for 1-year, 2-year, and 3-year eurodollars and a flat 9% for 1-year, 2-year, and 3-year French francs, the same interest rates as the original coupon rates of the swap.

Thus, with 3 years left, the market value of the dollar payments of $60,000 for 3 years, plus the principal payment of $1,000,000, given the flat 6% dollar yield curve, is $1,000,000 (= $60,000/1.06 + 60,000/1.06^2 + 1,060,000/1.06^3). Similarly, the value of the payments of FF450,000 for 3 years plus the FF5,000,000 principal payment is FF5,000,000. Note that the assumption of a flat discount yield curve equal to the coupon rate means that the value of a bond is equal to its par value.

Now if the spot exchange rate is 5 FF/$ at this time, the swap value is 0, since the present values of the two sides of underlying cash flows balance each other. If, instead, the spot exchange rate were 6 FF/$ at this time, the FF5,000,000 value of the French franc cash flows would only be equivalent to a dollar value of $833,333.33. The value of the swap, from the viewpoint of the long position on French francs is thus $833,333.33 – $1,000,000 = –$166,666.67. This MTM valuation is diagrammed in Figure 6-7 (panel A).

In this case, the French franc has depreciated from the spot exchange rate at the time of origination, and the long position on French francs has lost value in the amount of $166,666.67. Now, if the party with the long position on French francs wants to liquidate his swap position in the open market, essentially finding a third party to assume the long position on French francs, the third party would expect an initial payment (at time 2) of $166,666.67 as compensation to take the negatively valued swap.

Example 6-4 implicitly demonstrates an important point that we'll use later on in Chapter 10. Note in Example 6-4 that the French franc has appreciated in value by 25% (from 0.20 $/FF to 0.25 $/FF) and the MTM gain on the swap from the point of view of the long position has been 25% of the face value of the swap. The point is that, all else the same, the *MTM gain/loss on the swap from the point of view of the long position on the foreign currency is the same*

EXAMPLE 6-4

Continue the text example, demonstrating the value of the swap to the long position on French francs after the second payment, if the spot exchange rate were 4 FF/$, but all else remains the same.

Solution 6-4   At a time 2 exchange rate of $X^2_{FF/\$}$ = 4 FF/$, the present value, after the second notional interest settlement, of the remaining French franc cash flows, is FF5,000,000 and is equivalent to FF5,000,000/(4 FF/$) = $1,250,000. Thus, the value of the swap from the viewpoint of the long position on French francs is $1,250,000 – $1,000,000 = $250,000. The party that is currently long on the French francs would require a compensation payment of $250,000 to turn his swap position over to a third party, given the assumed current spot exchange rate of 4 FF/$ and the time 2 dollar and French franc interest rates. In this case, the French franc has appreciated relative to what the exchange rate was when the swap originated, and the swap's long position on French francs increased by $250,000 in value because of the appreciation of the French franc.

A. Interests Rates (Market) Equal to Coupon Rates of Currency Swap

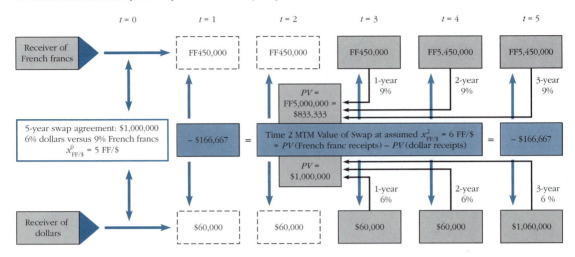

Mark-to-market valuation of 6% U.S. dollar for 9% French franc fixed-for-fixed currency swap on $1,000,000 at time 2. Swap originated at time 0, when spot exchange rate was $x^0_{FF/\$}$ = 5 FF/$. Cash flows at times 1 and 2 already settled (represented by dashed lines). Time 2 value of swap to long position on French francs (receiver of French franks), assuming $x^2_{FF/\$}$ = 6 FF/$, is PV (remaining French franc receipts) − PV (remaining dollar payments) = FF5,000,000/(6 FF/$) − $1,000,000 = $833,333 − $1,000,000 = −$166,667.

B. Interests Rates (Market) Not Equal to Coupon Rates of Currency Swap

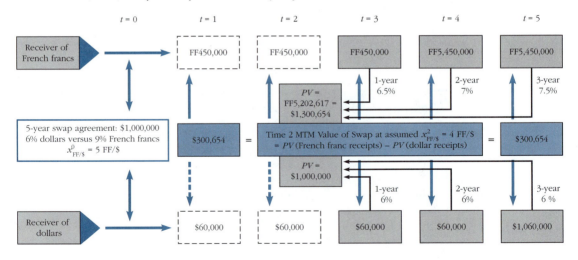

Mark-to-market valuation of 6% U.S. dollar for 9% French franc fixed-for-fixed currency swap on $1,000,000 at time 2. Swap originated at time 0, when spot exchange rate was $x^0_{FF/\$}$ = 5 FF/$. Cash flows at times 1 and 2 already settled (represented by dashed lines). Time 2 value of swap to long position on French francs (receiver of French franks), assuming $x^2_{FF/\$}$ = 4 FF/$, is PV (remaining French franc receipts) − PV (remaining dollar payments) = FF5,202,617/(4 FF/$) − $1,000,000 = $1,300,654 − $1,000,000 = $300,654.

FIGURE 6-7 Mark-to-Market (MTM) Valuation of Fixed-for-Fixed Currency Swaps

percentage of the notional principal as the percentage of appreciation/depreciation of the foreign currency.

Of course, changes in interest rates will have an effect on swap values, also. For example, what would be the swap value in Example 6-4 if the time 2 euroFrench franc interest rates were 1 year, 6.5%; 2 year, 7%; and 3 year, 7.5%? The time 2 value of the remaining French franc payments, given the new assumed interest rates, would be FF450,000/1.065 + FF450,000/1.07² + FF5,450,000/1.075³ = FF5,202,617. At the assumed spot exchange rate in Example 6-4 of $X_{FF/\$}^2$ = 4 FF/$, the present value of the French franc payments has a dollar value of FF5,202,617/(4 FF/$) = $1,300,654. Thus, the value of the swap from the viewpoint of the long position on French francs is $1,300,654 −$1,000,000 = $300,654.

In this case, the value of the swap has increased from time 0 for two reasons. First, the French franc has appreciated relative to the dollar from $X_{FF/\$}^0$ = 5 FF/$ at the swap's origination to $X_{FF/\$}^2$ = 4 FF/$ after the second payment. Second, the recipient of French franc payments benefits from the lower market rates of interest assumed to prevail for French francs at time 2. This MTM valuation is also diagrammed in Figure 6-7 (panel B).

Summary

This chapter has covered an instrument in widespread use in global financial management, the currency swap. Currency swaps are used to help widen financing alternatives, permitting firms to hedge their currency exposure when issuing low-cost financing in foreign currencies. It can be said that currency swaps played a significant role in globalizing the world's financial markets.

Through currency swaps and other market innovations, corporate financial management has gradually learned that the choice of market, type of instrument, and currency in which debt is raised can be totally divorced from the type of liability it ultimately wishes to assume.

Currency swaps, like forward exchange contracts, may be viewed in the context of physical delivery of cash flows pertaining to underlying financial instruments. A fixed-for-fixed currency swap is essentially an exchange of fixed coupon bond payments in one currency for those of another currency. A fixed-for-floating currency swap, also called a cross-currency swap, is essentially an exchange of fixed coupon bond payments in one currency for floating rate payments of another currency.

Like forward exchange contracts, currency swaps often involve cash settlement with difference checks. In fact, a fixed-for-fixed currency swap is really nothing more than a package of off-market forward exchange positions of various maturities and payment sizes, since the principal payment is much larger than the interest payments. The valuation of currency swaps was covered from the point of view of valuing the underlying financial instruments represented in the swap.

Glossary

At-Market Swap: A swap whose present value is zero and involves no time 0 cash flow to initiate a position.

Back-to-Back Loan: A precursor to currency swaps, involving "loan" payments by a parent company in country A to the subsidiary of a parent firm from country B, and vice versa, even though the loan proceeds "canceled" and thus are not exchanged.

Bilateral Closeout Netting: The settlement of a swap cash flow with a difference check, rather with an exchange of the contract cash flows.

Circus Swap: A fixed-for-fixed currency swap that is synthetically constructed from a cross-currency swap and an interest rate swap.

Contract Exchange Rate: The forward exchange rate for an underlying payment of a currency swap.

Cross-Currency Swap: See *Fixed-for-Floating Currency Swap.*

Exchange Market Swap: An exchange of currencies for a set amount of time, or more precisely, a combination of a spot exchange transaction and a forward exchange transaction in the opposite directions.

Fixed-for-Fixed Currency Swap: An exchange of periodic cash flows based on the concept of exchanging fixed coupon bond payments in one currency for those of another currency.

Fixed-for-Floating Currency Swap: Also called a cross-currency swap, an exchange of periodic cash flows based on the concept of exchanging fixed coupon bond payments in one currency for floating rate payments of another currency.

Forward Swap: A swap in which there is a delay between the date on which the swap is contracted and the date of the first cash flow.

Interest Rate Swap: A fixed-for-floating swap in the same currency.

Mark-to-Market Valuation (of Swaps): The economic amount that must be paid to the long position in a swap to assume that position. The amount may be negative.

Notional Principal: The fictional amount of bond principal, upon which a swap's payment amounts are based.

Off-Market Swap: A swap whose present value is not zero and involves an immediate cash flow to initiate a position.

Outright Forward Exchange Contract: The same as a forward exchange contract (Chapter 4); the outright term implies that the contract was constructed from an exchange market currency swap combined with a spot exchange transaction.

Parallel Loan: A precursor to currency swaps, a parallel loan involves a loan by a parent company in country A to the subsidiary of a parent firm from country B, and vice versa.

Swap Points: The difference between a forward exchange rate and the corresponding spot exchange rate, often times 100.

Swap Rate: The difference between a forward exchange rate and the spot exchange rate, expressed as a percentage of the spot exchange rate, in simple annualized terms.

Swap-Driven Financing: The use of swaps as a planned part of a financing scheme.

Discussion Questions

1. Explain the advantages of a parallel loan arrangement in a world of segmented financial markets.

2. Explain why a currency swap accomplishes the same objectives as a parallel loan arrangement, but in a better way.

3. Explain why a firm might wish to engage in swap-driven financing.

Problems

1. You wish to enter into a 6-year fixed-for-fixed currency swap, such that the cash flow stream you are receiving is in Japanese yen and the cash flow stream you are paying is in U.S. dollars. The swap is to be based on a principal of $1,000,000. What are the cash flows upon which the currency swap is based, if the swap is an at-market swap and the 6-year par coupon rates are 7% for dollars and 7% for yen, and if the spot exchange rate is currently $X_{¥/\$}^0 = 140$ ¥/$?

1. You would be receiving ¥9,800,000 per year for 6 years and a principal payment of ¥140,000,000 at year 6.

2. Extend the previous problem, continuing to assume that the time 0 spot exchange rate is $X^0_{¥/\$}$ = 140 ¥/$. Suppose you still want to make the future payments on a 6-year, 7% coupon par U.S. dollar bond, but instead of receiving based on a 6-year, 7% coupon yen par bond, you wish to receive based on a 6-year, 12% coupon, yen bond. Assume that the market-required yield to maturity on 6-year, 12% coupon, yen bonds is 10%. Would you have to pay or receive a time 0 payment and how much?

3. Consider a 6-year fixed-for-fixed currency swap of 7% U.S. dollars for 7% Japanese yen. The current (time 0) spot exchange rate is 140 ¥/$, which is also the contract exchange rate. The notional principal is $1,000,000. Find the difference check settlement, from the party long on yen to the party short on yen, if the yen appreciates to 120 ¥/$ at time 1 (the time of the first payment).

4. What would be the settlement of principal at maturity of the swap in the previous problem if the spot exchange rate at that time is $X^6_{¥/\$}$ = 150 ¥/$?

5. Consider a 6-year, fixed-for-fixed currency swap of 5% U.S. dollars for 8% British pounds at the current spot exchange rate of $X^0_{\$/£}$ = 1.60 $/£ on notional principal of $1,000,000. Find all the difference check settlements, including the final one on the notional principal, if the dollar-pound spot exchange rate is 1.80 $/£ at every settlement time in the future.

6. What is the MTM value, after 3 payments, of a 6-year $1,000,000 5% fixed dollar versus 7% fixed yen currency swap that originated as an at-market swap when the spot exchange rate was 140 ¥/$. Assume a spot exchange rate of $X^3_{¥/\$}$ = 112 ¥/$ at time 3, that market interest rates on 1-year, 2-year, and 3-year euroyen are all 7% at time 3, and similarly that market interest rates on 1-year, 2-year, and 3-year eurodollars are all 5% at time 3.

7. Rework the previous problem assuming that the euroyen interest rates after the third settlement are 1 year, 8%; 2 year, 8.5%; and 3 year, 9%. Every other assumption still holds.

The next two problems are not represented by chapter coverage, but are provided as advanced problems for the eager student.

2. You should make a time 0 payment of $87,105 (or ¥12,194,700).

3. The net payment to the long position on yen is $11,666.67.

4. The long position on yen settles the principal on the swap at maturity with a difference check of $66,666.67 to the short position on yen.

5. The long position would receive 6 payments of $40,000 from the short position to settle the notional interest payments and would also receive $125,000 from the short position on pounds at time 6 to settle the notional principal.

6. The swap has a dollar value of $250,000.

7. $188,141.

8. Assume that U.S. Tyroid issues £2,500,000 in sterling-denominated FRNs at LIBOR plus 75 basis points and simultaneously takes a currency swap position to receive sterling at 1-year sterling LIBOR flat and pay dollars at 5% fixed. At the time of the financing the spot exchange rate is 2.00 $/£. Assume that U.S. Tyroid would have to pay a 6% coupon rate on a par issue of dollar bonds. Suppose that one year after the swap-driven financing is placed, the 1-year sterling LIBOR is 10%. What is Tyroid's savings at year 2 from the swap-driven financing, if the exchange rate is still 2.00 $/£ at time 2?

9. Assume that the discount yield curve is a flat 8% in both British pounds and U.S. dollars and the current spot exchange rate is 2.00 $/£. Find the time 0 payment of a $1,000,000, 4-year, off-market, cross-currency swap of 8% fixed coupon British pounds versus floating rate dollars at LIBOR plus 1.5%. What is the value of the swap after 1 year to the floating dollar receiver, if the pound interest rates have not changed, the dollar discount yield curve has dropped to a flat 5%, and the exchange rate is $X^1_{\$/£} = 1.75$ $/£?

The following problem and answer relate to material presented in the appendix.

A-1. Assume that the current spot dollar/pound exchange rate is $X^0_{\$/£} = 1.60$ $/£, while the 1-year forward exchange rate is $F_{\$/£} = 1.50$ $/£. How would the "swap rate" (for exchange market swaps) be quoted? If the 1-year eurodollar LIBOR is 8%, what is the interest rate differential between the sterling LIBOR and the dollar LIBOR; relate this differential to the swap rate quote.

8. The net benefit of the swap-driven financing at time 2, given $X^2_{\$/£} = 2.00$ $/£, is $12,500.
9. The value of the swap to the floating dollar receiver is $165,849.
A-1. The sterling interest rate is 15.2%; the dollar is at a forward premium.

EXCHANGE MARKET
CURRENCY SWAPS

An *exchange market currency swap* refers to an exchange of currencies for a set amount of time, or more precisely, a spot exchange transaction and a simultaneous forward exchange transaction in the opposite direction.

For example, suppose Citibank wants to borrow £1,000,000 to service some retail customers, and Citibank is willing to lend the equivalent amount in dollars. Assume a term of one year. Citibank finds a partner in the interbank market, exchanges dollars into pounds in the spot exchange market, and simultaneously executes a 1-year dollar-denominated short forward position on pounds with the same other bank. Thus, at time 0, Citibank acquires the pounds and contracts at the current 1-year forward exchange rate to deliver pounds back 1 year from now. The two banks in this illustration have used the currency market to swap the use of pounds for the use of dollars for one year.

This discussion implies that an exchange market currency swap is a "synthetic" instrument constructed from basic "building block" transactions, namely, a spot exchange and a forward exchange contract. However, the market actually developed with spot exchange transactions and swap transactions as the fundamental trades. A forward exchange transaction was actually the derivative in the market, constructed synthetically by combining a swap with a spot exchange transaction. Such a forward contract is referred to as an *outright forward* and was a product developed to meet the needs of corporations along the lines described in Chapter 4.

For this reason, forward exchange rates are often quoted via the so-called *swap rate*. The swap rate is the difference between the forward exchange rate and the spot exchange rate, expressed as a percent of the spot exchange rate, in simple annualized terms. For example, assume that the spot exchange rate is $X^0_{\$/£}$ = 2.00 $/£ and the 1-year forward exchange rate is $F_{\$/£}$ = 2.05 $/£. Thus, the pound is at a forward premium. In this example the 1-year swap rate is (2.05 $/£ − 2.00 $/£)/(2.00 $/£) = 0.05/2.00 = 0.025 or 2.5%.

The difference between the forward exchange rate and the spot exchange rate (0.05 $/£), when multiplied by 100, is often referred to as the *swap points*. In this example the market would quote 5 *swap points*. Given a swap rate or points quote, traders know which currency is at the forward premium and which is at the forward discount by the magnitudes of the bid versus the ask.

The swap rate represents a way to express the interest rate differential in the two currencies. Extending the example, given that $X^0_{\$/£}$ = 2.00 $/£ and $F_{\$/£}$ = 2.05 $/£, if the 1-year dollar interest rate is $r_\$$ = 12%, then the 1-year pound interest rate is $r_£$ = [(2.00 $/£)(1.12)/(2.05 $/£) − 1] = 0.0927, or about 9.27%, according to the covered interest parity condition (see Chapter 4). The 2.5% quoted swap rate may be used to link the two interest rates, since 1.0927(1.025) = 1.12.

Thus, the swap rate expresses (multiplicatively) the interest rate differential between the two currencies. Thus, if Lloyd's lends Citibank pounds for 1 year and Citibank correspondingly lends Lloyd's dollars for 1 year, the swap rate simply expresses the interest rate differential that Lloyd's must pay, as impounded in the forward exchange rate, due to the higher interest rate on dollars prevailing in the global market.

▣ EXAMPLE 6A-1

The spot exchange rate for French francs is 5 FF/$, while the 1-year forward exchange rate is 5.50 FF/$. How would the 1-year swap points and swap rate be quoted? If the 1-year eurodollar LIBOR is 4%, find the interest rate differential between the French franc LIBOR and the dollar LIBOR; relate this differential as a swap rate quote.

Solution 6A-1   The quoted swap points would be 100(5.50 - 5.00) = 50. The quoted swap rate is (5.50 FF/$ − 5.00 FF/$)/(5.00 FF/$) = (0.50 FF/$)/(5 FF/$) = 0.10, or a 10%, with 1-year forward French franc at a discount. If $r_\$$ is 4%, then covered interest rate parity dictates that the 1-year r_{FF} is [(5.50 FF/$)(1.04)/(5.00 FF/$) − 1] = 0.144, or 14.4%. The (multiplicative) interest rate differential is (1.144/1.04) − 1 = 0.10, the swap rate quoted on the 1-year French franc.

chapter 7

TOPICS IN STRUCTURED GLOBAL FINANCING AND THE USE OF OPTIONS

Structured financing is the use of derivatives positions embedded into, or in combination with, conventional financing instruments. The use of structured financing has grown tremendously in the 1990s, due largely to the opportunities of the global financial markets. Structured financing is generally motivated by an issuer's desire to reduce financing costs.

One approach has been to offer investors a package with features that appeal directly to the investors' appetites, but the features are otherwise not available to the investors. For supplying the features, the issuer gets paid a premium by the market, in the form of reduced financing costs. If the issuer does not like the risk exposure created by the inclusion of the features, the issuer's investment bank will often be able to develop a low-cost method for the issuer to offset the unwanted exposure, as part of the financing deal.

Sometimes, the issuer will want to retain the exposure of the derivatives features if the features can reduce the credit risk borne by the investors. The reduction in the investors' risk means that the investors will require a lower rate of return, and thus the financing cost to the issuer is lowered.

The previous three chapters have introduced examples of structured global financing within the topics of forward contracts, eurobonds, and currency swaps. This chapter extends the coverage of structured global financing even further. After a brief discussion of interest rate swaps and commodity swaps, the topic of options is covered in detail.[1]

Options, such as puts, calls, and variations of puts and calls, have played a significant role in global finance. This chapter reviews the basics of options and discusses some of the important aspects of option usage in global financial management.

Interest Rate Swaps and Commodity Swaps

INTEREST RATE SWAPS

An *interest rate swap* is a fixed-for-floating swap in the same currency. The first interest rate swaps were constructed synthetically out of two currency swaps. For example, an interest rate swap to receive floating U.S. dollars and pay fixed U.S. dollars may be synthetically constructed from a fixed-for-fixed currency swap to pay fixed coupon dollars and *receive* fixed coupon French francs and simultaneously a fixed-for-floating currency swap to *pay* fixed coupon French francs and receive floating dollars. The net position is one of paying fixed coupon dollars and receiving floating rate dollars.

Convention in the interest rate swap market is to define the long position as the receiver of floating interest payments and the payor of fixed rate payments. Correspondingly, the short position in an interest rate swap receives fixed interest payments and makes floating rate payments. Recall that in swap parlance, positions are called counterparties. Thus, one having the long position in an interest rate swap is called the long counterparty. Often, it is easier simply to define the two counterparties in an interest rate swap as the pay fixed (or receive floating) position and the receive fixed (or pay floating) position.

After the initial interest rate swaps were synthetically constructed, the direct intermediation of interest rate swaps developed rapidly, exploiting the global interbank network; global banks competed vigorously to provide intermediation services to potential users, located around the globe, of interest rate swaps. The size of the interest rate swap market soon grew much larger than that of the currency swap market.

Many corporate clients wanted long positions in interest rate swaps to effectively convert floating rate debt into fixed rate debt. For example, the market is often more receptive to buying floating rate notes that a company issues than the company's fixed coupon bonds, especially during volatile interest rate times. This receptive market may be in another country. Even

---

[1]In addition to the citations in footnote 4 of Chapter 5, insights on the topic of structured debt are in Leland Crabbe and Joseph D. Argilagos, "Anatomy of the Structured Note Market," *Journal of Applied Corporate Finance*, Fall 1994, pp. 85–98.

though the company itself may not want the interest rate risk of making floating rate interest payments on FRNs, it may find that by issuing the FRNs and then taking a long position in an interest rate swap to hedge that risk, the company can synthetically convert to fixed coupon debt that is at a lower effective financing cost than issuing actual fixed coupon debt directly into an unreceptive market. See panel A of Figure 7-1.

On the other side, many financial institutions have an asset structure that produces income that naturally fluctuates with interest rates, due to the short-term nature of the loans made to customers. While some of a financial institution's liabilities are short term (the deposits of customers), much of a financial institution's capitalization is long term. This situation creates interest rate risk out of this mismatch of maturities. Thus, financial institutions often like short positions in interest rate swaps to pay floating coupon interest and receive fixed coupon interest. Such positions allow the institutions to synthetically convert fixed coupon liabilities into effective floating rate liabilities, which more directly match assets in terms of maturities.[2] See panel B of Figure 7-1.

Most, but not all, interest rate swaps use a LIBOR interest rate as the floating rate. The quotes in Figure 6-2 imply that a long position in an at-market, 5-year, U.S. dollar interest rate swap would have received payments based on

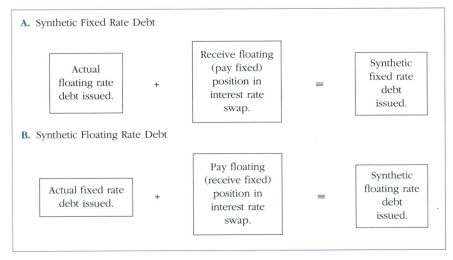

FIGURE 7-1   Synthetic Fixed Rate and Floating Rate Debt

---

[2]An excellent discussion of this practice may be found in Ben Esty, Peter Tufano, and Jonathan Headley, "Banc One Corporation: Asset and Liability Management," *Journal of Applied Corporate Finance*, Fall 1994, pp. 33–51. Also see the commentaries following that article.

LIBOR (flat) and paid fixed interest based on an annual coupon rate of 9.26%. A short position would have made payments based on LIBOR (flat) and received level dollar payments based on an annual coupon rate of 9.20%.

Interest rate swaps are generally settled semiannually via a difference check. The time $t + 1$ cash flow to the long position is known one period before and is found by multiplying the swap's notional principal by the difference between the time t 6-month floating rate and the fixed coupon rate, and then dividing by 2, because of the semiannual feature. For example, assume you have a long position in the 5-year interest rate swap, mentioned in the prior example, with a notional principal of $1,000,000. The first 6-month payment is known at the time the swap is originated and is based on the 6-month LIBOR at that time. If the 6-month LIBOR at time 0 was 7%, then the long position cash flow at time 1 is $1,000,000(0.07 − 0.0926)/2 = −$11,300. The negative number means that the long position (floating receiver) pays the short position (fixed receiver) $11,300 to settle the swap cash flows at time 1. If the 6-month LIBOR at time 1 is 11%, then the settlement at time 2, from the viewpoint of the long counterparty, is $1,000,000(0.11 − 0.0926)/2 = $8700.

In an interest rate swap there is no need to consider the principal payment at the maturity of the swap. The par value of the floating component is in the same currency and in the same amount as the par value of the fixed component in an interest rate swap. Thus, the principal amounts at maturity are ignored, because they are assumed to cancel each other exactly. In contrast, the principal components on currency swaps (covered in the prior chapter) do not cancel, because the exchange rate at the maturity is generally different from the contract exchange rate.[3]

COMMODITY SWAPS

Commodity swaps are based on a notional agreement to ship fixed quantities of a commodity for a fixed price in a currency, over a number of periods. While the agreement is ultimately the same as if the commodity were physically delivered, commodity swaps in practice are settled with difference checks, based upon the spot price of the commodity at the time of the notional periodic shipment.

---

[3]For helpful discussions on the uses of interest rate swaps, see Laurie S. Goodman, "The Uses of Interest Rate Swaps in Managing Corporate Liabilities," *Journal of Applied Corporate Finance*, Winter 1990, pp. 35–47, and Robert Einzig, "Swaps at Transamerica: Applications and Analysis," *Journal of Applied Corporate Finance*, Winter 1990, pp. 48–58. Some theory of the interrelationships between interest rate swaps, cross-currency swaps, and fixed-for-fixed swaps is in Rudy Yaksick, "Swaps, Caps, and Floors: Some Parity and Price Identities," *Journal of Financial Engineering*, June 1992, pp. 105–115. Additional insight may be obtained from Donald J. Smith, "The Arithmetic of Financial Engineering," *Journal of Applied Corporate Finance*, Winter 1989, pp. 49–58.

For example, suppose you enter into a commodity swap to receive copper and pay dollars, which is regarded as a long position in the swap on copper. Assume that the contract size is 2000 tons of copper per period and the contract price is $100,000 per ton. If the actual price of copper at the time of one of the "shipments" is $120,000 per ton, then you would receive (2000 tons)($120,000/ton − $100,000/ton) = $40,000,000 in a cash settlement. If the price of copper is instead $70,000 per ton, then you would "receive" (2000 tons)($70,000/ton − $100,000/ton) = −$60,000,000 in a cash settlement. Since your receipt is negative, you would pay $60,000,000 to the swap counterparty that is short on copper.

Figure 7-2 demonstrates the role of both commodity swaps and interest rate swaps in a fascinating global financing problem.[4] The examination of this financing case provides a vivid picture of the role of financial engineering in global finance. The problem begins in the lower left-hand corner of the chart with the Latin American copper mining company, Mexicana de Cobre.

In 1989, Mexcobre was a recently privatized company in need of $210 million in financing. Since the Latin American capital markets were not developed enough to provide financing, Mexcobre sought the financing in the form of a syndicated loan from several global banks representing developed countries.

However, the banks were nervous about lending money in Latin America, given the region's history of political upheaval and the threat of nationalization and/or default. A deal was put together by the French bank Banque Paribas, which specializes in commodity swaps. The deal involved a sales contract between Mexcobre and the Belgian copper fabricator, SOGEM, for 4000 tons of copper per month, roughly one-third of Mexcobre's monthly output.

Instead of sending payments for the copper back to Mexcobre, SOGEM agreed to forward payments to an escrow account in New York. These payments were "floating" in that the amounts depended on the world price of copper, as reflected in the London Metals Exchange (LME) price. Banque Paribas executed a commodity swap on 4000 tons of copper with the escrow account, in which the escrow account would pay the floating side and receive the fixed amount of $2000 per month.

Thus, the escrow account would receive a fixed amount of dollars per month and would thus guarantee timely repayments of interest and principal

---

[4] The flowchart in Figure 7-2 was graciously provided by the Risk Management Research Group of the Chase Manhattan Bank. The original appeared in an article by Paul B. Spraos in *Corporate Risk Management*, which is no longer in print. Details of the case may be found in Gregory J. Millman, "Financing the Uncreditworthy: New Financial Structures for LDCs," *Journal of Applied Corporate Finance*, Winter 1991, pp. 83–89, and in Laurent Jacque and Gabriel Hawawini, "Myths and Realities of the Global Market: Lessons for Financial Managers," *Journal of Applied Corporate Finance*, Fall 1993, pp. 81–90.

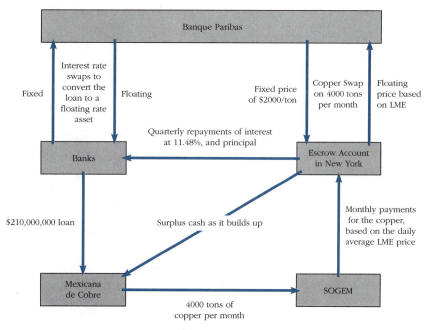

FIGURE 7-2   The Role of Commodity and Interest Rate Swaps in a Global Financing Problem

Source: Originally published in *Corporate Risk Management.* Reprinted by permission of *CFO Magazine,* holder of rights.

to the syndicate banks, and at an interest rate that the banks could not resist, 11.48%. In effect, the banks received servicing and repayment of the loan without the risk inherent in receiving payments directly from Mexcobre. Since the $2000 per month on 4000 tons is more than enough to make quarterly payments on an 11.48%, $210 million loan, the difference was forwarded to Mexcobre as its profit. Banque Paribas thus ultimately took on and managed the commodity price risk involved, which is a business in which the bank specializes.

Currency Options

Options are derivative instruments, just as currency swaps are. Like currency swaps, currency options are often used to manage exchange rate exposure and to help arrange financing deals in such a way as to allow a firm to lower its cost of capital.

The two basic types of options are calls and puts. You may have studied these instruments in other courses. These two basic options are reviewed in the paragraphs that follow, and some of their uses in global financial man-

Structured global financing, like that arranged for the copper mining company, Mexcobre, helps overcome segmentation and facilitates international commerce.

agement are demonstrated. In addition, the appendix to this chapter provides some coverage of *exotic options*, which is a general label that has evolved to refer to the many creative adaptations of basic calls and puts.

CALLS AND PUTS

A *call option* gives its owner the right to buy a stated amount of a commodity at a stated price, while a *put option* gives its owner the right to sell a stated amount of a commodity at a stated price. Options are traded on a very wide variety of commodities, including shares of stock, foreign currencies, and physical commodities, such as oil, or even "undeliverable" commodities, such as stock indexes and inflation indexes. Foreign currency options are emphasized in this chapter, but there is also some discussion of oil options and stock index options.

The stated price at which a call (put) permits the underlying instrument to be bought (sold) is referred to as the *exercise price*, or often the *strike price*. This contractually set price should not be confused with the market-determined price that the option buyer must pay for the option itself, which is often called the *option premium*, but is also referred to simply as the option price.

An option owner is not required to exercise an option. In the case of a call option, if the market price of the commodity is below the exercise price of the call, it would be irrational for the call option owner to exercise and purchase the commodity at the exercise price when the commodity could be purchased in the open market at a lower price. In the case of a put option, if the market price of the commodity is above the strike price of the put, it would be irrational for the put option owner to exercise and sell the commodity at the exercise price when the commodity could be sold in the open market at a higher price.

If exercise of an option is rational, the exercise of an option is often merely a cash settlement rather than an actual exercise. For example, assume that you own a currency call option contract that is denominated in U.S. dollars, and the underlying commodity is British pounds sterling. Assume that the size of the call option contract is 10,000 British pounds and that the exercise price is 1.50 $/£. If the spot exchange rate were 1.60 $/£ in the actual market, then your option contract technically gives you the right to purchase pounds for $1.50, and you could turn right around and sell them for $1.60, for a gain of $0.10 per pound.

Rather than go through the procedure implied by the exercise mechanics, of actually buying and selling the pounds, the option market may simply allow you to receive $0.10 per pound sterling in cash, when you make the exercise decision. In this example, the total dollar proceeds from the exercise is £10,000(0.10 $/£) = $1000. Whether or not these cash proceeds from the exercise represent a *net* profit depends on the amount paid for the call option contract when you bought it. Note that had the exchange rate been below 1.50 $/£, it would not be rational to exercise the call option.

In general, the exercise value of a dollar-denominated call on currency C is given by equation (7-1):

$$V_C = C\#(X^e_{\$/C} - K_{\$/C}), \text{ if } X^e_{\$/C} > K_{\$/C}$$

$$= 0, \text{ otherwise}$$

where

V_C = the exercise value of the call option

$C\#$ = the contract *size*, in units of currency C

$X^e_{\$/C}$ = the exchange rate at the exercise time, expressed in direct terms from the point of view of the currency in which the contract is denominated

$K_{\$/C}$ = the exercise price of the option, expressed in direct terms from the point of view of the currency in which the contract is denominated.

Figure 7-3 shows the exercise values for the call option in our example for various possible spot exchange rates. A payoff diagram of these exercise values is also shown. Note that below the strike price, the call option is val-

---

EXAMPLE 7-1

(a) Find the exercise value of the call option in the text example, if the exchange rate is 1.75 $/£ at the time of exercise. (b) Find the exercise value of the call option in the text example, if the exchange rate is 1.25 $/£ at the time of exercise.

Solution 7-1 (a) $V_C = £10,000(1.75 \ \$/£ - 1.50 \ \$/£) = \$2500$.
(b) Since $£10,000(1.25 \ \$/£ - 1.50 \ \$/£) = -\$2500$, which is negative, the exercise value of the call is 0.

---

ueless, while above the strike price, the option increases in value linearly and proportionately to increases in the dollar price of the pound (the $/£ exchange rate). Options generally have a deadline for exercise, referred to as the *expiration time* of the option. Often options have an expiration time a few months into the future, but many expire several years into the future. When a corporation sells options with long expiration times, the options are sometimes referred to as *warrants*. Some foreign currency exchange warrants are discussed later in the chapter.

Sometimes, an option may only be exercised at the expiration time, but not before. Such an option is referred to as a European-style option, or simply a *European option*. An option that can be exercised anytime prior to the expiration time is referred to as an *American option*. These terms do not imply geographical location, since there are many European options traded in the United States and many American options traded in Europe. (In the spirit of "fair" representation for significant economic areas in the global market, one

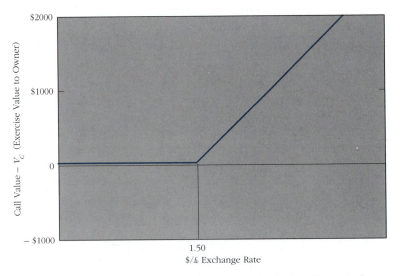

FIGURE 7-3 Exercise Values for the Call Option in Our Example for Various Possible Spot Exchange Rates

of the exotic options covered in the appendix to this chapter has come to be called an *Asian option.*)

In many cases, the privilege of early exercise of an American option has little or no value, in and of itself. The reason is that the fair market value for the option is often higher than the exercise value, and thus it would be better for the option owner to *sell* the option rather than to exercise it, if the option owner wanted to liquidate the option position. For example, if the market value of the call option on the British pounds in the example earlier had a market value of 0.12 $/£, then selling it for that price would be better than exercising it for 0.10 $/£.

*T*HE DERIVATIVES DEBATE: ARE DERIVATIVES GOOD OR BAD?

Derivatives generally refer to forward contracts, swaps, options, and their variations. Some variations on swaps were mentioned in Chapter 6, while some variations on options and forwards are discussed in the appendix to this chapter. In addition, there are a host of other variations beyond the scope of this text, such as indexed coupon swaps, participating currency caps, multirate forward extendible swaps, spreadlock swaps, reverse zero-cost collars, and so forth.

As you should be able to tell from Chapters 4 through 7, derivatives have been useful in (1) integrating global financial markets, (2) enabling financing that otherwise would not be possible, and (3) managing risk. In addition, by themselves, derivatives are used by many speculators. Informed speculation has a desirable economic function of increasing the efficiency of financial markets, but uninformed speculation is gambling. Unfortunately, the opportunity to take excessive, and often unauthorized, risks in derivatives speculation has created a number of problems for many organizations, including the headline cases of Allied Lyons, Procter & Gamble, Orange County, and Barings Plc.

Currently, there is a debate over derivatives. Some argue that derivatives should be regulated, so that the problems making the headlines cannot occur. Others believe strongly that the benefits of unregulated derivatives far outweigh the drawbacks. The latter position is the one that we see in "The Financial Economists Roundtable Statement on Derivatives Markets and Financial Risk," signed by 33 of the world's most distinguished financial economists, including three Nobel Prize winners, and appearing in the *Journal of Applied Corporate Finance,* Fall 1994, pp. 4–7.

OPTION WRITING

For every option owner, or buyer, there is an option seller, often referred to as the *option writer.* The option writer has no option to exercise, but instead must play a passive role against the owner's exercise decision. However, the option writer receives the premium from the option buyer as compensation for giving the buyer the exercise option. The buyer pays a premium to the call writer to buy the option, and it is the call option writer's responsibility to pay the exercise value.

The option writer's gain is the option buyer's loss, and vice versa. The net profit/loss to the writer and the buyer depends upon the exercise value of the option when it is exercised and how much the option buyer paid the writer for the option when the contract was originated. The written option position is sometimes referred to as the short position in the option, as opposed to the buyer's position, which is often called the long position in the option.

Figure 7-4 depicts the exercise payoff profile from the point of view of the writer of the call option of Figure 7-3. Note that below the strike price, the call

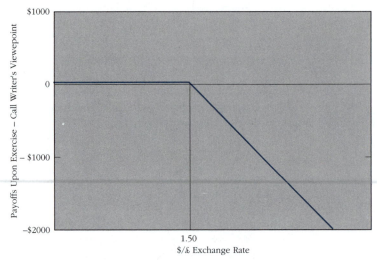

FIGURE 7-4 The Exercise Payoff Profile from the Point of View of the Writer of the Call Option of Figure 7-3

EXAMPLE 7-2

You write a dollar-denominated call option on ¥1,000,000 with a strike price of 0.008 $/¥. At the time you write the call, the option premium is 0.0003 $/¥. If the exchange rate is 100 ¥/$, what is the exercise value of the call option? What would be your net profit/loss if a rational exercise decision is made? What if the exchange rate were instead 140 ¥/$?

Solution 7-2 The call gives the owner the right to buy ¥1,000,000 from you at 0.008 $/¥, and the owner can sell the yen for 1/(100 ¥/$) = 0.010 $/¥. The exercise value of the option is V_C = ¥1,000,000(0.010 $/¥ – 0.008 $/¥) = $2000. This is the amount you would have to pay to cash settle your written call option position. Since you received a premium of 0.0003 $/¥, you took in ¥1,000,000(0.0003 $/¥) = $300 when you wrote the call. Your net loss is thus $1700. If the spot exchange rate were 140 ¥/$, then exercising would involve selling yen for a lower price, specifically, 1/(140 ¥/$) = 0.00714 $/¥, than purchasing. Thus, exercise by the owner is not rational, and the option's exercise value is zero. In this situation, your net profit/loss is a $300 gain, the amount of initial premium from the option write.

option entails no exercise liability to the writer, since it would not be rational for the owner to exercise. Above the strike price, the option writer's value decreases linearly and proportionately to increases in the dollar price of the pound (the $/£ exchange rate), reflecting the increase in the exercise value of the call option.

Foreign currency options are traded in significant volume in the global over-the-counter interbank market. In addition, foreign currency options are traded on exchanges in various financial centers of the world. In these markets, if it is understood in context that the base currency is dollars, the call option in the example might be referred to as a "pound call." However, to avoid ambiguity with the British perspective of a pound-denominated call option on dollars, we'll refer to the option in this example as a dollar-denominated call option *on* pounds.

PUTS

In general, the exercise value of a dollar-denominated put on currency C is given by equation (7-2):

$$V_P = C\#(K_{\$/C} - X^e_{\$/C}), \text{ if } X^e_{\$/C} < K_{\$/C}$$

$$= 0, \text{ otherwise}$$

For example, consider a put option on 10,000 British pounds, and the exercise price of the put is 1.50 $/£. If the exchange rate were 1.35 $/£ in the actual market, the exercise value of the put option is £10,000(1.50 $/£ – 1.35 $/£) = $1500.

Your option contract technically gives you the right to sell pounds for $1.50, and you can buy them for $1.35, for a gain of $0.15 per pound. Rather than go through the procedure of actually buying and selling the pounds, you may accept a settlement of $0.15 in cash, per pound, when you make the exercise decision. In this example, the total cash proceeds from exercise is £10,000(0.15 $/£) = $1500. Whether or not these cash proceeds from the exercise represent a *net* profit depends on the amount that you paid for the put option when you bought it.

Figure 7-5a shows the exercise values for the put option in the text exam-

---

EXAMPLE 7-3

You own an American put option on 10,000 British pounds and the exercise price is 1.50 $/£. (a) If the exchange rate were 1.25 $/£ in the actual market, what is the exercise value of the put option? (b) If the exchange rate were 1.75 $/£ in the actual market, what is the exercise value of the put option?

Solution 7-3 V_P = £10,000(1.50 $/£ – 1.25 $/£) = $2500. (b) If the exchange rate were above 1.50 $/£, it would not be rational to exercise the put option.

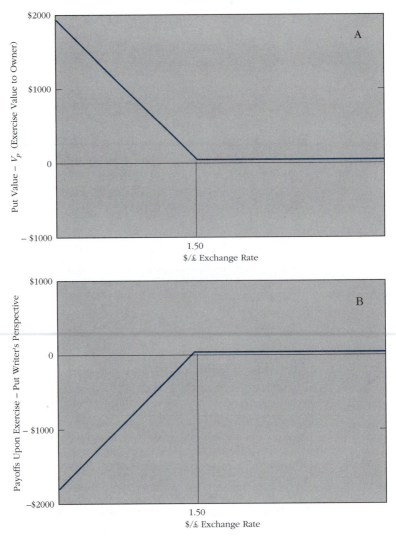

FIGURE 7-5 • Exercise Values for a Put Option for Various Possible Spot Exchange Rates (A) and the Corresponding Payoffs upon Exercise from the Put Writer's Perspective (B)

ple and Example 7-3 for various possible spot exchange rates. Note that above the strike price, the put option is valueless, while below the strike price, the option increases in value linearly and proportionately to decreases in the dollar price of the pound (the $/£ exchange rate).

The put writer's payoffs are the reciprocal of the owner's. Figure 7-5b depicts the payoff profile from the point of view of the writer of the put option of Figure 7-5a. Note that above the strike price, the put option entails no exercise liability to the writer, since it would not be rational for the owner to exercise. Below the strike price, the option writer's value decreases linearly and proportionately to decreases in the dollar price of the pound (the $/£ exchange rate), reflecting the increase in the exercise value of the put option.

When the market price of the currency (or other commodity underlying a call option) exceeds the exercise price of a call option, the call is said to be *in the money*. By the same token, when the market price of the commodity is less than the exercise price of a call option, the call is said to be *out of the money*. Similarly, an in-the-money put option describes a situation where the exercise price of the put exceeds the current market value of the commodity, whereas an out-of-the-money put describes the opposite situation. An *at-the-money* option is one where the market price of the commodity is equal to the strike price of the option. All else equal, the lower the strike price of a call, the higher the premium that must be paid to purchase the call. By the same token, the higher the strike price of a put, the higher the premium that the buyer of the put must pay to the writer.

OPTIONS AND TRANSACTION EXPOSURE TO FOREIGN EXCHANGE RISK

Corporate treasurers like to employ currency options in the management of currency exposure for a number of reasons. At this time, we consider one of the most prominent motivations, the hedging of transaction exposure without the loss of "upside potential."

In Chapter 4, the topic of transaction exposure was introduced. It was demonstrated at that point that this exposure may be managed via forward exchange contracts. However, the use of forward exchange contracts, while eliminating "downside risk," involves giving up the possible opportunity gains from exchange rate movements. Many corporate treasurers prefer to pay a premium for an option that eliminates downside exposure while allowing the "upside" opportunity gains.

For example, consider a U.S. dollar-based company with a natural receivable of DM100,000, due in 3 months. Instead of going short a 3-month dollar forward contract on marks to hedge the natural long exposure of the receivable to the value of the mark, what would happen if a 3-month dollar-denominated put on 100,000 marks is purchased with a strike price of 0.625 $/DM? The answer is that a minimum value DM100,000(0.625 $/DM) = $62,500 is assured on the combined receivable-plus-put position.

To see this point, note that if the spot dollar value of the mark is below 0.625 $/DM at the expiration time in 3 months, then the put option pays off the difference between 0.625 $/DM and the actual spot value, times DM100,000. This payoff will compensate for the value of the receivable being less than $62,500. For example, if the exchange rate turns out to be 1.75 DM/$, which is equivalent to 1/(1.75 DM/$) = 0.5714 $/DM, the put pays off V_P = DM100,000(0.625 $/DM - 0.5714 $/DM) = $5360. The mark receivable is worth DM100,000(0.5714 $/DM) = $57,140. Thus, the total payoff on the receivable-plus-put is $57,140 + $5360 = $62,500. In combination, the payoff on the put and the dollar value of the receivable will total to $62,500 for any expiration time value of the mark below 0.625 $/DM. Example 7-4 demonstrates this for another exchange rate.

EXAMPLE 7-4

If the exchange rate turns out to be 2.00 DM/$, demonstrate that the receivable plus the put is worth $62,500.

Solution 7-4 If the exchange rate turns out to be 2.00 DM/$, which is equivalent to 1/(2.00 DM/$) = 0.50 $/DM, the put pays off V_P = DM100,000(0.625 $/DM − 0.50 $/DM) = $12,500. The mark receivable is worth DM100,000(0.50 $/DM) = $50,000. Thus, the total payoff on the receivable-plus-put is $50,000 + $12,500 = $62,500.

If the value of the mark is above 0.625 $/DM at the expiration time, then the put is worthless and the owner simply lets the option expire unexercised. The higher the value of the mark, the higher the dollar value of the mark receivable. The upside opportunity gain is thus obtained, while a downside floor is established.

For various values of the mark, Figure 7-6 shows (a) the natural dollar-based long transaction exposure of the mark receivable; (b) the flat, hedged position when short forward positions are used (a forward exchange rate of 0.625 $/DM is assumed); (c) the payoff profile on the long put position by itself; and (d) the payoffs that result from a combination of (a) and (c) together to create an "insured" long position on marks, that is, when the put option on marks is used to hedge the natural long transaction exposure.

There is an analogous situation for a firm that must make a natural payment in the future in foreign currency. Such a firm has a natural short position in the foreign currency; if the currency appreciates in value, the payable will cost the firm more base currency to make. As we know, this transaction exposure may be eliminated with a long forward position on the foreign currency, but the benefits of a depreciation of the foreign currency would be forgone. If the firm wanted to retain those benefits enough to justify paying the option premium, the firm could buy base currency–denominated calls on the foreign currency. If the foreign currency appreciated in value, the firm would have no worry about the higher base currency value of the natural payable, because that erosion in value would be compensated for by a gain in the call option. If the foreign currency depreciated, the call is not exercised and is worthless, but the company gains by making a lower base currency payment on the natural foreign currency payable.

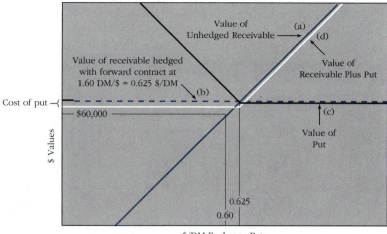

FIGURE 7-6 The Use of a Long Put Option with a Foreign Currency Receivable to Hedge the Downside Risk of Lower Foreign Currency Values and to Allow the Capture of the Upside Benefit of Higher Foreign Currency Values

Figure 7-7 depicts (a) a natural dollar-based short transaction exposure to marks; (b) the flat, hedged position when a long forward position is used to hedge the exposure; (c) the payoff profile on a long call option position by itself; and (d) the combination of subtracting the gains on the call (see c) from the natural payouts (see a) to create an "insured" short position on marks.

The motivations for hedging with options in lieu of forward contracts are diverse. Some treasurers cannot psychologically handle the regret of looking back and thinking "If I only had not hedged, I could have made a big profit from currency conversion." Other treasurers think the following way: "If I hedge with forwards and my competitor does not, and if my competitor incurs opportunity gains that I do not, then my competitor can use his profits to somehow gain a competitive advantage over my company."[5] Merck, Inc., is a company that employs options to manage currency exposure for this reason.[6]

For still other corporate treasurers, avoiding downside risk while capturing upside potential ensures an apparent "no-lose" situation. Of course, for

---

[5]Some examples of this motivation are discussed in G. J. Millman, *The Floating Battlefield: Corporate Strategies in the Currency Wars* (New York: AMACOM, The American Management Association, 1990).

[6]Merck's case serves as a classic introduction to the corporate problem of currency exposure. See J. C. Lewent and A. J. Kearney, "Identifying, Measuring, and Hedging Currency Risk at Merck," *Journal of Applied Corporate Finance*, Winter 1990, pp. 19–28.

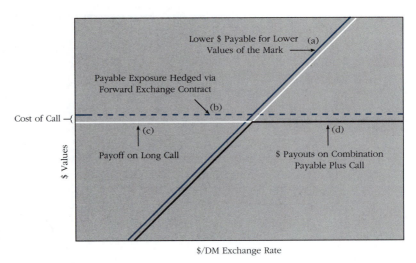

FIGURE 7-7 The Use of a Long Call Option with a Foreign Currency Payable to Hedge the Downside Risk of Higher Foreign Currency Values and to Allow the Capture of the Upside Benefit of Lower Foreign Currency Values

this attractive benefit, we know that the option buyer must pay a price, the premium for the option.

Options are also employed in so-called *selective hedging* strategies. Selective hedging is a speculative approach to hedging based on judgment, or a "view," as to the future direction of exchange rates. Suppose, for example, that a dollar-based treasurer anticipating a receipt of DM100,000 strongly believes that the mark will appreciate in value by the time that the marks will be paid. In this circumstance, the treasurer may wish to buy a dollar-denominated put option on marks, in lieu of a short forward position on marks, to capture the benefits of the mark appreciation while still hedging downside exposure, "just in case" the beliefs were erroneous. If the treasurer believes that the mark will depreciate, then the hedging strategy would employ a short forward position on marks, to avoid paying a premium for the option.

The Swedish shipping company, Argonaut, has reported that it employs a selective hedging strategy in exactly the fashion described: For its natural long foreign currency exposure, Argonaut employs short forward positions when the treasury group takes a bearish view on the value of the foreign currency relative to the base currency, the Swedish krona (SKr).[7]

When its view on the value of the foreign currency is bullish, Argonaut turns to the use of currency put options. Argonaut also employs two other

---

[7]The Argonaut policies are explained in D. Hambrick, "In Search of the Golden Fleece," *Risk*, April 1991, pp. 17–19.

Companies like the Swedish shipping company Argonaut are employing options to manage foreign exchange exposure.

strategies, based on exotic options, in situations when they are less definite about the direction of exchange rates; these strategies are covered in the appendix to this chapter.

Finally, consider the role of options in *contingent hedging,* typified by the following scenario. Suppose you are U.S. dollar-based and have placed a bid of £5,000,000 for a piece of real estate in England. If the pound appreciates and you get the bid, the expense in terms of dollars is larger. Thus, you may consider going long a forward exchange contract on pounds, but then if you do not get the bid, you will lose on the forward exchange contract if the pound depreciates.

If, instead, you buy a call option on pounds, then you'll be covered against an appreciation of the pound if you get the bid. If the pound depreciates, then you will not lose if you do not get the bid, as you would have with a long forward exchange contract position.

The Role of Options in Global Financing

The prior section attempted to demonstrate the range of applications for currency options in the management of transaction exposure to foreign exchange risk. Options have also played an important role in global financing in that many corporate securities have built-in, or embedded, options.

The most obvious option in corporate financing is the often-found call provision in corporate debt issues. In the callability feature, the issuing company has the option to recall (buy) the debt for a set price. As is well known, such a recall may be advantageous if interest rates drop after the debt is issued, such that the market value of the debt increases. In effect, the bond-holders have implicitly written a call option on the bond to the company issuing the bond.

Another rather common built-in option in eurobonds is the convertibility into common stock. Bonds that are convertible into stock have been around since well before eurobonds. However, as was pointed out in Chapter 5, investors in the eurobond market have had a very large appetite for bonds that carry the option to convert into common stock at the discretion of the bondholder. The convertibility feature is like having a call option on the common stock with the added feature that the bond can also fluctuate in value due to the influence of interest rate changes.

*F*OREIGN CURRENCY EXCHANGE WARRANTS

To test the notion that the use of options by corporations in financing deals is advantageous, consider the study performed on a number of corporate issues of *foreign currency exchange warrants (FCEWs)*. FCEWs are much the same as currency options, but are generally for longer terms and are cash-settled only; that is, physical delivery of foreign currency is not permitted. The study found that the FCEWs were generally overvalued to the end-user investors. In one example cited, the Student Loan Marketing Association (Sallie Mae) in 1987 was able to price 2 million FCEWs on yen to the public at $4.375 per warrant. After paying an underwriting fee of $0.35 per warrant to Morgan Stanley, Sallie Mae's proceeds were 2,000,000($4.375 − $0.35) = $8,050,000. Sallie Mae effectively aggregated the demand by retail investors, who had no access to the interbank currency option market. On the same date, Sallie Mae purchased 2 million currency options from Bankers Trust Company at a price of $3.3675 per warrant, for a net cost of $6,735,000. The currency options had the same contract specifications as the warrants. The size of the trade made it possible for Sallie Mae to obtain a price from Banker's Trust that was considerably below the offering price of the FCEWs. Sallie Mae made a net arbitrage profit of $1.315 million.

The study and the Sallie Mae example are in Richard J. Rogalski and James K. Seward, "Corporate Issues of Foreign Currency Exchange Warrants: A Case Study of Financial Innovation and Risk Management," *Journal of Financial Economics,* December 1991, pp. 347–366.

CURRENCY OPTION BONDS

In addition to the rather well-known features of callability and convertibility, global financial markets have responded well to the inclusion of many other innovative option features in corporate financing packages. One important example is the *currency option bond,* which is a bond denominated in one currency, but which gives the owner the option to receive payment in another currency, based upon a contractual exchange rate that is usually close to the spot exchange rate at the time the bond is issued. In effect, the ownership of a currency option bond is the same as owning a straight bond plus a call option on a foreign currency. To see this point, consider the following numerical example.

EXAMPLE 7-5

You can issue a 3-year, zero-coupon, dollar-mark currency option bond at a 3% yield to maturity. The currency option bond gives its owner the right to accept the principal repayment in dollars or in marks at 2.00 DM/$, which is the assumed exchange rate at the time the bond is issued. Show that the right to receive the principal payment in the form of either $1,000,000 or DM2,000,000 (investor's choice) is equivalent to giving the investor a 3-year, U.S. dollar, zero-coupon bond for principal of $1,000,000 plus a call option on DM2,000,000 with a strike price of 0.50 $/DM (= 2.00 DM/$). To demonstrate, compare what the investor will have under both approaches if the spot exchange rate ends up at 0.60 $/DM in three years.

Solution 7-5   The bond owner has the U.S. dollar zero-coupon bond plus a call on DM2,000,000 at a strike of 0.50 $/DM. If the mark is valued at 0.60 $/DM at the bond's maturity, for example, the bond owner will get $1,000,000 in principal plus DM2,000,000(0.60 $/DM – 0.50 $/DM) = $200,000. The total value of the bond and the option is $1,000,000 + 200,000 = $1.2 million. This is the same as taking the principal payment in the form of DM2,000,000 and exchanging it into dollars at 0.60 $/DM, which is DM2,000,000(0.60 $/DM) = $1.2 million. If the value of the mark at the bond's maturity is less than 0.50 $/DM, then the call option would not be exercised. The rational nonexercise of the call is economically equivalent to accepting the principal repayment of the currency option bond in the form of $1,000,000 instead of DM2,000,000.

Why are option features like that of currency option bonds popular? One reason is that many institutional portfolio charters restrict the outright purchase of options. But if a charter does not restrict the positioning of bonds with a few "bells and whistles," then managers of the portfolio can get in on the "betting action" of currency plays without specifically trading options, per se. If the issuing company can take advantage of its ability to sell options in this way, a profitable implicit price may be charged for the option feature. Indeed, if the issuer can buy the same option in the interbank market at a lower price than the implicit price of the option feature sold in the bond issue, then the company has employed financial engineering to find an arbitrage opportunity and lower its financing costs.

The next example demonstrates this idea and extends Example 7-5. Also see Figure 7-8.

Of course, the reason that the company in Example 7-6 is able to exploit the opportunity in the market is that the bond's buyers are not able to buy the currency options themselves directly in the market.

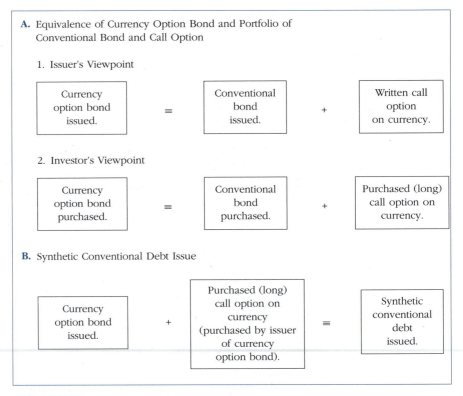

FIGURE 7-8 Currency Option Bonds

*B*ULL AND BEAR NOTES

Option features in global financing packages are not always related to exchange rates. For a while, the inclusion of warrants of the Nikkei-Dow Japanese stock market were popular features of eurobond issues. The reasoning was the same; some bond portfolio managers were able to "play" the volatile Japanese stock market moves, even though charters and regulations might prohibit such speculation directly for both funds.

Consider the details of the issue by the kingdom of Denmark in 1986 of FF800 million worth of notes, with payoffs linked to the performance of the French stock market. The issue consisted of two separate tranches—one called *Bulls* and the other *Bears*—of FF400 million each. The annual coupon rate of the notes was 4.5%. Each *Bear* note combined a 5-year, FF450 annuity (4.5% of FF10,000 of face value for 5 years) and a 5-year European put option on the French stock index with an exercise price of 896.45. (At the time of the issue the stock market index was at 405.97.) The *Bull* note consisted of a 5-year, FF450 annuity plus a long position in the stock market index minus a 5-year European call option with an exercise price of 896.45. (The latter call option gave the issuer the option to call the *Bull* notes at FF23,200 if the stock market reached 896.45, effectively capping the notes' value.)

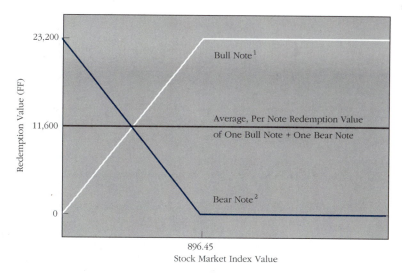

FIGURE 7-9   Bull-Bear Notes: Redemption Value as a Function of Stock Market Index Value

[1]The redemption value of the Bull note equals 25.88 times the Index value, up to a maximum redemption value of FF23,200 when the index reaches 896.45 or above.
[2]The redemption value of the Bear note equals FF23,200 minus the redemption value of the Bull note.

Together, one *Bull* and one *Bear* note had a fixed redemption value of FF23,200 and annual interest payments of FF900 for FF20,000 worth of face value, implying a yield to maturity of 7.27%. At the same time, 5-year AAA French franc fixed coupon debt would require an 8% interest rate. By issuing the *Bull* and *Bear* package, the kingdom of Denmark was able to innovatively issue synthetic fixed coupon bonds, but at a reduced financial cost relative to an actual issue of fixed coupon bonds. Had options on the French stock market otherwise been available to investors at the time, the *Bull* and *Bear* notes would not have been able to be sold with a scarcity premium on the options. As it was, however, the kingdom of Denmark was able to profit from the recognition of the market demand for specific option instruments on the French stock market index.

This description and Figure 7-9 are taken from Laurent Jacque and Gabriel Hawawini, "Myths and Realities of the Global Market: Lessons for Financial Managers," *Journal of Applied Corporate Finance*, Fall 1993, pp. 81–90. Figure 7-9 reprinted by permission.

OIL OPTIONS IN THE SONATRACH DEAL[8]

In 1989 Algeria's state-owned oil company, Sonatrach, borrowed $100 million from a syndicate of lenders in an innovative financing arranged by Chase

[8]This case is abstracted from Charles W. Smithson and Donald H. Chew, "The Uses of Hybrid Debt in Managing Corporate Risk," *Journal of Applied Corporate Finance*, Winter 1992, pp. 79–89 Figure 7-10 is reprinted with permission.

Investment Bank in London. Sonatrach was not considered to be very credit-worthy from the viewpoint of the syndicate banks, who would have therefore required a very high coupon rate on straight debt, a rate too high for Sonatrach to pay.

EXAMPLE 7-6

Assume that your company wishes to raise debt capital and desires the liability to be in the form of a straight 3-year, zero-coupon liability with a face value of $1,000,000. The market yield to maturity for the zero would be 6%. You could issue the currency option bond in Example 7-5, with a lower yield to maturity of 3%, but you do not want the exposure to the $/DM exchange rate. You find that you can buy 3-year currency call option on marks with strike = 0.50 $/DM for a price of 0.03 $/DM. Which is a better strategy: (1) Issue the straight zero, or (2) issue the currency option bond and hedge the exposure, creating a synthetic straight zero-coupon bond via financial engineering?

Solution 7-6   If you issue the currency option bond, you can cover your exposure by buying the call, essentially converting your short currency option bond position into a short straight 3-year zero. The cost of the currency option at time 0 would be DM2,000,000(0.03 $/DM) = $60,000. If you issue the 3% currency option bond, the proceeds at time 0 are $1,000,000/$1.03^3$ = $915,141.66. Thus, the net proceeds from the hedged currency option bond financing would be $915,141.66 − $60,000 = $855,141.66. Compare this to a straight 3-year zero proceeds of $1,000,000/$1.06^3$ = $839,619.28. The synthetic zero offers more proceeds per $1,000,000 of time 3 liability than the straight bond and thus represents a lower-cost financing alternative.

However, the rate that was charged to Sonatrach was low, 1% over LIBOR for the life of the debt. The reason that the low coupon was charged was that two option kickers were included in the package: (1) If the price of oil rises above a specified level, lenders receive additional payments from Sonatrach, which would presumably be in a position to meet the higher payment with its additional oil revenues. (2) If oil prices drop below a specific level, the syndicate lenders receive an additional payment from Chase to compensate for the presumably more risky position of the oil price–dependent Sonatrach.

The LIBOR + 1% pricing of the debt depended on Sonatrach granting Chase a series of call options on oil. Chase, in turn, wrote the puts and calls on oil to the syndicate members, as mentioned in the previous paragraph. Chase also managed the mismatch of the options—that is, the mismatch between the calls obtained from Sonatrach and those sold to the syndicate members—by trading in the market that exists for oil puts and calls. The Sonatrach financing deal is diagrammed in Figure 7-10.

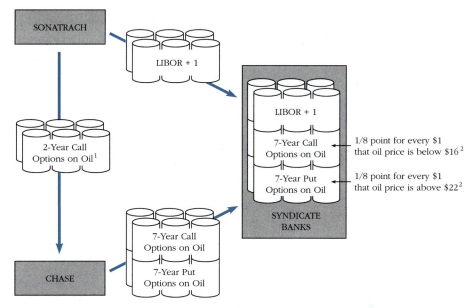

FIGURE 7-10 The Sonatrach Financing Deal

[1] During the first two years, if the price of oil exceeds $23, Sonatrach will pay a supplemental coupon to Chase.

[2] In the first year, the syndicate receives additional interest if the price of oil falls outside the range of $16–22. In year 2, the range widens to $15–23, then $14–24 in year 3, and to $13–25 in years 4–7.

EQUIVALENCE OF CALLS AND PUTS FROM CURRENCY PERSPECTIVE

Because the right to buy yen with dollars is the same as the right to sell dollars for yen, a dollar-denominated call on yen is the same instrument as a yen-denominated put on dollars, and a dollar-denominated put on yen is the same instrument as a yen-denominated call on dollars.

More precisely, a dollar-denominated call option on x yen is equivalent to a yen-denominated put on y dollars, where y is derived by converting x at the exercise exchange rate. For example, consider a dollar-denominated call option contract on x = 100,000 French francs with a strike price of 0.125 $/FF. Next consider a French franc–denominated put option contract on dollars with a strike price of 1/(0.125 $/FF) = 8 FF/$ and a contract size of y = FF100,000/(8 FF/$) = $12,500.

To see that these two options are equivalent, compare their exercise values if the present spot exchange rate is 7 FF/$. Since 7 FF/$ is equivalent to 0.1429 $/FF, the dollar-denominated call on French francs is worth FF100,000(0.1429 $/FF – 0.125 $/FF) = FF100,000(0.01786 $/FF) = $1,786. The French franc–denominated put on dollars is worth $12,500(8 FF/$ – 7 FF/$) = FF12,500. Note that at the exchange rate of 7 FF/$, the payoff on the put on dollars (FF12,500) is equivalent to the payoff on the call on French francs [$1,786 = FF12,500/(7 FF/$)].

Summary

A significant portion of the chapter focuses on currency options and their applications in managing transaction exposure to foreign exchange risk and in global corporate financing. In general, the chapter concluded the text's section on global financing and financial engineering. The Sonatrach deal demonstrates a global financing arrangement that otherwise would not have been possible without the derivatives, innovation, and financial engineering. The same may be said for the Mexcobre deal covered earlier in the chapter. These examples are highlights of a chapter that attempts to convey the role of financial engineering and derivatives in the globalization of the financial marketplace.

Glossary

American Option: An option that can be exercised anytime prior to the expiration time.

Asian Option: An exotic option whose payoffs are based on the average value of the underlying commodity's price over the life of an option.

At-the-Money Option: An option where the market price of the underlying commodity is equal to the strike price of the option.

Barrier Options: A type of exotic, path-dependent option that has a barrier on the validity of the option. See *Knock-out* and *Knock-in Options*.

Call Option: A derivative instrument that gives its owner the right to buy a stated amount of a commodity at a stated price.

Currency Option Bond: A bond denominated in one currency, but which gives the owner the option to receive payment in another currency, based upon a contractual exchange rate.

Cylinder: A type of exotic option constructed by combining a purchased put on a foreign currency and writing a call on the same currency with a higher exercise price than on the put.

European Option: An option that may only be exercised at the expiration time.

Exercise Price: The stated price at which a call (put) permits a commodity to be bought (sold). Also called the strike price.

Exotic Options: A general reference to many creative adaptations of basic calls and puts.

Expiration Time: The deadline for exercise of an option.

Foreign Currency Exchange Warrants (FCEWs):   The same as currency options, but are generally for longer terms and are cash-settled only; that is, the physical delivery of foreign currency is not permitted.

In-the-Money Call: When the market price of the underlying commodity is greater than the exercise price of the call option.

In-the-Money Put: When the market price of the underlying commodity is less than the exercise price of the put option.

Knock-in Call Option: An exotic option that is not in effect to the buyer unless the value of the underlying commodity falls below the knock-in price; this option is also known as a *down-and-in call.*

Knock-in Put Option: An exotic option that is not in effect to the buyer unless the value of the underlying commodity rises above the knock-in price; this option is also known as an *up-and-in put.*

Knock-out Call Option: An exotic option that becomes void to the buyer if the value of the underlying commodity falls below a contractual knock-out price; this option is also known as a *down-and-out call.*

Knock-out Put Option: An exotic option that becomes void to the buyer if the value of the underlying commodity rises above the knock-out price; this option is also known as an *up-and-away put.*

Lookback Option: A type of exotic, path-dependent option that specifies payoffs based upon values that have been taken by the underlying commodity during the life of the option.

Out-of-the-Money Put: When the market price of the underlying commodity is greater than the exercise price of the put option.

Option Premium: The market-determined price that the option buyer must pay for the option, also referred to simply as the option price.

Participating Forward: By reducing the size of the written call position in a conventional range forward, the company can retain a proportion of the upside potential of an appreciation of the foreign currency above the call's strike price.

Path-Dependent Options: A class of exotic options whose payoffs depend not only on the difference between the value of the commodity and the exercise price at the time the exercise decision is made, but also on the path that the value of the commodity takes over time during the life of the option.

Put Option: A derivative instrument that gives its owner the right to sell a stated amount of a commodity at a stated price.

Range Forward: A combination of a cylinder with a long forward position on the foreign currency.

Selective Hedging: A speculative approach to hedging based on judgment as to the future direction of exchange rates.

Strike Price: The stated price at which a call (put) permits a commodity to be bought (sold). Also called the exercise price.

Strike-out Price: The price at which a knock-out option becomes invalid.

Warrants: Options issued by companies and having long expiration times.

Zero-Cost Cylinder: A special cylinder where the strike prices are structured such that the proceeds from selling the call option are exactly equal to the outlay that will be necessary to purchase the put option.

Discussion Question

1. Do you think derivatives should be regulated?

Problems

1. Assume that you own a currency call option contract that is denominated in U.S. dollars, and the underlying commodity is German marks. Assume that the size of the call option contract is 10,000 German marks and that the exercise price is 0.6667 $/DM. (a) If the spot exchange rate were 1.60 DM/$ in the actual market, what is the exercise value of the call? (b) Find the exercise value of the call option, if the exchange rate is 1.25 DM/$ at the time of exercise.

2. You write a dollar-denominated call option on £10,000 with a strike price of 1.50 $/£. At the time you write the call, the option premium is 0.05 $/£. (a) If the exchange rate is 1.75 $/£, what is the exercise value of the call option? What would be your net profit/loss if a rational exercise decision is made? (b) What if the exchange rate were instead 1.25 $/£?

3. You own an American put option on 10,000 German marks and the exercise price is 0.6667 $/DM. (a) If the exchange rate were 1.25 DM/$ in the ac-

---

1. (a) zero; (b) $1333.
2. (a) –$2000. (b) $500.
3. (a) zero. (b) $952.38.

tual market, what is the exercise value of the put option? (b) If the exchange rate were 1.75 DM/$ in the actual market, what is the exercise value of the put option?

4. Consider a U.S. dollar–based company with a natural payable of DM100,000, due in three months. The company is evaluating a 3-month call option on 100,000 marks with a strike price of 0.80 $/DM. If the exchange rate turns out to be 1.15 DM/$, (a) what is the company's inflow from the call, and (b) what is the company's net dollar payments on the payable-plus-call option?

5. You can issue a 3-year, zero-coupon dollar-pound currency option bond at a 4% yield to maturity. The currency option bond gives its owner the right to accept the principal repayment in dollars or in pounds at 1.50 $/£, which is the assumed exchange rate at the time the bond is issued. The face value of the bond is $1,000,000. Assume that the spot exchange rate ends up at 1.60 $/£ in three years. (a) What is the dollar value of the principal repayment to the bondholder at maturity? (b) Show that this amount is the same as that of a 3-year, U.S. dollar zero-coupon bond for principal of $1,000,000 plus a call option on £666,667 with a strike price of 1.50 $/£.

6. Assume that your company wishes to raise debt capital and desires the liability to be in the form of a straight 3-year, zero-coupon liability with a face value of $1,000,000. The market yield to maturity for the zero would be 5%. You could issue the currency option bond in Problem 5, with a lower yield to maturity of 4%, but you do not want the exposure to the $/£ exchange rate. You find that you can buy 3-year currency call option on pounds with strike = 1.50 $/£ for a price of 0.05 $/£. Which is a better strategy: (a) Issue the straight zero, or (b) issue the currency option bond and hedge the exposure, creating a synthetic straight zero-coupon bond via financial engineering?

7. The dollar-denominated call on 10,000 marks in Problem 1 is the same as a mark-denominated put on how many dollars, with what strike price? Find the expiration time value of the put if the spot exchange rate were 1.25 DM/$ in the actual market and show that this value should be equivalent to that of the call in Problem 1.

4.   (a) $6960; (b) $80,000.

5.   (a) $1,066,667. (b) The total value of the straight zero-coupon bond and the call option is $1,000,000 + $66,667 = $1,066,667.

6.   The net proceeds from the hedged currency option bond financing would be $855,663, less proceeds per $1,000,000 of time 3 liability on the straight bond.

7. $6667; 1.50 DM/$; $1,333.33.

EXOTIC OPTIONS

The global financial marketplace has been extremely creative in its financial engineering and applications with options. In general, options beyond basic calls and puts have come to be called exotic options, or simply *exotics*. While there are as many different exotics as one's imagination will allow, we categorize some commonly found exotics along three lines: (1) combinations, (2) path-dependent options, and (3) other specific-purpose options.

Combinations of calls and puts can be engineered by treasurers to accomplish specific purposes. A *cylinder* is constructed by combining a purchased put on a foreign currency and writing a call on the same currency with a higher exercise price than on the put. The company with a natural long exposure that employs a cylinder is then protected against a decline in the value of the foreign currency below the strike price of the put, but it can take advantage of any appreciation of the foreign currency up to and including the call's strike price. If the foreign currency appreciates above the strike price of the call option, the call will be exercised and the company must sell the foreign currency at the call's strike price. Thus, there is both a floor and a cap on the company's exposure to the foreign currency.

The Swedish shipping company Argonaut has reported that it employs this strategy to manage its natural exposure when it has a "neutral to slightly bearish view" on the future direction of the foreign currency. Figure 7-A1 shows the idea of using a cylinder to manage currency risk.

Cylinders are often assembled by banks and sold as a product "off the shelf" to corporate treasurers, but treasurers can sometimes "manufacture" the cylinder themselves. Whether a treasurer purchases this product or assembles one on his or her own, the strategy frequently takes the form of a *zero-cost cylinder*. Since the premium that an option will sell for depends upon the option's strike price, the strike prices of a cylinder may be structured such that the proceeds from selling the call option are exactly equal to the outlay that will be necessary to purchase the put option. Thus, the strategy, in effect, creates the desired protection against a depreciation of the foreign currency, but requires no out-of-pocket cost to the company. The cost of the put is paid for by giving up the potential rewards for the most extreme foreign currency appreciation levels. Since the company can still benefit from some currency appreciation, these cylinders are popular, especially when the treasury group believes that there does not exist much likelihood that the currency will appreciate beyond the call's strike price.

Banks also market a related product, which combines a cylinder with a long forward position on the foreign currency. This product is known as a *range forward*. In effect, the payoffs on a range forward position look like the payoffs of a natural long exposure plus a cylinder.

It is also popular to fine-tune the risk-reward scenario in other ways. For example, by reducing the size of the written call position in a conventional cylinder, the company can retain a proportion of the upside potential of an appreciation on the foreign currency above the call's strike price. When this approach is an adjustment to a range forward, the product is called a *participating forward*. Argonaut reportedly employs a participating forward strategy when the treasury group has a "neutral to slightly bullish view" on the future value of the foreign currency.

Path-dependent options are a class of exotics whose payoffs depend not only on the difference between the value of the commodity and the exercise price at the time the exercise decision is made, but also on the path that the

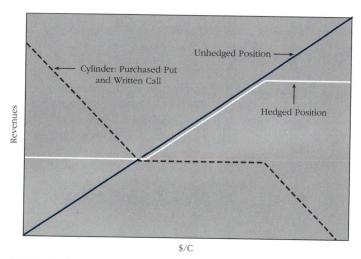

FIGURE 7-A1   A Cylinder and Its Impact on Risk Exposure

value of the commodity takes over time during the life of the option. We'll briefly describe three types of path-dependent exotics: (1) barrier options, (2) lookback options, and (3) average rate ("Asian") options.

Barrier options are also known as *knock-out* and *knock-in options*. There are four basic types of barrier options. A knock-out call option becomes void to the buyer if the value of the underlying commodity falls below a contractual knock-out price, referred to as the *strike-out rate*; this option is also known as a *down-and-out call*. Analogously, a knock-out put option becomes void to the buyer if the value of the underlying commodity rises above the knock-out price; this option is also known as an *up-and-away put*.

These options set limits within which the option is valid, and such options are cheaper to buy for managers who wish to hedge currency exposure. For example, in September 1992 a $1 million, 3-month down-and-out call on pounds sterling, with a strike price of 1.75 $/£ and a strike-out rate of 1.71 $/£, cost around $18,000 (1.8%). By comparison, a $1 million, 3-month regular call option, with a strike price of 1.75 $/£, cost $27,000 (2.7%).[1]

A knock-in call is not in effect to the buyer unless the value of the underlying commodity falls below the knock-in price; this option is also known as a *down-and-in call*. Analogously, a knock-in put option is not in effect to the buyer unless the value of the underlying commodity rises above the knock-in price; this option is also known as an *up-and-in put*.

Barrier options are employed in refined situations about views on the future direction of currency value changes. In addition, the premiums on barrier options are lower than those on basic calls and puts, because of the reduced flexibility involved with barrier options.

Some treasurers, especially those who have problems with giving up the opportunity gains of exchange rate changes, would love to always be able to look back in hindsight and know that they made the best decision possible. For example, suppose a treasurer, at the time a call option expires, could look back and exercise the call for the difference between the highest value achieved by the underlying commodity. Such *lookback options* are readily available in today's global marketplace.

Other types of lookback options are those where one can, at the option's expiration time, set the strike price at the most advantageous price of those experienced by the underlying commodity (the lowest price touched for a call and the highest price touched for a put). Still other types of lookback calls pay off the difference between the highest price and the lowest price experienced by the underlying commodity during the life of the option.

Asian options are popular for purposes of hedging ongoing income streams rather than single transactions, because the payoffs of Asian options are based on the average value of the underlying commodity's price over time.

---

[1]See "Lost in a Maze of Hedges," *The Economist*, October 3, 1992.

For exchange rates, such an average is often used in computing the base currency equivalent of a foreign currency income stream over a specific period of time. There are two basic types of Asian options. The first pays off based on the comparison of the average commodity value over the life of the option relative to a stated exercise price. The second pays off based on a comparison of the commodity's price at the exercise time and the average commodity value.

part III

CORPORATE

EXPOSURE TO

FOREIGN

EXCHANGE RISK

chapter 8

OPERATING EXPOSURE TO EXCHANGE RATE RISK

The measurement and management of the economic exposure of a company to exchange rate risk is a central issue in global financial management. *Economic exposure* to exchange risk is defined to be the variability in a firm's value, or in its ongoing cash flows, caused by uncertain exchange rate changes. Economic exposure is a much more complex problem than *transaction exposure* (covered in Chapter 4), which is the exposure of a single, already-arranged transaction. If reference is to the firm's operating cash flows, economic exposure is called *operating cash flow exposure*, or sometimes simply *operating exposure*. If reference is to the firm's equity value, economic exposure is called *equity exposure*.

This chapter deals with the components and fundamental economic determinants of a firm's operating cash flow exposure, while Chapter 9 deals with a firm's equity exposure and its relationship with operating exposure, financial leverage, and the currency or currencies in which the firm's debt and equity are denominated. In Chapter 10, we'll get into accounting issues and their relationship to a firm's economic exposure.

All three of the chapters in Part III discuss many real-world cases and scenarios. To develop some tools for quantitative analysis, the chapters also employ a number of hypothetical examples that capture the fundamental issues of real-world problems. In this chapter, we begin with the development of those tools; then, as the chapter progresses, we make references to actual companies.

The Measurement of Operating Exposure

Consider XYZ Co., which does business in Germany but whose owners live in the United States. XYZ Co. is assumed to generate cash flows in German marks. Since XYZ's owners have U.S. dollars as their base currency, the owners are ultimately concerned with the dollar equivalent of the mark-denominated cash flows. For example, if the foreign currency cash flows are DM2,000,000 per year and the exchange rate is 2.00 DM/$, the foreign currency cash flows are equivalent to base currency cash flows of DM2,000,000/(2 DM/$) = $1,000,000 per year.

In this example, the base currency equivalent to the mark cash flows are clearly subject to currency exposure, even if the magnitude of the mark cash flows is unaffected by exchange rate changes. For example, assume that the mark depreciates to 2.5 DM/$ and that the mark cash flows are unaffected. Then the equivalent base currency cash flows drop to DM2,000,000/(2.5 DM/$) = $800,000 per year. See Figure 8-1

Thus, from the point of view of the U.S. owners, the base currency equivalent of XYZ's cash flow stream declines as the mark depreciates. Even if the cash flows are not directly converted to dollars each year, a decline in the base currency equivalent of the foreign currency cash flows implies a decline in the base currency market value that the owners would receive from selling the operation.

The exposure problem of XYZ Co. is typical of many companies in the global economy. One actual company that will be mentioned several times is the U.S. pharmaceutical company, Merck. Merck does about 50% of its business in overseas markets, and changes in exchange rates influence the level of Merck's base currency (dollars) cash flows for given levels of foreign cur-

Base Currency ($) Cash Flow Equivalent

$1,000,000 per year if exchange rate = 2.00 DM/$
$800,000 per year if exchange rate = 2.50 DM/$

Foreign Currency Cash Flows

DM2,000,000 per year

FIGURE 8-1 Base Currency Cash Flow Stream Equivalent of a Foreign Currency Cash Flow Stream

rency cash flows.[1] To analyze actual situations, such as Merck's, we must first develop some tools.

The analysis that follows assumes that a firm's flow variables (like operating revenues, costs, or cash flows) are expected to be level perpetuities of annual amounts. Although the realized amount of a flow variable will deviate from the expectation, the exposure of a firm's flow variable to a foreign currency is defined as the percentage change in the *expected* level of the flow variable per year, for a given percentage change in a spot exchange rate. To repeat, we define exposure with respect to changes in *expectations* of flows, rather than with respect to changes in realized flow amounts or to deviations of realized flow amounts from expected flow amounts.

Consider the actual exchange rate at the present point in time, time 0. This exchange rate, in direct terms from the base currency point of view, will be denoted X^0. At time 0, and based upon the time 0 exchange rate, analysts form a subjective *expectation*, or prediction, about the firm's stream of future operating revenues, costs, and cash flows, with the first of those future flows to be realized at the next point in time, which is time 1. Remember that we assume for simplicity that the analysts expect that the future stream of a flow variable is a level perpetuity.

The expected stream of future base currency operating cash flows at time 0, which is based upon the observed time 0 exchange rate, will be denoted O^0. The "0" superscript denotes that the expectation is formed at time 0 and is based upon the spot exchange rate prevailing at time 0, even though the first of the operating cash flows will not be realized until time 1.

Similarly, at time 1, *after* the actual time 1 operating cash flow is realized, analysts are assumed to observe a new spot exchange rate, X^1, and to revise their expectations about the future base currency operating cash flow stream as a result of observing the time 1 spot exchange rate. Thus, as of time 1, the firm expects to receive base currency operating cash flows of O^1 each year into perpetuity, beginning with time 2.

The reason for putting the analysis in terms of expected streams of *future* cash flows is to facilitate the link to valuation, since value will be modeled (in Chapter 9) as the present value of expected future cash flows. In Chapter 10, when we get into accounting issues, we'll discuss the matter of accounting for actually realized cash flows. Of course, factors other than exchange rates can influence the level of a firm's expected and actually realized operating flows (like the state of the global economy, for example). Such other factors are held constant in the analysis that follows, to focus only on the effects of exchange rate movements.

---

[1]The Merck case is discussed in Judy C. Lewent and A. John Kearney, "Identifying, Measuring, and Hedging Currency Risk at Merck," *Journal of Applied Corporate Finance*, Winter 1990, pp. 19–28.

The percentage change in a company's financial accounts, relative to the percentage change in the value of a foreign currency, is elasticity, the analytical basis of measuring economic exposure to exchange rates.

OPERATING CASH FLOW EXPOSURE

Operating cash flows consist of operating revenues (from sales) minus operating costs. Financial costs, like interest on debt, are not relevant in determining operating cash flows. *Operating cash flow exposure* to a foreign currency is defined as the percentage change in the level of the expected base currency operating cash flows for a given percentage change in the base currency value of a foreign currency.

Denote the percentage deviation in O^1 from O^0 as $\%\Delta O = (O^1 - O^0)/O^0 = O^1/O^0 - 1$. Denote the percentage deviation in the new exchange rate from the initial exchange rate as $\%\Delta X = (X^1 - X^0)/X^0 = X^1/X^0 - 1$. Formally, *operating cash flow exposure*, denoted B_O, is the percentage deviation in O^1 from O^0, given the percentage deviation in X^1 from X^0. Thus, $B_O = \%\Delta O/\%\Delta X$, or

$$B_O = \frac{O^1/O^0 - 1}{X^1/X^0 - 1} \qquad (8\text{-}1)$$

Equation (8-1) may be rearranged to give the operating cash flow exposure an interpretation as a multiplier. Given (1) the initial expected base currency operating cash flows (given the current exchange rate), O^0, (2) the operating cash flow exposure, B_O, and (3) the percentage deviation in the time 1 exchange rate from the time 0 exchange rate, $X^1/X^0 - 1$, the new expected base currency operating cash flows per year, O^1, are

$$O^1 = O^0 [1 + B_O (X^1/X^0 - 1)] \qquad (8\text{-}2)$$

The term $B_O(X^1/X^0 - 1)$ in equation (8-2) represents the percentage change in the expected base currency operating cash flows. That percentage change is equal to the operating cash flow exposure, B_O, times the percentage change in the exchange rate, $X^1/X^0 - 1$. Equation (8-2) expresses the new expected base currency operating cash flows, O^1, as equal to the original base currency operating cash flows, O^0, times 1 plus the percentage change (in decimal form) in the expected base currency operating cash flows.[2]

EXAMPLE 8-1

Consider an operation called DEF Co., operating in Germany (or elsewhere), that has U.S. base currency ownership. Let the current exchange rate be 1.50 DM/$, and let the expected future base currency operating cash flows be $500,000 per year. Assume that DEF has an operating cash flow exposure, B_O, of 2.40 to the mark. If the exchange rate goes to 1.80 DM/$ in the next period, by what percentage will the expected base currency operating cash flows change? What will be the new level of future expected base currency operating cash flows?

Solution 8-1   Since the exchange rates are quoted in European terms, they must be converted into direct terms from the base currency (U.S. dollar) point of view. Thus, $X^0 = X^0_{\$/DM} = 1/X^0_{DM/\$} = 1/(1.50\ DM/\$) = 0.667\ \$/DM$, while new exchange rate, X^1 is $1/(1.80\ DM/\$) = 0.556\ \$/DM$. Thus, the percentage change in the mark value is $(0.556\ \$/DM)/(0.667\ \$/DM) - 1 = -0.1667$, or a mark depreciation of 16.67%. Given the operating cash flow exposure of 2.40, the base currency operating cash flows should change by $2.40(-0.1667) = -0.40$, or minus 40%, to $300,000 per year. Using equation (8-2), the new base currency operating cash flows are O^1 $= \$500,000\{1 + 2.4[(0.556\ \$/DM)/(0.667\ \$/DM) - 1)]\} = \$500,000[1 + 2.4(-0.1667)] = \$500,000(0.60) = \$300,000$ per year.

We'll see that a firm's operating cash flow exposure to a foreign currency can be virtually any number. Operating cash flow exposure may be positive or negative, and it may be relatively high or low. Figure 8-2 shows some possible linear relationships between the percentage change in expected operating cash flows ($\%\Delta O$) and the percentage change in the value of a foreign currency ($\%\Delta X$). The slope of a given relationship is the operating cash flow exposure in that situation. Later in the chapter, various real-world and hypothetical scenarios are discussed that relate to various magnitudes of B_O. For the time being, we continue to develop our analytical framework.

---

[2]An elasticity approach to operating exposure is discussed in Christine R. Hekman, "Don't Blame Currency Values for Strategic Errors: Protecting Competitive Position by Correctly Assessing Foreign Exchange Exposure," *Midland Corporate Finance Journal*, Fall 1986, pp. 45–55.

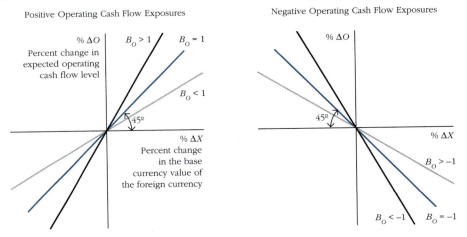

FIGURE 8-2 Possible Operating Cash Flow Exposures

OPERATING CASH FLOW EXPOSURE, OPERATING REVENUE EXPOSURE, AND OPERATING COST EXPOSURE

Since operating cash flows are equal to operating revenues minus operating costs, a firm's operating cash flow exposure to a given currency has three basic components:

1. Operating revenue exposure
2. Operating cost exposure
3. Expected operating cash flow margin

The expected *operating cash flow margin* is defined to be the ratio of expected operating cash flows to expected operating revenues. In this section we establish the relationship between a firm's operating cash flow exposure to a currency and the three components.

Let R^0 and C^0 denote the time 0 expectation of the level of the firm's future base currency operating revenues and operating costs, respectively, given the current exchange rate. The time 0 expected future base currency operating cash flows, O^0, is equal to $R^0 - C^0$. Also, the new level of expected base currency operating cash flows, O^1, is equal to $R^1 - C^1$, where R^1 and C^1 are the new expected levels for the base currency operating revenues and operating costs, respectively, given the new exchange rate.

Operating revenue and cost exposures are defined with similar elasticities as operating cash flow exposure. Operating revenue exposure is $B_R = \%\Delta R/\%\Delta X = (R^1/R^0 - 1)/(X^1/X^0 - 1)$. Operating cost exposure is $B_C = \%\Delta C/\%\Delta X = (C^1/C^0 - 1)/(X^1/X^0 - 1)$.

Equation (8-3) expresses the relationship between a firm's operating cash flow exposure and its components:[3]

$$B_O = B_R \left(\frac{R^0}{O^0} \right) - B_C \left(\frac{C^0}{O^0} \right) \qquad (8\text{-}3)$$

Note that the currently expected operating cash flow margin is O^0/R^0, which is simply the reciprocal of the first bracketed term in equation (8-3). Thus, if $O^0/R^0 = 0.20$, then R^0/O^0 equals 5. Since $C^0 = R^0 - O^0$, then $C^0/O^0 = R^0/O^0 - 1$, which means that the second bracketed term is always equal to the first bracketed term minus 1. If $R^0/O^0 = 5$, then $C^0/O^0 = 5 - 1 = 4$. Thus, both of the bracketed terms in equation (8-3) can be determined by simply knowing the expected operating cash flow margin, O^0/R^0.

EXAMPLE 8-2

Let us illustrate equation (8-3) with a numerical example. Assume an operation has base currency of U.S. dollars and has an operating cash flow exposure to the German mark. Assume that the currently expected base currency operating revenues, R^0, are $1,200,000 per year and that expected base currency operating costs, C^0, are $700,000 per year, given an observed current exchange rate of 1.50 DM/$. Thus, $O^0 = \$1,200,000 - \$700,000 = \$500,000$ per year. Let the operating revenue exposure, B_R, be 1 and the operating cost exposure, B_C, be 0. What is the operating cash flow exposure?

Solution 8-2   Equation (8-3) says that the operating cash flow exposure is $B_O = 1(\$1,200,000/\$500,000) - 0(\$700,000/\$500,000) = 2.4$. Had one only been given the expected operating profit margin of 0.41667 (= $500,000/\$1,200,000), then the computation would have been performed as $1(1/0.41667) - 0[(1/0.41667) - 1]$. (Of course, there is really no need to worry about the C^0/O^0 term in this example since B_C is 0, but it may be useful to specify it here anyway, while one is still getting used to equation (8-3).)

---

[3]There are a number of methods to derive equation (8-3). One simple one is as follows. Note that $O^0 + C^0 = R^0$. Thus, R^0 may be thought of as a portfolio of O^0 and C^0, and any percentage change in R may be expressed as a weighted average of the percentage changes in O and C, where the weights are O^0/R^0 and C^0/R^0, respectively. Thus, we have that $\%\Delta R = \%\Delta O(O^0/R^0) + \%\Delta C(C^0/R^0)$. Multiplying both sides by R^0, we have that $\%\Delta R(R^0) = \%\Delta O(O^0) + \%\Delta C(C^0)$, which rearranges to $\%\Delta O(O^0) = \%\Delta R(R^0) - \%\Delta C(C^0)$. Dividing both sides of the last expression by $\%\Delta X$ and by O^0, and substituting for the definitions of the three pertinent exposures, B_R, B_C, and B_O, equation (8-3) results.

Note that in Example 8-2, a firm with a B_R of 1 and a B_C of 0 has an operating cash flow exposure, B_O, of 2.40, given the expected operating cash flow margin of $500,000/$1,200,000 = 0.41667, or 41.667%. We'll see later in the chapter that this exposure magnification is due to operating leverage.

Since Example 8-2's operating cash flow exposure, exchange rate, and expected future operating cash flow stream are the same as those for DEF Co. in Example 8-1, let us reconcile DEF's new expected future operating cash flow stream (O^1 = $300,000 per year in Example 8-1) through the operating cash flow statement for the firm in Example 8-2, given a 16.67% depreciation of the mark to 1.80 DM/$. Given an operating revenue exposure, B_R, of 1, a 16.67% depreciation of the mark to 1.80 DM/$ means that the new expected base currency operating revenues will be $R^1 = R^0(1 - 0.1667) = $1,200,000(0.8333) = $1,000,000 per year.

Since the new expected base currency operating costs, C^1, will remain at the original expected level of $700,000 per year, by virtue of the zero operating cost exposure, the new expected base currency operating cash flows are $O^1 = R^1 - C^1 = $1,000,000 - $700,000 = $300,000 per year. Thus, the new expected base currency operating cash flow level is consistent with the answer in Example 8-1 for an operating cash flow exposure of B_O = 2.4 and a 16.67% depreciation of the mark.

The Economic Determinants of Operating Exposure

CONVERSION EXPOSURE

Conversion exposure is the uncertainty in the base currency equivalent of a given stream of foreign currency cash flows due to the uncertainty in the exchange rate at which the foreign currency cash flows are converted into the base currency equivalent. Pure conversion exposure results in situations where a firm has cash flows generated in a foreign currency and where none of the economic determinants of the cash flows, like product prices and volume of sales, is influenced by exchange rate changes.

The exposure of Merck, Inc., mentioned previously, is a case of conversion exposure. As exchange rates change, Merck does not change its foreign product prices, nor is the demand for Merck's products affected by economic conditions. Thus, the portion of Merck's base currency operating revenues that are generated overseas are subject to pure conversion exposure.

The next example demonstrates pure conversion exposure analytically. In the example, the firm's expected *foreign currency* operating revenues are *not* affected by exchange rate changes, and the expected *base currency* operating revenues change by the same percentage as the value of the foreign currency; that is, B_R = 1.

A firm's operating cost exposure will depend on the geographical distribution of its production operations and of its suppliers. A firm with purely domestic production and with no imports of raw materials could have an operating cost exposure of zero, $B_C = 0$, to any foreign currency. However, even for a company with domestic suppliers, the prices of the raw materials could be indirectly linked to exchange rates, particularly if the domestic suppliers themselves have operating cost exposures and pass this exposure along.

EXAMPLE 8-3

Consider a German firm, GRE Co., with a base currency of marks. The firm sells products in the United States. GRE expects to do a volume of 500,000 units per year at $2.00 per piece, if the exchange rate maintains its initial level, 1.50 DM/$. Assume that the product's dollar price and expected sales volume do not change as the exchange rate changes. Demonstrate that if the dollar depreciates by 15%, then GRE's expected base currency operating revenues also decline by 15%, that is, that GRE's B_R is 1.

Solution 8-3   The European terms quote is in direct terms from the point of view of the mark as the base currency. Thus, a 15% depreciation of the dollar would imply a new exchange rate of $X^1 = (0.85)(1.50 \text{ DM/\$}) = 1.275 \text{ DM/\$}$. GRE's initial expected foreign currency operating revenues are ($2.00/unit)(500,000 units) = $1,000,000 per year. Initially, the expected foreign currency operating revenues convert to a base currency equivalent of $R^0 = \$1,000,000(1.50 \text{ DM/\$}) = \text{DM}1,500,000$ per year. Since the foreign currency operating revenues are unaffected by the exchange rate change, the new expected base currency operating revenues are $R^1 = \$1,000,000(1.275 \text{ DM/\$}) = \text{DM}1,275,000$ (per year). Thus, the expected base currency operating revenues fall from DM1,500,000 to DM1,275,000, a decline of 15%.

On the other hand, consider the parent with a subsidiary that produces entirely overseas with raw materials that are neither imported nor price linked to exchange rates. From the parent's view, the operating cost exposure of the subsidiary is a case of pure conversion exposure, that is, $B_C = 1$, to the foreign currency of the country in which the production occurs. Alternatively, suppose the subsidiary imports raw materials produced in the parent's country, possibly even by the parent. In this case, from the parent's point of view, the raw materials used by the subsidiary have an operating cost exposure of 0. The subsidiary's foreign currency labor costs may have an operating cost exposure of 1 from the parent's point of view.

The operating cost exposure posed by a firm's imported raw materials may be viewed as the opposite of the exporter's operating revenue exposure. For example, consider GRE's pure conversion exposure, $B_R = 1$, in Example

8-3. The U.S. importer of GRE's products faces stable dollar prices, and thus has an operating cost exposure of $B_C = 0$.

PRICE EXPOSURE

The influence of exchange rate changes is often more complex than a simple conversion effect, because exchange rate changes may lead to changes in the magnitude of the foreign currency cash flows. In some cases, a firm has the power to change its product's price to fully pass through the exchange rate changes with no effect on sales volume. In this case the base currency operating revenues will not change because the foreign currency operating revenues change in such a way as to precisely offset the effect of conversion exposure. In other cases, however, the adjustment of a product's price to an exchange rate change may be nonexistent or only partial.

The case of U.S.-based Vulcan Materials Co. illustrates the scenario where an overseas subsidiary actually poses no operating revenue exposure to its parent.[4] Vulcan's U.K. subsidiary sells metals whose currency of determination is the U.S. dollar. The U.K. subsidiary was able to fully change its products' pound-denominated prices to reflect changes in $/£ exchange rate, with no change in expected sales volume. Thus, from its base currency point of view (the U.S. dollar), Vulcan's operating revenue exposure, B_R, is 0, even though the subsidiary's operating revenues (in pounds) were volatile.

Here is a hypothetical example to explain this type of situation. Suppose a U.S. firm imports parts from the hypothetical German company, Mannheim Co. Assume that the exchange rate is currently 1.50 DM/$ and that the current price charged by Mannheim to the U.S. importer is $2.00/unit, for operating revenues of DM3.00/unit to Mannheim. Suppose the dollar depreciates to 1.25 DM/$; if Mannheim raises the dollar price to $2.40/unit, Mannheim's base currency operating revenues are stabilized at DM3.00/unit.

In this case, the German exporter, Mannheim, has *no exposure* in its base currency operating revenues, even though the revenues are produced in a foreign currency and must be converted. The reason is that, without losing sales, the German exporter is assumed to be able to adjust the foreign currency sales price for exchange rate changes to keep the effective mark sales price, and the expected base currency operating revenues, constant.

For the German exporter to have the power to adjust dollar prices with no change in U.S. volume, it must be true that (i) there are no other viable competing suppliers in the selling market and (2) the U.S. importer's demand is extremely inelastic. An extremely *inelastic demand* is one where the user is willing to order the same volume of products at virtually any price.

These conditions imply that an increase in the dollar selling price, with no

---

[4]The Vulcan Materials case is covered in C. Kent Garner and Alan C. Shapiro, "A Practical Method of Assessing Foreign Exchange Risk," *Midland Corporate Finance Journal*, Fall 1984, pp. 6–17.

loss of expected sales volume, causes Mannheim's foreign currency operating revenue level to increase by an amount that exactly offsets the loss of base currency conversion value due to the depreciation of the foreign currency, and vice versa. Thus, Mannheim's $B_R = 0$. Mannheim Co. is in a completely different situation from the German exporter, GRE Co., in Example 8-3. In Example 8-3, GRE Co. had to accept a stable foreign currency price for its product (dollars), due to the existence of viable competing suppliers from countries other than Germany, especially U.S. domestic suppliers. As we saw, the GRE's operating revenue exposure, B_R, is equal to 1 in Example 8-3, due to a pure conversion effect.

Correspondingly, a U.S. importer of Mannheim's products faces operating cost exposure for the raw materials purchased from Mannheim. In the numerical example, the mark appreciates from 1.50 DM/\$ (= 0.667 \$/DM) to 1.25 DM/\$ (= 0.80 \$/DM), representing a percentage increase of (0.80 \$/DM)/(0.667 \$/DM) − 1 = 0.20, or 20%. As a result, the U.S. importer's cost per unit rises from \$2.00 to \$2.40, also an increase of 20%. The U.S. importer's operating cost exposure, B_C, is 1 for these raw materials.

The term *currency of determination* is often used to indicate the currency in which, due to the particular economic conditions, prices are effectively set, even if the billing is actually denominated in another currency. Thus, in the case of GRE Co. in Example 8-3, the currency of determination is the dollar, while in the case of Mannheim Co. the currency of determination is the mark.

Figure 8-3 and the following table are provided as a reference to the points made on the currency of determination:

If the currency of determination is:

	Exporter's	*Importer's*
then the Exporter's B_R is	0	1
and the Importer's B_C is	1	0

The cases covered so far are extreme ones in which the economic conditions that are assumed make the currency of determination unambiguous. In the real world of global business, the issue is far more complex due to price elasticities of demand and multiple competitors from many currency bases. In such cases, B_R and B_C may be between 0 and 1. One approach that may be useful in this environment is to estimate *the degree to which* an exchange rate change can and/or will be reflected in a product's sales price. Such a system is used by a European chemicals subsidiary of a U.S.-based multinational discussed in the box on page 235.

Consider the following illustration of the reciprocal relationship between an exporter's operating revenue exposure and an importer's operating cost exposure, when the product's price exposure is between 0 and 1. The illus-

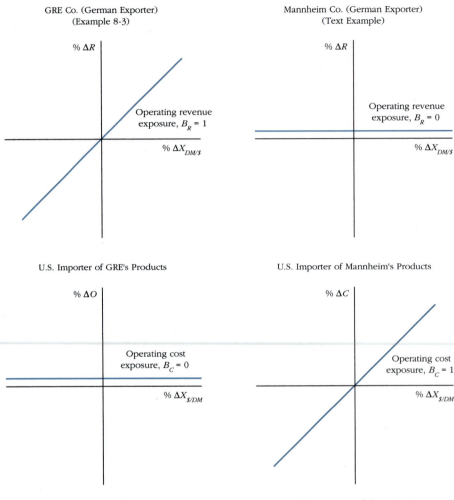

FIGURE 8-3 Operating Revenue Exposure, Operating Cost Exposure, and Currency of Determination: Conversion Exposure Scenarios

tration is based on the relationship between the U.S. firm Caterpillar Co. and its Canadian distributor, Finning Co.[5]

---

[5]A description of Caterpillar-Finning is found in Gregory J. Millman, *The Floating Battlefield: Corporate Strategies in the Currency Wars* (New York: AMACOM, The American Management Association, 1990). For additional insights on the concept of currency of determination, which is also referred to as the *currency habitat of price*, see Eugene Flood, Jr., and Donald R. Lessard, "On the Measurement of Operating Exposure to Exchange Rates: A Conceptual Approach," *Financial Management*, Spring 1986, pp. 25–36.

If the U.S. dollar appreciates relative to the Canadian dollar, Caterpillar passes along some, but not all, of its operating revenue exposure in the form of higher Canadian dollar prices to Finning. If Caterpillar's prices to Finning are 60% stable in Canadian dollar terms, Caterpillar would have an operating revenue exposure of 0.60 in its sales to Finning. By altering 40% of the Canadian dollar prices with changes in the exchange rates, Caterpillar would be passing along 40% of the currency exposure to Finning, which would have an operating cost exposure of 0.40 to changes in the Canadian dollar value of the U.S. dollar.

*M*EASURING EXPOSURE IN THE REAL WORLD

Consider the system of measuring price exposure used by a large U.S. multinational firm. For a given product, the marketing managers are interviewed and asked to rate the stability of each product's price to currency movements.

A rating of 1 means a product's price in the foreign currency is completely stable and is unaffected by changes in the exchange rate. A rating of 0 means that none of the product's price in the foreign currency is stable, and thus that the foreign currency price fully adjusts to reflect the exchange rate change. A 0.60 rating means that 60% of the foreign currency price is stable and not subject to change with exchange rates, while the other 40% will fluctuate with the exchange rate.

Note that the extreme ratings of 0 and 1 imply that the currency of determination is unambiguously the base currency and the foreign currency, respectively. A rating of 0.60 implies that 60% of a product's price is determined by the foreign currency, while 40% is determined by the base currency. Given no changes in expected sales volume, the ratings are the operating revenue exposures, B_R, for particular products. A price exposure rating of 0.60, for example, indicates the operating revenue exposure for the exporter is 0.60.

This discussion is based on the report in John J. Pringle, "Managing Foreign Exchange Exposure," *Journal of Applied Corporate Finance*, Winter 1991, pp. 73–82.

DEMAND EXPOSURE

Additional complexity occurs if a firm's foreign sales volume changes in response to a change in the foreign currency selling price of a firm's product. Moreover, even if the foreign currency selling price is kept stable, the demand for a given firm's products could change with exchange rate movements, if the exchange rate movements cause changes in a country's wealth and/or other changes in the economic environment. The influence of exchange rate movements on the demand for a firm's output is called *demand exposure.*[6]

---

[6]The demand exposure idea (though not the term) is discussed in Gunter Dufey, "Corporate Finance and Exchange Rate Variations," *Financial Management*, Summer 1972, pp. 51–57.

An actual case of demand exposure is Western Mining Co., an Australian firm that produces and sells metals, whose U.S. dollar prices do not change as a result of exchange rate changes.[7] In one of Western Mining's largest markets, Europe, demand drops when the U.S. dollar appreciates relative to European currencies and thus when the metals' prices rise in European currency terms.

The idea behind Western Mining's demand exposure may be seen by considering a hypothetical firm POZ Co., which sells in Europe a product whose currency of determination is the U.S. dollar. Assume the $/ECU exchange rate is currently 1.20 $/ECU. Assume the company currently expects to sell 10,000 tons per year at $144/ton, so that the Europeans pay ($144/ton)/(1.20 $/ECU) = ECU120/ton as long as the exchange rate is 1.20 $/ECU. POZ's initially expected foreign currency operating revenues are thus (ECU120/ton)(10,000 tons) = ECU1,200,000 (per year), with a base currency equivalent of $R^0 =$ ECU1,200,000(1.20 $/ECU) = $1,440,000 (per year). Now let the ECU depreciate by 10% relative to the dollar. Thus, the new $/ECU exchange rate is $X^1 =$ 0.90(1.20 $/ECU) = 1.08 $/ECU. At the new $/ECU exchange rate, the same dollar price of $144/ton means that the Europeans are now charged ($144/ton)/(1.08 $/ECU) = ECU133.33/ton, instead of ECU120/ton.

Let us compare three different cases. Case I assumes that demand is somewhat inelastic. Case II is a special case where the decline in the volume of foreign sales offsets the increase in the sales price, and vice versa, such that the foreign currency operating revenues are unaffected by exchange rate changes. Case III demonstrates a case where demand is very elastic. Figure 8-4 summarizes the cases graphically.

Case I: Assume that demand is somewhat inelastic and that only 9500 tons per year are expected to be imported at the new price of ECU133.33/ton, instead of the expected volume of 10,000 tons assumed earlier. Then POZ's new expected foreign currency operating revenues would be (ECU133.33/ton)(9500 tons) = ECU1,266,667, which has a base currency equivalent of $R^1 =$ ECU1,266,667(1.08 $/ECU) = $1,368,000. In this case, POZ's operating revenue exposure is $B_R =$ ($1,368,000/$1,440,000 − 1)/[(1.08 $/ECU)/(1.20 $/ECU) − 1] = 0.50. The drop in foreign sales volume, accompanying the foreign currency price increase, partially impedes the role of the product's ECU price increase in offsetting the effect of the depreciation of the ECU. In this case, demand is not too elastic, and there is still some increase in expected foreign currency operating revenues (from ECU1,200,000 to ECU1,266,667). However, the conversion loss due to the depreciation of the ECU more than offsets this gain. The net result is an operating revenue exposure, B_R, of 0.50.

---

[7]The Western Mining Co. case is covered in Peter J. Maloney, "Managing Foreign Exchange Exposure: The Case of Western Mining," *Journal of Applied Corporate Finance*, Winter 1990, pp. 29–34.

Case II: If POZ's expected foreign sales volume instead drops to 9000 tons per year, the new expected foreign currency operating revenues would be (ECU133.33/ton)(9000 tons) = ECU1,200,000 per year, and the new expected base currency equivalent would be R^1 = ECU1,200,000(1.08 \$/ECU) = \$1,296,000 per year. In this case, POZ's operating revenue exposure is B_R = (\$1,296,000/\$1,440,000 − 1)/[(1.08 \$/ECU)/(1.20 \$/ECU) − 1] = 1. Thus, even though the currency of determination is the exporter's currency, the loss of sales volume, to 9000 units per year, completely offsets the higher foreign currency selling price, so that expected foreign currency operating revenues are *constant* at ECU1,200,000 per year. The constant expected foreign currency operating revenues, of course, are still subject to conversion exposure, and B_R = 1.

Case III: If POZ's expected foreign sales volume instead drops to 7500 tons per year, the new expected foreign currency operating revenues would be (ECU133.33/ton)(7500 tons) = ECU1,000,000 per year, and the new expected base currency equivalent would be R^1 = ECU1,000,000(1.08 \$/ECU) = \$1,080,000 per year. In this case, POZ's operating revenue exposure is B_R = (\$1,080,000/\$1,440,000 − 1)/[(1.08 \$/ECU)/(1.20 \$/ECU) − 1] = 2.50. Thus, even though the currency of determination is the exporter's currency, the loss of sales volume, to 7500 units, more than offsets the higher foreign currency selling price, so that expected foreign currency operating revenues decrease to ECU1,000,000 per year. The effect of the diminished expected foreign currency operating revenues is further compounded by conversion exposure.

Not all demand effects result in a positive operating revenue exposure. Consider the case of the now-defunct small British company Laker Airways, whose base currency was the pound sterling. Laker Air specialized in flying British vacationers to the United States at a time when the pound was over-valued in purchasing power terms relative to the dollar. However, when the dollar appreciated relative to the pound, the cost of a U.S. holiday rose, discouraging the use of the airline. Since this company's operating revenues rose as the base currency appreciated (and the foreign currency depreciated), and vice versa, the operating revenue exposure was negative. A negative exposure to foreign currencies, based upon the same reasoning, has also been reported for American Airlines.[8]

COMPETITIVE EXPOSURE

Often demand and price exposures are the result of a firm's competitive position, a situation that is termed *competitive exposure.* Consider the case of a

---

[8]The Laker Airways situation is reviewed in Millman, *The Floating Battlefield.* The American Airlines case is in John F. O. Bilson, "Managing Economic Exposure to Foreign Exchange Risk: A Case Study of American Airlines," New York University Salomon Center's *Conference on Exchange Rate Effects on Corporate Financial Performance and Strategies,* May 1992.

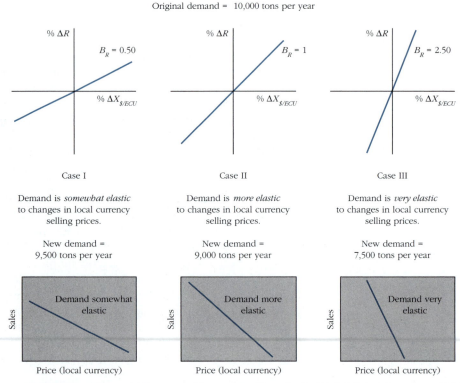

FIGURE 8-4 Demand Exposure Alternatives: Hypothetical U.S. Mining Company, POZ Co., Represents the Situation of the Actual Australian Firm, Western Mining Co.

U.S. company operating in Germany. Suppose the mark appreciates relative to the dollar, and as a result more U.S. companies become inclined to compete for business in Germany. The additional competition could result in a lower market share and a lower German sales volume. The competitive pressure could result in price exposure as well.

Competitive exposure exhibits itself very clearly in the U.S. automobile industry, where the yen appears to be the dominant currency of determination. When the yen depreciates relative to the dollar, Japanese auto manufacturers can afford to sell at lower dollar prices, forcing the U.S. auto manufacturers to lose revenues. Note that this situation also works in the other direction. When the yen appreciates relative to the dollar, and the Japanese raise the dollar prices of the autos that are sold in the United States, the U.S. auto producers raise their prices in the United States and increase profits.[9]

---

[9]See "With Auto Profits Up, Big Three Again Get a Major Opportunity," *The Wall Street Journal*, May 4, 1994, p. 1.

INDIRECT EXPOSURE

Consider the position of a company's suppliers. If a company's cash flows fall, due to an exchange rate change, the company may decide to cut back on its operations. Assuming that this cutback reduces the company's demand for raw materials, then the suppliers, whatever their nationality or base currency, may have a demand exposure to changes in the exchange rate that is termed an *indirect exposure*. Indirect exposure is an easy concept to grasp, but is often overlooked. A company could have volatile operating cash flows and not even realize that the reason is an indirect currency exposure.

Consider the case of a domestic supply company that has no direct foreign exchange exposure due to conversion, price, demand, or competitive effects. The firm could still have an indirect exposure as a supplier to firms with foreign currency risk. If the domestic currency appreciates and the profitability falls for the firm's customers that have direct exposures, so too may the customers' demand for supplier's product. Thus, the domestic supplier could see a decline in expected operating revenues due to an appreciation of its base currency, even if the firm has no direct exposure.

As an example, again consider the Canadian heavy equipment dealer, Finning Co., with its base currency of the Canadian dollar. Finning's customers, also with base currency in Canadian dollars, sell products primarily to U.S. firms, with the U.S. dollar as the currency of determination. Thus, when the U.S. dollar appreciates relative to the Canadian dollar, Finning's Canadian customers experience increased expected base currency (Canadian dollar) operating revenues and are more likely to place orders with Finning.

MULTIMARKET EXPOSURES

Consider the case of a firm that sells in both domestic and foreign markets. Such a firm may have a combination of different exposures in different markets. In the foreign market, the price and/or demand exposure—combined with the effect of conversion exposure—could be different than the competitive exposure in the domestic market. Kodak and Caterpillar are two major examples of the many modern firms with operating revenue exposure in multiple markets.[10]

For example, suppose the hypothetical U.S. firm SLM Co. sells products in both England and the United States, and SLM's base currency is the dollar. Assume SLM's British competition in England is significant, but in the domestic U.S. market is insignificant. In this case, currency of determination for the company's products in England may be the pound, but not in the United

---

[10]Both cases are discussed in Clifford W. Smith, Charles W. Smithson, and D. Sykes Wilford, *Managing Financial Risk* (New York: HarperBusiness, 1990). Caterpillar is also found in Millman, *The Floating Battlefield.*

States. For example, if the product's currency of determination in the U.S. market is the dollar, then the U.S. operation has an operating revenue exposure of 0. SLM's overall operating revenue exposure depends on the relative expected base currency operating revenue proportions from the two markets. For example, if SLM generates 30% of its business in England and the other 70% domestically, then the firm's overall operating revenue exposure will be $B_R = 0.30(1) + 0.70(0) = 0.30$.

The British firm Rolls-Royce may typify this last numerical example, but with a base currency of pounds instead of dollars.[11] Rolls-Royce reported that 41% of its operating revenues were derived from overseas sales in the United States, with the dollar as the currency of determination. Assuming the other 59% of operating revenues were from domestic U.K. sales and did not fluctuate with changes in the $/£ exchange rate, the firm's operating revenue exposure (to the dollar) would have been $B_R = 0.41(1) + 0.59(0) = 0.41$.

SCENARIOS OF OPERATING EXPOSURE

Note that the operating cash flow exposure in Examples 8-1 and 8-2 is greater than 1, even though the operating revenue exposure is 1 and the operating cost exposure is 0. The demonstration that operating cash flow exposure may be greater than 1 may be surprising, but the situation may be representative of an ordinary exporter, which sells products overseas, but which has operating costs that are domestic. In general, an exporter's operating cash flow exposure will typically be greater than 1, as long as the firm's operating costs are not very significantly exposed.

The reason that an exporter's operating cash flow exposure may typically exceed 1 is that, in effect, all unexposed domestic operating costs may be viewed as *fixed costs* when changes in exchange rates are the issue. Thus, the exposure of operating *revenues* is magnified into an even greater exposure of *operating cash flows* by an *operating leverage* effect, which you may recall from your introductory financial management course. The degree of this magnification depends upon the proportion of the base currency operating costs (playing the role of the fixed operating costs) to other operating costs and to expected operating cash flows.

Let us consider a hypothetical illustration of operating cash flow exposure as it might apply to Merck, Inc., whose overseas business is assumed to have an operating revenue exposure of 1 due to a conversion effect, and much of whose production costs are effectively in the base currency (U.S. dollars). Assume that Merck's overseas business comprises 50% of total operating cash flows and that Merck's currently expected operating cash flow margin is 20%. Thus, if $O^0/R^0 = 0.20$, then R^0/O^0 equals 5, and $C^0/O^0 = R^0/O^0 - 1 = 5$

---

[11]The Rolls-Royce situation is discussed in Gunter Dufey and S. L. Srinivasulu, "The Case for Corporate Management of Exchange Risk," *Financial Management*, Winter 1983, pp. 54–62.

$- 1 = 4$. Assuming that Merck's domestic operating revenues are not subject to currency exposure, then Merck's overall operating revenue exposure is 0.50 and, applying equation (8-3), the overall operating cash flow exposure is $B_O = 0.50(5) - 0(4) = 2.50$. Since Merck does overseas business in a number of other countries, the operating cash flow exposure computed here may be regarded as exposure to a basket of foreign currencies or exposure to a general appreciation of the dollar relative to other currencies.

Next, consider again the situation of the Australian company Western Mining Co., whose base currency is the Australian dollar (A$). Western's operating revenues are denominated in U.S. dollars and thus Western has an operating revenue conversion exposure, $B_R = 1$, to changes in the rate of exchange between the Australian dollar and the U.S. dollar. Since all production takes place in Australia, it may be reasonable to assume that Western's operating cost exposure is 0. Given this exposure environment, Western's operating cash flow exposure to changes in the A$/$ exchange rate must be greater than 1, assuming positive expected operating cash flows. At a 20% operating cash flow margin, for illustration, Western Mining's B_O would be $1(5) - 0(4) = 5$. (The interaction of Western Mining's conversion exposure with its demand exposure to the $/ECU exchange rate, mentioned previously, makes it difficult to analyze the currency exposure situation for Western Mining Co. Accordingly, further analysis is deferred until Chapter 13.)

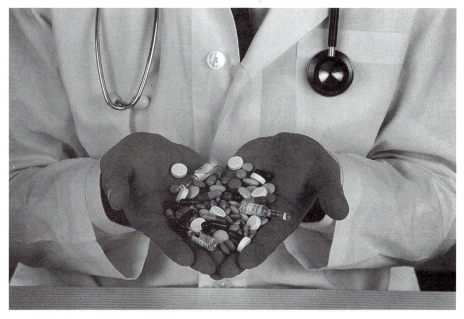

Companies like Merck, Inc., believe that the understanding of economic currency exposure is crucial to their future.

Next consider a firm that markets products abroad and has an operating revenue exposure of 1. But instead of having base currency operating costs, assume that the production operations are also abroad and that all operating costs are incurred in the same foreign currency as the operating revenues and not subject to the influence of changing exchange rates. In this case, $B_C = 1$ instead of 0, as was assumed to be the case above for an exporter.

We can see from equation (8-3) that if both B_R and B_C are equal to 1, then the operating cash flow exposure, B_O, is equal to $R^0/O^0 - C^0/O^0$, which is simply 1 (since $R^0 - C^0 = O^0$), regardless of the expected operating cash flow margin.

This example represents a possible scenario of a parent firm's exposure to an overseas subsidiary that conducts both sales and production in the same foreign country. Given the scenario, it may be reasonable for such an overseas subsidiary to have an operating exposure of 1, from the parent's point of view, to the currency of the country in which the subsidiary operates.

The intuition to this scenario is that if all the operating costs are in the foreign currency and, therefore, if all the base currency operating costs change with changes in currency values, then there are no fixed base currency operating costs relative to exchange rate changes. Thus, there is no magnifying operating leverage effect; given that B_C is equal to 1, then B_O will be 1, since B_R is assumed to be 1.

EXAMPLE 8-4

Consider a subsidiary of a U.S. firm that sells products in England and the currency of determination is the pound. Thus, the firm's operating revenue exposure from its subsidiary is $B_R = 1$. Let us say that at the current exchange rate, the subsidiary has an expected operating cash flow margin of 25%. If all operating costs are incurred in pounds with the pound as the currency of determination, what is the operating cash flow exposure, B_O?

Solution 8-4   Given the preceding discussion, one could simply state that the answer is $B_O = 1$. From the data, the solution would be as follows. If the expected operating cash flow margin, O^0/R^0, is 25%, then $R^0/O^0 = 1/0.25 = 4$. Moreover, since $C^0 = R^0 - O^0$, then $C^0/O^0 = R^0/O^0 - 1 = 4 - 1 = 3$. Since $B_C = 1$, equation (8-3) tells us that the operating cash flow exposure, B_O, is $1(4) - 1(3) = 1$.

The scenario in Example 8-4 also demonstrates an important point concerning managing corporate foreign exchange exposure strategically. Comparing this scenario with the firm in Examples 8-1 and 8-2, representing an exporter whose $B_O > 1$, the difference is that the currency of the operating costs has been changed from the base currency to the foreign currency. This strategic move reduces the firm's operating exposure significantly, from 2.40

to 1. However, even when *all* operating costs are shifted to the exposed currency, the operating cash flow exposure is still 1 and cannot be made to go lower than 1 (as long as $B_R = 1$).

Of course, not all overseas subsidiaries pose an operating exposure of 1 to their parent. Many subsidiaries are international in scope, exporting finished products and importing raw materials. Consider again, for example, the case of the U.S. parent, Vulcan Materials. Vulcan's U.K. subsidiary sells and produces in England. However, the currency of determination for the product is not the pound but is instead the U.S. dollar. Thus, as was pointed out previously the parent's operating revenue exposure is 0 (roughly). Moreover, Vulcan is also able to adjust its raw materials costs in concert with the changes in the pound prices of its output, so that the raw materials have an approximate operating cost exposure of 0 from the viewpoint of the parent firm's base currency, the dollar. Since the raw materials are substantially Vulcan's most significant operating cost, equation (8-3) may be used to see that the parent Vulcan's overall operating cash flow exposure from the subsidiary is insignificantly different from 0, even though the subsidiary operates (sales and production) totally outside of the United States.

Let us now consider an example of the operating exposure of a classic importer with conversion exposure in its operating costs. Suppose, for example, that BAM Co. is a hypothetical U.S. company with purely domestic sales. Assume that BAM has no operating revenue exposure, including competitive or indirect exposures. Assume further that BAM has an expected operating cash flow margin of 10% and that raw materials imported from Japan make up 40% of operating costs. Thus, if 40% of operating costs have a conversion exposure of 1, B_C for total operating costs is 0.40. Since the expected operating cash flow margin is 10%, expected operating revenues are 10 times the expected operating cash flows, while the expected operating costs are 90% of expected operating revenues and thus 9 times the expected operating cash flows. Thus, the operating cash flow exposure would be $B_O = 0(10) - 0.40(9)$ $= -3.6$. This case represents the classic importer of raw materials with a foreign currency of determination. The operating cost exposure to the currency leads to a negative, or a natural short, operating cash flow exposure.

The next example considers other combinations of operating cost exposure and operating revenue exposure. Consider a hypothetical U.S. firm, RAM Co., that (1) imports raw materials from Japan with prices determined in yen and (2) has purely domestic sales. RAM has an operating cost exposure to the Japanese yen due to a conversion effect, but also has Japanese-based competition in its domestic market. Since the competitors' position weakens as the yen appreciates, the operating revenue and cost exposures will naturally offset each other to some degree. The situations for BAM and RAM are depicted in Figure 8-5.

Another example of operating exposure where there are both revenue and cost exposures is the real-life example of Laker Airways. In the Laker case the operating revenue and cost exposures reinforced each other. Laker's negative operating revenue exposure to the dollar has already been discussed. Since Laker acquired its airplanes from a U.S. supplier and was billed in dollars for the planes, Laker also had an operating cost exposure to the dollar. Thus, Laker's operating cash flow exposure to the dollar had multiple nega-

---

◼ EXAMPLE 8-5

Suppose that RAM Co. has an expected operating cash flow margin of 12.5%. Assume the product's currency of determination is the Japanese yen, resulting in a competitive operating revenue exposure of 1. Assume that raw materials imported from Japan make up 30% of operating costs. Thus, 30% of operating costs have a conversion exposure of 1. What is RAM's operating cash flow exposure?

Solution 8-5 In this case $R^0/O^0 = 1/0.125 = 8$. Thus, $C^0/O^0 = 7$. Since $B_R = 1$ and $B_C = 0.30$, $B_O = 1(8) - 0.30(7) = 5.90$. To some degree, the conversion exposure of the raw materials serves to naturally hedge the competitive exposure in the operating revenues. However, the firm's overall operating cash flow exposure is still a relatively high 5.90, partly due to the relatively low expected operating cash flow margin of 12.5%.

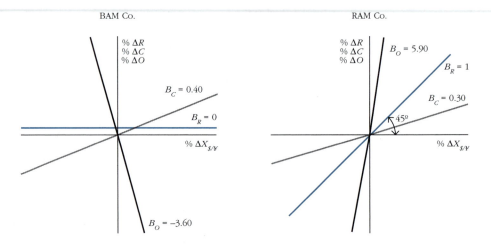

Expected operating cash flow margin = 10%

● Both BAM Co. and RAM Co. import goods from Japan and thus have positive operating cost exposure to the yen.

● BAM Co. has no operating revenue exposure to the yen and thus has a large negative operating cashflow exposure to the yen.

● RAM Co. has operating revenue exposure to the yen of $B_R = 1$ and thus has a positive operating cash flow exposure to the yen.

FIGURE 8-5 Operating Cash Flow Exposure Scenarios

tive components. When the dollar appreciated against the pound, Laker Airways' losses were so great that the company went out of business.

Note that if one assumes a negative or zero expected operating cash flow margin, then the operating cash flow exposure measure in equation (8-3) is meaningless. However, the operating cash flow margin envisioned here is meant to be applied to long-term conditions, not temporary distress conditions. If a negative or zero operating cash flow margin is expected for the long haul, the operation's very viability is questionable and should be reevaluated.[12]

Summary

Operating exposure to a given currency depends upon the exposures of both operating revenues and operating costs to the currency as well as the expected operating cash flow margin. This chapter has covered the relationship between operating cash flow exposure and its three components: operating revenue exposure, operating cost exposure, and the expected operating cash flow margin. There is more to a firm's long-term economic exposure than just operating cash flow exposure. Ultimately, the concern is with the exposure of a firm's stock value to currency fluctuations, which depends on not only the operating cash flow exposure, but also the amount and types of foreign currency financing. These issues are addressed in the next chapter.

Glossary

Base Currency Operating Cash Flow: Either (1) the base currency equivalent of a foreign currency cash flow or (2) the operating cash flow of a domestic firm that is subject to competitive or indirect currency exposure.

Competitive Exposure: Long-term economic exposure due to the effects of changes in a firm's competitive environment on its operating cash flows, where the competitive changes are due to exchange rate changes.

Conversion Exposure: Exchange rate exposure due to converting given foreign currency cash flows to base currency equivalent.

Currency of Determination: Term used to indicate the currency in which, due to the particular economic conditions, prices of goods are effectively set.

---

[12]For additional discussion of real-world corporate scenarios of currency exposure, see Donald R. Lessard and John B. Lightstone, "Volatile Exchange Rates Can Put Foreign Operations at Risk," *Harvard Business Review*, July–August 1986, pp. 107–114.

Currency Habitat of Price: Synonym for currency of determination.

Demand Exposure: The effect of a change in an exchange rate on an operation's sales volume, including the effects due to changes in selling prices for the products.

Economic Exposure: The variability in a firm's value, or in its ongoing cash flows, caused by uncertain exchange rate changes.

Indirect Exposure: Long-term exposure of a firm due to its relationships with other firms that are subject to currency exposure.

Inelastic Demand: A situation described when users of a product are willing to order the same volume of the product at virtually any price.

Operating Cash Flows: Operating revenues (from sales) minus operating costs.

Operating Cash Flow Exposure: A type of economic exposure that focuses on the variability in a firm's ongoing operating cash flows, caused by uncertain exchange rate changes.

Operating Cost Exposure: The variability in a firm's ongoing operating costs, caused by uncertain exchange rate changes.

Operating Revenue Exposure: The variability in a firm's ongoing operating revenues, caused by uncertain exchange rate changes.

Price Exposure: The variability in a product's selling price caused by uncertain exchange rate changes.

Transaction Exposure: The exposure of a single transaction to exchange risk.

Discussion Questions

1. Explain in words why a classic exporter may have a positive operating cash flow exposure to a currency and why a classic importer would be likely to have a negative operating cash flow exposure.

2. Explain in words the circumstances for how an overseas subsidiary would *not* impose any economic exposure to foreign exchange risk to its parent. (Hint: Use the Vulcan scenario discussed in the chapter.)

3. Explain in words how a company can have an operating exposure greater than 1. Could a purely domestic company, with no foreign trade or foreign exchange transactions, have an operating exposure greater than 1? Explain.

Problems

1. Assume the base currency is British pounds. Let the current spot exchange rate be 1.50 $/£ and the expected base currency operating revenues be £500,000 per year. Assume that if the value of the pound changes to 1.80 $/£, the expected base currency operating revenues would change to £750,000 per year. What is the operating revenue exposure?

2. Consider an Australian company with base currency operating revenues of A$500,000 per year, given a current exchange rate of 0.6667 A$/$, and an operating revenue exposure to changes in the A$/$ exchange rate of $B_R = 0.6$. Then, if the U.S. dollar appreciates by 20%, what will be the new expected base currency operating revenues?

3. Assume a base currency of U.S. dollars. Let the current spot exchange rate be $X^0_{\$/£} = 1.50$ $/£ and the currently expected future base currency operating cash flows be $500,000 per year. Assume that if the value of the pound changes to $X^1_{\$/£} = 1.80$ $/£, the expected base currency operating cash flows would change to $750,000 per year. What is the operating cash flow exposure?

4. Assume a firm has a base currency of U.S. dollars and expected foreign currency operating cash flows of FF1,000,000 per year. The current exchange rate is 5 FF/$. If the firm's operating cash flow exposure is 1, what will be the expected base currency operating cash flows if the French franc depreciates by 10% relative to the dollar?

5. Find the operating cash flow exposure to a currency if the operating revenue exposure to the currency is 1, the operating cost exposure to the currency is 0.50, and the expected operating cash flow margin is 0.10. What would be the percentage change in the expected base currency operating cash flows if the foreign currency depreciates by 7% relative to the base currency?

6. Consider an English firm with base currency of pounds. The firm sells products in the United States. The firm expects to do a sales volume of

---

1. $B_R = -3.0$. The negative operating revenue exposure represents a case like those discussed in the text for Laker Airways and American Airlines.

2. $R^1 = $ A$560,000.

3. 2.50.

4. $180,000 per year.

5. $B_O = 5.5$; a 38.5% decrease.

6. The base currency operating revenues increase from £666,667 to £733,333, which is an increase of 10%.

500,000 units at $2.00 per unit. The exchange rate is currently $X^0_{\$/\pounds} = 1.50$ $\$/\pounds$. Assume that the product's dollar price and expected volume of sales do not change as the exchange rate changes. Demonstrate that if the dollar appreciates by 10%, the expected base currency operating revenues for the English firm (in pounds) also increase by 10%.

7. Your firm is a domestic firm in Japan with no overseas sales. The base currency is the yen. However, your domestic market has a dominant U.S.-based competitor, and the currency of determination for the products is the U.S. dollar. Assume that your firm currently has sales volume of 1000 units at a selling price of ¥100,000 per unit. Assume the dollar appreciates by 15% from the current exchange rate of $X^0_{¥/\$} = 120$ ¥/$. What is the operating revenue exposure for your firm to the yen/dollar exchange rate? If the U.S. competitor raises its yen selling price, while maintaining the same base currency operating revenues at the same volume, what will be the new expected operating revenues for your firm?

8. Extend the POZ example on demand exposure in the text by finding POZ's operating revenue exposure assuming that sales demand falls to 8700 units.

9. If 30% of a firm's expected base currency operating revenues have an exposure of 1 to a currency, 20% have an exposure of −0.44 to the same currency, and the other 50% have an exposure of 0 to the same currency, what is the firm's operating revenue exposure to the currency? Assume that 15% of the firm's operating costs have a pure conversion exposure to the currency, while another 25% are raw materials that have 40% of their price determined by the foreign currency as the currency of determination. Find the operating cost exposure to the currency.

10. Laker Airways, discussed in the text, had more exposure than the indirect negative operating revenue exposure to the dollar. Laker also had significant dollar-based operating costs in the form of airplanes ordered from an American airplane manufacturer and priced (currency of determination) in U.S. dollars. When the dollar appreciated, not only did Laker lose customers (a pure demand effect), but a significant portion of its costs had conversion exposure. Let us fabricate some hypothetical numbers. Let the expected operating cash flow margin at the current $/\pounds$ exchange rate be 25%. Let the operating revenue exposure, B_R, be −0.35, and let the dollar-based costs, with $B_C = 1$, be 60% of expected operating costs. What is the operating cash flow exposure?

7. $B_R = 1$.
8. $B_R = 1.30$.
9. $B_R = 0.212$; $B_C = 0.25$.
10. −3.20.

11.   Consider a subsidiary of a U.K. firm that sells products in the United States, and the currency of determination is the dollar. Thus, the firm's operating revenue exposure from its subsidiary is $B_R = 1$. Let us say that at the current exchange rate, the firm has an expected operating cash flow margin of 25%. If all operating costs are incurred in dollars with the dollar as the currency of determination, what is the operating cash flow exposure, B_O.

12.   Consider the case of a Japanese firm that sells products in the United States, and competitive forces cause the selling price to be 60% determined by the dollar and 40% by the yen. Assume no demand exposure. Let us say that at the current exchange rate, the firm has an expected operating cash flow margin of 25%. Raw materials imported from the United States, with the dollar as the currency of determination, constitute 30% of the firm's expected operating costs. If all other operating costs are incurred in Japan (and not subject to any currency exposure), what is the firm's operating cash flow exposure?

13.   Your firm is a multimarket firm with a base currency of U.S. dollars with (a) domestic operations in the United States and only a small amount of U.K. competition and (b) foreign sales in the United Kingdom subject to significant competition, especially from U.S. firms. Assume that the currency of determination mix for the domestic sales is 78% the dollar and 22% the pound, while for U.K. sales it is 65% the pound and 35% the dollar. If one-third of your firm's expected base currency operating revenues are generated in the United Kingdom and the other two-thirds are generated in the domestic U.S. market, find the firm's operating revenue exposure.

As a challenging extension, assume that your firm currently has U.K. sales of 1000 units at a selling price of £100/unit and U.S. sales of 2000 units at $150/unit. Assume that the dollar appreciates by 25% from the current exchange rate of 1.50 $/£. Assuming that new product prices are determined in both markets by the currencies of determination with no changes in sales volume, what will be the new expected operating revenues for your firm? Verify the company's operating revenue exposure directly using the change in the company's base currency operating revenues.

11.   1.

12.   1.50.

13. $B_R = 0.3633$; $R^1 = \$417,300$.

DYNAMIC NATURE
OF OPERATING
EXPOSURE

Note that a firm's operating cash flow exposure may not be stable over time. Consider the operating cash flow exposure for DEF Co. in Examples 8-1 and 8-2, after the mark depreciates by 16.67% relative to the dollar and after the expected base currency operating revenues drop to $R^1 = \$1,000,000$ per year. The new expected base currency operating cash flow margin is $O^1/R^1 = \$300,000/\$1,000,000 = 0.30$. Since it is reasonable to assume that B_R and B_C have stable values of 1 and 0, respectively, the firm's new operating cash flow exposure at time 1 is $1(\$1,000,000/\$300,000) - 0(\$700,000/\$300,000) = 3.33$, which is higher than the operating cash flow exposure of 2.4 at time 0.

Note from this example and from Example 8-6 that a higher operating cash flow exposure corresponds to a lower operating cash flow margin, and vice versa.

EXAMPLE 8A-1

Let WUV Co. be a U.S. firm with initial expected base currency operating revenues of $R^0 = \$1,000,000$ per year and expected operating costs of $C^0 = \$750,000$ per year. Thus, the initial expected base currency operating cash flows are $O^0 = R^0 - C^0 = \$1,000,000 - \$750,000 = \$250,000$ per year. Assume that the operating revenue exposure to the Japanese yen, B_R, is 0.15 and that the operating cost exposure to the yen, B_C, is 0. Then, initially, the operating cash flow exposure is $B_O = 0.15$ $(R^0/O^0) - 0(C^0/O^0) = 0.15(\$1,000,000/\$250,000) - 0(\$750,000/\$250,000) = 0.60$. Assuming that the operating revenue and cost exposures are stable, what will be WUV's new operating cash flow exposure at time 1 if the yen depreciates by 10% relative to the dollar from time 0 to time 1?

Solution 8A-1   If the yen depreciates by 100%, then the expected base currency operating revenues will change by $0.15(-0.10) = -0.015$, or will decrease by 1.5%. The time 1 expected base currency operating revenues will thus be $0.985(\$1,000,000) = \$985,000$. The new operating cash flow exposure will be $0.15(R^1/O^1) - 0(C^1/O^1) = 0.15(\$985,000/\$235,000) - 0(\$750,000/\$235,000) =$

chapter 9

CAPITAL STRUCTURE AND EXPOSURE TO FOREIGN EXCHANGE RISK

ROLES OF FOREIGN CURRENCY DEBT

Recall that Chapter 5 covered the notion that the corporate use of foreign currency debt financing is becoming increasingly common. In Chapter 5, the question was asked: "Why would a company want to issue foreign currency debt?" One answer, given in Chapters 5 and 6, is that an issue of foreign currency debt, along with the appropriate derivatives positions to cover the currency exposure, can represent a synthetic issue of base currency debt; such a financial structure is worth examining for the possibility that it might entail a lower financing cost than an actual issue of base currency debt. While finding different financing costs for two equivalent financing structures should not be possible in a theoretical "perfect market," such situations have occurred regularly in reality during the time that the global financial markets have been in the process of integrating.

Another reason for issuing foreign currency debt instead of base currency debt would be if the issuer believed that the foreign currency would depreciate relative to the base currency in the future. However, this strategic use of foreign currency debt is speculative, and the issuer must bear the risk that the foreign currency might appreciate instead.

In this chapter, we consider a third reason for issuing foreign currency debt: the hedging of operating cash flow exposure. If a company has a positive operating cash flow exposure to a currency ($B_O > 0$), the company may wish to issue foreign currency debt, instead of base currency debt, as part of a program of managing the firm's currency exposure. One objective would be to reduce or eliminate the company's *net cash flow exposure* to currency fluctuations, where net cash flow is defined to be the "bottom line," or operating cash flows minus interest paid on debt financing.[1] Another objective would be to reduce or eliminate the exposure of the company's equity value, or stock price, to currency fluctuations.

As you may recall from your introductory financial management course, the use of debt financing entails a *financial leverage effect*, in that the fixed cost of debt interest magnifies the variability of operating cash flows into an even greater variability of net cash flows. This chapter reasserts this effect in the topic of currency exposure. In the case of foreign currency debt, both a financial leverage effect and a *currency exposure hedging effect* are involved. The interplay between these two effects is somewhat complex, as you will discover in this chapter.

SHOULD COMPANIES MANAGE CURRENCY EXPOSURE?

As you deal with the analysis in this chapter, you may wonder about two questions. The first is: "Should companies be concerned about their foreign currency exposure?" The second question is: "*Are* companies concerned about their foreign currency exposure?"

The answer to the first question is the subject of a debate among academics. Some argue that corporate management of currency exposure is unnecessary, because the effects of currency fluctuations on a firm's financial accounts and its stock price will average out over the long run. There are others who also take the position that corporate management of currency exposure is unnecessary, but for a different reason. This group believes that a company's shareholders can and should manage this risk if they want it managed. This "irrelevancy argument" is similar to the one that some theorists have used to doubt the usefulness of corporate diversification, since investors can easily diversify for themselves.

On the other hand, a number of scholars have contended that the corporate management of risk exposures, like currency exposure, interest rate exposure, and commodity price exposure, *is* important. For example, the argu-

---

[1]For purposes of simplifying the exposition, corporate taxes are assumed to be included in operating costs. As interest expense is usually deductible for tax purposes, this simplifying assumption implies that we are disregarding the tax shield benefit of debt interest in our analysis. However, this simplification will allow us to focus more clearly on the main issues of foreign currency debt financing relative to base currency debt financing. Moreover, as we'll see in Chapter 11, disregarding the tax shield benefit in cash flows is standard in capital budgeting, since the benefit is accounted for in the cost of capital. Additional details are laid out in Chapter 11.

ment has been made that risk exposure management ensures the viability of firms' capital investment programs.[2]

The answer to the second question is: "Some firms are actively managing currency exposure, and some are not." The firms that are trying to manage their currency exposure are trying to understand their economic exposures and to measure them, and such firms are employing foreign currency debt and derivatives strategies. Many case write-ups of firms that are trying to manage risk exposures have appeared in the literature and are discussed in this text, like Merck, Western Mining Company, Vulcan Materials Co., Caterpillar Corp., American Airlines, and so forth. On the other hand, some firms have taken the position, at least for now, that exposure management is not for them. Some of these firms may be reluctant to begin a risk management program, because of fear of the potential abuses of derivatives speculation. (See "The Derivatives Debate" in Chapter 7.)[3]

Debt Financing, Operating Cash Flow Exposure, and Net Cash Flow Exposure

In this section we demonstrate the ideas of the financial leverage effect and the currency exposure hedging effect with debt financing. For this purpose, we define the concept of net cash flow exposure in a similar fashion to the definition of operating cash flow exposure in the last chapter. Let a firm's expected base currency net cash flow stream, assuming that the time 0 exchange rate prevails, be denoted N^0, and let a firm's expected base currency net cash flow stream, assuming the time 1 exchange rate prevails, be denoted N^1. Then net cash flow exposure, which will be denoted B_N, is measured as the per-

---

[2]See Kenneth A. Froot, David Scharfstein, and Jeremy Stein, "A Framework for Risk Management," *Harvard Business Review*, November–December 1994, pp. 91–102. This article is reprinted in the *Journal of Applied Corporate Finance*, Fall 1994, pp. 22–32, and clarifies the more formal version by the same authors in "Risk Management: Coordinating Corporate Investment and Financing Policies," *Journal of Finance*, December 1993, pp. 1629–1658. More on the debate may be found in Maurice D. Levi and Piet Sercu, "Erroneous and Valid Reasons for Hedging Foreign Exchange Rate Exposure," *Journal of Multinational Financial Management*, Vol. 1 no. 2, 1991, pp. 25–35.

[3]Early evidence supports the notion that the investment markets do appreciate and reward risk management initiatives by companies. See, for example, Walter Dolde, "The Trajectory of Corporate Financial Risk Management," *Journal of Applied Corporate Finance*, Fall 1993, pp. 33–41; Deana R. Nance, Clifford W. Smith, Jr., and Charles W. Smithson, "On the Determinants of Corporate Hedging," *Journal of Finance*, March 1993, pp. 267–284; and Charles W. Smithson and Christopher M. Turner, "Financial Price Risk, Hedging and Share Price Behavior," Risk Management Research Working Paper, Chase Manhattan Bank, 1994. Some considerations about implementing a risk management program may be found in Joseph Bauman, Steve Saratore, and William Liddle, "A Practical Framework for Exposure Management," *Journal of Applied Corporate Finance*, Fall 1994, pp. 66–72.

centage deviation in N^1 from N^0 given the percentage deviation in the new exchange rate from the initial exchange rate.

Formally,

$$B_N = \frac{N^1/N^0 - 1}{X^1/X^0 - 1} \qquad (9\text{-}1)$$

Equation (9-1) will be employed in the following scenario, which is also summarized in Figure 9-1. Consider a hypothetical firm, Interex Corporation, that initially has expected base currency operating cash flows of $1,000,000 per year. Assume that the firm's operating cash flow exposure to the pound

---

Time 0 Assumptions for Interex Corporation
  Initial expected base currency operating cash flows: $1,000,000 per year
  Operating cash flow exposure to the pound: $B_O = 1$
  Assumed time 0 exchange rate: 1.50 $/£

Case I: Base Currency Debt Financing, $7,500,000 at 5% interest

Initial expected base currency operating cash flows		$1,000,000
− Interest expense [0.05($7,500,000)]		− 375,000
Initial expected base currency net cash flows		$625,000
If time 1 exchange rate is	$1.35 $/£	1.65 $/£
	(−10%)	(+10%)
New expected operating cash flows	$900,000	$1,100,000
− Interest expense	− 375,000	− 375,000
New expected net cash flows	$525,000	$725,000

B_N = ($725,000/$625,000 − 1)/(0.10) = 1.60

Case II: Foreign Currency Debt Financing, £5,000,000 at 5% interest
  (Note: £5,000,000 is equivalent to $7,500,000 at $X^0_{\$/£}$ = 1.50 $/£.)

Initial expected base currency operating cash flows		$1,000,000
− Interest expense		− 375,000*
Initial expected base currency net cash flows		$625,000
If time 1 exchange rate is	$1.35 $/£	1.65 $/£
	(−10%)	(+10%)
New expected operating cash flows	$900,000	$1,100,000
− Interest expense	337,500†	412,500‡
New expected net cash flows	$562,500	$687,500

B_N = ($687,500/$625,000 − 1)/(0.10) = 1.00

*(0.05)(£5,000,000)(1.50 $/£).
†(0.05)(£5,000,000)(1.35 $/£).
‡(0.05)(£5,000,000)(1.65 $/£).

FIGURE 9-1 Net Cash Flow Exposure and Debt Financing

is $B_O = 1$. Thus we know from Chapter 8, if the value of the pound (relative to the dollar) depreciates by 10% between time 0 and time 1, Interex's expected base currency operating cash flow stream will drop by 10% (since $B_O = 1$) to $900,000 per year. Correspondingly, if the value of the pound (relative to the dollar) appreciates by 10% between time 0 and time 1, Interex's expected base currency operating cash flow stream will increase by 10% to $1,100,000 per year. Now consider two cases.

CASE I: BASE CURRENCY DEBT FINANCING AND THE FINANCIAL LEVERAGE EFFECT

In Case I, Interex is assumed to employ $7,500,000 in debt financing, and the debt carries a coupon interest rate of 5%. Thus the company's debt interest is $0.05(\$7,500,000) = \$375,000$ per year, and we know that the company's net cash flow stream will be $N^0 = \$1,000,000 - \$375,000 = \$625,000$ per year as long as the exchange rate does not change. If the value of the pound (relative to the dollar) depreciates by 10% between time 0 and time 1, Interex's expected base currency net cash flow stream will drop to $N^1 = \$900,000 - \$375,000 = \$525,000$ per year. Correspondingly, if the value of the pound (relative to the dollar) appreciates by 10% between time 0 and time 1, Interex's expected base currency net cash flow stream will increase to $1,100,000 - $375,000 = $725,000 per year.

On a percentage basis, the variation in expected base currency net cash flows is greater than the variation in expected base currency operating cash flows. Indeed, Interex's net cash flow exposure, by applying equation (9-1), is $B_N = (\$525,000/\$625,000 - 1)/(-0.10) = (\$725,000/\$625,000 - 1)/(0.10) = 1.60$. Thus, we see that Interex's net cash flow exposure ($B_N = 1.60$) exceeds its operating cash flow exposure ($B_O = 1.0$). This analysis demonstrates the basic financial leverage effect of debt financing that you covered in your financial management course.

CASE II: FOREIGN CURRENCY DEBT FINANCING AND BOTH THE CURRENCY EXPOSURE HEDGING EFFECT AND THE FINANCIAL LEVERAGE EFFECT

In Case II, Interex is assumed to employ £5,000,000 in debt financing instead of $7,500,000. At time 0, the assumed exchange rate is $X^0_{\$/£} = 1.50$ $/£, and thus the £5,000,000 of sterling debt is equivalent in amount to the $7,500,000 amount of base currency debt assumed in Case I. Assume that the sterling debt carries a coupon interest rate of 5%. Thus the company's debt interest is $0.05(£5,000,000) = £250,000$ per year. As long as the exchange rate does not change, the company will need £250,000(1.50 $/£) = $375,000 to meet the sterling interest payments, and the company's expected base currency net cash flow stream will be $N^0 = \$1,000,000 - \$375,000 = \$625,000$ per year.

If, however, the pound depreciates by 10% to $X_{\$/£}^1 = 1.35$ $/£, and if that is the best-guess exchange rate forecast for the future after that, then Interex's expected future interest payments will be £250,000(1.35 $/£) = $337,500 per year. Accordingly, the expected base currency net cash flow stream will drop to N^1 = $900,000 − $337,500 = $562,500 per year. Correspondingly, if the value of the pound (relative to the dollar) appreciates by 10% between time 0 and time 1 to $X_{\$/£}^1 = 1.65$ $/£, then Interex's expected future interest payments will be £250,000(1.65 $/£) = $412,500 per year. Accordingly, the expected base currency net cash flow stream will rise to $1,100,000 − $412,500 = $687,500 per year.

On a percentage basis, the variation in expected base currency net cash flows is less than the variation in case I, where base currency debt is used. This finding reveals the currency exposure hedging effect of using pound-denominated debt financing when the operating cash flows are positively exposed to changes in the value of the pound. In fact, in this case the percentage variation in net cash flows is the same as the percentage variation in expected base currency operating cash flows, and the net cash flow exposure is equal to the operating cash flow exposure, since B_N = ($562,500/$625,000 − 1)/(−0.10) = ($687,500/$625,000 − 1)/(0.10) = 1.

Note that the currency hedging effect of the foreign currency debt has resulted in a lower net cash flow exposure than if an equivalent amount of base currency debt is employed. However, in this case, the foreign currency debt amount has not eliminated the firm's net currency exposure, or even reduced

---

▣ EXAMPLE 9-1

Suppose Interex's operating cash flow exposure were 1.50 instead of 1. What would be the company's net cash flow exposure in Cases I and II?

Solution 9-1 If B_O = 1.50, then a 10% appreciation in the pound would imply that O^1 = $1,150,000. For case I, where base currency debt is used ($7,500,000 at 5% interest), N^1 = $1,150,000 − $375,000 = $775,000. Thus, B_N = ($775,000/$625,000 − 1)/(0.10) = 2.40. (The reader may verify that the same exposure is computed if one uses the 10% depreciation scenario.)

For Case II, where foreign currency debt is used (£2,500,000 at 5% interest), the net cash flow exposure should be less than in Case I, according to the discussion presented previously. Let's see. A 10% appreciation of the pound results in a base currency interest expense that is the same as in the text example, $412,500. Thus N^1 = $1,150,000 − $412,500 = $737,500, and B_N = ($737,500/$625,000 − 1)/(0.10) = 1.80. The net cash flow exposure is lower than in the Case I scenario (2.40), but is higher than the firm's assumed operating exposure (1.50). The financial leverage effect causes a magnification of the operating exposure, but not as large a magnification as with use of an equivalent amount of base currency debt. The reason is that the currency exposure hedging effect partially offsets the financial leverage effect.

the net cash flow exposure relative to the operating cash flow exposure. The reason is that the financial leverage effect is also still involved.

Although you probably would not realize it yet, the assumption that B_O is 1 in the Interex example is the reason that $B_N = 1$ in case II. To see that B_N is usually different from B_O, even in foreign currency debt situations, Example 9-1 is provided. Problem 1 at the end of the chapter is a scenario where the use of foreign currency debt *does* result in a lower net cash flow exposure than operating cash flow exposure. In that problem the currency exposure hedging effect of the foreign currency debt is stronger than the financial leverage effect.

The Framework for Equity Exposure

This section extends the analysis to the exposure of the value of a firm's common equity. We examine the influence of debt financing, particularly with respect to the currency in which the debt is denominated. We'll see that there exist many situations where foreign currency-denominated debt can be used to eliminate a firm's equity exposure and many other situations where this strategy may not be viable, in which case the use of derivatives to eliminate equity exposure may be considered.

A model is constructed in this section where the basic determinants of a firm's equity exposure are (1) the operating cash flow exposure, (2) the relative level of debt financing, and (3) the currency denomination(s) of the debt. The model is based upon the valuation framework of Modigliani and Miller.[4]

MEASUREMENT OF EQUITY EXPOSURE

Equity exposure is measured here as the percentage change in a company's base currency equity value for a percentage change in the value of the foreign currency relative to the company's base currency. Dividends are assumed to be included in changes in equity values.

Let a firm's base currency equity value, observed while the time 0 exchange rate prevails, be denoted S^0, and let the base currency equity value, given the new spot exchange rate, be denoted S^1. Then equity exposure, which will be denoted B_S, is measured as the percentage deviation in S^1 from S^0 given the percentage deviation in the new exchange rate from the current exchange rate.

Formally,

$$B_S = \frac{S^1/S^0 - 1}{X^1/X^0 - 1} \qquad (9\text{-}2)$$

[4]Franco Modigliani and Merton Miller, "The Cost of Capital, Corporation Finance, and the Theory of Investment," *American Economic Review*, June 1958, pp. 261–297.

As with the exposures defined in Chapter 8, the role of equity exposure as a multiplier may be emphasized by rearranging equation (9-2) into $S^1 = S^0[1 + B_S(X^1/X^0 - 1)]$, where the percentage change in the equity value is determined by the equity exposure as a multiplier on the percentage change in the exchange rate. For example, assume that a firm's base currency equity value is currently $S^0 = \$5,000,000$ and the equity exposure, B_S, is 2. Let the percentage change in the (direct terms) exchange rate be 12%. Then the base currency equity value should increase by $2(0.12) = 0.24$, or 24%. The new base currency equity value is thus $S^1 = \$5,000,000(1.24) = \$6,200,000$.

EQUITY VALUE, DEBT VALUE, AND TOTAL VALUE

We will now state an identity that should be very familiar to anyone who has been introduced to basic accounting. Let D^0 represent the base currency value of the firm's debt, or liabilities, at the present time. Then the firm's base currency total value is equal to the base currency equity value plus the base currency value of the debt. In symbols, the base currency total value of the firm, denoted V^0, is simply

$$V^0 = S^0 + D^0 \qquad (9\text{-}3)$$

However, while the identity in equation (9-3) is an accounting concept, the values we'll be referring to here are economic values, not the historical book values used in published financial statements. Sometimes we'll refer to these economic values as market values.

> ### EXAMPLE 9-2
>
> Suppose that XYZ Co. has a base currency of dollars. Assume that XYZ's equity value is currently $S^0 = \$900,000$, while the debt value is currently $D^0 = \$600,000$. Thus, total value is currently $V^0 = S^0 + D^0 = \$1,500,000$. Let an exchange rate change cause a 10% increase in the firm's equity value. Find the percentage increase in the firm's total value, assuming that the exchange rate change has no effect on the firm's debt value.
>
> *Solution 9-2*   The equity value increases by 10% of $900,000, or $90,000, to $S^1 = \$990,000$, and by the identity in equation (9-3), the firm's total value increases to $V^1 = S^1 + D^1 = \$990,000 + \$600,000 = \$1,590,000$. Thus, total value increases by $\$1,590,000/\$1,500,000 - 1 = 0.06$, or 6%, given the 10% change in the equity value and the constant debt value. See Figure 9-2, situation A.

While the identity in equation (9-3) is useful as a starting point, we are going to employ the identity from a different viewpoint. We are going to start with the firm's total value, and given the amount of debt, determine the firm's equity value as a residual. Thus, we rearrange equation (9-3) into $S^0 = V^0 - D^0$. Suppose we begin with the same current conditions as in Example 9-2, that XYZ Co. has base currency of dollars and that currently $V^0 = \$1,500,000$, $D^0 = \$600,000$, and $S^0 = \$900,000$. Let an exchange rate change cause the base currency total value of the firm to drop by 15%, but cause no change in the base currency debt value. If total value drops by 15%, then it drops to $V^1 = 0.85(\$1,500,000) = \$1,275,000$. Since debt value stays at \$600,000, the new equity value for the firm must be $S^1 = \$1,275,000 - \$600,000 = \$675,000$. The percentage change in equity value is $S^1/S^0 - 1 = \$675,000/\$900,000 - 1 = -0.25$, or a 25% decrease. In short, a 15% decrease in total value has resulted in a 25% decrease in equity value, given the amount of debt and the assumption that the debt value does not change with the exchange rate change. See Figure 9-2, situation B.

CHANGES IN DEBT VALUE

If the company's debt is denominated in a foreign currency, then the base currency market value of the debt increases if the foreign currency appreciates relative to the base currency, and vice versa.

Let the base currency market value of a firm's debt, if the current exchange rate prevails, be denoted D^0, and let the base currency debt value, if the new spot exchange rate prevails, be denoted D^1. Let B_D denote the percentage deviation in D^1 from D^0, given the percentage deviation in the new exchange rate from the current exchange rate.

Formally,

$$B_D = \frac{D^1/D^0 - 1}{X^1/X^0 - 1} \qquad (9\text{-}4)$$

For example, if a firm with a base currency of dollars has £2,000,000 in debt outstanding and the exchange rate is $X^0 = X^0_{\$/£} = 2.00 \ \$/£$, then the base currency value of the debt is $D^0 = £2,000,000(2.00 \ \$/£) = \$4,000,000$; if the pound appreciates by 20% to $X^1_{\$/£} = 2.40 \ \$/£$, then the base currency value of the debt increases to $D^1 = £2,000,000(2.40 \ \$/£) = \$4,800,000$, representing an increase of 20%.

From this example, we see that the percentage change in the base currency market value of foreign currency debt will change by the same percentage that the exchange rate changes. Thus, the behavior of the base currency value of foreign currency debt is a situation of pure conversion exposure, and may thus be represented notationally as $B_D = 1$, *if the debt financing is foreign currency debt.*

If the debt is base currency debt, however, we assume that the base currency market value does not change with changes in exchange rates. Thus, $B_D = 0$, *if the debt is base currency debt.*

A. Example 9-2: XYZ Co.

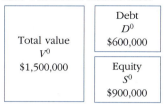

Time 0 Economic Balance Sheet

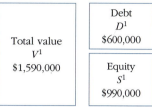

Time 1 Economic Balance Sheet

Total value is up 6%.   Equity value is up 10%.
Debt value is unchanged.

Note: In Example 9-3, it is shown that if $\%\Delta X = 12\%$, then this example is consistent with $B_O = 0.50$, $B_S = 0.833$; and $D^0/V^0 = D/V^0 = 0.40$, where the debt is denominated in the firm's base currency.

B. Text Example following Example 9-2: XYZ Co.

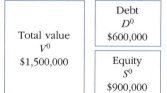

Time 0 Economic Balance Sheet

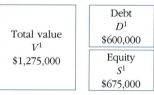

Time 1 Economic Balance Sheet

Total value is down 15%.   Equity value is down 25%.
Debt value is unchanged.

Note: This example is consistent with $\%\Delta X = -10\%$, $B_O = 1.50$, and $D^0/V^0 = D/V^0 = 0.40$, where the debt is denominated in the firm's base currency. From equation (9-6), $B_S = 1.50/(1 - 0.40) = 2.50$.

FIGURE 9-2   Changes in Total Value and Equity Value; Exchange Rates Change, Debt Value Does Not Change

CHANGES IN TOTAL VALUE AND OPERATING EXPOSURE

We now establish a simple theoretical link between changes in exchange rates and changes in a firm's *total value*. To accomplish this, we are going to assume that a firm's total value, in base currency terms, is equal to the present value of its expected base currency operating cash flows. As in Chapter 8, let a firm's expected stream of future base currency operating cash flows, if the current exchange rate prevails, be denoted O^0, and let the expected stream of future base currency operating cash flows, given the new spot exchange rate, be denoted O^1. We continue to assume that the expected base currency operating cash flow stream is a level perpetuity. Assume further that the expected base currency operating cash flows should be capitalized at a discount rate, or *cost of capital*, that is a constant and denoted by the symbol k. Then an operation's time 0 base currency total value is given by

$$V^0 = \frac{O^0}{k} \tag{9-5}$$

For example, assume that at time 0 a firm's expected base currency operating cash flows are \$1,000,000 per year. If the cost of capital is 10%, then the base currency total value, from equation (9-5) is $V^0 = \$1,000,000/0.10 = \$10,000,000$. If the base currency value of the firm's debt is \$4,000,000, the base currency equity value is $S^0 = \$10,000,000 - \$4,000,000 = \$6,000,000$.

The firm's cost of capital is assumed to be independent of exchange rates. Then the new total value of a firm after an exchange rate change is $V^1 = O^1/k$. The assumption that k is unaffected by exchange rate changes means that changes in a firm's total value are due solely to changes in expected base currency operating cash flows. Meanwhile, a firm's total value will change by the same percentage as the change in the stream of expected base currency operating cash flows, given a change in an exchange rate.

To see this point, note if the operating cash flow exposure, B_O, had been 1.20 in the example following equation (9-4), and if the foreign currency depreciates by 15%, then the expected base currency operating cash flows will change by $1.20(-0.15) = -0.18$, or decline by 18%. Thus, the new expected base currency operating cash flows become $O^1 = 0.82(\$1,000,000) = \$820,000$. Given that k does not change, the new base currency total value becomes $V^1 = \$820,000/0.10 = \$8,200,000$. Thus, total base currency value has changed by $V^1/V^0 - 1 = \$8,200,000/\$10,000,000 - 1 = -0.18$, or declined by 18%, the same as the percentage change in the expected future operating cash flow stream.

Thus, given that k does not depend on the exchange rate, we can say that the exposure of the firm's total base currency value to exchange rate changes, in percentage terms, is the same as the firm's operating cash flow exposure, B_O. Since the exposures of both total base currency value and the expected stream of future base currency operating cash flows are the same, given our assumed framework, both will simply be referred to together as operating exposure from this point on. Thus, operating exposure can be expressed as $B_O = (V^1/V^0 - 1)/(X^1/X^0 - 1)$. With this established framework, we can move on to develop some relationships and insights on the use of debt financing.

Operating Exposure, Debt Financing, and Equity Exposure

In the case where all the financing for a company is in the form of base currency equity, equity exposure is trivially the same as operating exposure, since

Companies like the Western Mining Company (Australia) are concerned about the exposure of their equity value to exchange rate changes.

the market value of equity and the total value of the firm are always the same amount. A more interesting case is the use of debt financing in a foreign currency. But before we get to that case, it will be useful to consider the financial leverage impact of using base currency debt financing.

FINANCIAL LEVERAGE

Assume that a firm has base currency debt financing that has a current market value of D. Since debt value in its own currency is assumed to remain the same when exchange rates change, there is no need for a time superscript on

D. Thus, $S^0 = V^0 - D$, and $S^1 = V^1 - D$. For this base currency debt case, some algebraic manipulation leads to the following relationship between operating exposure, equity exposure, and the ratio between the value of the firm's debt and the total value of the firm.[5]

BASE CURRENCY DEBT CASE: RELATIONSHIP BETWEEN EQUITY EXPOSURE AND OPERATING EXPOSURE

$$B_S = \frac{B_O}{1 - D/V^0} \qquad (9\text{-}6)$$

In words, equation (9-6) says that equity exposure is equal to operating exposure divided by one minus the *debt ratio*, in market value terms, assuming that the debt is base currency debt. For example, assume that the operating exposure is 1, that all financing (other than base currency equity) is exclusively base currency debt financing, and that the debt-to-market-value ratio, D/V^0, is 75%. Then the equity exposure, B_S, using equation (9-6), is $B_S = 1/(1 - 0.75) = 4$. In this example, the operating exposure of 1 has been magnified 4 times by the fact that the equity represents only one-fourth of the firm's cap-

---

■ EXAMPLE 9-3

For XYZ Co. in Example 9-2, recall that $V^0 = \$1,500,000$, $D = \$600,000$, and $S^0 = \$900,000$. Assume that the exchange rate change that caused the total value to increase by 6% was a 12% appreciation of the foreign currency. Since the debt value did not change when the exchange rate changed, it is reasonable that the debt was implicitly not foreign currency debt, at least not debt denominated in the same currency as the operating exposure. Reconcile the 10% increase in the firm's equity value with equation (9-6).

Solution 9-3 Since we now know that it was a 12% appreciation of the foreign currency that led to the 6% increase in total firm value, we know that XYZ's B_O is $\%\Delta V/\%\Delta X = 0.50$. Since $D/V^0 = \$600,000/\$1,500,000 = 0.40$, equation (9-6) says that equity exposure, B_S, should be $0.50/(1 - 0.4) = 0.50/0.60 = 0.8333$, and thus that equity value should rise by $0.8333(12\%) = 10\%$, in response to a 12% appreciation of the foreign currency.

---

[5]The derivation of equation (9-6) is as follows: Consider the firm's total value as a portfolio mix of debt and equity. Thus, any percentage change in total value will be a weighted average of the percentage changes in the debt and equity components where the weights are D/V^0 and S^0/V^0, respectively. Thus, $\%\Delta V = \%\Delta D(D/V^0) + \%\Delta S(S^0/V^0)$. Divide both sides of this last expression by $\%\Delta X$ and use the definitions of B_O, B_D, and B_S, and obtain $B_O = B_D(D/V^0) + B_S(S^0/V^0)$. Substituting 0 for B_D, equation (9-6) follows easily.

ital financing and by the fact that the other three-fourths is debt whose value is constant when exchange rates change. This *financial leverage* effect, of the magnification of the percentage changes in operating results, should be familiar to anyone with an introductory background in financial management.

DEBT FINANCING IN THE CURRENCY OF THE OPERATING EXPOSURE

The use of debt financing in exposed currencies is widely regarded as a natural way to hedge long operating exposures. We now develop a formula for assessing that view. The market value of the debt in *foreign currency* terms is assumed to remain constant in the face of exchange rate changes. As has been pointed out, if the foreign currency appreciates relative to the base currency, then the base currency value of the debt increases, and vice versa.

Let D_c represent the (assumed constant) value of the foreign currency debt in its own currency. At the current exchange rate, X^0, the base currency value of the foreign currency debt is $D^0 = D_c X^0$. As has been pointed out, too, the base currency value of the debt has a conversion exposure of $B_D = 1$. The new base currency value of foreign currency debt, given an exchange rate change, is $D^1 = D_c X^1$.

The following relationship between equity exposure and operating exposure holds for the case where the debt financing is in the exposed foreign currency.[6]

FOREIGN CURRENCY DEBT CASE: RELATIONSHIP BETWEEN EQUITY EXPOSURE AND OPERATING EXPOSURE

$$B_S = \frac{B_O - D^0 V^0}{1 - D^0 V^0} \tag{9-7}$$

Equation (9-7) reveals that when debt is denominated in the same currency as the operating exposure, there are two effects on the equity exposure. One effect, seen in the numerator, is the *currency exposure hedging effect*; the negative sign in front of the D^0/V^0 term implies that the use of relatively more debt will tend to reduce the equity exposure from what it would be if no debt were employed. The other effect, seen in the denominator, is the same *financial leverage effect* already observed in equation (9-6); the financial leverage effect causes an increase in the equity exposure for higher relative levels of debt, which is in the opposite direction of the influence of the currency exposure effect. The ultimate influence of foreign currency debt on a firm's equity exposure depends upon how the two effects combine. We'll see that this ultimate influence differs for different levels of operating exposure.

---

[6]The derivation of equation (9-7) follows that for equation (9-6), substituting D^0 for D, and deriving that $B_O = B_D(D^0/V^0) + B_S(S^0/V^0)$. Substituting 1 for B_D, equation (9-7) follows easily.

A. Text Example

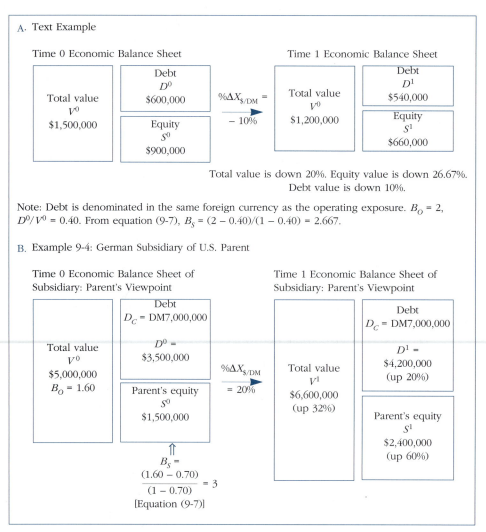

Note: Debt is denominated in the same foreign currency as the operating exposure. B_O = 2, D^0/V^0 = 0.40. From equation (9-7), B_S = (2 − 0.40)/(1 − 0.40) = 2.667.

B. Example 9-4: German Subsidiary of U.S. Parent

FIGURE 9-3   Operating Exposure and Equity Exposure: Debt Is Denominated in the Foreign Currency of Operating Exposure

Let us demonstrate equation (9-7) with a numerical example, also depicted in Figure 9-3, panel A. Assume that V^0 = $1,500,000, D^0 = $600,000, and S^0 = $900,000, and that the debt is denominated in the same foreign currency that the firm's operating cash flows are exposed. Thus, D^0/V^0 = $600,000/$1,500,000 = 0.40. Assume that if the foreign currency depreciates by 10%, the total value of the firm drops by 20%. Thus, B_O is 2.0, and using equation (9-7), the equity exposure, B_S, should be (2.0 − 0.40)/(1 − 0.40) = 1.60/0.60 = 2.667. Let us reconcile this result in detail.

If total value drops by 20%, then it drops to V^1 = 0.80($1,500,000) =

$1,200,000. Since the debt is foreign currency debt and the base currency value of the debt has a conversion exposure of $B_D = 1$, the base currency debt value drops by 10%, to $D^1 = 0.90(\$600,000) = \$540,000$. The new equity value for the firm thus is $S^1 = V^1 - D^1 = \$1,200,000 - \$540,000 = \$660,000$. The percentage change in equity value is $S^1/S^0 - 1 = \$660,000/\$900,000 - 1 = -0.2667$, or a 26.67% decrease. In short, a 10% depreciation in the foreign currency has led to a 26.67% decrease in equity value, consistent with the 2.667 result for B_S found using equation (9-7).

EXAMPLE 9-4

Consider the U.S. parent company of a German subsidiary. The parent's base currency is U.S. dollars. The currently expected stream of future base currency operating cash flows is $O^0 = \$500,000$ per year. Assume that the cost of capital for the expected base currency operating cash flow stream is 10%, making the total dollar value of the subsidiary equal to $V^0 = \$500,000/0.10 = \$5,000,000$. Assume that the parent company's operating exposure to the subsidiary's operations is 1.60. Also given is the current time 0 exchange rate of 2 DM/$. (See Chapter 8 for a discussion of conditions that can lead to $B_O > 1$.) Suppose a portion of the subsidiary is financed with mark debt whose market value is $D_c = \text{DM7,000,000}$. The rest of the subsidiary is financed with the parent's base currency equity. Find the equity exposure of the subsidiary, from the parent's point of view. Suppose the mark appreciates by 20%; find the parent's new equity value in the subsidiary.

Solution 9-4 Since the mark debt has an initial base currency debt value of $D^0 = \$3,500,000$ at the current exchange rate of 2 DM/$, the parent's base currency equity value in the subsidiary, in dollars, is currently $S^0 = V^0 - D^0 = \$5,000,000 - \$3,500,000 = \$1,500,000$. Equation (9-7) indicates that the exposure of the parent's equity is $B_S = (1.60 - 0.70)/(1 - 0.70) = 3$. Thus, by the definition of equity exposure, the equity value should increase by $3(0.20) = 0.60$, or 60%, from $S^0 = \$1,500,000$ to $S^1 = 1.60(\$1,500,000) = \$2,400,000$, given the 20% appreciation of the mark. By virtue of the assumed operating exposure of 1.60 and the appreciation of the mark by 20%, the total value of the subsidiary increases by $1.60(0.20) = 0.32$, or by 32%, from $V^0 = \$5,000,000$ to $V^1 = 1.32(\$5,000,000) = \$6,600,000$. The base currency (dollar) value of the mark debt rises from $D^0 = \$3,500,000$ to $D^1 = 1.20(\$3,500,000) = \$4,200,000$. Thus, the base currency equity value of the subsidiary rises to $S^1 = V^1 - D^1 = \$6,600,000 - \$4,200,000 = \$2,400,000$. Thus, for the 20% appreciation of the mark, the dollar value of the equity increases by $\$2,400,000/\$1,500,000 - 1 = 0.60$, or 60%. This increase, of three times the percentage increase in the mark's value, corresponds to the computed equity exposure of $B_S = 3$.

Equation (9-7) is a key result, because it provides guidance on determining the level of a firm's residual equity exposure, given the operating exposure and the proportionate level of foreign currency debt financing. Although equation (9-7) is based on simplified assumptions, the equation still conveys an important basic idea.

By comparing equations (9-6) and (9-7), we see that the use of foreign currency debt results in a lower exposure than the use of the same level of base currency debt. Had, for example, the debt in Example 9-4 been base currency debt, the equity exposure would be $B_S = 1.60/(1 - 0.70) = 5.33$. Thus, relative to the use of the same level of base currency debt, the use of foreign currency debt does tend to produce a lower equity exposure (3 compared to 5.33).

However, note that even in the case of foreign currency debt financing, the equity exposure of 3 is still greater than the operating exposure of 1.60. The reason is that, in this case where B_O is assumed to be greater than 1, *the foreign currency debt's financial leverage effect has dominated its currency exposure hedging effect.*

CORPORATE SCENARIOS OF EQUITY EXPOSURE

Let us further explore the relationship between equity exposure, operating exposure, and debt financing by examining five possible scenarios for operating exposure: (1) $B_O > 1$, (2) $B_O = 1$, (3) $1 > B_O > 0$, (4) $B_O = 0$, and (5) $B_O < 0$.

Keep in mind that the equity value referred to here is market value, not book value. Note first from equation (9-7) that for equity exposure, B_S, to be equal to zero, the amount of foreign currency debt must be such that the ratio of debt-to-total-value, D^0/V^0, is equal to the operating exposure, B_O.

1. Operating Exposure Greater than 1 ($B_O > 1$)

Consider the situation of Western Mining Co., the Australian firm with operating costs that are in the company's base currency, the Australian dollar (A$).[7] Here we ignore the firm's demand exposure to the $/ECU exchange rate, as was discussed in Chapter 8, and focus only on Western Mining's conversion exposure of its operating revenues to changes in the A$/$ exchange rate. Assuming that Western Mining's operating revenue and cost exposures to the U.S. dollar are $B_R = 1$ and $B_C = 0$, respectively, we should expect that the operating exposure, B_O, is greater than 1. In Chapter 8 an operating cash flow exposure of $B_O = 5$ for Western Mining Co. was hypothetically discussed.

Even though Western Mining issued U.S. dollar debt in hopes of hedging its operating exposure to the dollar, the firm was reported to have a residual exposure problem. Viewing equation (9-7), given $B_O > 1$, we may be able to understand why. From equation (9-7), we see that if operating exposure is

---

[7]The information about Western Mining Co. is taken from Peter J. Maloney, "Managing Foreign Exchange Exposure: The Case of Western Mining," *Journal of Applied Corporate Finance*, Winter 1990, pp. 29–34.

greater than 1, then the base currency equivalent of the foreign currency debt would have to *exceed the market value of the firm itself* to eliminate the firm's equity exposure. In other words, D^0/V^0 would have to be greater than 1, for the equity exposure to be 0. If B_O is 5, then to hedge the operating exposure to a zero equity exposure, Western Mining Company would have to have U.S. dollar debt in the amount of five times the total value of the firm!

Next let us look at two other implications of equation (9-7) in the case where both $B_O > 1$ and $D^0 < V^0$:

(1) As long as the base currency value of the debt, D^0, is less than the firm's total value, V^0, equity exposure will exceed operating exposure.

(2) The greater the amount of foreign currency debt financing, for a given B_O greater than 1, the greater will be the equity exposure.

These results may be counterintuitive at first. However, we've seen the first result already in the magnification effect in Example 9-4. The second result may be easily demonstrated by extending Example 9-4: Had the debt ratio in that example been assumed to be higher, say, 80% instead of 70%, then the equity exposure would be even higher than 3, since it would be $B_S = (1.60 - 0.80)/(1 - 0.80) = 4$.

When a company has an operating exposure in excess of 1, it appears that it is not practical to try to manage this exposure with a foreign currency debt position on the balance sheet. However, a company may wish to consider a currency swap position. In our hypothetical estimate of 5 for the Western Mining operating exposure, consider a short currency swap position on U.S. dollars, to pay U.S. dollars and receive Australian dollars. Assume a notional principal amount of five times the value of the firm. The expected value of each of the future periodic foreign currency cash flows is offset by one of the interest settlements on the swap, and the changes in the *present value* of the expected future foreign currency cash flows would be offset by changes in the mark-to-market value of the currency swap.

Of course, the hedge with the currency swap would not be perfect, since a company's actually realized foreign currency cash flows will deviate from those that are expected. Moreover, interest rate changes will have an impact on the mark-to-market value of the swap, as seen in Chapter 6, but probably would not have the same impact on the company's expected operating revenues.[8]

Still, the basic idea is that the currency swap position would accomplish the same hedging objective as foreign currency debt, namely, the relative sta-

---

[8]This problem is potentially manageable with floating rate swaps and/or with floating rate/foreign currency debt. The development of this idea is beyond the scope here, but some thoughts on the use of floating rate/foreign currency debt are expressed in John J. Pringle and Robert A. Connolly, "The Nature and Causes of Foreign Currency Exposure," *Journal of Applied Corporate Finance*, Fall 1993, pp. 61–72.

bilization of the expected base currency net cash flow stream and of the firm's equity value, given the inherent instability in the expected operating cash flow stream and in the firm's total value. The main advantage of a currency swap over foreign currency debt is that a firm's balance sheet is not affected by a currency swap.

Note that, in general, it is not advisable to try to hedge an entire present value with a single, short-horizon derivative, such as a forward exchange con-

*M*ETALLGESELLSCHAFT: THE DERIVATIVES DEBATE CONTINUED

Metallgesellschaft is a large German metals and oil conglomerate. In 1991, as a marketing strategy, Metallgesellschaft's American subsidiary, MG Refining and Marketing, offered some American customers fixed price contracts for 5 to 10 years for heating oil and gasoline. To protect itself from the possibility that oil prices would rise above its guaranteed selling prices, MG Refining hedged with futures contracts, which are essentially the same as forward contracts, on oil. MG Refining's broker required no cash settlements on the derivatives positions, as long as the contracts were "rolled over" from period to period. Thus, when oil prices fell, MG Refining had losses in their derivatives positions, but would be able to cover those losses with the large future operating profits when the lower-cost oil would be sold at the fixed prices.

However, MG Refining did have to post cash deposits, or margins, on its futures contracts, and the margin requirement increased as the losses in the derivatives grew. These margins were to be made from a $1.50 billion standby line of credit from MG Refining's parent, Metallgesellschaft. By December 1993, MG Refining's paper losses had grown to $1.30 billion. Metallgesellschaft's supervisory board, dominated by its largest shareholder and largest creditor, Deutsche Bank, "pulled the plug." The supervisory board refused to let MG Refining use the standby line of credit, dismissed virtually the entire management of Metallgesellschaft and MG Refining, and ordered the derivatives contracts liquidated. The paper losses were not only turned into real losses, but MG Refining's future operating cash flows were no longer hedged against the risk that oil prices would rise. Oil prices then *did* rise, causing losses on the long-term delivery contracts, a classic "double whammy."

Where does the blame lie? One could argue that the MG Refining team had established a clever and productive financial hedging arrangement, and was not speculating. If this were the case, then the interference by Deutsche Bank and the supervisory board may be blamed, in particular because of the timing to liquidate the derivatives position at the low point for oil prices. However, within the overall hedging strategy, MG Refining may have embedded some speculation as well. Deutsche Bank and the supervisory board believed that the team at MG Refining was speculating. What if, for example, MG Refining's customers reneged on their agreements to buy oil from MG Refining at the fixed prices?

The Metallgesellschaft debacle has added fuel to the derivatives debate, but is somewhat different in concept from the Baring's situation. In the Baring's case, derivatives were clearly being abused for speculative purposes. In the Metallgesellschaft case, the degree to which the firm was speculating rather than hedging is not clear.

tract, for example. The reason is that the entire settlement on the derivative may have to be in cash, which might not be available. For example, suppose one tried to hedge the entire exposed present value of the hypothetical Western Mining's expected operating cash flows with a single 1-year short forward exchange position on the foreign currency. If the value of the firm falls due to a depreciation of the foreign currency, the company is not unhappy because it has an offsetting gain in the forward exchange contract.

Of course, if the value of the firm rises due to an appreciation of the foreign currency, the company has an offsetting loss in the forward exchange contract. While the economic gain on the firm's value offsets the economic loss on the forward exchange contract, the gain on the value is not a cash inflow at time 1, but the company will, in principle, need cash at time 1 to settle its loss on the forward exchange contract.

It is possible that the cash settlement may be avoided by "rolling over" the forward contract, but two problems still exist. One is that cash deposits, or margins, are often required, and these margins will be raised as the unrealized losses in forward contracts mount. Such margin increases will be a cash drain for the hedging firm, even if the forward contracts do not have to be fully settled in cash. The other problem is the appearance of the unrealized losses on the firm's books, which may create its own problems, as you will understand by reading the real-world case on Metallgesellschaft described in the box. A similar real-world situation, Kashima Oil, is found in the next chapter, when the accounting issues for derivatives are covered in more detail.

2.   Operating Exposure Equal to 1 ($B_O = 1$)

Consider the scenario of an overseas subsidiary whose sales and production operations are both located in the same foreign country. Assume further that the currency of determination for *both* the subsidiary's products and its operating costs is the foreign currency. This scenario describes a situation where the subsidiary poses an operating exposure of $B_O = 1$ to the parent. (See Chapter 8.)

From equation (9-7), it can be seen that if a firm's operating exposure, B_O, is equal to 1, then the equity exposure, B_S, will be equal to 1, no matter what level of foreign currency debt financing is being employed. The substitution of $B_O = 1$ into equation (9-7) permits this result to be easily seen.

If, on the other hand, a firm's operating exposure to a currency is 1 and the firm issues debt denominated in the *base currency*, then the equity exposure, by equation (9-6), will be greater than 1. For example, if $D/V^0 = 0.60$, then $B_S = 1/(1 - 0.60) = 2.50$. In this case, the financial leverage effect magnifies the operating exposure of 1 to an equity exposure of 2.50.

Thus, the use of foreign currency debt to finance an overseas subsidiary *will* tend to reduce a parent's equity exposure, *relative to the use of the same amount of base currency debt*. However, as long as $B_O = 1$, the equity exposure can never be driven below 1, no matter how much foreign currency debt is used relative to equity financing. Once again, a currency swap position may hold the answer to managing fully the currency exposure.

3. Operating Exposure Positive, But Less than 1 ($1 > B_O > 0$)

Situations also exist where operating exposure could be fractional between 0 and 1. For example, an overseas subsidiary might be able to partially pass along some exchange rate changes in the form of changes in product prices. Another example is a company with a relatively small proportion of business derived in an overseas market. Other examples were discussed in Chapter 8.

In this case, it *is* possible for a level of foreign currency debt less than the total value of the operation to completely hedge the operating exposure and produce an equity exposure of $B_S = 0$. The choice of a debt-to-market-value ratio (D^0/V^0) equal to B_O will establish an equity exposure of 0. (See Figure 9-4, which depicts the scenario of Example 9-5.)

It may be possible to employ this result in managing operating exposure with foreign currency debt, when an overseas subsidiary's B_O is greater than or equal to 1, if a parent company can borrow the debt against some of its *other* assets. For example, consider a parent with a total firm value of $3,000,000, of which $2,000,000 is the value of an unexposed domestic operation and $1,000,000 represents the base currency value of a foreign subsidiary. Assume, further, that the subsidiary poses an operating exposure of $B_O = 2.0$. The overall operating exposure for the firm is a weighted average of the exposures of the domestic operation and of the overseas subsidiary,

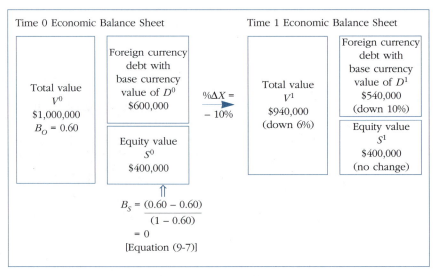

FIGURE 9-4 Elimination of Equity Exposure if $0 < B_O < 1$ by Employing a Debt Ratio Equal to B_O (Example 9-5)

EXAMPLE 9-5

Suppose that a firm's operating exposure, B_O, is 0.60 and that foreign currency debt is employed equal to 60% of the total value of the operation; that is, $D^0/V^0 = 0.60$. Let the base currency total value of the operation be $1,000,000, and let the foreign currency depreciate by 10%. Show that B_S is 0 using equation (9-7). Also demonstrate that the equity value after the currency change is the same as before the change.

Solution 9-5 From equation (9-7), the equity exposure is $B_S = (0.60 - 0.60)/(1 - 0.60) = 0$. The total value will decline by 0.60 times 10%, or 6%, to $0.94($1,000,000) = $940,000$, since $B_O = 0.60$. Since $D^0/V^0 = 0.60$, the initial base currency debt value is $600,000, while $S^0 = V^0 - D^0 = $1,000,000 - $600,000 = $400,000$. The new base currency debt value becomes $D^1 = 0.90($600,000) = $540,000$, so that the new base currency equity value becomes $S^1 = V^1 - D^1 = $940,000 - $540,000 = $400,000$, the same as before the change.

---

where the weights are the percentage of the firm's total market value represented by the market value of each portion. Thus, B_O for the total firm would be $0($2,000,000/$3,000,000) + 2.0($1,000,000/$3,000,000) = 0.667$.

The overall operating exposure of the firm suggests that the firm can eliminate its equity exposure problem by borrowing two-thirds of its total value (i.e., two-thirds of $3,000,000), or $2,000,000, in foreign currency–denominated debt. Since the value of the subsidiary is only $1,000,000, the parent would have to borrow some of the foreign currency debt against the value of the domestic portion of the firm.

4. Operating Exposure Equal to Zero ($B_O = 0$)

Consider the case of Vulcan Materials, whose U.K. subsidiary did not actually present the U.S. parent with any appreciable operating exposure to the pound.[9] If the operating exposure, B_O, is equal to 0, then there is no hedging role for foreign currency debt to play, and thus the use of foreign currency debt will create a negative equity exposure which may be calculated using equation (9-7), substituting 0 for B_O. For example, if $B_O = 0$, and the firm employs foreign currency debt financing such that the debt-to-market-value ratio is 0.25, an equity exposure will be created in the amount of $B_S = (0 - 0.25)/(1 - 0.25) = -0.333$.

Prior to the analysis that revealed $B_O = 0$, Vulcan considered having its U.K. subsidiary issue debt denominated in British pounds to try to hedge the

---

[9]The Vulcan case is described in C. Kent Garner and Alan C. Shapiro, "A Practical Method of Assessing Foreign Exchange Risk," *Midland Corporate Finance Journal*, Fall 1984, pp. 6–17. Also see Chapter 8.

foreign exchange exposure to the pound that the parent had originally (and mistakenly) perceived was posed by its British subsidiary. Had the sterling-denominated debt been issued, a negative equity exposure would have been created.

5. Operating Exposure Less than Zero ($B_O < 0$)

If a company's operating exposure is less than zero, the use of foreign currency debt will exacerbate the resultant negative equity exposure. For example, if a firm has a natural short operating exposure of $B_O = -1.25$ and a debt-to-market-value ratio of 0.25, the firm's equity exposure, from equation (9-7), is $B_S = (-1.25 - 0.25)/(1 - 0.25) = -2$. Thus, a "classic importer" cannot use foreign currency debt to manage its exposure problem.

Operating exposure was also negative for the now-defunct British firm Laker Airways, which had a negative operating exposure to the U.S. dollar. Thus, had Laker Airways issued U.S. dollar debt, it would have had a negative equity exposure that was even greater in absolute value than its operating exposure. Similarly, American Airlines would not be hedging its reportedly negative currency exposure by issuing foreign currency debt.[10]

EQUITY EXPOSURE AND NET CASH FLOW EXPOSURE

One may wonder why we do not view equity exposure by taking percentage changes in a company's bottom-line net income. After all, net income is the residual income belonging to the equityholders. It can appear reasonable, without thorough analysis, that changes in net income would be the same as changes in equity value.

However, the exposure of net income to exchange rate changes is *not* equal to the exposure of the equity. One issue is the definition of net income in the accounting sense, which is an issue dealt with in the next chapter. For now let us think in terms of a firm's expected stream of future base currency *net cash flows*, denoted N, and defined earlier to be base currency operating cash flows minus the base currency equivalent of the interest payments on debt. If the debt is foreign currency debt, then let I_c represent the foreign currency interest payments and let I represent the base currency equivalent to I_c. Thus, $N = O - I$.

It is *not* the case that the net cash flow exposure is equal to the equity exposure, given that the cost of capital for the total firm, k, is assumed to be

---

[10] Laker Airways is discussed in Gregory J. Millman, *The Floating Battlefield: Corporate Strategies in the Currency Wars* (New York: AMACOM, the American Management Association, 1990). American Airlines is discussed in John F. O. Bilson, "Managing Economic Exposure to Foreign Exchange Risk: A Case Study of American Airlines," New York University Salomon Center's *Conference on Exchange Rate Effects on Corporate Financial Performance and Strategies*, May 1992.

Companies like airlines are conducting analyses to better understand their residual exposure.

independent of exchange rate changes, despite the fact that a firm's equity value can be viewed as the capitalized value of the expected base currency *net* cash flows, where the capitalization rate is often referred to as the cost of equity or the required rate of return on equity.

Let us illustrate this issue by extending the scenario in Example 9-4, where the subsidiary is initially expected to generate base currency operating cash flows of $500,000 per year and the mark debt, D_c, is DM7,000,000, is at par, and carries a 5% coupon interest rate. The annual interest expense in marks is $I_c = 0.05(\text{DM7,000,000}) = \text{DM350,000}$. If the mark interest is converted to dollars at the time 0 exchange rate of 2 DM/$, the base currency interest on the mark-denominated debt would be DM350,000/(2 DM/$) = $175,000. Thus, the initially expected base currency *net* cash flows of the subsidiary are $N^0 = \$500,000 - \$175,000 = \$325,000$ per year.[11]

Given that $B_O = 1.60$, the expected base currency operating cash flows increase by 1.60(0.20) = 0.32, or 32%, to $O^1 = 1.32(\$500,000) = \$660,000$, if the mark appreciates by 20%, from $X^0 = 0.50$ \$/DM to $X^1 = 0.60$ \$/DM. At the

---

[11]The conversion of future foreign currency interest payments at the current spot exchange rate is not exactly a correct procedure, but it allows the point to be made here relatively simply. Conversion of forecasted future cash flows with forecasted exchange rates is covered in Chapter 12.

new spot exchange rate, the new mark-denominated interest converts to DM350,000(0.60 $/DM) = $210,000. The new expected base currency *net* cash flows are $N^1 = \$660,000 - \$210,000 = \$450,000$.

Thus, the expected base currency net cash flows increase from $325,000 to $450,000, which represents an increase of $450,000/$325,000 − 1 = 0.3846, or 38.46%, and the net cash flow exposure is $B_N = \%\Delta N/\%\Delta X = 0.3846/0.20 = 1.923$. Contrast this computed net cash flow exposure of 1.923 with the equity exposure that has already been determined in Example 9-4 to be 3 using equation (9-7).

The reason for the difference between net cash flow exposure and equity exposure is that equity value is influenced by changes in both expected net cash flows and the equityholders' cost of *equity* capital. For the firm's overall cost of capital to remain at 10%, given the exchange rate change, the cost of equity capital rate must decrease as the financial leverage decreases and

---

EXAMPLE 9-6

Assume that a firm has a base currency of U.S. dollars and initial expected base currency operating cash flows of $O^0 = \$200,000$. Assume that the current exchange rate is $X^0_{FF/\$} = 5$ FF/$. If the firm's operating exposure is $B_O = 1.20$, and it has financed the operation with a combination of base currency equity and FF5,000,000 of 4%-coupon debt, currently at par, what will be the expected base currency *net* cash flows if the French franc depreciates by 10% relative to the dollar? Demonstrate that, in general, the net cash flow exposure is not equal to the equity exposure. (Assume, for simplicity, that the future foreign currency interest expense is converted to base currency with the spot exchange rate prevailing at the time the future cash flows are being predicted.)

Solution 9-6 Since the annual interest expense is $I_c = 0.04(\text{FF}5,000,000) = $ FF200,000, the initially expected base currency interest expense is FF200,000/(5 FF/$) = $40,000 per year. The initially expected base currency net cash flows are $N^0 = \$200,000 - \$40,000 = \$160,000$ per year. If the French franc depreciates by 10%, then since operating exposure is 1.20, the new expected base currency operating cash flows are $O^1 = \$200,000[1 + 1.20(-0.10)] = \$176,000$. $X^1 = 0.90[1/(5 \text{ FF}/\$)] = 0.90(0.20 \$/\text{FF}) = 0.18 \$/\text{FF}$. The new expected base currency interest expense is FF200,000(0.18 $/FF) = $36,000. The new expected base currency net cash flows, after the French franc depreciates by 10%, from 0.20 $/FF to 0.18 $/FF, are $N^1 = \$176,000 - \$36,000 = \$140,000$. The expected base currency net cash flows thus change by $(N^1/N^0) - 1 = (\$140,000/\$160,000) - 1 = -0.125$, or decrease by 12.5%. This percentage change, given the 10% depreciation of the French franc, implies that the net cash flow exposure is $B_N = (-0.125)/(-0.10) = 1.25$. The equity exposure, on the other hand, could be anything, depending on the company's debt ratio. If, for example, the FF5,000,000 debt represents 50% of the firm's initial total value, the initial equity exposure would be $B_S = (1.20 - 0.50)/(1 - 0.50) = 1.40$, by equation (9-7).

increase as the financial leverage increases. In this situation, the financial leverage of the subsidiary changes, in base currency terms, from $D^0/V^0 = \$3,500,000/\$5,000,000 = 0.70$, to the new ratio of $D^1/V^1 = \$4,200,000/\$6,600,000 = 0.6363$.

Thus, in addition to higher expected base currency net cash flows, $N^1 = \$450,000$ versus $N^0 = \$325,000$, equityholders also require a lower expected rate of return due to their decreased financial leverage. Given the specific cost of capital and interest rate assumptions employed here, it works out that the equity capitalization rate changes such that the equity exposure, B_S, in the example is 3, when accounting for both the net cash flow exposure and the impact of the change in financial leverage.

EXCHANGE RATES, INTEREST RATES, AND CAPITALIZATION RATES

Exchange rates may change for a number of reasons that do not involve changes in interest rates. Hence, the assumption just employed, of independence between exchange rates and debt values in their denominated currencies (and between exchange rates and capitalization rates), has some basis.

For example, consider the asset market view in Chapter 3 that an increase in the short-term interest rate of a currency, all else constant, results in an increase in the value of the currency in the spot market, and vice versa. Let us speculate on what impact this relationship might have in our analysis.

Consider, first, the case where the foreign currency interest rates change, with all else remaining the same, including the base currency interest rates and capitalization rates. In this case, an appreciation of the foreign currency would accompany an increase in the interest rate in the foreign currency. Thus, the market value of any foreign currency debt would decline in its own currency. This drop in value would tend to *reduce the equity exposure* problem to some extent, since the decline in the market value of the debt in its own currency tends to offset, to some degree, the increase in the base currency value of the debt, caused by the currency appreciation.

But next consider the case where an appreciation of the foreign currency is driven by a decrease in base currency interest rates. It is reasonable to expect that the base currency cost of capital will decline along with the decline in interest rates. In this case, a company with a positive operating exposure will see the base currency total value of the operation increase for two reasons: (1) a lower cost of capital and (2) a higher level of expected base currency operating cash flows, due to the higher foreign currency value. These two forces will be reinforcing, and the total value will increase by a higher percentage than the expected base currency operating cash flows. Thus, the operating exposure, as the elasticity of the operation's total value to exchange rate changes, is higher than the operating cash flow exposure in this case. Since the foreign currency market value of any foreign currency debt is unaffected, the net result in this circumstance is a *larger equity exposure*.

In summary, we really cannot predict the relationship between interest rate changes and equity exposure.

Summary

This chapter has covered some aspects of economic exposure from the viewpoint of a firm's residual base currency investors. A simple model of equity exposure was formulated in terms of operating cash flow exposure, the proportionate use of debt financing, and whether the denomination of the debt is base currency or foreign currency. The simple framework allows us to clearly see some important basic relationships.

Whether or not foreign currency debt can be used, by itself, to satisfactorily hedge operating exposure was explored with the model. We found that there exist situations where the use of foreign currency debt can result in zero equity exposure, if the operating exposure is positive but less than 1. (However, attention must be paid to the dynamic nature of the situation, as is shown in the appendix.)

We also found that the use of foreign currency debt will not completely eliminate equity exposure in cases where the operating exposure is positive and greater than or equal to 1, and assuming that the amount of debt is not allowed to exceed the market value of the operation generating the cash flows.

In the next chapter, we consider the accounting dimensions of the exposure issue, especially with regard to the hedging of currency exposure via financial instruments like forward exchange contracts and currency swaps.

Glossary

Cost of Capital: The capitalization rate, or discount rate, applied to the expected base currency operating cash flows, to determine the total value of an operation.

Currency Exposure Hedging Effect (to Debt Financing): The effect of the choice of currency of a company's debt financing on its residual exposure; the other effect of debt financing is the financial leverage effect.

Debt Ratio: The ratio of debt value to a firm's total value.

Dynamic Hedging: A program of continually trading in financial instruments to achieve a target position (such as a hedged position) that, without which, the target position cannot be maintained due to changes in underlying variables (such as exchange rates.)

Equity Exposure: A type of economic exposure that focuses on the variability in a firm's equity value, caused by uncertain exchange rate changes.

Financial Leverage Effect (to Debt Financing):   The leverage effect of a company's debt financing on its equity exposure, regardless of the currency in which the debt is denominated; the other effect of debt financing is the currency exposure hedging effect.

Net Cash Flow: Operating cash flow minus interest.

Net Cash Flow Exposure: The percentage change in net cash flows relative to the percentage change in the exchange rate.

Total Value (of a Firm):   The market value of a company's expected future stream of operating cash flows; the value of the firm's total capital, debt plus equity, as opposed to the value of the firm's equity alone.

Discussion Questions

1.   Can you think of some reasons that corporations might be able to do a better job at managing currency exposure than their investors?

2.   Do you think companies are better able to diversify internationally than their shareholders? Discuss.

3.   Try to explain in your own words why a company's net cash flow exposure is not equal to its equity exposure.

4.   Would issuing foreign currency debt be an effective risk management tool for a company with a negative operating exposure? Explain. What about a short position in a currency swap to pay the foreign currency and receive the base currency? What about a long position in a currency swap to receive the foreign currency and pay the base currency?

5.   What is your opinion about the Metallgesellschaft debacle and the derivatives debate in general?

Problems

1.   Refer to the Interex example in the text. Assume that Interex's operating cash flow exposure to the pound is 0.60. Case I: With $6,000,000 of debt issued at a 6% interest rate, what would be Interex's net cash flow exposure?

---

1.   In Case I, $B_N = 0.9375$. In Case II, $B_N = 0.375$. Note that in this example, the currency hedging effect of the foreign currency debt has resulted in a lower net cash flow exposure than if an equivalent amount of base currency debt is employed, and has also reduced the net cash flow exposure relative to the operating cash flow exposure.

Case II: With the equivalent amount of sterling debt (at $X_{\$/\pounds}^0 = 1.50$ \$/£), instead of base currency debt, what would be the firm's net cash flow exposure? Assume the interest rate on the sterling debt is 6%. Hint: As in the text, compare the pro forma cash flow results for the no-change and 10% pound appreciation scenarios.

2. Assume that the percentage change in the (direct terms) exchange rate is 10% and that the equity exposure is –0.60. What is the new equity value if the original value is £1,000,000?

3. Consider an Australian company with expected base currency operating cash flows of A$1,000,000 per year. If the capitalization rate for the expected base currency operating cash flows is 12.5%, and if the market value of the liabilities is, in base currency terms, A$3,000,000, what is the initial base currency equity value of the operation? If the base currency operating cash flow exposure to the U.S. dollar is 0.80, what is the percentage change in the total value of the company if the Australian dollar appreciates by 25%? Assuming that the exchange rate change has no effect on the debt value, what is new equity value of the company if the Australian dollar appreciates by 25% relative to the U.S. dollar? (Hint: Recall that the percentage change in the Australian dollar does not equal the percentage change in the foreign currency.)

4. Assume a firm's operating exposure is 1.60 and financing (other than base currency equity) is exclusively base currency debt financing, with a debt to market value ratio of 40%. What is the firm's equity exposure?

5. If $B_O = 1.60$ and 40% of the financing is debt issued in the same currency to which the operating results are exposed, then what is the equity exposure? What if 70% of the financing is debt issued in the same currency to which the operating results are exposed.

6. Assume a company has operating exposure of 0.40. What amount of foreign currency debt should the firm employ if the total market value is currently $2,500,000 and the firm wishes to eliminate equity exposure?

7. Assume that a firm has base currency of U.S. dollars. The firm's expected future base currency operating cash flows are a level perpetuity of $1,600,000 per year. The cost of capital is 10%. The current exchange rate is 1.60 \$/£.

2. £940,000.

3. Minus 16%. S^1 = A$3,720,000.

4. 2.667.

5. 2; 3.

6. $1,000,000.

7. The net cash flow exposure is 1.588. The equity exposure is 1.714.

Assume the firm's operating exposure to the pound is 1.50. Assume that the pound depreciates by 15% relative to the dollar. Assume that the firm has £3,000,000 (in market value) of sterling debt outstanding at time 0. If the coupon rate on the sterling debt is 5%, what is the firm's net cash flow exposure? Compare this result to the equity exposure. (Assume, for simplicity, that the future foreign currency interest expense is converted to base currency with the spot exchange rate prevailing at the time the future cash flows are being predicted.)

The following problem and answer relate to material presented in the appendix.

A-1. Suppose a company's original base currency market value is ¥1,000,000 and its operating exposure is 0.40. The company has issued foreign currency denominated debt to help finance the operation, with a current base currency worth of ¥400,000, leaving a base currency equity value of ¥600,000. If the foreign currency depreciates by 10%, then what is the new debt ratio (in market value terms) and what changes must be made in the capital structure to reestablish an equity exposure of 0? Assume that the operating exposure does not change.

A-1. The new debt-to-market-value ratio is 0.375. The company should issue ¥24,000 in additional debt.

DYNAMIC HEDGING
AND CAPITAL STRUCTURE

Maintaining a zero equity exposure from period to period, regardless of how the zero equity exposure is achieved initially, may require some effort. Suppose that a firm has issued foreign currency debt and has established a debt ratio equal to its operating exposure, as in Example 9-5. After an exchange rate change, the debt ratio will more than likely be some number different than the operating exposure.

One reason for this difference is that, even if operating revenue and cost exposures remain the same while exchange rates change, a change in the expected base currency operating revenues and/or operating costs may change the expected operating cash flow margin, and the expected operating cash flow margin is a factor determining operating exposure. (This notion is established in the appendix to the previous chapter.)

Another reason is that the debt ratio, in market value terms, will not be stable. To see this point, simply consider Example 9-5. Whereas the original debt ratio was 0.60, the new debt ratio, after the currency depreciates by 10%, is D^1/V^1 = \$540,000/\$940,000 = 0.5745. Note that the changes in the operating exposure and the debt ratio will *not* tend to be offsetting. If the foreign currency depreciates, operating exposure will tend to increase (see the appendix to Chapter 8), while the debt ratio, in market value terms, tends to decrease, as was just illustrated.

This situation presents a problem if the firm wishes to *maintain* a constant or zero equity exposure. To reestablish an equity exposure of 0, the amount of foreign currency debt must be adjusted as the exchange rate changes. As an example of the necessary adjustment, again consider Example 9-5. For simplicity, we'll ignore the change in the operating exposure and assume that the operating exposure stays the same at 0.60. First, ask the question, after the exchange rate changes: What amount of new debt would reestablish a debt ratio of 0.60, given the new total firm value of $940,000? The answer is 0.60($940,000) = $564,000.

Next, ask, What financial transactions would be necessary to increase the debt level from its current amount of $540,000 to a new level of $564,000, while leaving total firm value at its new level of V^1 = $940,000? The answer is that additional foreign currency debt must be issued such that the base currency amount is $24,000 ($564,000 minus $540,000). To maintain total firm value at $940,000, the proceeds from the debt issue, $24,000 in base currency, must be used to retire some shares of stock. This transaction lowers the value of the equity by $24,000.

If the foreign currency should appreciate in value relative to the base currency, the reverse will occur in this example. The base currency debt value will rise by a greater percentage than the total firm value, and the debt ratio will exceed 0.60. If this happens, some new equity must be issued and the proceeds from the issue must be used to retire some of the outstanding debt, if an equity exposure of zero is to be reestablished.

The amount of the equity issue/debt retirement must be determined such that the new debt ratio will again be equal to 0.60, the assumed (constant) operating exposure. The amount of the transaction depends on how much the value of the foreign currency changes. Thus, if a firm has an operating exposure that is positive but less than 1, or can arrange it, it can use foreign currency debt to naturally hedge and to eliminate residual equity exposure. That good news is accompanied by the bad news that such a strategy will involve a program of continually trading in the debt to readjust the debt ratio as the exchange rate changes. Such a program is an example of what is called *dynamic hedging.*

We do not mean to suggest that it is practical for a firm to practice dynamic hedging for minor amounts of debt as exchange rates change every instant. Each firm would have to work out its own strategy of how often to readjust, given how concerned it is over the currency exposure. In particular, management may have to use discretion about the timing of adjustments if actual stock prices do not reflect their correct values.

EXAMPLE 9A-1

Suppose FEH Co. is a U.S. company with an initial base currency total value of $V^0 = \$1,000,000$. Assume that FEH's operating exposure to the mark is $B_O = 0.40$. FEH currently has $D_c = $ DM800,000 in debt outstanding (market value). The current exchange rate is 2 DM/\$. Demonstrate that FEH's equity exposure is zero. If the mark appreciates by 20%, what transactions will reestablish an equity exposure of zero, assuming that the operating exposure is still 0.40?

Solution 9A-1 At 2 DM/\$, the current base currency value of the mark debt is $D^0 = D_c(X^0) = $ DM800,000(0.50 \$/DM) $= $ DM800,000/(2 DM/\$) $= \$400,000$. Since $B_O = 0.40$ and $V^0 = \$1,000,000$, a base currency debt value of \$400,000 means that $D^0/V^0 = 0.40$, which is equal to the assumed value for B_O. Thus, the equity exposure is 0 before the mark appreciates. Given the 20% appreciation of the mark, the base currency total value of the firm increases by 0.40(0.20) = 0.08, or 8%, by virtue of an operating exposure of $B_O = 0.40$. Thus, the new total firm value, V^1, becomes 1.08(\$1,000,000) = \$1,080,000. The mark debt has a conversion exposure of $B_D = 1$, so that the base currency debt value becomes $D^1 = \$480,000$. Thus, one can see that $S^1 = V^1 - D^1 = \$1,080,000 - \$480,000 = \$600,000$, which is the same as S^0. Thus, the hedge worked for one period against the currency change. However, the new debt-to-market-value ratio is $D^1/V^1 = \$480,000/1,080,000 = 0.444$. Assuming that FEH's B_O has not changed, \$48,000 worth of the debt must be retired and equity issued, since 0.40(\$1,080,000) = \$432,000. Thus, to reduce the base currency value of the foreign currency debt from \$480,000 to \$432,000, \$48,000 in base currency value of mark debt must be retired to reestablish the debt ratio that eliminates equity exposure, given an assumed constant operating exposure equal to 0.40.

chapter 10

ACCOUNTING ISSUES IN CORPORATE EXPOSURE TO FOREIGN EXCHANGE RISK

Financial accounting is based on historical, or book, values, which are often different from market, or economic, values. For this reason, accounting for exchange rate changes has created confusion and controversy. Many managers believe that investors do not find it easy to understand the market/book value discrepancies that occur.

These valuation issues underlie management's more severe concern over the accounting requirements for reporting corporate earnings. Consider a company that wishes to use foreign currency debt and/or derivatives to hedge economic operating exposure. There are frequently times when changes in a firm's expected future cash flows and thus in the market value of the total firm, induced by changes in exchange rates, cannot be measured and, therefore, *cannot* be reported as income. However, at the same time, accounting rules require that the corresponding economic gains/losses on the hedging vehicles (the changes in the base currency value of the debt and/or the mark-to-market gains/losses on the derivatives) be reported on the income statement, at least on the portions of such positions that cannot be shown to correspond to the *book values* of foreign assets.

As will be shown in this chapter, the issues with regard to reported earnings imply two distinct problems:

1. Corporate efforts to manage economic exposure with foreign currency

debt and/or derivatives can create volatility in reported earnings. This volatility is disconcerting to management, if not to investors and boards of directors. As such, the situation poses an impediment for companies that want to manage their economic exposure to foreign exchange risk.

2. In some circumstances a company's financial statements can represent the firm as having more exposure than actually exists in an economic sense. In such cases, corporations may feel compelled to "hedge" the *apparent* exposure in the financial statements, in which case an economic exposure is actually created by the activity of hedging the accounting exposure!

The details of the accounting issues are laid out in this chapter. The issues, which are presently under debate in the accounting and financial communities, are larger than the exposure to exchange rate changes, since interest rate risk and commodity price risk are also involved in the debate. However, we limit our scope to the issues in a currency exposure context.

Accounting and Foreign Currency Transactions

We start with the very basic case of a company with no operating transactions denominated in foreign currencies and whose assets and sales are 100% located in the United States and are denominated in U.S. dollars. Although the company's sales are assumed to all be on U.S. soil, with no foreign sales of any kind, the company's operating revenues are assumed to be sensitive to changes in the $/£ exchange rate due to the actions of British competitors operating in the United States. Thus, the company is assumed to have a competitive economic exposure to the pound.

This scenario may represent the situation of many smaller domestic companies. Moreover, even though the scenario does not encompass all the problems of exporters and large multinationals, the situation does allow the clearest focus on the general issues. We assume that the company wishes to manage the exposure with foreign currency debt or currency derivatives.

Assume that the company, which we'll call PDC Co., currently (time 0) expects a stream of future operating cash flows $O^0 = \$1,000,000$ per year into perpetuity and has a cost of capital of 10%. The total economic value of the company at time 0 is thus $V^0 = \$1,000,000/0.10 = \$10,000,000$. Assume that the firm has $D_C^0 = £3,000,000$, in both par and market value, of sterling debt outstanding at time 0. Say the time 0 exchange rate is $X_{\$/£}^0 = 2.00$ $/£; thus, the dollar value of the sterling debt at time 0 is $D^0 = (£3,000,000)(2 \ \$/£) = \$6,000,000$. Assume further that the firm's operating exposure to changes in the British pound, B_O, is 0.60.

Assets (Total Value)		Liabilities and Net Worth	
		Foreign currency debt	$ 6,000,000
		Common equity	4,000,000
Total	$10,000,000	Total	$10,000,000

FIGURE 10-1 PDC Co. Time 0 Economic *and* Reported Balance Sheet

THE ECONOMIC BALANCE SHEET VERSUS THE REPORTED BALANCE SHEET

Let us assume, for the sake of argument, that at time 0, the firm's economic balance sheet and its reported balance sheet look identical. In other words, the market values of the firm's accounts are equal to the book values. Then PDC's time 0 economic balance sheet and reported balance sheet both appear as in Figure 10-1.

Now suppose the foreign currency (the pound) appreciates by 20% relative to the dollar, to $X^1_{\$/\pounds} = 1.20(2.00 \ \$/\pounds) = 2.40 \ \$/\pounds$, *just prior* to time 1 occurring. Thus, the operating exposure of 0.60 dictates that at time 1 the new expected future operating cash flows are $1,120,000 per year and the new total value of the company, V^1, is $1,120,000/0.10 = $11,200,000, given that we are assuming no change in the cost of capital.

The dollar value of the sterling debt increases by the full 20% that the value of the pound increases and is now $D^1 = 1.20(\$6,000,000) = \$7,200,000$. PDC's new (time 1) economic balance sheet appears as shown in Figure 10-2. Note that the period's actually realized net cash flow (operating cash flow minus interest) is not shown and is assumed to be paid out to shareholders in the form of dividends.

The economic value of PDC Co.'s equity is the same at time 1 as at time 0, $S^1 = S^0 = \$4,000,000$. This result is consistent with the assumption that the firm's debt-to-total-market-value ratio at time 0, D^0/V^0, is $6,000,000/$10,000,000, which is equal to the assumed operating exposure (0.60).

However, now consider how the reported balance sheet will appear at time 1. The firm's reported balance sheet is required by accounting rules to

Assets (Total Value)		Liabilities and Net Worth	
		Foreign currency debt	$ 7,200,000
		Common equity	4,000,000
Total	$11,200,000	Total	$11,200,000

FIGURE 10-2 PDC Co. Time 1 Economic Balance Sheet

show domestic assets and liabilities at book (historical) value. Thus, the time 1 reported value of the firm, that is, the book value of the firm's assets, is the same as the time 0 book value, $10,000,000. (For simplicity, depreciation is being ignored here.) However, the sterling-denominated debt is defined by accounting rules as a *foreign currency transaction*, and the new U.S. dollar value must be reported on the balance sheet using the time 1 exchange rate, the current exchange rate at the time of the reporting. Thus, the sterling liability will be reported at the new dollar value of $7,200,000.

The foreign currency debt account is thus charged $1,200,000, an accounting entry that actually does represent the proper base currency economic change in the foreign currency liability due to the appreciation of the pound. Since the total book value of the firm's assets remains at $10,000,000, the accounted-for loss on the sterling debt must be reflected in a decrease somewhere else on the right-hand side of the balance sheet. The loss, as we'll see in the next section, is required to flow through the income statement, and is then deducted from retained earnings, part of the reported equity. Thus, the reported balance sheet for PDC Co. at time 1 would appear as in Figure 10-3.

As one can see in Figure 10-3, the reported (book) equity of the firm has fallen from $4,000,000 to $2,800,000, because of the accounting treatment of the foreign currency debt. Recall, for comparison, that the economic value of the equity is stable, at $4,000,000 from time 0 to time 1, reflecting the economic hedging property of the sterling debt in the face of the firm's operating exposure.

The reason why the time 1 *reported* value of PDC Co.'s equity in the example here ($2,800,000) understates the time 1 economic value of the equity ($4,000,000) is that, while the restatement of the dollar value of the sterling debt is a proper reflection of the new economic value (in base currency), the increase in the economic value of the firm cannot be reflected in the time 1 book value of the firm's assets, which are denominated in the base currency and thus must be reported at time 1 at the historical (time 0) book value of $10,000,000.

REPORTED EARNINGS

Now let us look at the influence on reported earnings. The gains/losses on foreign currency transactions, such as the use of foreign currency debt in the PDC example, are required by accounting rules to be included in the compu-

Assets (Total Value)		Liabilities and Net Worth	
		Foreign currency debt	$ 7,200,000
		Common equity	2,800,000
Total	$10,000,000	Total	$10,000,000

FIGURE 10-3 PDC Co. Time 1 Reported Balance Sheet

tation of reported income. For simplicity we are going to think of the accounting gains/losses on the foreign currency debt as a noncash adjustment to net cash flow to arrive at the "bottom-line" reported earnings, which we'll call net income. For simplicity, taxes are assumed to be in the operating costs.

Let us examine the effect on the time 1 income statement of PDC's loss on its foreign currency debt. Assume that the debt interest rate is 5%. The actual foreign currency interest paid at the end of the year is 0.05(£3,000,000) = £150,000. At the assumed time 1 exchange rate of 2.40 $/£, PDC's dollar interest expense is (£150,000)(2.40 $/£) = $360,000.[1]

Assume further that the actually realized base currency operating cash flow for the year, reported at time 1, turns out to be just as was expected at time 0, $1,000,000, given the exchange rate of 2.00 $/£ that prevailed until almost the end of the year. The relevant portion of the income statement is shown in Figure 10-4.

The choice of an amount for the actually realized operating cash flow is arbitrary; one could choose $759,000, $1,235,000, and so on, since the flow is a random variable. The lesson in this section would not be altered by this choice. The $1,000,000 amount was chosen as the best guess at time 0 of the amount to be realized over the course of the next year, given that the exchange rate stayed at 2.00 $/£. The assumption that the exchange rate changed to 2.40 $/£ *just prior to* time 1 caused a new expectation for the future operating cash flows beginning at time 2 and a new market value for the firm at time 1.

Our concern is with the last two lines on the income statement in Figure 10-4. We see that the company reports a $560,000 net loss for the year, even though its net cash flow was positive in the amount of $640,000. As was pointed out earlier, the accounting gains/losses on foreign currency debt figure into the reported earnings. This example demonstrates the general principle that reported income may be significantly more volatile for a company when the economic exposure of a company's total value (as the present value

Operating cash flow	$1,000,000
Debt interest (5%)	360,000
Net cash flow	$640,000
Gain/(loss) on foreign currency transactions	(1,200,000)
Net income/(loss)	($560,000)

FIGURE 10-4   PDC Co. Time 1 Income Statement

---

[1] In reality, income statement items in foreign currencies that are steady streams over the accounting period are converted at an average exchange rate over the accounting period. We'll report the actual dollar interest here, but this line is not the subject of our real concern anyway.

of its stream of all expected future operating cash flows) *is not reflected* in current earnings, but the use of foreign currency debt to hedge that economic exposure involves changes in economic value that *are reflected* in current earnings, making it look like an exposure exists, when in fact the exposure has been hedged. Example 10-1 compares the results, in both economic and accounting terms, of three alternative financing scenarios. Figure 10-5 summarizes the results visually.

ECONOMIC EXPOSURE, ACCOUNTING EXPOSURE, AND MARKET PERCEPTIONS

The effects of changes in currency values on a company's reported earnings and its balance sheet are aspects of *accounting exposure*. The example demonstrates the general rule that base currency gains/losses on foreign currency transactions, not pertaining to an overseas subsidiary, must go through the income statement and be reflected on the balance sheet in changes to the retained earnings account and thus the equity account. When accounting exposure pertains to situations involving accounting for an overseas subsidiary, the exposure is referred to as *translation exposure*, and the implications are covered later.

The PDC Co. and Macrotek (Example 10-1) examples demonstrate the basic problem with financial statement reporting when there exists an economic exposure to exchange rate changes that cannot be accounted for within the framework of accounting rules and conventions; the company's reported income may not reflect the true economic income, and the book value of equity can drop even though the economic value of the equity was hedged and remained stable.

According to the most orthodox version of the efficient market hypothesis, rational investors are able to see behind accounting conventions and to understand the firm's true economic situation. In this view, rational investors are believed to comprehend fully PDC's use of the foreign currency debt as a hedge of economic exposure, even though accounting exposure affects the reported balance sheet and income statement.

However, despite the large academic following behind the efficient market hypothesis, many managers (and many accountants) believe that investors are not as capable of seeing through the accounting as assumed in the theory and, instead, rely upon financial statements as sources of fundamental information. In other words, it sometimes may be impossible for investors to accurately discern when financial statements reflect the true economic values and when not. Managers thus believe that accounting exposure tends to confuse investors and that investors actually perceive the accounting exposure as a real problem in itself. In addition to a concern about accounting exposure from the investors' viewpoint, management is also concerned from its own viewpoint in the many situations where compensation is tied to reported performance.

Macrotek Corporation is a purely domestic operation with no overseas sales. At time 0 you expect that the future operating cash flows will be $5,000,000 per year, given an assumed current spot exchange rate of 2 $/£. The company's cost of capital is 8%. You estimate that the company has an operating exposure to the British pound of 0.40. Assume that just prior to time 1, the pound depreciates by 20%.

Consider three possible scenarios: (1) no debt is in the capital structure at time 0, (2) the company has $25,000,000 of 5% coupon U.S. dollar debt outstanding (trading at par) at time 0, and (3) the company has £12,500,000 of 5% sterling debt outstanding at par at time 0. Assume that the economic value of the firm at time 0 is equal to the book value of the firm's assets. If the actually realized operating cash flow at time 1 turns out to be the amount that was expected at time 0, then under current accounting requirements, what will be the reported "net income" (using the framework here) at time 1 for each of the scenarios? Assuming that all the company's net cash flow is paid out in dividends, what are the theoretical economic and book values of the company's equity at time 1 for each of these scenarios? (Scenarios 1 and 2 are meant to set up a comparison with scenario 3.)

Solution 10-1 The total economic value of the firm at time 0 is $V^0 = \$5,000,000/0.08 = \$62,500,000$. The total economic value of the firm at time 1 is $V^1 = [1 + 0.40(-0.20)](\$62,500,000) = \$57,500,000$.

(1) If no debt is used at time 0, the time 1 net income is the same as the net cash flow, which is the same as the realized operating cash flow, assumed to be $5,000,000. The time 1 economic value of the equity is $57,500,000. The book value is the historical amount reported originally at time 0, $62,500,000.

(2) If, instead, $25,000,000 of 5% U.S. dollar debt is part of the capital structure at time 0, the interest expense at time 1 is 0.05($25,000,000) = $1,250,000, and the time 1 net cash flow is $5,000,000 − $1,250,000 = $3,750,000, which is also the "net income."

The time 0 debt-to-market-value ratio is $25,000,000/$62,500,000 = 0.40. The time 0 economic value and reported value of the equity are both $62,500,000 − $25,000,000 = $37,500,000. The debt is base currency debt, so its value at time 1 is the same as at time 0, $25,000,000. The time 1 economic value of the equity is $57,500,000 − $25,000,000 = $32,500,000. The book value of the equity is still $62,500,000 − $25,000,000 = $37,500,000. Note that the book value of Macrotek's equity overstates the economic value at time 1.

(3) If £12,500,000 ($25,000,000) of 5% sterling debt is used at time 0, the time 1 interest expense is (0.05)(£12,500,000)(1.60 $/£) = $1,000,000, and thus the net cash flow is $5,000,000 − $1,000,000 (in interest expense) = $4,000,000. Since the pound depreciates by 20%, the dollar value of the sterling debt declines by 20%, from $25,000,000 to $20,000,000, representing a gain for the firm's equityholders of $5,000,000. To get reported net income, we add the gain on the debt, $5,000,000, to the net cash flow to get $4,000,000 + $5,000,000 = $9,000,000. The time 0 debt-to-market-value ratio is $25,000,000/$62,500,000 = 0.40. Since the ratio equals the operating exposure, the equity value ($62,500,000 − $25,000,000 = $37,500,000) should be hedged for a period. Indeed, $57,500,000 (the time 1 total economic value) minus $20,000,000 (the time 1 debt value) equals $37,500,000, the time 1 economic value of the equity. The book value of the equity will now include the gain of $5,000,000, reflecting the accounting gain on the sterling debt in the face of the depreciation of the pound. The total time 1 book value of the firm's equity is $42,500,000, which exceeds the economic value of $37,500,000.

Time 0 ($X^0_{\$/£} = 2.00$ \$/£)   Time 1 ($X^1_{\$/£} = 1.60$ \$/£)

Economic and Reported Balance Sheet | Economic Balance Sheet | Reported Balance Sheet | Net Cash Flow and Income Statement

1. No Debt in Capital Structure

Time 0 — Economic and Reported Balance Sheet

Total value V^0 / Total assets	Equity value S^0 / Equity book value
$62,500,000	$62,500,000

$B_O = 0.40$ $B_S = 0.40$

%ΔX = −20%

Time 1 — Economic Balance Sheet

Total value V^1	Equity value S^1
$57,500,000	$57,500,000

Reported Balance Sheet

Total assets	Equity book value
$62,500,000	$62,500,000

Net Cash Flow and Income Statement

Operating cash flow	$5,000,000
− Interest expense	− 0
Net cash flow	$5,000,000
+ Gain/loss on FX	− 0
Net income	$5,000,000

2. $25,000,000 of U.S. Dollar Debt (5%)

Time 0 — Economic and Reported Balance Sheet

Total value V^0 / Total assets	Debt value D^0 / Debt book value
$62,500,000	$25,000,000
	Equity value S^0 / Equity book value
	$37,500,000

$B_O = 0.40$ $B_S = 0.667$

%ΔX = −20%

Time 1 — Economic Balance Sheet

Total value V^1	Debt value D^1
$57,500,000	$25,000,000
	Equity value S^1
	$32,500,000

Reported Balance Sheet

Total assets	Debt book value
$62,500,000	$25,000,000
	Equity book value
	$37,500,000

Net Cash Flow and Income Statement

Operating cash flow	$5,000,000
− Interest expense	1,250,000*
Net cash flow	$3,750,000
+ Gain/loss on FX	0
Net income	$3,750,000

3. £12,500,000 in Sterling Debt (5%) (equivalent to $25,000,000 at time 0)

Time 0 — Economic and Reported Balance Sheet

Total value V^0 / Total assets	£12,500,000 Debt value D^0 / Debt book value
$62,500,000	$25,000,000
	Equity value S^0 / Equity book value
	$37,500,000

$B_O = 0.40$ $B_S = 0$

%ΔX = −20%

Time 1 — Economic Balance Sheet

Total value V^1	£12,500,000 Debt value D^1
$57,500,000	$20,000,000
	Equity value S^1
	$37,500,000

Reported Balance Sheet

Total assets	£12,500,000 Debt book value
$62,500,000	$20,000,000
	Equity book value
	$42,500,000

Net Cash Flow and Income Statement

Operating cash flow	$5,000,000
− Interest expense	− 1,000,000†
Net cash flow	$4,000,000
+ Gain/loss on FX	+ 5,000,000
Net income	$9,000,000

*(0.05)($25,000,000).
†(0.05)(£12,500,000)(1.60 \$/£).

FIGURE 10-5 Results of Alternative Financing Strategies (Example 10-1) Macrotek Corporation

The understanding of the relationship between a firm's economic exposures and its accounting exposures requires thought and analysis.

On the other hand, managers agree that some investors do have some comprehension of the influence of exchange rates on economic values beyond that which is captured in financial reports and, furthermore, that this comprehension is reflected in market prices. For example, a *Wall Street Journal* article (January 3, 1992) once reported Merck, Inc., was a good play due to a weak dollar. (This suggestion presumes that Merck has not hedged its operating exposure.)

Since managers do believe that exchange rates influence stock prices in this fashion, and for purposes of stabilizing base currency cash flows, managers *are* concerned about economic exposure as well as accounting exposure. However, managers believe that the misunderstanding created by accounting exposure discourages the proper management of economic exposure.

There also exist situations where a firm's economic business is dictated by its reported balance sheet. For example, computed ratios from firms' reported financial statements are used by banks and investment analysts in credit and investment decisions. Thus, balance sheet appearances could impede a firm's ability to raise capital at times when capital should be raised. Also consider regulated industries. For example, the book value of an insurance company's equity dictates how much new insurance business a firm is allowed to write by insurance regulators. Here, again, accounting exposure forms the basis of an economic exposure.

ACCOUNTING ISSUES AND DERIVATIVES

Management has tried to find ways to hedge economic exposure without creating potentially confusing accounting exposure. One early solution was *off-balance-sheet* transactions in derivative products, such as forward exchange contracts, currency swaps, and options.

Currency Forwards and Swaps For example, we know from Chapters 5 and 6 that synthetic foreign currency debt can be created via a combination of base currency debt and forward exchange positions or currency swap positions. For some time, accounting rules required that only *realized* gains/losses on forwards/swaps be reported. For currency forward and swap positions with longer maturities than the current reporting period, the mark-to-market (MTM) gains/losses on the positions were permitted by accounting rules to be treated as contingent liabilities, discussed in notes to the financial statements, but not reported in the earnings statement or in balance sheet accounts. In this arrangement, it was possible to hedge economic exposure and avoid accounting exposure. One reason for this treatment was that the initial value of an at-market currency swap or forward exchange position is zero, making it difficult to book onto the balance sheet at historical cost.

However, the off-balance-sheet approach to synthetic foreign currency debt has been eliminated by accounting and regulatory authorities. These authorities now require that the mark-to-market gains/losses on these instruments be reported directly in a company's financial statements. Given this situation, the mark-to-market gains/losses on the forward/swap positions in the synthetic debt have effectively the same impact on a firm's reported income and on the book value of the firm's equity as if the actual foreign currency debt were used.

For example, suppose that instead of sterling debt, the PDC Co. in the earlier example employs U.S. dollar debt at time 0 and simultaneously takes an at-market short position in a fixed-for-fixed currency swap to pay pounds at 5% and receive dollars at 5%, with a notional principal of $6,000,000

(£3,000,000). The swap's periodic interest settlement to be paid by PDC Co. is 0.05(£3,000,000) = £150,000, and the contract exchange rate for interest settlements is 2.00 $/£, the spot exchange rate at time 0, since the swap's coupon rates are assumed to be equal. When the pound appreciates by 20% at time 1, the difference check that PDC would need to send to the swap counterparty would be (£150,000)(2.40 $/£ − 2.00 $/£) = $60,000. Assuming that interest rates have not changed, the new present value of the stream of payments that PDC owes in pounds has a new time 1 value in dollars of (2.40 $/£)(£3,000,000) = $7,200,000, while the present value of its future receipts of dollar flows from the swap is still $6,000,000. Thus, the mark-to-market value of the currency swap is $7,200,000 − $6,000,000 = $1,200,000, from the viewpoint of the counterparty long on sterling. This mark-to-market value represents a loss of $1,200,000 from time 0 to time 1 from the standpoint of PDC's short position on sterling.

The mark-to-market loss is currently required by accounting practice to be reported on the firm's income statement and will reduce the firm's retained earnings, just as the loss of $1,200,000 did in the earlier example where sterling debt was used. In this case, there is no direct charge to the debt account, since the debt is actually denominated in the base currency. However, the $1,200,000 is booked as an unrealized liability in the debt section, and the common equity (in the retained earnings account) is reduced by $1,200,000 to reflect the mark-to-market loss. PDC's time 1 reported balance sheet and earnings statement would appear as in Figure 10-6.

Thus, given the same level of debt as before, if PDC had tried to hedge the operating exposure synthetically, by a short position on pounds in a currency swap, the reported time 1 earnings would show a loss of $560,000, and the equity account on the reported balance sheet would show $2,800,000, just

Assets (Total Value)		Liabilities and Net Worth	
		Base currency debt	$ 6,000,000
		Unrealized MTM loss	1,200,000
		Total liabilities	$ 7,200,000
		Common equity	$ 2,800,000
Total	$10,000,000	Total	$10,000,000

Relevant Portion of Time 1 Income Statement	
Operating cash flow	$1,000,000
Debt interest (5%)	− 300,000
Realized net swap payment	− 60,000
Net cash flow	$640,000
Mark-to-market gain/(loss) on currency swap	(1,200,000)
Net income/(loss)	($560,000)

FIGURE 10-6   PDC Co. Time 1 Reported Balance Sheet

EXAMPLE 10-2

Extend Example 10-1 to yet another scenario. Assume that Macrotek has $25,000,000 of 5% U.S. dollar debt outstanding (trading at par) at time 0 and an at-market short position in a fixed-for-fixed currency swap on sterling, with coupons of 5% for both dollars and pounds and a maturity that matches the maturity of the debt. The top scenario in Figure 10-7 also relates to the example.

Solution 10-2 The interest expense is $0.05(\$25,000,000) = \$1,250,000$, as in Example 10-1(2). However, there is a difference check received from the swap position in the amount of $-(\pounds625,000)(1.60 \; \$/\pounds - 2.00 \; \$/\pounds) = \$250,000$, which is a realized cash inflow. The company's net cash flow is the same as if sterling debt had been issued, $4,000,000 (= \$5,000,000 - \$1,250,000 + \$250,000.)$ The short swap position on pounds will also have a mark-to-market gain of 20% of the notional principal of the swap, given a 20% depreciation of the pound and no other changes. This unrealized MTM gain of $5,000,000 is reported on the income statement and goes to retained earnings. The impact on the income statement is effectively the same as if foreign currency debt had been used. On the reported balance sheet, there is an increase of $5,000,000 in the book value of the equity and a $5,000,000 offset of unrealized liabilities. The effective impact on the book value of equity is the same as if foreign currency debt had been used, an increase to $42,500,000. Since the synthetic sterling debt behaves economically like actual sterling debt, the economic value of the firm's equity is hedged in the same fashion discussed in Example 10-1(3) and is, thus, $37,500,000.

as it does in Figures 10-3 and 10-4 for the case where actual foreign currency debt is used. A similar analysis would demonstrate similar results of creating synthetic foreign currency debt via a strip of forward positions.

The earnings volatility caused by the accounting for mark-to-market derivatives valuation in reported financial statements, in situations where the economic exposure being hedged cannot itself be accounted for in the same financial statements, can create severe problems. To appreciate this point, read the real-world scenario on Kashima Oil on page 297.

Options Until a ruling by the SEC in 1992, the off-balance-sheet management of economic exposure by a firm was sometimes possible with long-dated currency options, widely available and traded in the global over-the-counter interbank market. Indeed this market owes much of its depth to the corporate use of options for this purpose.

The techniques for using options to hedge economic exposure and to create synthetic securities are much more complex than are those for forwards and swaps. However, corporations have often used options anyway to manage economic exposure, because (until 1992) the *Financial Accounting Standards Board (FASB)* rules on the treatment of futures and swaps did not mention options. Thus, the FASB silently, if inadvertently, "OKed" the use of

KASHIMA OIL

Kashima Oil refines imported oil for the Japanese market. In the early 1990s, the strong yen meant cheap inputs and high profits. Concerned that the dollar would appreciate, and thus that the price of oil would rise in yen terms, Kashima took long forward exchange positions on the U.S. dollar to hedge its anticipated future oil purchases. However, the dollar continued to depreciate against the yen. While this depreciation was good news in terms of Kashima's anticipated future operating costs and operating cash flows, it was bad news in terms of its forward exchange positions. These results would seem to be expected given the hedging strategy.

However, Kashima was apparently trying to hedge multiple periods of future operating cash flows with short-horizon forward exchange contracts. When the dollar depreciated, Kashima found that it had unrealized losses of ¥153 billion ($1.50 billion), which dwarfed the company's total annual pretax profit of ¥12.5 billion. The loss on the forward exchange contacts was an unrealized accounting loss that was only on paper and did not require cash. However. the accounting loss was nevertheless measured, while the corresponding economic gains on the present value of the anticipated future revenue stream was not, and could not be, accounted for "on paper." As a result of this problem, the firm had to sell ¥100 billion worth of property and securities, and four parent firms and 29 banks had to infuse fresh capital.

---

currency options for hedging economic exposure without having to report unrealized mark-to-market gains/losses as income or changes to retained earnings. However, this "OK" did not really condone the practice, but instead reflected the situation that the accounting authorities had not yet finished deciding on how to account for options.

An American Institute for Certified Public Accountants (AICPA) issues paper, *Accounting for Options*, did make suggestions on how options should be treated in 1986. However, since this issues paper was not an official FASB ruling, reporting for options continued to be controversial and regarded as a "gray area" by some companies, and many companies continued the off-balance-sheet use of options for economic hedging until the elimination of this practice in 1992.

Thus, for a while, the use of options for managing economic exposure represented a "loophole" that permitted the hedging of economic exposure without accounting exposure ramifications. When this loophole was closed by the SEC ruling in 1992, firms like the hypothetical PDC Co. had to begin reporting the unrealized mark-to-market gains/losses on options in the same fashion as with forwards and swaps.

Currency-Indexed Debt   Consider another approach to dealing with the accounting exposure problem, with so-called currency-indexed debt. Currency-indexed debt is technically (in the "legal" sense) denominated in base currency, but the interest and/or principal are "indexed" on an exchange

Time 0 ($X^0_{\$/£} = 2.00$ \$/£)
Economic and Reported
Balance Sheet

Time 1 ($X^1_{\$/£} = 1.60$ \$/£)
Economic Balance
Sheet

Reported Balance
Sheet

Net Cash Flow and
Income Statement

4. $25,000,000 of U.S. Dollar Debt (5%)

Pay sterling (5%)/receive dollars (5%) fixed-for-fixed currency swap
≡ synthetic £12,500,000 in sterling debt (5%).

Total value V^0 Total assets	Debt value D^0 Debt book value* $25,000,000		
$62,500,000	Equity value V^0 Equity book value $37,500,000		

%ΔX = −20%

$B_O = 0.40$ $B_S = 0$

Total value V^1	Debt value D^1 $20,000,000†
$57,500,000	Equity value S^1 $37,500,000

Total assets	Debt book value‡ $20,000,000
$62,500,000	Equity book value $42,500,000

Operating cash flow $5,000,000
− Interest expense −1,250,000
+ Difference check + 250,000
Net cash flow $4,000,000
+ MTM gain/(loss) 5,000,000
Net income $9,000,000

*Currency swap position in "notes."
†MTM gain on currency swap position reflected in value of debt.
‡MTM gain on currency swap position reflected in book value of debt.

5. $25,000,000 of U.S. Dollar Structured Debt

5% coupon linked to \$/£ exchange rate; principal also linked to \$/£ exchange rate.

Total value V^0 Total assets	Debt value D^0 Debt book value $25,000,000		
$62,500,000	Equity value V^0 Equity book value $37,500,000		

%ΔX = −20%

$B_O = 0.40$ $B_S = 0$

Total value V^1	Debt value D^1 $20,000,000
$57,500,000	Equity value S^1 $37,500,000

Total assets	Debt book value $25,000,000
$62,500,000	Equity book value $37,500,000

Operating cash flow $5,000,000
− Interest expense 1,000,000*
Net cash flow $4,000,000
+ Gain/(loss) on FX 0
Net income $4,000,000

*(0.80)($1,250,000).

FIGURE 10-7 Results of Alternative Financing Strategies (Continued from Examples 10-2 and 10-3), Macrotek Corporation

rate. As pointed out in Chapter 5, for example, if both the principal and interest are indexed in a direct proportion to an exchange rate, then currency-indexed debt is economically the same as foreign currency debt.

Thus, if PDC Co. were to employ U.S. dollar bonds, with interest and principal indexed in *direct proportion* to the $/£ exchange rate, this bond would behave economically the same as a sterling-denominated bond, but an argument could be made that the bonds are legally denominated in dollars and should be accounted for as such. This argument is assumed to hold in Example 10-3 below and is the concept behind the "Disney Notes," discussed on page 300. However, an accounting philosophy has recently evolved that if a financing technique is economically equivalent to a situation for which there is a clear rule for required treatment, then that treatment should be followed.

■ EXAMPLE 10-3

Extend Examples 10-1 and 10-2 to the following additional scenario: Assume that instead of the scenarios already described, Macrotek has $25,000,000 of 5% U.S. dollar currency-indexed bonds outstanding, with coupons and principal indexed in direct proportion to the dollar-pound exchange rate, trading at par at time 0 and considered to be U.S. dollar bonds by accounting rules. The lower scenario in Figure 10-7 also relates to the example.

Solution 10-3   With bonds whose coupon payments and principal are currency indexed in direct proportion to an exchange rate, the company is assumed to have issued foreign currency debt in an economic sense. However, if the accounting authorities recognize the bonds as technically denominated in dollars, then no unrealized gains/losses need to be figured in reported earnings or be reflected in the reported balance sheet. In short, the bonds would be base currency bonds in an accounting sense. The base currency interest expense, though, is the same as if sterling debt were issued, $1,000,000; see Example 10-1(3). Thus, the company's reported net income is equal to its net cash flow, which is $5,000,000 – $1,000,000 = $4,000,000. The economic value of the bond behaves like foreign currency debt and drops by 20% in U.S. dollar terms. The book value of the bond is carried at $25,000,000, since the bond is regarded for accounting purposes as being denominated in U.S. dollars. The economic value and book value of the equity at time 1 are thus both the same as at time 0, $37,500,000. The time 1 economic value of the equity is $57,500,000 – $20,000,000 = $37,500,000. The time 1 reported value of the equity is $62,500,000 – $25,000,000 = $37,500,000.

HEDGE ACCOUNTING

If a company could convince its accountants and the accounting authorities that it has a legitimate exposure, it may seek permission to use a technique called *hedge accounting*. With hedge accounting, a firm can use foreign cur

*T*HE DISNEY NOTES

In 1992, in the wake of the SEC's closing of the option loophole, Disney Co. began to issue dollar-denominated notes whose coupon interest payments were indexed on exchange rates. The first was on the dollar-pound exchange rate. The instrument's stated purpose was to hedge the portion of Disney's operating revenue stream that is denominated in British pounds. Disney planned similar issues tied to the dollar–French franc and dollar-yen exchange rates to hedge other currency exposures created by Euro Disneyland and Tokyo Disneyland.

To avoid the economic equivalence with a foreign currency bond, Disney did not set a proportional index factor for the coupon payments, and the principal in the Disney notes was *not* indexed on the exchange rate. Thus, the bonds would not behave economically exactly like a foreign currency bond. (Moreover, the notes have some built-in caps and floors on coupon payments.) However, the index factor for the coupon payments was geared so that the instrument would gain/lose dollar value more like a fixed coupon foreign currency bond than, say, like a dual currency bond with principal in dollars and fixed coupon interest in pounds.

The idea behind the notes is the hedging of economic exposure and the avoidance of accounting exposure. Although the economic value of the Disney notes behaves as if denominated in a foreign currency, Disney and its investment bankers would claim that the notes are technically denominated in Disney's base currency (dollars) and are not subject to accounting exposure.

rency debt and/or financial derivatives to hedge economic exposure, and the gains/losses on the hedge do not have to be recognized until the gains/losses on the assets being hedged are realized. The philosophy is that the accounting for hedge instruments should match the accounting for the underlying item. Thus, except for an amount that matches the current income generated by the assets being hedged, hedge accounting allows the gains/losses on hedging vehicles to avoid appearing as income/loss and/or being reflected in changes in the book value of the company's equity.

Thus, suppose that PDC Co. in the previous examples is able to convince accounting authorities that there exists an economic exposure that would be prudently hedged with a specific amount of foreign currency debt or derivatives transactions and that the company should be allowed to use hedge accounting for those specific debt/derivatives positions. The gains/losses on the book value of the debt and/or the MTM gains/losses on the derivatives would *not* have to appear on the income statement, nor would they be reflected on the balance sheet. Instead, the gains/losses would be simply explained in the "Notes" to the financial statements.[2]

---

[2]For an insightful discussion of hedge accounting, see J. Matthew Singleton, "Hedge Accounting: A State-of-the-Art Review," *Bank Accounting and Finance*, Fall 1991, pp. 26–32.

A firm with a situation like PDC Co.'s would not be able to simply dictate to authorities that it is hedging an economic exposure and assume that hedge accounting treatment would be allowed for its hedging instruments. Even though the firm has an economic operating exposure to the pound, the exposure is in its *future* cash flows, which are necessarily anticipatory in nature. Accounting principles do not recognize actual transactions in economic hedging instruments as hedges of anticipated cash flows. Instead, the transactions would be viewed by accounting authorities as speculative unless specifically proven otherwise.

If a firm's situation does not qualify for hedge accounting treatment, then the gains/losses on hedging instruments must appear on the reported income statement, in addition to the effects on the reported balance sheet demonstrated earlier. Thus, unless hedge accounting permission is obtained, the gains/losses on PDC's hedging instruments would be regarded as income, as has been shown.

If a company's exposure is to a foreign currency that does not permit liquid trading in hedging instruments, the firm may wish to *cross-hedge* with instruments denominated in a different foreign currency that is highly correlated with the actual currency of the exposure. Hedge accounting rules require that the company be able to prove the correlation between the actual currency of the exposure and the currency selected as the hedging vehicle.

It should be stated that the authorities are not purposely trying to impede firms like PDC Co. from managing economic exposure. Instead, the authorities are concerned that more liberal rules would open the door to speculation in derivatives in excess of positions necessary to manage exposure. Regulators worry that such speculation could harm investors. The concern of the authorities is well founded, as many companies have found their international treasury groups trying to become profit centers via speculation in the currency markets—sometimes with disastrous results for the firms and thus their investors. Indeed, disastrous reports of speculation often cite the use of options; this situation was no doubt the reason behind the 1992 SEC ruling, which curtailed the unqualified hedge accounting treatment of the unrealized gains/losses on options.

Without hedge accounting permission, a firm can hedge economic exposure if it wants with foreign currency debt or derivative products, but the gains/losses on these transactions must appear on the income statement, while the changes in economic value that are being hedged may not. This situation makes reported earnings more volatile than management desires.

Foreign Subsidiaries and Translation Exposure

The accounting exposure posed by an overseas subsidiary to its parent is related in many respects to the foregoing discussion. However, there are some distinctions in the accounting rules. Moreover, some of the issues are different from those encountered in the previous section. For purposes of clarity, we'll assume a simple scenario where the subsidiary's operations are based in a foreign country and denominated in the currency of that country.

The guiding authority for current procedures in financial reporting when overseas subsidiaries are involved is *FASB 52*, promulgated in 1981. FASB 52 requires that the parent choose a *functional currency* for any overseas subsidiary. For many subsidiaries, this is the currency of the country in which the subsidiary operates. The initial investment into the subsidiary's assets is carried on the subsidiary's books at historical cost and denominated in the foreign currency.

Then, each accounting period, the subsidiary's balance sheet and income statement items are consolidated with the parent's. Assuming that the functional currency is different than the reporting currency (generally the base currency), the consolidation is accomplished by translating the book value items at the *current* exchange rate. The fluctuations in the base currency book values of the subsidiary's assets, liabilities, and net worth create an accounting exposure situation for the parent's consolidated financial statements that is called *translation exposure*.

Translation exposure is proportional to the percent change in the foreign currency. That is, if the functional currency of a subsidiary is foreign and appreciates by 20%, then the book value of a parent's equity investment into the subsidiary will increase by 20%. Prior to 1981, under *FASB 8*, firms were required to report accounting gains and losses on the accounts of foreign subsidiaries according to a somewhat more complex method that also forced a significant amount of the translation gains/losses on a parent's equity in a foreign subsidiary to be reported on the income statement.

The situation under FASB 8 made reported bottom-line income extremely volatile for many firms with foreign subsidiaries. Despite protests by "efficient market" believers that investors could see through any aspect of that translation exposure that was not a true economic exposure, corporate management objected to the interpretation of such changes in value as income, and to their highly volatile earning reports.

These objections led to a significant change in accounting rules for overseas subsidiaries in FASB 52. Under FASB 52, the translation gains/losses on a parent's equity in foreign subsidiaries do not have to be reported on the income statement (nor reflected in retained earnings), but are instead taken directly to an account called the *cumulative translation account (CTA)* in the equity section of the balance sheet. This rule was designed to eliminate management's problem with highly volatile reported earnings.

Moreover, current hedge accounting rules put into effect after 1981, but under the general framework of FASB 52, permit the gains/losses on transactions that hedge the accounting gains/losses in the book value of a parent's equity in a foreign subsidiary to also avoid appearance on the income statement. In other words, hedge accounting permission is "automatic" for transactions in specific foreign currency hedging vehicles that offset a specific book value of a parent's equity in a foreign subsidiary.

Thus, if PDC Co. had a British subsidiary, it could have used sterling debt (or derivatives) *on its own books* to hedge the book value of its equity into the subsidiary, and the translation gains/losses on both the equity and the hedge could avoid the income statement. However, since PDC Co. has no foreign subsidiary on its books, then unless PDC could obtain special hedge accounting permission, accounting rules would not consider either sterling debt or currency derivatives as hedges, but as transactions whose gains/losses would have to be reported on the income statement, in addition to being reflected in reported net worth, as was demonstrated.

In ideal circumstances, translation exposure would represent an economic exposure. However, in this section we'll discuss examples where the translation exposure is not equal to the corresponding economic exposure, in an effort to point out the differences. The first example is one where the subsidiary poses a pure conversion exposure to the parent, but where a subsidiary's economic value does not equal its book value. Subsequent examples consider situations where book values and economic values are initially the same, but the subsidiary poses an operating exposure that is different than 1.

Companies like Disney have looked for creative means to manage economic exposure to foreign exchange risk without reporting misleading information in the financial statements.

ECONOMIC VALUE NOT EQUAL TO BOOK VALUE

Consider a U.S. parent, PRT Co., of a German subsidiary, called DMK Co. The *total* historical book value of the subsidiary is assumed to be DM6,000,000. Assume further that DM2,000,000 was borrowed by the subsidiary to help the financing and that the U.S. parent, PRT Co., supplied the other DM4,000,000. Assume that the total *economic* value of the subsidiary is DM8,000,000. Thus, the economic value of the subsidiary's *equity* is DM8,000,000 − DM2,000,000 = DM6,000,000.

The reported and economic balance sheets assumed for the subsidiary DMK at time 0 are shown in Figure 10-8. The subsidiary's equity value is viewed as a foreign currency asset from the perspective of PRT. For purposes of accounting for the book value of DMK's equity onto PRT's consolidated financial statements, the book value in marks is translated at the current spot exchange rate. Assuming an exchange rate of 2.00 DM/$ at time 0, the book value of PRT's investment into DMK's equity (DM4,000,000) is equivalent to $2,000,000.

Assume that PRT's other assets are domestic U.S. assets and have a book value of $5,000,000. For simplicity, assume that the economic value of PRT's other assets is also $5,000,000 and that PRT is an all-equity company. Thus, with the subsidiary's financials *translated* at the exchange rate of 2 DM/$, and with economic values *converted* at 2 DM/$, the parent's book value of total assets is $7,000,000. Since the economic value of PRT's ownership of the DMK equity is DM6,000,000/(2 DM/$) = $3,000,000, the total economic value of the parent's assets is $8,000,000. The parent's time 0 reported and economic balance sheets are shown in Figure 10-9.

Regardless of the economic operating exposure posed by the subsidiary to the parent, if the mark depreciates to 2.50 DM/$ (= 0.40 $/DM), the parent's *reported balance sheet* for time 1 would appear as in the top panel of

Time 0 Reported Balance Sheet			
Assets		*Liabilities and Net Worth*	
		Debt	DM2,000,000
		Equity	4,000,000
Total	DM6,000,000	Total	DM6,000,000

Time 0 Economic Balance Sheet			
Total Value of Firm		*Liabilities and Net Worth*	
		Debt	DM2,000,000
		Equity	6,000,000
Total	DM8,000,000	Total	DM8,000,000

FIGURE 10-8 DMK Overseas Subsidiary Co.

Time 0 Reported Balance Sheet			
Assets		*Liabilities and Net Worth*	
Subsidiary	$2,000,000	Debt	$ 0
Other	5,000,000	Equity	7,000,000
Total	$7,000,000	Total	$7,000,000
	Time 0 Economic Balance Sheet		
Total Value of Firm		*Liabilities and Net Worth*	
Subsidiary	$3,000,000	Debt	$ 0
Other	5,000,000	Equity	8,000,000
Total	$8,000,000	Total	$8,000,000

FIGURE 10-9 PRT Co.

Figure 10-10. The translation exposure, proportional to the percentage change in the value of the foreign currency, applies to the book value of the parent's investment into the subsidiary. Assuming that the currency of determination for the subsidiary's operating revenues and costs is the German mark, then the parent's operating exposure from the subsidiary is 1, and if the mark depreciates to 2.50 DM/$ at time 1, then the parent's time 1 *economic balance sheet* appears as shown in the bottom panel of Figure 10-10. The percentage change in book value is equal to the percentage change in economic value, but the value of the subsidiary on the parent's books is not the same as the economic value of the subsidiary. Thus, the parent would not be able to hedge all its

Time 1 Reported Balance Sheet			
Assets		*Liabilities and Net Worth*	
Subsidiary	$1,600,000	Debt	$ 0
		Cumulative translation account	(400,000)
Other	5,000,000	Other equity	7,000,000
Total	$6,600,000	Total	$6,600,000
	Time 1 Economic Balance Sheet		
Total Value of Firm		*Liabilities and Net Worth*	
Subsidiary	$2,400,000	Debt	$ 0
Other	5,000,000	Equity	7,400,000
Total	$7,400,000	Total	$7,400,000

FIGURE 10-10 PRT Co.

economic exposure without some income statement effects of the kind outlined above.

Specifically, PRT could alter its capital structure by issuing its own mark-denominated debt (and retiring some of its own equity) and would be permitted by accounting rules to regard up to $2,000,000 worth of foreign currency debt, the amount of the book value of its time 0 investment into the subsidiary, as a hedge of its foreign currency asset. In this case, the book value of PRT's foreign currency asset has a defined translation exposure. The gains/losses on debt issued to hedge this defined exposure would be allowed to flow directly to the cumulative translation account, bypassing the income statement, just as the gains/losses on the foreign subsidiary asset account under FASB 52.

However, PRT actually has $3,000,000 of total economic value that is subject to economic exposure, not $2,000,000. Thus, $1,000,000 worth of its

---

EXAMPLE 10-4

Suppose PRT Co. alters its capital structure at time 0, issuing $3,000,000 worth of mark-denominated debt and simultaneously retiring a similar amount of its own equity. Thus, PRT has an equity book value of $4,000,000 at time 0. The economic value of the firm's equity is $8,000,000 − $3,000,000 = $5,000,000 at time 0. Find the time 1 income if PRT's consolidated net cash flow is $200,000 (after interest). Find the economic and book values of PRT's equity, assuming that net cash flow is paid out as dividends. Recall that the time 1 exchange rate is assumed to be 2.50 DM/$.

Solution 10-4 At time 1, the DM6,000,000 debt liability is worth $2,400,000 instead of the time 0 worth of $3,000,000. In economic terms, the time 1 equity value is $7,400,000 − $2,400,000 = $5,000,000, the same as at time 0. Thus, the economic value of the firm's equity is hedged by the mark-denominated debt. Under FASB 52, the translation loss on PRT's investment into the foreign subsidiary's equity ($400,000) bypasses the income statement and would be taken directly to the cumulative translation account. In this case, there is also a translation gain on $2,000,000 (DM4,000,000) of PRT's own mark debt; since this DM4,000,000 of mark debt is worth DM4,000,000/(2.5 DM/$) = $1,600,000, the gain is $400,000 and is also taken to the CTA account, offsetting the translation loss on the asset investment into the subsidiary. The remaining DM2,000,000 ($1,000,000 at time 0) of PRT's debt must be treated differently however. This portion of the debt is now worth only DM2,000,000/(2.5 DM/$) = $800,000, representing a gain to PRT of $200,000. Since this portion of PRT's mark debt does *not* hedge a defined asset amount in book value terms, the gain must be reported as income and be added to retained earnings. The book value of total assets is $6,600,000 (see Figure 10-10); since the debt will appear as $2,400,000, the book value of the equity is $6,600,000 − $2,400,000 = $4,200,000, which is the time 0 book value of $4,000,000 plus the addition to retained earnings of $200,000. Net income is the net cash flow ($200,000) plus the currency gain ($200,000), but since net cash flow is assumed to be paid out as dividends, the addition to retained earnings is $200,000.

economic exposure to the foreign currency cannot be hedged with foreign currency debt or currency swaps/forwards, without PRT having to report the unrealized conversion and/or mark-to-market gains/losses of the hedging instrument on the income statement.

OPERATING EXPOSURE NOT EQUAL TO 1

If the operating exposure of the economic value of a subsidiary is not equal to 1, then translation effects will not reflect economic exposure, even if the book and economic values are the same at time 0. For example, assume that a subsidiary poses an operating exposure of 0 to its parent, instead of the pure conversion exposure of 1 assumed in the PRT/DMK example above. (See the case of Vulcan Materials Co. and its British subsidiary, cited in prior chapters.)

In this case, the parent's economic balance sheet would not change as exchange rates change, and no economic hedging is necessary. However, the parent is still subject to the same translation exposure discussed in the last example. Here it is useful that FASB rules prevent the translation gains/losses on the equity investment into the subsidiary from having to be represented as current income on the parent's consolidated income statement. However, the equity section of the balance sheet does reflect translation exposure through the cumulative translation account.

Management has sometimes believed that it should hedge its translation exposure, whether or not it is an accurate reflection of economic exposure. Such hedging of translation exposure that is without economic counterpart is antithetical to the efficient market hypothesis, but management may believe that investors (and/or directors) will *not* be able to see through the reported translation gains/losses. For companies whose translation exposure is greater than the economic exposure, this hedging activity will actually create economic exposure where none was present.

For example, if the operating exposure of a foreign subsidiary is 0, and the parent tries to hedge the translation gains/losses on book values by issuing foreign currency debt, and/or trading in forward exchange contracts or currency swaps, then the gains/losses on those hedge positions will generate *real* gains/losses, even though the balance sheet equity book value would be "hedged" against changes in the *book value* of the parent's investment into the subsidiary. Ironically, those real gains/losses on the hedging vehicles would *not* have to be reported on the income statement, because the transactions would be considered to be proper hedges under current accounting rules. Note that an ideal situation for the domestic company, PDC Co., in the earlier section of the chapter, would be to acquire Vulcan's British subsidiary. PDC Co. could issue sterling debt against its British assets and have the debt treated as a hedge for accounting purposes. The debt would actually be hedging PDC's own domestic economic exposure.

If a parent's economic exposure to a foreign subsidiary is positive but less than 1, then there may be a "good news and bad news" situation. The "good news" is that it may be possible to put on an economic hedge without having to report any income statement gains/losses on the hedging vehicle. For example, assume that the operating exposure of a subsidiary is 0.40. Then the parent could establish an economic hedge of equity exposure by using foreign currency debt in the amount of 40% of the total market value of the subsidiary. As long as the book value of the parent's investment into the subsidiary is not less than 40% of the market value, the parent can issue the appropriate economic level of debt and still have that amount be considered a hedge of book value under current accounting rules.

The "bad news" is that any excess of book foreign asset value over the book debt value will show up as a translation exposure of the firm's reported equity value on the balance sheet, even though economic exposure of the firm's equity has been hedged. Such translation-driven changes in the "excess" book equity values do not have any economic meaning, just as in the case mentioned earlier of the subsidiary whose operating exposure is 0.

For example, assume that the market value of a parent's holdings of a subsidiary is $10,000,000. Assume that the book value of the subsidiary is $6,000,000 and the economic operating exposure is 0.40. The parent can employ 0.40($10,000,000) = $4,000,000 in debt denominated in the foreign currency to put on a correct economic hedge that eliminates its equity exposure. However, the gains/losses from exchange rate changes for *the amount of book value not hedged*, which is $6,000,000 − $4,000,000 = $2,000,000, will have to be reflected on the reported balance sheet in the CTA and thus as a change in the book value of the equity.

Had the book value of the investment been $3,000,000, instead of $6,000,000, then using $4,000,000 in foreign currency debt would have still hedged the economic exposure, but the excess of foreign currency debt over the book value of the investment, $4,000,000 − $3,000,000 = $1,000,000, would be regarded as a foreign currency *transaction* (not a translation) by accounting rules. As such, the treatment discussed in the earlier part of the chapter applies: the changes in the value of $1,000,000 worth of the foreign currency debt would have to be reflected in the reported earnings in addition to the balance sheet. The other $3,000,000 in debt is regarded as a proper hedge of the $3,000,000 worth of foreign currency assets (at book value).

Summary

To the extent that changes in book values reflect changes in economic values, accounting rules reflect the impact of currency changes on the financial position of investors. Even if changes in book and economic values were equal, management might object to such changes in value being regarded as "income"—to be represented on the income statement. However, in the special case of overseas subsidiaries with equal market and book values, both the "net" balance sheet and income statement effects (under FASB 52) are eliminated with the hedging of the economic exposure.

However, some problems occur when book values do not reflect market values, yet a firm has economic exposure it wishes to manage. In such cases, management feels that it must consider how investors will perceive reported balance sheet changes, and especially how investors would perceive losses/gains on hedging vehicles reported as income without the corresponding economic gains/losses in asset values reported as income.

Glossary

Accounting Exposure: The changes in a firm's reported financial statements, required by accounting rules, due to changes in exchange rates.

Cumulative Translation Account (CTA):   An account designed to reflect the cumulative gains and losses from translating the value of a parent's ownership of foreign assets at different exchange rates.

FASB 8:   Accounting rules in effect prior to FASB 52 requiring firms to include translation gains and losses on foreign currency–denominated assets as reported earnings.

FASB 52:   Accounting rules superseding FASB 8, with the general impact that translation gains/losses on foreign assets do not have to be reflected in current earnings but are instead taken directly to the CTA on the balance sheet.

Functional Currency: The currency of the primary economic environment in which a corporation's subsidiary generates and expends cash.

Hedge Accounting: An accounting technique, permitted when it can be shown that hedging vehicles are truly being employed as hedges, that allows the gains/losses on the hedging vehicles to be reported gradually, as the earnings of the underlying assets being hedged are realized, allowing the mark-to-market gains/losses on the hedging vehicles to avoid inclusion in currently reported earnings.

Off Balance Sheet: The reflection of certain transactions, notably in financial derivatives, as contingent liabilities discussed in a financial statement's notes, but not directly on the balance sheet.

Translation Exposure: The restatement, as exchange rates change, of the base currency equivalent of accounting values for ownership of foreign assets.

Discussion Questions

1. Consider a company that has an economic operating exposure, but does nothing to hedge that exposure. Do you think that the market would correctly account for the equity exposure in the company's stock prices?

2. Consider a company that has an economic operating exposure that does get reflected in the financial statements. If the company were to use "off-balance-sheet" derivatives positions to hedge the economic exposure and create an equity exposure of zero, do you think that the market would recognize that the company has hedged its economic exposure with derivatives? Do you think stock prices would reflect the zero equity exposure?

3. Consider a situation where a company has an economic operating exposure, and this exposure does *not* get reflected in the financial statements, perhaps because the exposure is of the competitive variety. If the company were to use "off-balance-sheet" derivatives positions to hedge the economic exposure and create an equity exposure of zero, do you think that the market would recognize that the company is using derivatives to hedge an economic exposure? Do you think stock prices would reflect the zero equity exposure? Since the economic exposure does not show up in the accounting reports, do you think that the earnings volatility caused by the mark-to-market rules for the derivatives would influence stock prices?

4. Consider a situation where the economic operating exposure is zero, but that accounting exposure exists, as in the discussion of Vulcan Materials in the text. Do you think that the market regards the changes in the financial reports due to exchange rate changes as information and that stock prices are thereby affected?

Problems

1. Your company is a purely domestic company with no foreign sales or subsidiaries. At time 0 your company expects operating cash flows of $1,000,000 per year into perpetuity. The company's cost of capital is 10%. You estimate that your company has an operating exposure to the yen of 0.75. Assume that the exchange rate at time 0 is $X^0_{¥/\$} = 100$ ¥/$. Assume that at time 0, the company's economic values and book values are the same. Between time 0 and time 1 the yen appreciates by 20%. Consider five possible scenarios: (a) no

---

1. The total value at time 1 is $11,500,000. (a) The time 1 economic equity value is $11,500,000; the time 1 book equity value is $10,000,000. (b) If $7,500,000 of U.S. dollar-denominated debt is used, the time 1 economic value of the equity is $4,000,000; the book value is still $2,500,000. (c) If yen-denominated debt is used, the economic equity value at time 1 is $2,500,000. The book value is $1,000,000. (d) The book loss of $1,500,000 is reflected in an unrealized liability account. The economic impact is the same as if foreign currency debt has been used. (e) With currency-indexed bonds, the economic value and book value of the equity at time 1 are both $2,500,000.

debt is in the capital structure at time 0; (b) the company has $7,500,000 of 5% coupon U.S. dollar debt outstanding (trading at par) at time 0; (c) the company has ¥750,000,000 of 5% yen debt outstanding at par at time 0; (d) the company has $7,500,000 of 5% U.S. dollar debt outstanding (trading at par) at time 0, and has an at-market short position on yen in a 5% dollar–for–5% yen (fixed-for-fixed) currency swap, with a maturity that matches the maturity of the debt; and (e) the company has $7,500,000 of a 5% U.S. dollar-denominated currency-indexed bond outstanding, with coupons and principal proportionately indexed to the dollar-yen exchange rate, trading at par at time 0. What are the theoretical economic and book values of the company's equity at time 1 for each of these scenarios?

2. This example extends the previous problem. Your company does not have hedge accounting status. If the operating cash flow at time 1 turns out to be the amount that was expected at time 0, then under current accounting convention requirements, what will be the reported "net income" (using the framework of the text) at time 1 for each of the scenarios?

3. For practice with translation exposure issues for foreign subsidiaries, use the PRT scenario in the text and find what both PRT's time 1 reported balance sheet and time 1 economic balance sheet would look like if the time 1 exchange rate (in American terms) had turned out to be $X^1_{\$/DM} = 0.30$ \$/DM.

4. Assume that PRT's operating exposure to its investment in DMK were 0.60 (instead of 1) in the previous problem and that PRT employs $1,800,000 worth of mark-denominated debt to hedge the economic exposure of its $3,000,000 market value investment. How much of the debt can PRT count as a hedge? With the debt in place does PRT have translation exposure? Does PRT have any other exposure in the accounting sense? Is there any economic exposure?

5. Assume that PRT's operating exposure to its investment in DMK were 0.80 (instead of 0.60) in the previous problem and that PRT employs $2,400,000 worth of mark-denominated debt to hedge the economic exposure of its $3,000,000 market value investment. How much of the debt can PRT count as a hedge? With the debt in place, does PRT have translation exposure? Does PRT have any other exposure in the accounting sense? Is there any economic exposure?

2.   (a) $1,000,000; (b) $625,000; (c) -$950,000; (d) the impact is the same as if foreign currency debt has been used, −$950,000; (e) $550,000.

3.   For the reported balance sheet, the left-hand side would show $6,200,000; the right-hand side would show debt of zero, CTA of ($800,000), and common equity of $7,000,000, for a total of $6,200,000. For the economic balance sheet, the left-hand side would show a total of $6,800,000; the right-hand side would show debt of zero, and common equity of $6,800,000, for a total of $6,800,000.

4. $200,000 is subject to translation exposure. There is no other exposure in the accounting sense, and economic exposure has been hedged.

5.   There is no translation exposure. A sum of $400,000 is subject to exposure in the accounting sense, with its implications for reported earnings. Economic exposure has been hedged.

part IV

GLOBAL CAPITAL

BUDGETING AND

OTHER TOPICS

chapter 11

INTRODUCTION TO CAPITAL BUDGETING IN GLOBAL FINANCIAL MANAGEMENT

Capital budgeting is one of the major topics that you covered in your introductory financial management course. The most important issues in capital budgeting in general are (1) the identification of the relevant expected future cash flows to be employed in the analysis of a proposed project and (2) the determination of the proper capitalization rate for finding the present (time 0) value of the project's expected cash flows.

After these two tasks have been satisfactorily accomplished, capital budgeting boils down to finding a project's *net present value*, or *NPV*, which you should recall is the difference between the present value of the project's expected future cash flows and the time 0 investment outlay for the project. Applying the NPV criterion in a global capital budgeting analysis is the same as in traditional capital budgeting: If the present value of a project's expected future cash flows exceeds the time 0 investment outlay, then the NPV is positive, and the project should theoretically be accepted because its NPV is positive.

The scenario for the global capital budgeting exposition here is a parent company in one country that is evaluating an investment of its own funds into a foreign subsidiary. To keep the presentation simple, the parent's investment into the foreign subsidiary constitutes 100% of the subsidiary's equity. The foreign subsidiary may borrow additional funds on its own. As we shall see, there are a number of issues in capital budgeting in a global setting that do not appear in a purely domestic capital budgeting problem:

- Should the cash flows in the analysis be defined from the point of view of the subsidiary as a whole or from the point of view of the receipt by the parent?
- How should taxes be treated, given both foreign and domestic taxation?
- How should future exchange rates be forecasted for purposes of converting expected future foreign currency cash flows?
- Is the foreign exchange exposure of the expected future cash flows a risk factor that requires additional expected return as compensation?

The global capital budgeting topic is covered in two chapters. This chapter focuses in part on identifying the relevant cash flows for global capital budgeting analyses. In the first part of this chapter, the parent is assumed to know its traditional *weighted average cost of capital (WACC)* and wishes to employ that cost of capital as a "hurdle rate" or capitalization rate for net present value analyses. To justify this scenario, the subsidiary is assumed to operate in the same line of business as the parent company, and after conversion of its cash flows to the parent's base currency, the subsidiary's business risk is assumed to be the same as the parent company's.

Later in the chapter we address the issue of the determination of risk-adjusted capitalization rates to apply when the risk of the foreign subsidiary (or any other project) is not the same as the parent's existing risk. In Chapter 12, we address the topic of forecasting future spot exchange rates for purposes of converting a subsidiary's expected foreign currency cash flows into the equivalent amounts in the base currency of the parent and complete the capital budgeting analysis.

Cash Flow Identification in Global Capital Budgeting

Before going into the issues in global capital budgeting, let us start by reviewing some important basic aspects of capital budgeting that you dealt with in introductory financial management.

REVIEW OF THE WEIGHTED AVERAGE COST OF CAPITAL

We take as given that the parent company knows its own weighted average cost of capital, or WACC. Furthermore, we take as given that the company wishes to employ the WACC as the hurdle rate for new projects whose risk are the same as that of the company.

The WACC is often denoted k_w and expressed as

$$k_w = \left(\frac{D}{V}\right)k_d\,(1-t) + \left(\frac{S}{V}\right)k_e \tag{11-1}$$

where

D/V = the firm's debt-to-market value ratio

k_d = the firm's "cost of debt" (before taxes)

t = the firm's corporate tax rate

S/V = the ratio of the firm's equity (market value) to total value

k_e = the firm's "cost of equity"

The cost of equity for the firm, k_e, is the equity market's required expected rate of return on the company's stock, based upon the equity market's opportunity cost of forgoing investment in other stocks of the same risk. In addition to the business risk of the company's operations, the cost of equity depends upon the firm's relative debt level, D/V, since the degree of financial leverage influences the risk of the equity. Note that D/V plus S/V sum to 1, since $D + S = V$. Thus, D/V and S/V are weights on the component costs of capital, which is why the term "weighted average" is used.

As you may recall from financial management, the factor $(1 - t)$ is applied to the before-tax cost of debt, k_d, as a reflection of the fact that interest on corporate debt is an expense that is accounted for before the computation of corporate taxes; that is, interest on corporate debt is tax deductible.

📋 EXAMPLE 11-1

Suppose a firm's debt has a market value of $2,000,000 and its equity has a market value of $6,000,000. If the firm's cost of debt (before tax) is 8%, the cost of equity (given this degree of financial leverage) is 12%, and the corporate tax rate is 25%, what is the WACC?

Solution 11-1 $V = D + S = \$2,000,000 + \$6,000,000 = \$8,000,000$. $D/V = \$2,000,000/\$8,000,000 = 0.25$. $S/V = \$6,000,000/\$8,000,000 = 0.75$. Using equation (11-1), $k_w = (0.25)(0.08)(1 - 0.25) + 0.75(0.12) = 0.105 = 10.5\%$.

AFTER-TAX OPERATING CASH FLOWS

Since the present value of the expected cash flows will be found by using the WACC as the capitalization rate, it turns out to be logical that the definition of the cash flows is related to the WACC. In particular, since the tax deductibility of interest on debt has been accounted for in the WACC definition, we should not account again for this deductibility in the definition of cash flow.

For this reason, standard capital budgeting analyses that use the WACC as the capitalization rate define a project's capital budgeting cash flows as the *after-tax operating cash flows*, which are

$$O = O_{bt}(1 - t) = O_{bt} - tO_{bt} \qquad (11\text{-}2)$$

where O_{bt} is the operating cash flow (before interest and taxes) and t is the corporate tax rate.

Note that in the definition of after-tax operating cash flows in equation (11-2), tO_{bt} overstates the amount of actual taxes that will be paid. Actual taxes are based on before-tax *net* cash flow, $O_{bt} - I$, where I is the interest on the firm's debt. Thus, a firm's actual taxes paid are $t(O_{bt} - I)$. The overstatement of the actual taxes paid in the capital budgeting analysis is due to the fact that the interest tax shield is being ignored in the cash flows. However, this procedure is proper, since as pointed out, the tax shield benefits of the interest deduction are accounted for in the WACC, and thus should be ignored in the cash flow definition, or else the interest tax shield would be "double counted." It may help to think of the after-tax operating cash flow, $O_{bt}(1 - t)$, as the after-tax operating cash flow of an all-equity firm, which would have no debt interest to shield taxes.[1]

FINANCIAL LEVERAGE OF A SUBSIDIARY

Although we wish to address a global capital budgeting problem involving a foreign subsidiary, an initial important issue may be presented more clearly without the complexity of foreign operations. The issue involves a subsidiary's use of its own debt, which therefore creates a levered cash flow stream to the parent, and the impact of this situation on the appropriate capitalization rate to employ in the capital budgeting analysis. We'll cover this issue first, before considering the additional complexities of overseas subsidiaries.

Thus, assume for the time being a parent firm that is considering establishing a new subsidiary in its *own* country. The parent plans to use its own funds to finance a *portion of* the subsidiary's total investment outlay, and will acquire such funds by issuing its own new debt and equity in amounts that keep its own capital structure ratios unchanged. The remainder of the subsid-

---

[1]To understand this point better, we demonstrate that $O_{bt}(1 - t)$ is the expected cash flow that the WACC capitalizes to the time 0 total value of the firm, by letting k represent the rate that discounts $O = O_{bt}(1 - t)$ back to V and showing that k must be the WACC. Thus, assume that $V = O/k = O_{bt}(1 - t)/k$ and, correspondingly, $kV = O_{bt}(1 - t)$. Note that $O_{bt}(1 - t)$ may also be expressed for convenience as $(O_{bt} - I)(1 - t) + I(1 - t)$. Since k_e capitalizes the net after-tax cash flows to the equity value, that is, $[(O_{bt} - I)(1 - t)]/k_e = S$, then $Sk_e = (O_{bt} - I)(1 - t)$. Substituting this expression and Dk_d for I, we get that $kV = Dk_d(1 - t) + Sk_e$. Dividing both sides by V demonstrates that k is indeed the WACC. Since k was defined to be the rate that capitalizes $O_{bt}(1 - t)$ to the total value of the firm, and since k is the WACC, then the WACC must be the correct capitalization rate for $O_{bt}(1 - t)$, and vice versa.

> ### ☐ EXAMPLE 11-2
>
> Assume that a company's expected operating cash flows (before interest and taxes) are $1,120,000 per year. Assume that the firm is financed by $2,000,000 in debt, paying an 8% interest rate, and that the rest of the financing is equity (in an amount that is not needed to be known for this problem). The corporate tax rate is assumed to be 25%. Find the expected after-tax operating cash flows that should be discounted using the WACC, for purposes of finding the total value of the firm. For purposes of understanding, compare the fictional taxes assumed to be paid in the definition of after-tax operating cash flows with the actual taxes that would be paid.
>
> *Solution 11-2*   The expected after-tax operating cash flows for capital budgeting analysis are $O = O_{bt}(1 - t) = \$1,120,000(1 - 0.25) = \$840,000$ per year. The fictional taxes assumed to be paid in this cash flow definition are $0.25(\$1,120,000) = \$280,000$. The actual taxes that would be paid are $0.25(\$1,120,000 - \$160,000) = \$240,000$, since I is $0.08(\$2,000,000) = \$160,000$.

iary's investment outlay is borrowed by the subsidiary itself. The subsidiary's own debt is assumed to *not* be guaranteed by the parent. The subsidiary (as a whole) is assumed to have the same operating risk as the parent firm (as a whole), since the subsidiary and the parent are assumed to be in the same business.

After the payments by the subsidiary to its own debtholders, any remaining cash flows generated by the subsidiary are paid to the parent company. These cash flows are the net cash flows from the viewpoint of the subsidiary, but the parent regards these cash flows as operating cash flows from its point of view. See Figure 11-1. The *question* is:

Which cash flow should the parent employ when performing the capital budgeting analysis:

1. the total operating cash flow of the subsidiary (before the subsidiary's own debt service) or

2. the cash flow to the parent (the subsidiary's net cash flow after the subsidiary's own debt service)?

While it is natural for a parent to think in terms of the cash flows it receives from the subsidiary after the subsidiary services its own debt (choice 2), it is generally easier to use the total operating cash flow of the subsidiary (choice 1) for a capital budgeting analysis. The reason is that since the subsidiary as a whole is assumed to have the same business risk as the parent firm as a whole, then the parent's cost of capital (the WACC) is the appropriate discount rate to use to find the present value of the expected *total* operating cash flows of the subsidiary. Thus, the appropriate discount rate to apply in the capital budgeting analysis is conveniently known, because the rate is the parent's WACC.

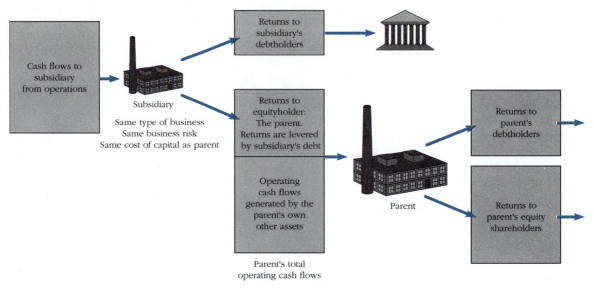

Figure 11-1 The Levered Returns by a Subsidiary to the Parent

By the same token, the parent's WACC is *not* the appropriate capitalization rate to find the present value of the expected cash flows to the parent (after the subsidiary's own debt service). The cash flow stream to the parent is *levered* by the subsidiary's own debt and therefore constitutes a more risky cash flow stream to the parent than the operating cash flows that the parent generates from its own operations.[2]

In principle, a capital budgeting analysis *may* be performed with the cash flows to the parent, but then the parent's WACC would have to be adjusted to reflect the degree of financial leverage imposed by the subsidiary's use of its own debt financing. This leverage adjustment is possible, but it is not very intuitive to perform. For this reason, as long as the parent knows its own cost of capital and the subsidiary has the same business risk as the parent, it seems easier to simply employ the parent's cost of capital, which is appropriate to apply to the after-tax operating cash flows of the subsidiary as a whole, *before* the subsidiary's own debt service. Moreover, this approach is more consistent with the standard capital budgeting practice in evaluating the parent's own projects.

Note that even though the NPV is found via an analysis of the subsidiary's total operating cash flows and not the net cash flows returned to the parent, *all* the NPV of a subsidiary accrues to the parent. To see this point, consider

---

[2]This point is correct except in the special case where the parent is merely a holding company "shell" and all the subsidiaries have the same degree of financial leverage.

a parent that supplies $2,000,000 to finance the equity of a subsidiary, while the subsidiary borrows $1,000,000 on its own. Thus, the total investment outlay for the subsidiary is $3,000,000. Next assume that the present value of the subsidiary's after-tax operating cash flows is $4,500,000. Thus, the subsidiary's NPV is $4,500,000 − $3,000,000 = $1,500,000. The present value of the subsidiary's equity, owned by the parent, may be viewed as the total value of the subsidiary minus the subsidiary's debt, $4,500,000 − $1,000,000 = $3,500,000. Thus, the NPV of the subsidiary's equity is the present value of the subsidiary's equity minus the parent's investment outlay into the subsidiary's equity, $3,500,000 − $2,000,000 = $1,500,000. Thus, the NPV of the parent's outlay is the same as the NPV of the subsidiary as a whole. Example 11-3 extends Example 11-1 to incorporate the issues covered thus far.

Of course, the issue just discussed also applies to overseas subsidiaries, but it was easier to make the point about the subsidiary's debt and the finan-

---

EXAMPLE 11-3

Following the information in Example 11-1, before the investment into the subsidiary, the parent is assumed to have $8,000,000 in total firm value and $2,000,000 of debt. Thus, the equity value of the parent company is $6,000,000 before the subsidiary investment. The proposal for the new subsidiary calls for a *total* investment outlay of $4,000,000. The parent plans to invest $3,000,000 of its own funds into the subsidiary as the subsidiary's equity, acquiring the funds by issuing its own new debt and equity such that its own capital structure ratios remain unchanged. The remaining $1,000,000 of the subsidiary's investment outlay is borrowed by the subsidiary itself by issuing its *own* debt. Assume for simplicity that the interest rate on the subsidiary's debt is the same as the parent's debt. Assume that the subsidiary is expected to generate total operating cash flows (before interest and taxes) of $600,000 per year. As given in Example 11-1, the corporate tax rate is 25%. Find the NPV of the subsidiary as would be found in a parent's capital budgeting analysis of the proposed subsidiary.

Solution 11-3   From Solution 11-1, the parent's cost of capital (WACC) is 10.5%. Since the subsidiary is assumed to have the same operating (business) risk as the parent, it is reasonable to apply 10.5% to the subsidiary's expected after-tax operating cash flows to find their present value. The subsidiary's expected after-tax operating cash flows are thus $600,000(1 − 0.25) = $450,000 per year. The present value of the expected after-tax operating cash flows is $450,000/0.105 = $4,285,714. Thus, $4,285,714 is the total value of the subsidiary. Since the total outlay for the subsidiary is $4,000,000, the subsidiary's NPV is $285,714. Since the subsidiary borrows $1,000,000 on its own account, the economic value of the subsidiary's equity is $3,285,714. This amount is also the economic value of the parent's investment into the subsidiary. The parent, in other words, gets all of the subsidiary's NPV, $285,714, viewing this NPV as the difference between the economic value of what it owns, $3,285,714, and its own outlay of funds, $3,000,000.

cial leverage to a parent in a domestic setting. Now let us begin considering specific issues in capital budgeting for *overseas* projects per se.

A conceptual matter concerns whether or not a foreign subsidiary's net cash flows are actually repatriated to the parent or instead are reinvested into the subsidiary. Even if a subsidiary's net after-tax cash flows are not repatriated, the parent still owns the equity in the foreign subsidiary. Thus, even if the subsidiary's net cash flows are not regularly repatriated to the parent on a periodic basis, it is reasonable to view them as ac-cruing to the parent anyway. Whether the subsidiary's net cash flows are repatriated or accrue to the parent's overseas investment, the point made here remains that it is easier to use the subsidiary's after-tax operating cash flows in capital budgeting analysis, to avoid having to adjust for the subsidiary's leverage in determining the discount rate.

TAXES

Now let's consider tax issues. A subsidiary must pay taxes to the government of the country in which it operates, and the parent may have to pay taxes to its own government on the subsidiary's returns, even if the taxes are not paid in cash but implicitly accrue to a later time. Logically, the subsidiary's expected after-tax operating cash flows, to which the parent's own cost of capital (WACC) applies, should be viewed net of all taxes, including (1) the foreign taxes on the subsidiary's cash flows, (2) the parent's taxes on the subsidiary's returns to the parent, and (3) any extra repatriation-of-funds taxes (or penalties) to the foreign government. Since the basic issues covered in this section do not depend on currency, it is useful to make our points by employing the device that the foreign subsidiary operates in, and keeps its books in, the same currency as the parent's base currency. Again, this is a fiction, but the simplification for now allows us to focus solely on the tax issue.

Thus, if a subsidiary's after-foreign-tax (including extra and repatriation taxes) operating cash flows are $600,000 per year, and if the parent must pay $50,000 in additional taxes to its own government on the subsidiary's cash flows, then the subsidiary's overall after-tax operating cash flows for capital budgeting should be $550,000. Because of this double taxation, and since the foreign and domestic tax rates are generally different, the treatment of taxes could be regarded as a major complexity in capital budgeting analysis for foreign projects. But is it really?

The answer is "No." It turns out that the treatment of taxes is really not as complex as it might seem. Fortunately, it may be reasonable to assume that the expected after-tax operating cash flows of the subsidiary, to be discounted at the parent's WACC, are simply the subsidiary's expected operating cash flows before interest and taxes, O_{bt}, times $(1 - t_p)$, where t_p is the *parent's* tax rate, *not* the foreign tax rate. The assumption is that the government of the corporate parent allows tax *credit* for foreign taxes paid by overseas subsidiaries.

This approach is based on the assumption that the two countries have a *tax neutrality treaty* that is designed to relieve double taxation. Tax treaties are relatively standard and are often based on the Organization for Economic Cooperation and Development (OECD) Model Tax Treaty. The approach discussed here is the *credit method*, which is based on the principle that the parent's total tax burden should be the same whether the parent earns income at home or abroad. The alternative is the *exclusion method*, where no taxes are paid to the parent's government. In the exclusion method, the effective tax rate is the subsidiary's country's corporate tax rate. With the exclusion method, a foreign-owned entity is being allowed to compete on an equal basis

Global subsidiary strategy often involves a global capital budgeting analysis of expected operating cash flows, taxes, and risks.

with domestic firms. However, the exclusion method may create an incentive for parents to export capital and employment to a low-tax country.

To see that the effective tax rate is the parent's tax rate with the credit method, consider the following explanation. Assume for the moment that the foreign country requires taxes of 20% (including any extra taxes and repatriation penalties) on the pretax cash flows of a foreign subsidiary. However, it is the parent's own domestic tax rate that is the effective tax rate for the subsidiary's cash flows. The reason is that the foreign taxes paid serve as a *tax credit* in the parent's country.

For example, assume that the parent's tax rate is 25%. In effect, for every $100 in pretax cash flow generated by the subsidiary in the foreign country, $20 is paid to the foreign government, and even though $25 would in principle be due to the parent's government, the $20 in foreign tax serves as a credit; thus, only $5 is owed in taxes by the parent to its own government on the earnings of its foreign subsidiary. Since a total of $25 is paid in taxes after all is considered, which is the amount based on the parent's tax rate applied to the subsidiary's before-tax operating cash flows, then from the parent's point of view, the effective tax rate applicable to the subsidiary's before-tax operating cash flows is the *parent's* corporate tax rate.

What if the foreign tax rate exceeds the parent's domestic tax rate. Say, for example, that the foreign tax rate is 40% while the parent's tax rate in its own country is 25%. Thus, for every $100 in pretax cash flow generated by the subsidiary, $40 in foreign tax is paid, but $40 in tax credits is allowed by the parent's government. Not only do these tax credits offset the $25 that would be otherwise owed in taxes by the parent to its government, but the parent can also use the remainder, $40 − $25 = $15, to offset taxes that would be paid on *other* foreign income. Since the parent can reduce taxes on other foreign income by $15, a net total of $25 is paid in taxes after all is considered. Since $25 is the amount based on the parent's tax rate, then from the parent's point of view, the effective tax rate applicable to the subsidiary's cash flows is again the parent's corporate tax rate.

Technically, one must assume that the parent actually *has* other foreign income to use the excess foreign tax credit against. Note also that by not repatriating a subsidiary's cash flows, a parent may be avoiding and/or deferring some of the foreign penalty taxes and the domestic taxes, and turning some taxes into capital gain taxes, which may be at a different rate. You may want to consider these complexities in real-world analyses, but the details of incorporating them here would obscure the task of illustrating the fundamental issue that the parent's tax rate generally applies to a foreign subsidiary's before-tax income, assuming the credit method of a tax neutrality treaty.

CURRENCY OF DENOMINATION IN GLOBAL CAPITAL BUDGETING

We now turn to the more general situation where a company's investment into an overseas plant or subsidiary is expected to generate future cash flows in a

> ### ▦ EXAMPLE 11-4
>
> Assume that the subsidiary is expected to generate operating cash flows (before interest and taxes) of $500,000 per year. Assume that the foreign tax rate on pretax cash flows is 35%, while the parent's corporate tax rate is 25%. Find the appropriate cash flows of the subsidiary to be capitalized at the parent's WACC, assuming that the credit method of a tax neutrality treaty applies.
>
> *Solution 11-4* $500,000(1 − 0.25) = $375,000.

foreign currency. For such an overseas project, one must make an important decision:

Which currency should be used for the capital budgeting analysis:

1. The foreign currency or
2. The parent company's base currency?

For example, consider a project in Germany that is expected to produce after-tax (at the parent's tax rate) operating cash flows of DM2,000,000 per year forever. Would it be better to perform the capital budgeting analysis with these cash flows denominated in the foreign currency, or would it be better to convert the expected future cash flows into the parent's base currency denomination using some predicted future spot exchange rates?

While it might seem that predicting future spot exchange rates might not be too difficult, Chapter 12 demonstrates that future spot exchange rates require some considerable effort to forecast rigorously. Thus, it would seem that the most convenient denomination for an overseas project's cash flows is the foreign currency. However, to perform the capital budgeting analysis in the foreign currency, one must use a cost of capital that applies to the foreign currency, which is *not* the parent's base currency WACC.

In other words, suppose that the parent company of a German subsidiary is based in the United States and has a cost of capital (WACC) of 10.5%, as the discount rate that capitalizes the parent's currently expected base currency after-tax operating cash flows to the total base currency value of the parent firm. Again assume that the after-tax operating cash flows of the German operation, when converted into dollars and considering the uncertainty in the exchange rate, would have the same risk as the cash flows generated by the U.S. parent's other assets. Then although it would be appropriate to apply the parent's known WACC to the subsidiary's expected operating cash flows when converted to U.S. dollars, it is not appropriate to use the parent's WACC to find the present value (in marks) of the subsidiary's expected operating cash flows that are denominated in *marks*.

Why not? To see the answer to this question, think about a cash flow stream that is certain (riskless) in the base currency. For example, assume that the U.S. dollar is the base currency, and consider a certain stream of $50 per year forever. Suppose 5% is the "long-term" risk-free rate in the base currency. Then 5% is the discount rate in the base currency that should be used to capitalize the certain dollar cash flow stream back to its present value. Thus, the value of the example cash flow stream would be $50/0.05 = $1000.

Now think about the *same cash flow stream* as if it were owned by a German citizen who will be converting each certain dollar payment into marks at the prevailing spot exchange rate each year in the future. Since the dollar stream is known with certainty, the mark stream is *not* certain due to the uncertainty about future exchange rates. Thus, the appropriate base currency discount rate, 5%, is *not* the appropriate discount rate that the German investor should apply to the asset's expected cash flows expressed in marks, if for no other reason than the mark cash flows are not riskless! Even if one's imagination stretched to consider the absence of exchange rate uncertainty, so that the mark cash flows were riskless, the riskless interest rate to apply to a cash flow stream that is certain in dollars is generally different from the riskless interest rate to apply to a cash flow stream that is riskless in marks, just as dollar LIBOR is generally different from mark LIBOR for any maturity.

The point, in general, is that the appropriate discount rate to find an asset's value in one currency should *not* simply be applied to the foreign currency version of the asset's cash flow stream as a means of finding the asset's value in the foreign currency. This reasoning applies to a corporation's base currency cost of capital and the rate that should be applied to expected foreign currency cash flows.

In practice, one sometimes encounters an ad hoc procedure where the discount rate that a parent applies to the expected foreign currency–denominated cash flows is the sum of the base currency cost of capital plus the differential between the riskless interest rates in the two currencies. Suppose, for example, that the riskless rate in the foreign currency is 8% and the riskless rate in the base currency is 5%. Do these assumptions imply that if the parent's own base currency WACC is 10.5%, then the rate that should be applied to foreign currency–denominated cash flows is 10.5% + (8% - 5%) = 13.5%? The answer is "No." It is not appropriate to find an asset's present value in a foreign currency with a discount rate found by simply adding the differential between the riskless interest rates in the two currencies to the appropriate base currency discount rate.

The reason why this procedure is inappropriate can be seen by again considering a riskless cash flow stream in the base currency, for which the assumed base currency riskless rate, 5%, is the correct discount rate. If the riskless interest rate differential, 3%, is added to the appropriate discount rate for the base currency riskless cash flow stream, 5%, we indeed get 8%. But this result does *not* mean that 8% should be used to discount the expected cash flows of the security when assessed from the viewpoint of the foreign currency. Rather, 8% is the rate that applies to a *riskless* cash flow stream in the foreign currency, whereas the foreign currency version of the riskless base currency stream is uncertain due to exchange rate uncertainty. Thus, the expected foreign currency version of the riskless base currency stream should not be discounted at 8%. In general, then, to find an appropriate capitalization rate for a cash flow stream in one currency, it is *not* appropriate to simply add the riskless interest rate differential to the rate appropriate for valuation when the cash flow stream is expressed from the viewpoint of the other currency.

It turns out that there is no easy answer for converting a cost of capital in one currency to the cost of capital to apply to the same asset's expected cash flows when converted into another currency. Thus, in practice, while a U.S. parent may well know its own cost of capital, to apply to a U.S. dollar–denominated expected cash flow stream, it may not have an easy way to know the appropriate foreign currency cost of capital to apply to the same expected cash flow stream when viewed from the foreign currency denomination. Therefore, in overseas capital budgeting, while the convenient information about cash flows is the cash flow stream denominated in the foreign currency, the difficulties in finding the appropriate foreign currency discount rate lead parent companies to conduct capital budgeting analyses after converting the expected foreign currency cash flows to their base currency. The forecasting of exchange rates for this purpose is a topic left to Chapter 12. Figure

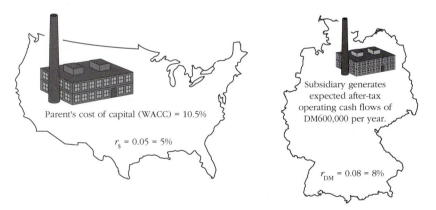

For the parent to find the *present value* of the foreign subsidiary's expected after-tax operating cash flow stream . . .

● Should the parent's WACC, 10.5%, be used, as in DM600,000/0.105 = ?
  Answer: No. The WACC here is a dollar rate, not a mark rate.

● Should the parent's WACC, 10.5%, be adjusted for the riskless interest rate differential, 8% − 5% = 3%, so that 10.5% + 3% = 13.5% is used, as in DM6000,000/0.135 = ?.
  Answer: No. This adjustment ignores the effects of future exchange rate uncertainty.

Result: Consider converting the expected mark cash flows to expected base currency cash flows with the help of forecasted future exchange rates.(See Chapter 12.) Then a base currency discount rate may be applied.

Figure 11-2   Problems of Discounting Foreign Currency Cash Flows Based on the Parent's Cost of Capital

11-2 summarizes the main results of this section. Next in this chapter we cover the subject of adjustments to discount rates for projects of different risk.

Global Asset Pricing Theory

In this section, we address the issue of finding risk-adjusted discount rates with a *global asset pricing model (GAPM)*.

A risk-adjusted discount rate is useful in finding the present value of an expected cash flow stream. Many companies may wish to assign different capital expenditure hurdle rates, or costs of capital, for different divisions or subsidiaries, based upon risk. For example, consider Grand Metropolitan, PLC (GrandMet), which is trying to estimate the cost of capital for each of its individual business segments by geographical area. GrandMet ranks among Britain's 10 largest companies and is a pure holding company for a group of business units that are widely diversified in terms of both global geography and in terms of products. GrandMet's three major operating sectors are foods, drinks, and retailing. GrandMet's operations include Pillsbury Brands (U.S.); Pillsbury Food Group (Europe); Haägen-Dazs (U.S., Europe, Far East); Alpo Pet Food (U.S.); drink brands like Smirnoff, Bailey's, J&B, and Cinzano (worldwide); Burger King (worldwide); and Pearle Vision (U.S., Europe, Far East). GrandMet's structure makes it a logical user of risk-adjusted discount rates. Like GrandMet, many global companies are faced with the desire to develop cost of capital estimates by business segment and by geographical area.

Asset pricing theory has been integrated into capital budgeting analysis for some time. The traditional approach in introductory financial management is to employ the capital asset pricing model (CAPM).

REVIEW OF THE CAPM

As you should recall, the traditional CAPM may be expressed as shown in equation (11-3)

$$k_i = r_f + \beta_i(k_m - r_f) \tag{11-3}$$

where

k_i = the equilibrium expected rate of return on the ith asset in the market portfolio

r_f = the risk-free rate

β_i = the beta of the ith asset relative to the market portfolio

k_m = the equilibrium expected rate of return on the market portfolio

The beta of the ith asset relative to the market portfolio, you may recall, measures the sensitivity of the ith asset's returns relative to those of the market portfolio and is the same as the slope coefficient in a simple linear regression of the ith asset's returns on the market portfolio's returns. The amount $k_m - r_f$ is viewed as the risk premium that the market portfolio is expected to earn in equilibrium to compensate investors for bearing that risk.

Introductory financial management texts and courses often stress the application of the CAPM to capital budgeting problems. A project's beta and an estimated risk premium on the market portfolio are used with equation (11-3) to estimate the expected rate of return that should be required on the project, given the observed valuation conditions in the market in the form of the risk-free rate and the estimated market risk premium.

To apply the CAPM to capital budgeting in a global setting, however, several questions arise:

- How should the market portfolio be defined: as the market portfolio of the base currency country, as the market portfolio of the subsidiary's country, as a combination of those two market portfolios, or as a global market portfolio?
- Should changes in currency values be included in that market portfolio's rate of return, or not?
- Since bill rates differ from country to country, what should be the appropriate risk-free rate?
- Should currency exposure of the proposed asset be taken into consideration as a risk factor that requires an expected return adjustment as compensation? If so, how?

These questions have been addressed by recent developments in global asset pricing theory. The rest of this section reviews some of the main results in this theory.[3]

THE GLOBAL ASSET PRICING MODEL

The theory of global asset pricing is based upon the idea of international diversification of investor portfolios, which is a concept that is increasingly found in reality. Given relatively thorough international diversification, the following global asset pricing model may in principle be used to find risk-adjusted required returns from the viewpoint of a given base currency:

$$k_i = r + \beta_{iG}(k_G - r) + \beta_{iQ}(k_Q - r) \qquad (11\text{-}4)$$

---

[3]We draw heavily from Bernard Dumas, "Partial Vs. General Equilibrium Models of the International Capital Market," NBER Working Paper #4446, September 1993.

where

r = the nominally risk-free rate of interest in the base currency, often thought of as that currency's LIBOR or the rate on that currency's government bills.

k_i = the expected rate of return that is, and should be, required on the ith asset, and on any and all assets that have "multiple regression betas" of β_{iG} and β_{iQ}.

β_{iG} and β_{iQ} measure the ith asset's risk as the sensitivities of the asset's nominal rate of return relative to (1) the rate of return of the global market portfolio, R_G, and to (2) the rate of change in a wealth-weighted index of exchange rates, R_Q, all measured in direct terms from the viewpoint of the base currency in which one is performing the valuation. (A numerical example of the currency index is covered later.) Thus, β_{iG} and β_{iQ} are the coefficients in a bivariate linear regression.

k_G is the expected rate of return that is and should be required on the global market portfolio, which depends upon the risk of that portfolio and upon the aggregate attitude of global investors to risk.

k_Q is the expected rate of change in the base currency value of a wealth-weighted portfolio of other currencies.

The relationship in equation (11-4) holds in any currency. In dollars, we are referring to the required nominal rate of return on the ith asset expressed in dollars, regardless of the home country of the asset. We are also referring to the dollar riskless interest rate, the rate of return on the global market portfolio expressed in dollars, and the dollar value of an index of currencies. Understanding this point clarifies the question about the relevant risk-free rate; if you apply the model to find the required rate of return for a foreign asset and you are performing the analysis with cash flows that have been converted into the parent's base currency, then the base currency risk-free rate is the relevant one to use.

Two differences stand out in the GAPM model of risk and expected return in equation (11-4), relative to the traditional relationship between risk and expected return in the well-known CAPM, equation (11-3):[4]

---

[4]This equation for risk-adjusted required returns is a global asset pricing equation adapted from Equation (2.9) in Dumas, "Partial Vs. General Equilibrium Models of the International Capital Market," under the assumption that the degree of risk aversion is the same in all countries. Equation (2.9) in the Dumas review is based upon the assumption that the purchasing power parity condition is consistently violated in reality. Dumas notes this result, as well as the fact that additional evidence and facts support global asset pricing theory that is derived from the assumption that purchasing power parity does not hold. If purchasing power parity is assumed to hold, then the inflation rate in every country would be the same after accounting for exchange rate changes. In this case, the asset pricing relationship may equivalently be expressed as either (1) the old CAPM, but with the market portfolio being the global market portfolio and the variables defined as "real," that is, inflation adjusted or (2) the same two-factor model for nominally defined variables as equation (11-4), but with the second factor being the global inflation rate.

1. The first difference, not surprisingly, is that the market portfolio is now interpreted as a global market portfolio.

2. The second and more striking difference, however, is that in the GAPM there are *two risk factors*, the one for market risk and the other for currency exposure risk. Correspondingly, in the GAPM, a risky asset has two betas that need to be measured, not just one. Moreover, the two betas, one measuring market risk and the other measuring currency risk, must be measured simultaneously via *multiple* regression. Multiple (bivariate) regression betas are different from the betas that would be estimated on the basis of simple single-variable regressions, because multiple regression takes into account the correlation between the independent variables in the regression, which in this case are the global market portfolio and the index of foreign currency changes. Students who have had an investments course may recognize that this model is similar to a two-factor arbitrage pricing theory (APT) model where the first factor is the global market portfolio and the second factor is the currency value index.

Before we apply the GAPM of equation (11-4) in a numerical example, let us explore the definitions of the variables at greater length.

RETURNS IN GLOBAL ASSET PRICING THEORY

In the GAPM, the rate of return on an asset or portfolio, whether domestic or foreign, is measured from the viewpoint of denomination in a base currency, after adjusting for exchange rate changes. Thus, for example, the rate of return on a French stock that is traded on the Paris Bourse, from the point of view of a U.S. investor who owns the stock, consists of two components: (1) the so-called domestic rate of return, which in this case is the rate of return on the French stock to French investors, that is, in French francs and (2) the rate of appreciation/depreciation of the French franc relative to the U.S. dollar.

The two components combine in a compound fashion. Let R_i denote the rate of return on the ith security from the viewpoint of a given base currency. If the security is denominated in currency C, with a domestic rate of return in currency C of R_{iC} and if x_c represents the rate of appreciation/depreciation of currency C relative to the base currency, then

$$R_i = (1 + R_{iC})(1 + x_c) - 1 \qquad (11\text{-}5)$$

For example, if LeTrec Industries stock on the Paris Bourse is trading at FF100/share at time 0, when the exchange rate is 5 FF/\$ (= 0.20 \$/FF), and the stock is trading at FF84/share at time 1, when the exchange rate is 4 FF/\$ (= 0.25 \$/FF), then the domestic rate of return is R_{FF} = FF84/FF100 − 1 = −0.16, while the rate of appreciation/depreciation of the French franc relative to the dollar is x_{FF} = (0.25 \$/FF)/(0.20 \$/FF) − 1 = 0.25. Thus, the rate of return on a U.S. investor's holding of LeTrec Industries is R_i = [1 + (−0.16)] (1 + 0.25) − 1 = 1.05 − 1 = 0.05, or 5%.

One can verify this answer given by equation (11-5) by starting with $100 at time 0, exchanging this amount into FF500, buying 5 shares of LeTrec, liquidating the LeTrec shares at time 1 for 5(FF84) = FF420, and then exchanging the FF420 back into FF420/(4 FF/$) = $105. In dollars, the rate of return was 105/100 − 1 = 0.05, or 5%.

Note from this example that the negative performance of LeTrec stock on the Paris Bourse was compensated for by the appreciation of the French franc relative to the dollar. The net effect was a positive rate of return for U.S. investors, due to the foreign currency appreciation. This example and the one in Example 11-5 are depicted in Figure 11-3.

THE MARKET PORTFOLIO IN GLOBAL ASSET PRICING THEORY

In the GAPM, the interpretation of the market portfolio is the global market portfolio, which is the portfolio of all risky assets of all countries in the world. Even though the global market portfolio contains assets from all countries, the rate of return on the global market portfolio, R_G, is expressed in terms of the relevant base currency. In other words, one does not simply combine the rates of return on all risky assets from the view of their own national markets, that is, in their own currencies. Instead, one must adjust all rates of return to one currency, the base currency in which one is conducting the analysis.

Thus, the rates of return on the global market portfolio will depend upon assets' rates of return in their own currencies, as well as the exchange rate changes. To understand the basic idea, assume for simplicity that there exist only two countries and two currencies. Let the rate of return on U.S. risky assets, in dollars, be 12%, and the rate of return on Japanese risky assets, in yen, be 30%. Assume that U.S. assets constitute 65% of the market value of the global market portfolio, and thus Japanese assets constitute 35%. Assume that

---

EXAMPLE 11-5

Consider a French investor's holding of shares of the U.S. stock Midwest Manufacturing, Inc. If Midwest stock goes from $50/share to $75/share from time 0 to time 1, while the exchange rate goes from 5 FF/$ to 4 FF/$, what is the rate of return on Midwest shares, from the point of view of the French investor with a base currency of French francs?

Solution 11-5   The rate of return on Midwest stock in dollars is $75/$50 − 1 = 0.50, or 50% The rate of appreciation/depreciation of the dollar relative to the French franc must be found using exchange rate quotes in direct terms from the point of view of the French franc as the base currency. Thus, $x_\$ = (4 \text{ FF}/\$)/(5 \text{ FF}/\$) − 1 = −0.20$, or −20%. Thus, the rate of return on Midwest stock, from a French investor's viewpoint, is $R_i = (1 + 0.50)[1 + (−0.20)] − 1 = 0.20$, or 20%.

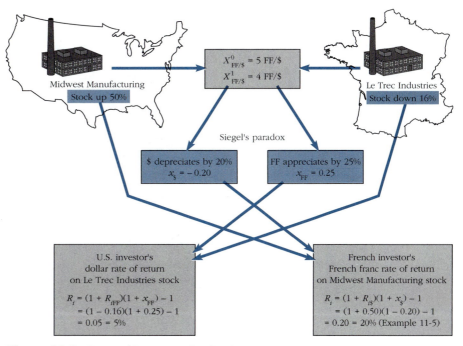

Figure 11-3   Rates of Return on Foreign Investments

EXAMPLE 11-6

Use the same information in the text example to find the rate of return on the global market portfolio from the yen perspective.

Solution 11-6   To find the rate of return on the U.S. market from the yen perspective, we must find the percentage change in the value of the dollar. (We know the dollar's appreciation is not 25%, from Siegel's paradox of Chapter 1.) Since we are not given exchange rates, but only that the yen depreciates by 25%, we have to invent some hypothetical exchange rates that correspond to a yen depreciation of 25% and then convert those exchange rates into direct terms from the point of view of the yen as the base currency. Say the value of the yen depreciates from 0.01 $/¥ to 0.0075 $/¥, which is a 25% depreciation. These hypothetical numbers may be used to find that the dollar appreciates from 100 ¥/$ to 133.33 ¥/$, an appreciation of 33.33%. Thus, the rate of return on the U.S. market from the Japanese perspective is $(1.12)(1.3333) - 1 = 0.4933$, or 49.33%. The rate of return on the global market portfolio from the Japanese perspective is thus $0.65(0.4933) + 0.35(0.30) = 0.4256$, or 42.56%.

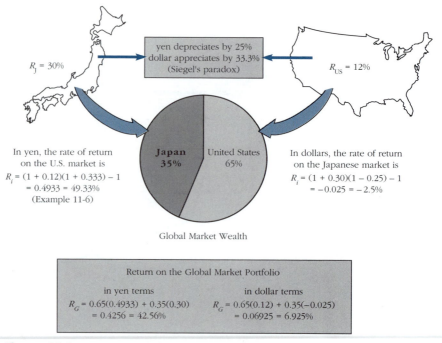

In yen, the rate of return
on the U.S. market is
$R_i = (1 + 0.12)(1 + 0.333) - 1$
$= 0.4933 = 49.33\%$
(Example 11-6)

In dollars, the rate of return
on the Japanese market is
$R_i = (1 + 0.30)(1 - 0.25) - 1$
$= -0.025 = -2.5\%$

$R_J = 30\%$

yen depreciates by 25%
dollar appreciates by 33.3%
(Siegel's paradox)

$R_{US} = 12\%$

Japan
35%

United States
65%

Global Market Wealth

Return on the Global Market Portfolio	
in yen terms	in dollar terms
$R_G = 0.65(0.4933) + 0.35(0.30)$	$R_G = 0.65(0.12) + 0.35(-0.025)$
$= 0.4256 = 42.56\%$	$= 0.06925 = 6.925\%$

Figure 11-4   Return on the Global Market Portfolio

the yen depreciates by 25% relative to the dollar. What is the rate of return on the global market portfolio from the dollar perspective? The rate of return on the Japanese assets from the dollar perspective is $(1.30)(1 - 0.25) - 1 = -0.025$, or -2.5%. Thus, the rate of return on the global market portfolio from the dollar perspective is $R_G = 0.65(0.12) + 0.35(-0.025) = 0.06925 = 6.925\%$.

Of course, managers in different countries want to view asset pricing from the point of view of their own currencies. The next example demonstrates the computation of the rate of return on the same global market portfolio as in the preceding example, but from the point of view of the yen as the base currency. Figure 11-4 depicts both the text scenario (dollars) and that in Example 11-6 (yen).

The Wall Street Journal publishes daily the dollar value of a world stock index. (See Figure 11-5.) This index could play a role in the future as the global market portfolio in applications of equation (11-4). The role would be similar to the one played by the S&P 500 as the market portfolio in the original CAPM in domestic U.S. analyses. In the latter analyses, historical stock returns published by Ibbotson and Sinquefield have often served as estimates of k_M. Perhaps analogous numbers for a global stock index will become readily available for application in equation (11-4).

DOW JONES WORLD STOCK INDEX

Friday, March 10, 1995

REGION/ COUNTRY	DJ EQUITY MARKET INDEX, LOCAL CURRENCY	PCT. CHG.	IN U.S. DOLLARS									
			CLOSING INDEX	CHG.	PCT. CHG.	12-MO HIGH	12-MO LOW	12-MO CHG.	PCT. CHG.	FROM 12/31	PCT. CHG.
Americas			114.45	+ 1.61	+ 1.43	114.45	105.21	+ 3.11	+ 2.79	+ 5.92	+ 5.46
Canada	114.33	+ 0.55	93.87	+ 0.65	+ 0.70	104.16	88.37	− 6.91	− 6.85	− 1.36	− 1.43
Mexico	118.34	+ 3.34	58.08	+10.28	+21.51	181.45	47.80	−112.26	− 65.90	−48.98	−45.75
U.S.	461.98	+ 1.31	461.98	+ 5.98	+ 1.31	461.98	416.31	+ 22.61	+ 5.15	+28.91	+ 6.68
Europe			115.69	− 1.57	− 1.34	121.15	110.89	− 1.87	− 1.59	− 0.01	− 0.01
Austria	99.43	− 0.52	106.76	− 2.06	− 1.89	113.96	95.91	− 2.16	− 1.98	+ 2.40	+ 2.30
Belgium	109.20	+ 0.63	117.15	− 1.43	− 1.21	123.30	111.37	− 1.20	− 1.01	+ 1.40	+ 1.21
Denmark	95.77	+ 0.85	99.71	− 0.24	− 0.24	107.35	92.02	− 5.64	− 5.35	+ 1.56	+ 1.58
Finland	211.25	+ 0.51	197.27	− 3.62	− 1.80	222.84	151.23	+ 23.78	+ 13.71	− 8.64	− 4.20
France	104.80	+ 0.75	107.65	− 0.88	− 0.81	120.91	104.68	− 11.32	− 9.51	− 1.52	− 1.39
Germany	117.85	− 0.32	126.04	− 2.22	− 1.73	134.14	112.48	+ 9.55	+ 8.20	+ 3.47	+ 2.83
Ireland	144.66	+ 0.03	121.65	− 3.06	− 2.45	130.08	106.32	+ 6.76	+ 5.89	− 0.94	− 0.77
Italy	138.89	− 2.38	102.37	− 3.73	− 3.52	143.55	98.43	− 7.42	− 6.76	− 7.17	− 6.54
Netherlands	131.84	+ 0.52	139.71	− 1.47	− 1.04	144.07	121.03	+ 10.91	+ 8.47	+ 5.83	+ 4.36
Norway	121.53	+ 1.96	114.59	− 0.09	− 0.08	123.93	101.45	− 1.01	− 0.87	− 8.00	− 6.53
Spain	114.00	+ 0.74	84.72	− 1.00	− 1.17	101.90	84.72	− 15.41	− 15.39	− 4.62	− 5.17
Sweden	158.39	+ 1.95	121.90	+ 1.10	+ 0.91	127.41	103.22	+ 5.31	+ 4.56	+ 2.48	+ 2.08
Switzerland	147.69	+ 0.31	169.57	− 1.79	− 1.05	181.32	149.77	+ 5.89	+ 3.60	+ 6.59	+ 4.04
United Kingdom	125.85	+ 0.97	105.83	− 1.65	− 1.54	113.27	100.94	− 4.55	− 4.12	− 1.51	− 1.40
Asia/Pacific			111.21	− 2.13	− 1.88	128.85	105.79	− 8.26	− 6.91	− 8.27	− 6.92
Australia	110.62	− 0.42	108.40	+ 0.06	+ 0.06	121.79	105.84	− 8.54	− 7.30	− 6.49	− 5.65
Hong Kong	178.90	− 1.50	179.81	− 2.77	− 1.52	231.17	158.20	− 51.36	− 22.22	− 4.12	− 2.24
Indonesia	176.96	− 1.51	158.28	− 2.43	− 1.51	210.12	156.97	− 51.39	− 24.51	−17.43	− 9.92
Japan	78.53	− 1.41	107.64	− 2.22	− 2.02	125.50	100.71	− 6.57	− 5.75	− 8.57	− 7.37
Malaysia	196.95	− 1.81	210.04	− 4.24	− 1.98	268.37	182.57	− 9.26	− 4.22	− 6.66	− 3.07
New Zealand	134.80	− 0.71	161.28	− 0.85	− 0.52	169.86	141.27	+ 4.99	+ 3.19	+ 5.42	+ 3.48
Singapore	148.71	− 0.86	169.76	− 1.96	− 1.14	191.35	139.96	+ 14.97	+ 9.67	− 8.30	− 4.66
Thailand	185.42	− 2.23	176.54	− 3.90	− 2.16	237.09	176.16	− 17.02	− 8.80	−31.11	−14.98
Asia/Pacific (ex. Japan)			149.95	− 1.86	− 1.23	181.63	140.27	− 20.48	− 12.02	− 7.62	− 4.83
World (ex. U.S.)			111.32	− 1.67	− 1.48	124.28	108.30	− 6.84	− 5.79	− 5.26	− 4.51
DJ WORLD STOCK INDEX			113.47	− 0.46	− 0.40	119.86	109.40	− 2.05	− 1.78	− 0.47	− 0.41

Indexes based on 6/30/82=100 for U.S., 12/31/91=100 for World.   ©1995 Dow Jones & Co. Inc., All Rights Reserved

Figure 11-5   Dow Jones World Stock Index
Source: The Wall Street Journal, March 10, 1995. Reprinted by permission of *The Wall Street Journal*, © 1995 Dow Jones & Company, Inc. All Rights Reserved Worldwide.

THE CURRENCY INDEX IN THE GAPM

Here is a numerical example of how the base currency value of the index of foreign currencies is constructed. For simplicity, assume that there exist only four countries: Japan, Germany, England, and the United States. Assume that Japan's wealth is 25% of global wealth, Germany's is 20%, and England's is

15%. Thus, the U.S. wealth is 40% of global wealth. Assume that at time 0 the exchange rates are 100 ¥/$, 1.60 DM/$, and 1.40 $/£. Given $100, assume that you hold $40 in dollars, buy $25 worth of yen (¥2500), $20 worth of marks (DM32), and $15 worth of pounds [($15)/(1.40 $/£) = £10.71]. A total of $60 is thus invested into the foreign currencies. Assume that, relative to the dollar, the value of the pound appreciates by 6% [to 1.06(1.40 $/£) = 1.484 $/£], the value of the mark appreciates by 22% [to 1.22(0.625 $/DM) = 0.7625 $/DM], and the value of the yen depreciates by 8% [to 0.92(0.01 $/¥) = 0.0092 $/¥]. In dollars, the entire currency portfolio, including the $40, is now worth $40 + £10.71(1.484 $/£) + DM32(0.7625 $/DM) + ¥2500(0.0092 $/¥) = $103.33. The percentage change in the dollar value of the currency portfolio "index" is 103.33/100 − 1 = 0.0333, or 3.33%. As stated previously, the percentage change in the currency index is denoted R_Q, and the expectation in equilibrium is denoted k_Q.

The easy way to find R_Q is by taking a "weighted average," but the weights do not add to 1 in this case. In the preceding example, R_Q may be found as 0.25(−0.08) + 0.20(0.22) + 0.15(0.06) = 0.033, or 3.3%. The weights in the foreign exchange index do not add to 1, since total wealth includes the wealth of all countries, including that of the country of the pricing currency. The rate of change in the currency index measures the rate of change in the value of a portfolio of all currencies relative to the base currency.

As noted, the percentage change R_Q has the expectation in equilibrium of k_Q. Assume that, relative to the dollar, the value of the pound is *expected* to appreciate by 8%, the value of the mark is expected to depreciate by 10%, and the value of the yen is expected to appreciate by 4%. Then k_Q is 0.25(0.04) + 0.20(−0.10) + 0.15(0.08) = 0.002, or 0.2%.

▥ EXAMPLE 11-7

Assume a base currency of U.S. dollars. Assume that U.S. assets constitute 25% of the global market portfolio. Assume that there exist three other "countries," (1) Europe, (2) Asia, and (3) Australia, with currencies called (1) ECU, (2) yen, and (3) Australian dollar. Assume also that European assets constitute 40% of the global market portfolio, Asia 30%, and Australia 5%. If, relative to the dollar, the ECU is expected to appreciate by 5%, but actually appreciates by 12%, the yen is expected to depreciate by 4%, but actually appreciates by 6%, and the Australian dollar is expected to appreciate by 2%, but actually depreciates by 4%, find k_Q and R_Q.

Solution 11-7 k_Q = 0.40(0.05) + 0.30(-0.04) + 0.05(0.02) = 0.009, or 0.9%. R_Q = 0.40(0.12) + 0.30(0.06) + 0.05(−0.04) = 0.064, or 6.4%.

While the foregoing explanation was intended to be instructive, you may find it burdensome to construct your own currency index for purposes of

The sensitivity of returns to an index of currencies is the second risk factor in the global asset pricing model.

applying the GAPM. A number of currency indexes are available, such as the J. P. Morgan Index, the Federal Reserve Bank Index, the U.S. Dollar Index (on which futures contracts are traded on the FINEX), the *New York Times* Index, and so forth. Generally, the existing exchange rate indexes are trade weighted, rather than asset market value weighted. However, values of a trade-weighted index may still provide a reasonably close "proxy" for R_Q anyway, until such time as a more precise time series of estimated R_Q values becomes readily available. Remember to be sure to apply the index in direct terms from the viewpoint of the currency in which you are working.

APPLYING THE GAPM

Now we move on to apply equation (11-4) to find a hurdle rate for a foreign project or subsidiary, which we demonstrate through the following numerical example. Assume that the potential rates of return represented by DMK Co.'s future operating cash flows, when valued in base currency (dollar) terms, would have multiple regression coefficients of β_{iG} = 1.05 (the sensitivity relative to the global market portfolio) and β_{iQ} = 0.45 (the sensitivity relative to changes in the dollar value of the wealth-weighted index of foreign currencies). Assume that the expected dollar rate of return on the global market portfolio, k_G, is 0.10 and the expected rate of change in the dollar value of the index of currencies, k_Q, is 0.0395. Assume that the dollar riskless rate is 6%. The appropriate capitalization rate for PRT Co. to apply to DMK's expected operating cash flows, in *dollar* terms, is k_i = 0.06 + 1.05(0.10 − 0.06) + 0.45(0.0395 − 0.06) = 0.0928, or 9.28%.

In principle, global asset pricing theory provides a model of the appropriate hurdle rate for either a foreign currency or base currency analysis. Thus, in principle, we could choose to denominate a project's cash flows in the foreign currency and use the theory to set a foreign currency hurdle rate. However, in this case, we would need to know the "betas" of the project's foreign currency returns with respect to the global market portfolio and the currency index, with *all* variables denominated from the viewpoint of the foreign currency. Naturally, it is more intuitive to think in terms of one's base currency.

Summary

This chapter has introduced the topic of global capital budgeting. First, under the assumption that firms wish to employ a standard WACC concept in dis-

---

EXAMPLE 11-8

Assume that the rates of return represented by DMK Co.'s potential future operating cash flows, when valued in base currency (dollar) terms, would have multiple regression coefficients of β_{iG} = 1.85 (relative to the global market portfolio) and β_{iQ} = 0.65 (relative to changes in the currency index). Assume that the expected dollar rate of return on the global market portfolio, k_G, is 0.10 and the expected rate of change in the dollar value of the index of currencies, k_Q, is −0.05. Assume that the dollar riskless rate is 4%. Find the appropriate capitalization rate for PRT Co. to apply to DMK's expected operating cash flows, in dollar terms.

Solution 11-8 k_i = 0.04 + 1.85(0.10 − 0.04) + 0.65(− 0.05 − 0.04) = 0.0925, or 9.25%.

counting cash flows, the appropriate after-tax operating cash flow concept was reviewed.

Second, we addressed whether cash flows should be defined from the viewpoint of a project as a whole or from the viewpoint of the receiving parent. While the parent's viewpoint is ultimately the relevant one, we found it easier to capitalize the project's overall expected operating cash flows, and then subtract the value of the project/subsidiary's own debt, to find the present value of the parent's investment. Capitalizing the expected cash flows received by the parent often would require adjusting the parent's WACC for the leverage created by the subsidiary's own debt.

Third, the issue of foreign taxes and home country taxes was covered, with the result that the after-tax operating cash flows are best found using the parent's domestic tax rate, even if the project is overseas and subject to foreign taxes, as long as the credit method of a tax treaty is applicable.

The difficulties in assessing risks and required returns in foreign currencies favors the conducting of global capital budgeting analyses in base currency terms. The drawback is that foreign currency cash flows must be converted to base currency cash flows for the analysis. Among other things, this conversion involves exchange rate forecasting. The next chapter takes up these issues and completes the topic of global capital budgeting.

Glossary

After-Tax Operating Cash Flows (for Capital Budgeting): The firm's operating cash flows minus a computed amount of taxes based on the assumption that no debt interest is deducted for purposes of shielding taxes.

Credit Method: A tax neutrality method that allows the parent credit for foreign taxes paid, based on the principle that the parent's total tax burden should be the same whether the parent earns income at home or abroad.

Exclusion Method: A tax neutrality method that permits a corporate parent to forgo paying taxes to its government on the earnings of a foreign subsidiary.

Global Market Portfolio: The portfolio of all risky assets of all countries in the world; the rate of return on the global market portfolio incorporates the rates of return on all risky assets in their own currencies, as well as currency value changes relative to the base currency in which one is conducting the analysis.

Tax Neutrality Treaty: An agreement between two countries to relieve the burden of double taxation on foreign operations' incomes.

Wealth-Weighted Index of Foreign Currencies: From the viewpoint of a given base currency, a weighted computation of changes in direct terms exchange rates with all foreign currencies, where the weights are the proportion of the foreign country's wealth in the global market portfolio.

Discussion Questions

1. Suppose a foreign government raises the tax rate on the earnings of foreign subsidiaries operating on its soil. Would this move discourage foreign investment. By the same token, would a reduction in that tax rate tend to encourage new foreign investment?

2. Suppose you were to perform two univariate regression analyses, first regressing an asset's returns on the returns of the global market portfolio, and then regressing an asset's returns on the percentage changes in the wealth-weighted currency index. Would the slope coefficients in the regressions (i.e., the "betas") be used with the GAPM? Explain.

Problems

1. Suppose a firm's debt has a market value of $3,000,000 and its equity has a market value of $5,000,000. If the firm's cost of debt (before tax) is 6%, the cost of equity (given this degree of financial leverage) is 16%, and the corporate tax rate is 30%, what is the WACC?

2. Assume that a company's expected operating cash flows (before interest and taxes) are $1,200,000 per year. Assume that the firm is financed by $3,000,000 in debt, paying a 6% interest rate, and that the rest of the financing is equity (in an amount that is not needed to be known for this problem). The corporate tax rate is assumed to be 30%. Find the expected after-tax operating cash flows that should be discounted using the WACC, for purposes of finding the total value of the firm. For purposes of understanding, compare the fictional taxes assumed to be paid in the definition of after-tax operating cash flows with the actual taxes that would be paid.

3. Following the information in Problem 1, before the investment into the subsidiary, the parent is assumed to have $8,000,000 in total firm value and $3,000,000 of debt. Thus, the equity value of the parent company is $5,000,000 before the subsidiary investment. The proposal for the new subsidiary calls for a *total* investment outlay of $3,000,000. The parent plans to invest $1,600,000 of its own funds into the subsidiary as the subsidiary's equity, acquiring the funds by issuing its own new debt and equity such that its own capital structure ratios remain unchanged. The remaining $1,400,000 of the subsidiary's investment outlay is borrowed by

---

1. 11.575%.
2. $840,000; $360,000 versus $306,000.
3. $23,758.

the subsidiary itself by issuing its *own* debt. Assume for simplicity that the interest rate on the subsidiary's debt is the same as the parent's debt. Assume that the subsidiary is expected to generate operating cash flows (before interest and taxes) of $500,000 per year. As given in Problem 1, the corporate tax rate is 30%. Find the NPV of the subsidiary as would be found in a parent's capital budgeting analysis of the proposed subsidiary.

4. Assume that the subsidiary is expected to generate operating cash flows (before interest and taxes) of $500,000 per year. Assume that the foreign tax rate on pretax cash flows is 20%, while the parent's corporate tax rate is 40%. Find the appropriate cash flows of the subsidiary to be capitalized at the parent's WACC. Assume the credit method of a tax neutrality treaty.

5. Consider a French investor's holding of shares of the U.S. stock Midwest Manufacturing, Inc. If Midwest stock goes from $75/share to $50/share from time 0 to time 1, while the exchange rate goes from 4 FF/$ to 5 FF/$, what is the rate of return on Midwest shares, from the point of view of the French investor with a base currency of French francs?

6. Assume that there exist only two countries and two currencies. Let the rate of return on U.S. risky assets, in dollars, be 20%, and the rate of return on European risky assets, in ECUs, be −12%. Assume that U.S. assets constitute 45% of the market value of the global market portfolio, and thus that European assets constitute 55%. Assume that the ECU appreciates by 18% relative to the dollar. What is the rate of return on the global market portfolio from the dollar perspective?

7. Assume a base currency of U.S. dollars. Assume that U.S. assets constitute 35% of the global market portfolio. Assume that there exist three other "countries," (1) Japan, (2) Germany, and (3) England, with currencies called (1) yen, (2) marks, and (3) pounds. Assume that Japan's assets constitute 30% of the global market portfolio, Germany's 20%, and England's 15%. If, relative to the dollar, the yen is expected to depreciate by 5% but actually appreciates by 6%, the mark is expected to depreciate by 4%, but actually appreciates by 6%, and the pound is expected to depreciate by 3%, but actually appreciates by 8%, find k_Q and R_Q.

8. Let DMK Co. be a proposed German subsidiary of the U.S.-based PRT Co. Assume that the rates of return represented by DMK Co.'s potential future operating cash flows, when valued in base currency (dollar) terms, would

4. $300,000.
5. −16.7%.
6. 11.11%.
7. k_Q = −2.75%; R_Q = 4.2%.
8. k_i = 14.2%.

have multiple regression coefficients of β_{iG} = 1.20 with respect to the global market portfolio and β_{iQ} = 0.40 with respect to changes in the indexed dollar value of the foreign currencies. Assume that the expected rate of return on the global market portfolio, k_G, is 0.12 when viewed in dollars and the expected rate of change in the indexed dollar value of foreign currencies is 0.07. Assume a riskless rate of 5% for dollars. Find the appropriate capitalization rate for PRT Co. to apply to DMK's expected operating cash flows, after conversion to dollar terms, assuming the GAPM model in equation (11-4).

chapter 12

EXCHANGE RATE FORECASTING AND GLOBAL CAPITAL BUDGETING

In Chapter 11, we argued that a capital budgeting analysis of an overseas project may be more easily accomplished in the analyst's base currency than in the foreign currency. Indeed, many companies actually do conduct their capital budgeting analyses in the base currency. However, this approach requires that we forecast future exchange rates for purposes of converting the expected stream of foreign currency cash flows into base currency terms.

Forecasting exchange rates is extremely difficult, perhaps even more difficult than forecasting stock prices. Often there are so many broad economic and political factors involved that forming a logical qualitative opinion is difficult, let alone a quantitative one. Although there is no easy solution for this problem, this chapter addresses the issues of exchange rate forecasting and of applying the forecasts in global capital budgeting analyses.

First, we review the economic fundamentals that should be considered. This review integrates material from Chapters 2 and 3. Second, we compare two formulas for forecasting exchange rates. The first is the uncovered interest parity condition of Chapter 3, and the second comes from the global asset pricing model (GAPM), introduced in Chapter 11. Although an equation is sometimes thought to be "valid" just because it has a mathematical form, one should understand that both of the formulas here are based on *equilibrium assumptions*. Therefore, for real-world applications, one should perhaps not expect too much from either formula. However, many analysts may want to learn about these formulas anyway, especially the GAPM formula. The GAPM formula for forecasting exchange rates is an extension of the uncovered interest parity condition, and as such, has all of the strong points, but fewer of the weak points of that parity condition.

Next in this chapter we apply exchange rate forecasts to multiperiod global capital budgeting analyses. If exchange rates are expected to change at a constant rate per period, and if a company's expected foreign currency cash flows are level or grow at a constant rate, then the expected base currency cash flows will change at a constant rate per period. In this circumstance, the *constant growth model* may be applied for purposes of valuing risky assets in the base currency.

If a company's operating cash flows have economic exposure to exchange rate changes beyond simple conversion effects, then a correlation effect between the foreign currency cash flows and the exchange rate may need to be accounted for when converting expected foreign currency cash flows to expected base currency cash flows using expected exchange rates. The computation of this correlation effect is discussed in the appendix.

Economic Fundamentals and Forecasting Exchange Rates

EQUILIBRATION AND THE LAW OF ONE PRICE IN THE GOODS MARKET

In Chapter 2, the international law of one price was introduced. The international law of one price is a theoretical relationship between goods prices and exchange rates that should hold if the goods prices and exchange rates are in equilibrium with each other.

As argued in Chapter 2, however, goods prices and exchange rates are often *not* in equilibrium with each other in reality, meaning that the international law of one price is often a theory that does not hold. For example, the yen might be overvalued relative to the dollar, and therefore the dollar undervalued relative to the yen, when the yen-dollar exchange rate is compared to goods market prices in Japan and the United States.

When currencies are misvalued relative to goods market prices, and thus when the international law of one price is violated, one factor that may influence the direction of future exchange rates is the pull towards equilibrium. One would forecast an overvalued currency to depreciate and an undervalued currency to appreciate, other things equal. If one wants to employ this misvaluation factor in forecasting exchange rates, then one would have to assess the degree of misvaluation. In this regard, information like the *Economist's* "Hamburger Standard" (Chapter 2) may be useful. Of course, one has no way of knowing how long a correction will take; the misvaluation may continue for some while and may even become larger, because a host of other factors will simultaneously be influencing exchange rates. There will also be pressure for goods prices to change, and these changes will have a bearing on the future currency value, as is discussed next.

INFLATION

In this section, we consider the role of future changes in goods prices, that is, inflation. If the international law of one price were to always hold, then an inflation differential could occur if one country expands its money supply at a faster rate than the other, relative to the growth in the two economies. In this case, the higher inflation rate will be accompanied by a depreciation of that country's currency. This result is the purchasing power parity condition (Chapter 2).

But we've already discussed the fact that the international law of one price is often violated, and we discussed in Chapter 2 the results of published studies that do *not* confirm the purchasing power parity condition empirically. Violations of the international law of one price will create their own pressure on goods prices. A country with an undervalued currency at time 0 may not only experience an appreciation of its currency back to equilibrium, but also experience *rising* goods prices (inflation) as part of the same equilibration process.

For example, many believe that the U.S. dollar was undervalued relative to the Japanese yen in early 1995. The high value of the yen was feared to cause Japanese auto manufacturers to raise the prices of their autos sold in the United States to recoup the losses in revenues from the slumping dollar. (See Chapter 8.) As U.S. auto manufacturers were expected to follow with their own price increases, there was concern that the undervalued dollar would *cause* domestic U.S. inflation in the form of higher auto prices as well as higher prices of other goods in general. Thus, while one might expect higher inflation in the United States and a *depreciation* of the dollar to go hand-in-hand if the purchasing power parity condition holds, one might instead see higher U.S. inflation accompany a dollar *appreciation* if both are part of the same process of equilibration toward the international law of one price that is violated. Thus, while the purchasing power parity condition contains some insight about exchange rate movements, the explanatory power of that condition in general is relatively weak, because the issues in reality are far more complex than the parity condition can handle by itself.[1]

---

[1]There is also a technical problem with using the purchasing power parity condition in a forecasting mode. Since the inflation rates over the time period of the model are "unknowns" at time 0, one is not mathematically justified in simply applying the condition in the following ad hoc "expectations form": $E(X^1_{\$/C}) = X^0_{\$/C}\{[1 + E(i_\$)]/[1 + E(i_C)]\}$, where the $E(\ )$ operator indicates expected value. Although often done, this application is ad hoc and technically incorrect when uncertainty is involved. The reason, which has the same mathematical basis as Siegel's paradox, is that the expected value of the reciprocal of a variable is not equal to the reciprocal of the variable's expected value. Thus, in this situation, it is not mathematically correct to assume that the expected value of the quotient of two random variables, $E[(1 + i_\$)/(1 + i_C)]$, is equal to the quotient of the expected values of the two random variables, $E(1 + i_\$)/E(1 + i_C) = \{[1 + E(i_\$)]/[1 + E(i_C)]\}$.

REAL INTEREST RATES AND ECONOMIC GROWTH

If a country is experiencing relatively high real investment returns, which may in part correspond to high real economic growth, then the country's currency should appreciate in value as foreign investors shift their investments to capture higher rates of return. This point was covered in Chapter 3. Thus other factors that one may wish to consider in forecasting future exchange rates are the real interest rate differentials and the economic growth rate differentials between the two countries of the exchange rate. As long as the real rate in one country is high (relative to the real rate in another country), the country's currency may appreciate *even if* the currency is already overvalued relative to goods market prices.

NOMINAL INTEREST RATES AND PORTFOLIO FLOWS

In the short run, as nominal interest rates rise, the value of the corresponding currency will rise, according to the asset market theory of exchange rates (Chapter 3). However, in equilibrium, which assumes among other things that *real* rates are equal across borders, the country with the higher nominal rate of interest is the one whose currency will be expected to gradually depreciate over time. This seemingly confusing situation was discussed in Chapter 3.

The nominal interest rates in the asset market theory are rates that are relatively near term and relatively riskless in nominal terms. Of course, there is more to the global asset markets than near-term, nominally riskless assets in the various currencies. In Chapter 3, we briefly covered the impact of long-term portfolio investors. We saw that in the case of the U.S. dollar in 1994, increases in U.S. dollar interest rates provoked foreign holders of long-term U.S. bonds to sell rather than to risk further price declines in their bonds. As the dollar proceeds from the bond sales were exchanged into the foreign investors' own currencies, the dollar depreciated in value.

Thus, we see that the asset market model of Chapter 3, which applies to near-term, nominally riskless assets, is not complex enough to capture the (perhaps irrational) activities of long-term foreign portfolio investors. In forecasting future exchange rates, the activity of global portfolio investors must be anticipated. This task may prove difficult as investors around the world are still in the process of diversifying internationally and deciding how much international diversification is best. More insight on the portfolio investment factor may be found in the accompanying exhibit, reprinted by permission from *The Wall Street Journal.*

*T*HE DOLLAR DEPRECIATION MYSTERY

The Mexican peso's precipitous fall has gotten a lot of attention lately. But the dollar's own depreciation is, in many respects, even more puzzling. Last year, the dollar fell 11% relative to the Japanese yen, 9% relative to the German mark and 6% relative to the British pound. While the dollar depreciated, the U.S. economy's performance continued to be much stronger and more vigorous than that of the European and Japanese economies whose currencies appreciated.

In contrast with those economies, U.S. gross domestic product growth has been rapid, unemployment has decreased, productivity and corporate profits have risen, prices have been stable, and the dollar's relative purchasing power has increased. Under these circumstances, one might have expected the dollar's exchange value to rise, rather than fall. Indeed, George Soros reportedly lost about $1 billion betting that this would happen.

The explanation usually offered is the U.S. current account deficit: the excess of U.S. outlays for imports of goods and services over receipts from exports. While this is surely a part of the explanation, the larger part lies in the size and *composition* of U.S. capital exports. Indeed, the U.S. has been the world's largest capital exporter at the same time that it has been the world's largest capital importer.

Underlying the surge of U.S. investment abroad has been the proliferation and expansion of international and "emerging market" global equity funds. Mutual fund managers tend to be less concerned with exchange-rate risks than with other considerations: the outlook for aggregate and sectoral growth in specific foreign countries; the competitive strength of specific foreign firms; the domestic, regional, and global market shares that these firms can acquire; their dividend policies and management capabilities; and the increased interest of U.S. mutual fund shareholders in risk diversification through investment in markets outside the U.S.

These major movers of U.S. capital outflow have been sufficiently bullish about buying into foreign holdings to be willing to pay a higher dollar price for foreign exchange.

But a larger share of capital imports into the U.S. represents foreign bank loans to U.S. banks, rather than equity investments. (U.S. tax withholding on earnings from equity investments reduces the incentives of foreign investors and portfolio managers to buy U.S. equities.) These bank IOUs tend to be responsive to changes in interest rates, and are more passive with respect to changes in exchange rates. They tend, therefore, not to have a major effect on exchange rates.

Thus, the net impact on the dollar's exchange rate is greater per dollar of capital exports than per dollar of capital imports. Capital exports can have this dramatic effect because they are so huge. In 1993, U.S. capital exports were the largest of any country, rising to $148 billion, principally due to this surge of U.S. investments in foreign equities by mutual funds, pension funds, and individuals (totaling $120 billion), as well as U.S. direct investment in places like Mexico.

For the first half of 1994, the corresponding figures are $50 billion for total U.S. capital outflows, of which $37 billion represents increased holdings of foreign securities, and $33 billion is direct investment abroad. (Reductions by U.S. banks in their claims on foreign banks account for most of the difference between total outflows in the first half of 1994, $50 billion, and the sum of portfolio and direct investment, $70 billion.)

U.S. capital imports have also been the world's largest, necessarily exceeding the magnitude of our capital exports by an amount sufficient to provide financing for the current account deficit. In 1993, total capital inflows into the U.S. reached $231 billion. Of this amount, more than 40% represented increased holdings by foreign governments and individuals of U.S. governments assets, with the remainder divided among foreign direct investment in the U.S., bank loans, and foreign investment in U.S. equities and bonds. For the first half of 1994 the corresponding figure for total capital inflows into the U.S. was $137 billion, of which about $20 billion consisted of increased foreign government holdings of U.S. assets, $60 billion represented loans to U.S. banks, and the remainder was divided among direct investment and increased holdings of U.S. securities.

On this reasoning, the dollar might continue to depreciate even if the U.S. current account deficit diminishes, because U.S. portfolio and direct investment abroad might continue to be large. However, to the extent that the most lucrative niches in foreign equity markets have already been, or soon will be, filled, and the next-best equities are less attractive, U.S. capital exports will recede and the dollar's value will appreciate. Also pointing in this direction is the plunge in the value of the Mexican peso. Mexico's setback may dim the luster of emerging markets, thereby reducing the flow of U.S. capital abroad.

To assess whether the dollar's foreign exchange value is more likely to rise or fall, look at the capital account, not just at the current account. The value of the dollar will depend on what happens to U.S. portfolio and direct investment abroad, rather than what happens to the current account deficit.

By Charles Wolf Jr.
   Mr. Wolf is dean of the RAND Graduate School of Policy Studies in Santa Monica, Calif.

Source: The Wall Street Journal, February 10, 1995. Reprinted by permission of The Wall Street Journal, © 1995 Dow Jones & Company, Inc. All Rights Reserved Worldwide.

Equilibrium Formulas for Exchange Rate Forecasting: A Comparison

Given the complexity of exchange rate forecasting in reality, one is tempted to hope that the process can be quantified with a mathematical formula. Unfortunately, the only potential candidates for a forecasting formula discussed below are two *equilibrium* formulas. As you might expect from the foregoing discussion, neither of the equilibrium formulas has been established as empirically valid in reality. Nevertheless, this section contains information about the formulas that may help you in forecasting exchange rates. The first formula is simply the uncovered interest parity condition, first encountered in Chapter 3. The second is an exchange rate forecasting formula based on the GAPM. The latter appears to dominate the former in terms of logic and robustness, but it is still based on the assumption that equilibrium holds.

THE FORWARD EXCHANGE RATE AND THE INTEREST PARITY CONDITION

Consider using the forward exchange rate as the "best guess" forecast of the future spot exchange rate. Such an approach is often taken based on the assumption that both the uncovered and the covered interest parity conditions are simultaneously valid. These two conditions were covered in Chapters 3 and 4 and are reexpressed in the paragraphs that follow.

In American terms, the *covered* interest parity condition, for dollars and currency *C*, is (for 1 year)

$$F_{\$/C} = X^0_{\$/C}\left(\frac{1+r_\$}{1+r_c}\right) \tag{12-1}$$

and the *uncovered* interest parity condition is

$$X^{1p}_{\$/C} = X^0_{\$/C}\left(\frac{1+r_\$}{1+r_c}\right) \tag{12-2}$$

As was pointed out in Chapters 3 and 4, the covered interest parity condition is a no-arbitrage condition that is a reasonably reliable relationship for many currencies in reality. Given the validity of the *covered* interest parity condition, the uncovered interest parity condition may be simply stated that the forward rate is equal to the expected spot exchange rate. However, the uncovered interest parity condition is a relatively naive economic theory that (1) requires market participants to be able to perform that complex task of forecasting future exchange rates "on average" and (2) does not adjust for risk. In addition, we now demonstrate that the uncovered interest parity condition suffers from a logical problem, based on *Siegel's paradox*, which has the following implication:

Siegel's Paradox

Under uncertainty, if the forward exchange rate were equal to the expected spot exchange rate when expressed in one currency direction, it is mathematically impossible for the equality to hold when the exchange rate is expressed in the other currency direction.

To demonstrate, assume a probability distribution for the time 1 spot exchange rate such that the rate can be either 1.00 $/£, 1.50 $/£, and 2.00 $/£, with equal probabilities. Clearly, the expected spot exchange rate, in direct terms from the point of view of the dollar as the base currency, is $E(X^1_{\$/£}) =$ (1/3)(1.00 $/£) + (1/3)(1.50 $/£) + (1/3)(2.00 $/£) = 1.50 $/£. For the sake of argument, suppose that the forward exchange rate, $F_{\$/£}$, is 1.50 $/£, so that it *appears* that the uncovered interest parity condition *is* valid (i.e., that the forward exchange rate is equal to the predicted exchange rate), at least expressing exchange rates in the direction of dollars per pound.

Then, in direct terms from the viewpoint of the *pound* as the base currency, the forward exchange rate would be quoted as $F_{£/\$} = 1/(1.50 \text{ \$/£}) =$ 0.667 £/$, while the probability distribution for the time 1 spot exchange rate

> ### ■ EXAMPLE 12-1
>
> Assume that the spot exchange rate for marks and dollars is 1.00 DM/$ at time 0. The future spot exchange rate at time 1 is, of course, unknown at time 0. However, assume that it is known at time 0 that the time 1 exchange rate will be either 2.00 DM/$ or 0.50 DM/$ with equal probabilities. Demonstrate the counterintuitive result that the value of the mark *and* the value of the dollar are *both expected* to appreciate by the same amount. Also demonstrate that while an assumed forward exchange rate of 1.25 DM/$ is equal to the expected exchange rate in DM/$, the reciprocal forward exchange rate of 1/(1.25 DM/$) = 0.80 $/DM is not equal to the expected exchange rate in $/DM.[2]
>
> *Solution 12-1*   The expected time 1 value of the dollar relative to the mark is 0.5(2.00 DM/$) + 0.5(0.50 DM/$) = 1.25 DM/$. The expected time 1 value of the mark relative to the dollar is 0.5[1/(2.00 DM/$)] + 0.5[1/(0.50 DM/$)] = 1.25 $/DM. Thus, the mark and the dollar are both expected to appreciate by 25% from their spot exchange values of 1 DM/$ and 1 $/DM at time 0. Clearly, although the forward exchange rate of 1.25 DM/$ equals the expected time 1 value of the dollar, the forward exchange rate of 0.80 $/DM does *not* equal the expected time 1 value of the mark.

is 1/(1.00 $/£) = 1 £/$, 1/(1.50 $/£) = 0.667 £/$, and 1/(2.00 $/£) = 0.50 £/$, with equal probabilities. The expected spot exchange rate, in direct terms from the point of view of the *pound* as the base currency, is $E(X^1_{£/\$}) = (1/3)(1$ £/$) + (1/3)(0.667 £/$) + (1/3)(0.50 £/$) = 0.72 £/$. This expected exchange rate is obviously *not* equal to the forward exchange rate of 0.667 £/$. Figure 12-1 summarizes this example.

This manifestation of Siegel's paradox is based on the mathematical issue that under uncertainty, the expected value of the reciprocal of a variable cannot be equal to the reciprocal of the expected value of the variable. Another aspect of the same paradox is that the rate of appreciation of one currency in an exchange rate is not equal to the rate of depreciation in the other currency of the exchange rate, as was first discussed in Chapter 1 and found throughout the text.

Siegel's paradox is a reason that the forward exchange rate cannot be equal to the expected spot exchange rate, but is not necessarily the only cause of differences between the forward exchange rate and the expected spot exchange rate. If markets are not risk neutral (and many people believe that markets are risk averse), then differences between the expected spot ex-

---

[2]This example is adapted from Fischer Black, "Universal Hedging: Optimizing Currency Risk and Reward in International Equity Portfolios," *Financial Analysts Journal*, July/August 1989, pp. 16–22.

Time 1 Exchange Rate Possibilities ($/£)	Probability	Time 1 Exchange Rate Possibilities (£/$)
1.00 $/£	1/3	1.00 £/$
1.50 $/£	1/3	0.667 £/$
2.00 $/£	1/3	0.50 £/$

$$E(X^1_{\$/£}) = 1.50 \ \$/£ \qquad\qquad E(X^1_{£/\$}) = 0.72 \ £/\$$$

$$= \searrow \qquad\qquad \nearrow \neq$$

$$F_{\$/£} = 1.50 \ \$/£ \longrightarrow F_{£/\$} = 0.667 \ £/\$$$

FIGURE 12-1   Siegel's Paradox and the Uncovered Interest Parity Condition

change rate and the forward rate may occur due to risk premia as well. A theory for these risk premia will be presented shortly.

Aside from the Siegel's paradox and risk premia issues, the empirical studies of the uncovered interest parity condition, and of the use of forward exchange rates as unbiased predictors of future exchange rates, do not support the validity of those concepts. Recall from Chapter 3 that according to the uncovered interest parity condition in equation (12-2), the currency with the higher interest rate is the one whose currency would be predicted to depreciate. However, consider the reported evidence in the following simulated experiment.[3]

Suppose one compared 1-month U.S. dollar and Canadian dollar interest rates each month over the period June 1973 to April 1993. Assume that each month one invested $1 million at the higher interest rate. If the U.S. interest rate was higher, one invested at that rate. If the Canadian interest rate was higher, one converted the $1 million into Canadian dollars at the spot exchange rate, earned the Canadian interest for a month, and then converted the resulting amount back into dollars at the end of the month at the spot exchange rate at that time.

If the uncovered interest parity condition provides a "best guess" about future exchange rates, then the experiment just described should yield no excess returns. The extra interest earned in Canadian dollars would be offset, on average, by the depreciation of the Canadian dollar relative to the U.S. dollar. However, this experiment reportedly would have yielded an average of $1072 per month of excess returns during the months of holding Canadian bills.

One reason for the excess returns may be that higher interest rates may reflect higher economic growth opportunities and not expected currency depreciation. As Chapter 3 argues, one should not put too much faith in the im-

---

[3]This material is adapted from Gregory P. Hopper, "Is the Foreign Exchange Market Efficient?" *Business Review, Federal Reserve Bank of Philadelphia*, May/June 1994, pp. 17–27.

plication of the uncovered interest parity condition that higher interest rates imply expected currency depreciation, because this reasoning ignores the influence of economic growth on interest rates and currency values.

Indeed, empirical evidence has been reported that when foreign interest rates rise above U.S. rates, the foreign currency tends to rise in value, rather than fall, and vice versa.[4] See Figure 12-2. In the 1973–1993 study of Canadian dollar versus U.S. dollar exchange rates, the forward value of the dollar, on average, tended to predict (1) too low of a spot value of the dollar when the value of the dollar was rising (panel A) and (2) too high of a spot value of the dollar when the dollar was depreciating (panel B).[5]

The reported results just outlined suggest that forward exchange rates are not useful *unbiased predictors* of future spot exchange rates. Despite these and other empirical results, however, the question of whether the forward exchange rate is an unbiased predictor of the spot exchange rate is still one of the most controversial issues among economists. Many economists argue that empirical results like those just discussed are due to statistical problems, like the *peso problem*, which refers to a condition where forward exchange rates do reflect proper probabilities of random events, but where the events do not happen. In this case, retrospective empirical analyses will observe and report that the forward exchange rate appears biased even when it is not.

The reason for the term "peso problem" is that in the early 1970s, the forward exchange rate between pesos and dollars reflected an expectation of a possible devaluation that did not occur. According to the argument, although the exchange rate was pegged, the market assigned some probability to a devaluation, and this probability was reflected in the forward exchange rate. But since the devaluation did not happen, empirical tests of the data appear to suggest that the forward exchange rate was a biased predictor when it actually might have been correctly incorporating the probability of a devaluation.

While empirical economists may debate the statistical issues for years, the fact is that the use of the forward exchange rate as a predictor still has two thorny theoretical problems—risk premia and Siegel's paradox. As we'll see, the GAPM approach to forecasting exchange rates does not have these two theoretical problems.

FORECASTING EXCHANGE RATES WITH THE GAPM

A more logical economic model of equilibrium exchange rate forecasts is the global asset pricing theory. That theory yields the following relationship. Let x_c represent the percentage change in the value of currency C from the viewpoint of a given base currency. Then the expected percentage change in the value of currency C, $E(x_c)$, is given by equation (12-3):

---

[4]See Kenneth A. Froot, "Short Rates and Expected Asset Returns," NBER Working Paper #3247, January 1990.

[5]Hopper, "Is the Foreign Exchange Market Efficient?"

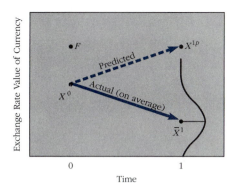

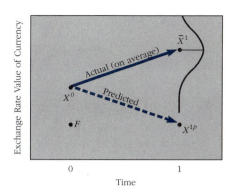

A. If the *forward* exchange value of a currency
is *greater than* the spot exchange value,
then the currency, on average, tends to
depreciate in value.

B. If the *forward* exchange value of a currency
is *less than* the spot exchange value,
then the currency, on average, tends to
appreciate in value.

FIGURE 12-2 Summary of Empirical Findings on Forward Exchange Rates and
Average Eventual Spot Exchange Rates

Source: As described in Gregory P. Hopper, "Is the Foreign Exchange Market Efficient?" *Business
Review, Federal Reserve Bank of Philadelphia*, May/June 1994, pp. 17–27.

$$E(x_c) = r - r_c + \beta_{cG}(k_G - r) + \beta_{cQ}(k_Q - r) \qquad (12\text{-}3)$$

where

$E(x_c)$ = the expected percentage change in the value of foreign currency C
relative to the base currency

r_c = the nominally riskless interest rate for foreign currency C

β_{cG} and β_{cQ} = the sensitivities of the percentage change in foreign currency C's value relative to (1) the rate of return of the global market
portfolio and (2) the rate of change in a wealth-weighted index of exchange rates, all from the viewpoint of the currency in which one is
performing the valuation

Thus, β_{cG} and β_{cQ} are the coefficients in a bivariate linear regression of
the percentage changes in the value of foreign currency C on both the nominal base currency rates of return on the global market portfolio and the percentage changes in the base currency value of the foreign exchange index.[6]
Clearly, the risk premia problem with the uncovered interest parity condition approach is solved by the GAPM approach of equation (12-3). Also

[6]This equation is adapted from Equation (2.10) in Bernard Dumas, "Partial Vs. General Equilibrium Models of the International Capital Market," NBER Working Paper #4446, September 1993.
Equation (12-3) follows from Dumas's Equation (2.20) under the assumption that the degree
of risk aversion is the same in all countries. Equation (2.10) in the Dumas review is based upon
the assumption that the purchasing power parity condition is consistently violated in reality.

solved is the Siegel's paradox problem, but a discussion of why this is the case is beyond our scope.[7]

Note that if a currency's value in base currency terms has risk coefficients that are zero, then the expected rate of change in the currency's value is $r - r_c$, the base currency riskless interest rate minus the currency C's riskless interest rate. This interest rate differential is essentially the same as the uncovered interest parity condition, equation (12-2).[8]

Let us now employ equation (12-3) to generate an exchange rate forecast in a numerical example. Suppose the 1-year eurosterling LIBOR is 8%, while the 1-year eurodollar LIBOR is 5%. Assume that you perform a multiple regression of the percentage changes in the dollar value of the pound against the nominal dollar rates of return on the global market portfolio and the percentage changes in the wealth-weighted global index of currencies, from the perspective of the dollar as the base currency. Assume that the coefficients in

Forecasting exchange rates is a key aspect in global capital budgeting analysis.

[7]The interested reader is encouraged to consult Dumas, "Partial Vs. General Equilibrium Models of the International Capital Market."

[8]The only difference is a technical one, that the time period for portfolio revision in the GAPM is assumed to be so small that $(1 + r)/(1 + r_c)$ is virtually equal to $r - r_c$. Often, one will see the interest parity condition expressed as the interest rate differential in this additive form, rather than in the multiplicative form of equation (12-2).

the regression are $\beta_{\text{£}G} = 0.40$ and $\beta_{\text{£}Q} = 0.20$. Assume that the expected dollar rate of return on the global market portfolio, k_G, is 0.10 and the expected rate of change in the index of currencies relative to the dollar, k_Q, is 0.03.

In this case, currency C is the pound and the base currency is the dollar. The expected rate of change in the value of the pound (relative to the dollar) is $E(x_{\text{£}}) = 0.05 - 0.08 + 0.40(0.10 - 0.05) + 0.20(0.03 - 0.05) = -0.014$, or -1.4%. The expected spot exchange rate for time 1, assuming that the current exchange rate, $X^0_{\$/\text{£}}$, is 1.40 $/£, is $X^0_{\$/\text{£}}(1 - 0.014) = (1.40 \text{ \$/£})(0.986) = 1.38 \text{ \$/£}$. Compare this answer to the forward exchange rate (found via the covered interest parity condition). From equation (12-1), the forward exchange rate, $F_{\$/\text{£}}$, is $(1.40 \text{ \$/£})(1.05/1.08) = 1.361 \text{ \$/£}$. The expected exchange rate is not the same as the forward exchange rate, due to the risk premia in the global asset pricing model forecast.

📋 EXAMPLE 12-2

Assume that the expected dollar rate of return on the global market portfolio, k_G, is 0.12 and the expected rate of change in the dollar value of the index of currencies, k_Q, is 0.07. Assume that the 1-year dollar LIBOR is the "riskless rate" in the base currency, dollars, and is 5%. Let the 1-year nominally riskless mark interest rate be 9%. Assume that the bivariate regression betas of percentage changes in the $/DM spot exchange rate on the dollar-denominated global market portfolio and the wealth-weighted index of the dollar value of foreign currencies are -0.60 and 1.35, respectively. What is the predicted time 1 exchange rate for the mark, given a time 0 spot exchange rate of 1.40 DM/$? Compare your answer to the ad hoc predicted time 1 exchange rate that would be forecasted by the forward exchange rate assuming that the uncovered interest parity condition holds.

Solution 12-2 Using equation (12-3), the expected percentage change in the dollar value of the mark is $E(x_{\text{DM}}) = 0.05 - 0.09 - 0.60(0.12 - 0.05) + 1.35(0.07 - 0.05) = -0.055$, or -5.5%. The mark is thus expected to depreciate in value in equilibrium by 5.5%, relative to the dollar, according to this model and these assumptions. Thus, the predicted time 1 dollar value of the mark is $(1 - 0.055)(0.7143 \text{ \$/DM}) = 0.675 \text{ \$/DM}$, which reciprocates to 1.481 DM/$. Using the European terms version of equation (12-1), the forward exchange rate, $F_{\text{DM}/\$}$, is $(1.40 \text{ DM/\$})(1.09/1.05) = 1.453 \text{ DM/\$}$. Clearly, the forward exchange rate of 1.453 DM/$ does not equal the GAPM forecast of 1.481 DM/$.

Like many asset pricing theories, the model represented in equation (12-3) is a single-period model. However, the model's results can be applied in multiperiod capital budgeting problems by envisioning the rates as expected period-by-period changes, as if the single-period model held during each of the time periods in the future. For expected exchange rates, the $E(x_c)$ term in equation (12-3) may be applied in a multiperiod context by viewing this percentage appreciation/depreciation of a currency's value as a rate that applies "per period" for a long horizon. This approach is taken shortly.

The empirical validity of the GAPM has yet to be decided by empiricists. It may turn out that the risk premia adjustments of the GAPM still do not add enough forecasting power to the interest rate differential to provide good predictions. It may turn out that the disequilibrium nature of the "real world" is too complex to capture with the equilibrium model of the GAPM. Still, the GAPM as a forecasting model appears to be a step in the right direction, relative to the interest parity condition.

Cash Flow Conversion in Capital Budgeting

As pointed out in Chapter 11, the base currency denomination is often preferred by practitioners for purposes of conducting global capital budgeting analysis. However, this preference is despite the fact that it is no simple matter to forecast future spot exchange rates. We now turn to the task of converting a project's expected foreign currency cash flows into the equivalent base currency form using forecasted exchange rates.

CURRENCY CONVERSION AND GROWING CASH FLOW STREAMS

To apply a forecasted single-period rate of appreciation of a currency, from equation (12-3), for example, in a multiperiod problem like capital budgeting, one must extrapolate the forecast. For example, assume that one forecasts that the mark will appreciate by 3% against the dollar and that one wishes to apply this result in a multiperiod analysis.

Assume that the time 0 exchange rate is $X_{DM/\$}^0 = 1.25$ DM/$. Recall that to think clearly about the value of the mark (as a foreign currency from the dollar perspective), the exchange rate must be expressed in direct terms from the dollar–as–base currency point of view. Thus, we express the time 0 exchange rate as $X_{\$/DM}^0 = 1/(1.25$ DM/$) = 0.80 $/DM.

Let $E_0(\ )$ represent an expectation held at time 0. Since at time 0 the mark is expected to appreciate in value by 3% per year, the forecasted time 1 exchange rate is $E_0(X_{\$/DM}^1) = (0.80$ $/DM$)(1.03) = 0.824 $/DM, the forecasted time 2 exchange rate is $E_0(X_{\$/DM}^2) = (0.824$ $/DM$)(1.03) = (0.80$ $/DM$)(1.03)^2 = 0.8487 $/DM, and so forth.

Assume that the German subsidiary of a U.S. firm is expected to generate DM600,000 in cash flows per year, with the first cash flow occurring at time 1. Since the mark is expected to appreciate by 3% per year, then the time 1 expected mark cash flow of DM600,000 converts to DM600,000(0.80 $/DM)(1.03) = DM600,000(0.824 $/DM) = $494,400, the time 2 expected mark

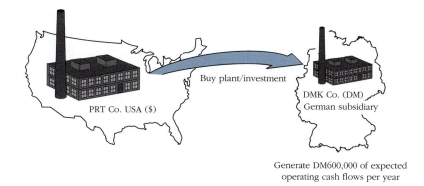

Expected base currency operating cash flow (in $)
= (Expected exchange rate $/DM)*(Expected operating cash flow [in DM]).
Note: Assumes $X_{\$/DM}$ and O_{DM} are independent.

FIGURE 12-3 Foreign Currency Cash Flow Stream

cash flow of DM600,000 converts to DM600,000(0.80 $/DM)(1.03)^2 = DM600,000(0.8487 $/DM) = $509,232, and so forth.[9] See Figure 12-3.

Recall that in prior chapters, we have for simplicity been assuming that cash flow streams are level. However, with currency values that are predicted to appreciate/depreciate over time, we can see now that the following view of cash flows may be taken: When converting a *level* expected perpetual foreign currency cash flow stream, the base currency cash flow stream will be growing at the same rate as the expected rate of appreciation of the foreign currency. See Figure 12-4, panel A.

In Example 12-3, since the dollar is expected to depreciate by 4%, the expected base currency cash flow stream is expected to decline by 4% per period (a growth rate of –4%); thus, given $E_0(O^1)$ = ¥192,000,000, $E_0(O^2)$ = ¥192,000,000(0.96) = ¥184,320,000, we may directly compute that $E_0(O^3)$ = ¥192,000,000(0.96)^2 = ¥176,940,000, and $E_0(O^4)$ = ¥192,000,000(0.96)^3 = ¥169,860,000. See Figure 12-4, panel B.

In general, the expected foreign currency cash flow stream may not be level. If the expected foreign currency cash flow stream is growing at the rate

---

[9]Technically, to say that an expected base currency cash flow is equal to the expected exchange rate times the expected foreign currency cash flow, one is required to make the assumption that the exchange rate and the foreign currency cash flow are independent. This assumption is implicitly made in the examples in this chapter, if not explicitly stated. However, it may not be realistic to make the independence assumption in many cases, especially when competitive exposure and/or price exposure is involved. (See Chapter 8.) In such cases, one should take into consideration the correlation between the exchange rate and the foreign currency cash flow. Further details are found in the appendix to this chapter.

EXAMPLE 12-3

Assume that a Japanese firm with a base currency of yen is considering buying a plant in the United States and establishing a subsidiary. The subsidiary is expected to generate operating cash flows in the amount of $2,000,000 per year, after the consideration of all taxes, including the parent's. If the dollar is expected to depreciate by 4% per year against the yen, find the expected operating cash flows of the subsidiary converted to base currency (yen), for times 1 through 4. Assume $X^0_{¥/\$} = 100$ ¥/$.

Solution 12-3　The time 0 exchange rate quote, in the conventional European terms format, is in direct terms from the point of view of the yen as the base currency. Thus, a 4% depreciation of the dollar means that $E_0(X^1_{¥/\$}) = (100$ ¥/$)(0.96) $= 96$ ¥/$, $E_0(X^2_{¥/\$}) = (100$ ¥/$)(0.96)^2 = 92.16$ ¥/$, $E_0(X^3_{¥/\$}) = (100$ ¥/$)(0.96)^3 = 88.47$ ¥/$, and $E_0(X^4_{¥/\$}) = (100$ ¥/$)(0.96)^4 = 84.93$ ¥/$. The expected base currency operating cash flows are $E_0(O^1) = $2,000,000(96$ ¥/$) $= ¥192,000,000$, $E_0(O^2) = $2,000,000(92.16$ ¥/$) $= ¥184,320,000$, $E_0(O^3) = $2,000,000(88.47$ ¥/$) $= ¥176,940,000$, and $E_0(O^4) = $2,000,000(84.93$ ¥/$) $= ¥169,860,000$.

g_c, and if the *growth rate* of the expected foreign currency cash flow stream is independent of the exchange rate, then the growth rate of the expected base currency stream, g, may be found via equation (12-4), where $E(x_c)$ is the expected rate of appreciation/depreciation of the foreign currency.

$$g = (1 + g_c)[1 + E(x_c)] - 1 \qquad (12-4)$$

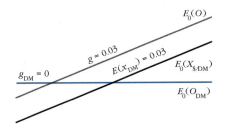

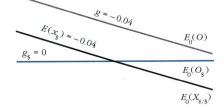

A. Base Currency (in $)

$E(x_{DM})$ = Expected rate of change in $X_{\$/DM}$ = 3%

g_{DM} = Expected rate of growth in foreign currency cash flow stream (O_{DM}) = 0

g = Expected rate of growth in base currency cash flow stream (O) = 3%

B. Base Currency (in ¥)

$E(x_\$)$ = Expected rate of change in $X_{¥/\$}$ = –4%

$g_\$$ = Expected rate of growth in foreign currency cash flow stream ($O_\$$) = 0

g = Expected rate of growth in base currency cash flow stream (O) = -4%

FIGURE 12-4 Expected Foreign Currency Cash Flows, Expected Rate of Currency Value Change and Expected Growth of Base Currency Cash Flows

For example, if $g_c = 0.08$ and $E(x_c) = -0.06$, then $g = (1.08)(0.94) - 1 = 0.0152$; that is, the growth rate of the expected base currency cash flow stream is 1.52%.

VALUATION WITH PERPETUAL GROWTH

If a change in the currency value is expected, and if this change is expected to continue each year for the infinite horizon, then the conditions imply that a present value analysis in the base currency may employ the *constant growth model*, which you should recall from your introductory financial management course.

Under the assumption of an infinite horizon, the present value of the expected base currency cash flows may be found with equation (12-5).

$$V = \frac{E_0(O^1)}{k_i - g} \tag{12-5}$$

where

V = the present value of all future expected base currency after-tax operating cash flows

$E_0(O^1)$ = the expected base currency after-tax operating cash flow for the first year

k_i = the discount rate to apply to the expected base currency after-tax operating cash flows

g = the growth rate of the expected base currency after-tax operating cash flows

For example, consider the base currency operating cash flow stream that starts with an expected time 1 amount of $E_0(O^1) = \$494,400$ and grows at 3% per year forever. (See the text example prior to Example 12-3.) The present value of this growing stream, if the discount rate is 10%, is $V = \$494,400/(0.10 - 0.03) = \$7,062,857$.

If the foreign currency is expected to depreciate in value relative to the base currency, then for a level expected foreign currency stream, the expected

---

EXAMPLE 12-4

Consider Example 12-3, where the base currency is yen and $E_0(O^1) = ¥192,000,000$. Assume that the expected dollar cash flow stream is a level perpetuity. If the discount rate is 12%, what is the present value of the yen cash flow stream that grows at the negative rate of 4% per year?

Solution 12-4 $V = ¥192,000,000/[0.12 - (-0.04)] = ¥1200$ million.

base currency cash flow stream will decline over time at a constant rate of negative growth. Mathematically, this situation involves plugging in the rate of depreciation of the foreign currency as a negative growth rate in equation (12-5). An illustration is given in Example 12-4.

NET PRESENT VALUE

Now we put all the elements of Chapters 11 and 12 together to perform net present value analysis of an overseas capital budgeting proposal. For purposes of relating to some of the topics in this and prior chapters, we'll use an example analysis for a hypothetical company called PRT Co., a U.S.-based parent that represents a prototypical parent company. PRT Co. is considering a proposed overseas investment into a German subsidiary, DMK Co., that represents the prototypical foreign subsidiary.

Once established, DMK is expected to generate DM800,000 in perpetual *before-tax* operating cash flows per year. Assume that PRT's tax rate is 25%. Assume that the time 0 spot exchange rate is $X_{DM/\$}^0 = 2.00$ DM/\$. Assume that the mark cash flows are *not* correlated with the exchange rate (see footnote 9). The subsidiary is to be financed with DM4,000,000 (\$2,000,000) from the parent, which is the subsidiary's equity financing, and with DM2,000,000 of mark-denominated debt with a coupon rate of 5%, borrowed directly by the subsidiary in Germany. Assume that the parent's cost of capital (WACC) is 10.5%. Assume that the mark is expected to appreciate by 3% per year relative to the dollar. Assume the credit method of taxation. What is the NPV of the project?

First, as discussed in Chapter 11, the parent's tax rate should be applied to DMK's expected before-tax operating cash flows of DM800,000 per year to find after-tax expected operating cash flows of DM800,000(1 − 0.25) = DM600,000 per year. The stream of expected after-tax operating cash flows could be valued if the appropriate mark cost of capital were known, but that is not the case. Instead, the general practice to convert the expected mark cash flow stream into an expected base currency (the dollar, in this case) cash flow stream is followed, using the expected future exchange rates for the conversion. Since the value of the mark is expected to appreciate by 3% per year, the expected time 1 exchange rate is $E_0(X_{\$/DM}^1) = (0.50 \ \$/DM)(1.03) = 0.515$ \$/DM, the expected time 2 exchange rate is $E_0(X_{\$/DM}^2) = (0.50 \ \$/DM)(1.03)^2 = 0.53045$ \$/DM, and so forth. The expected after-tax operating cash flow of the subsidiary for the first year, expressed in dollars, is $E_0(O^1) = $ DM600,000(0.50 \$/DM)(1.03) = \$309,000; the expected after-tax operating cash flow of the subsidiary for the second year, expressed in dollars, is $E_0(O^2) = $ DM600,000(0.50 \$/DM)(1.03)^2 = \$318,270 and so forth.

Thus, the expected after-tax operating cash flows generated by the subsidiary DMK, after computing taxes based upon the parent's tax rate and converting to base currency, begins with a time 1 quantity of \$309,000 and is expected to grow at the rate of 3% per year.

Given the assumptions in the example, an application of equation (12-5)

Companies like Grand Metropolitan, Plc, are developing their global capital budgeting procedures

yields that the total dollar value of the German subsidiary, DMK, is $V = \$309,000/(0.105 - 0.03) = \$4,120,000$. Given that the total investment outlay for the project is DM6,000,000, which is equivalent at time 0 to \$3,000,000, the NPV of the project is \$4,120,000 − \$3,000,000 = \$1,120,000. Let us demonstrate again, as in Chapter 11, that PRT receives 100% of this NPV, even though the analysis has been performed on the operating cash flows of the subsidiary as a whole and not on the cash flows to PRT. Recall that \$4,120,000 is the present value of DMK as a whole; in marks, DMK's total value at time 0 is \$4,120,000(2 DM/\$) = DM8,240,000. Since DMK employed DM2,000,000 in debt financing, the present value of PRT's equity is DM8,240,000 − DM2,000,000 = DM6,240,000. In dollars, the present value of PRT's equity is DM6,240,000/(2 DM/\$) = \$3,120,000. PRT's NPV on its \$2,000,000 investment is \$3,120,000 − \$2,000,000 = \$1,120,000.

The Current Spot Exchange Rate as a Forecast

What about simply using the current (time 0) exchange rate as the "best guess" of the forecasted exchange rate for future periods? Unfortunately, this approach is flawed, and it is *not* valid to convert an expected foreign currency cash flow stream into base currency terms using a currently observed spot ex-

📖 EXAMPLE 12-5

Assume that a Japanese firm with a base currency of yen is considering buying a plant in the United States and establishing a subsidiary. Assume that the Japanese parent has a cost of capital of 9% and a tax rate of 30%. Assume that the U.S. plant would cost $12,000,000, which the Japanese parent can finance in part by having the subsidiary borrow $3,000,000 on its own. The rest of the outlay for the plant must be supplied by the Japanese parent ($9,000,000). The time 0 exchange rate is 100 ¥/$, and the dollar is expected to depreciate by 4% per year; the U.S. plant is expected to generate a level operating cash flow stream (before taxes) of $2,000,000 per year into perpetuity. Assume the credit method of taxation. Find the NPV of the project from the Japanese parent's point of view.

Solution 12-5   The time 1 expected after-tax operating cash flow is $2,000,000 $(1 - t_p) = \$2,000,000(1 - 0.30) = \$1,400,000$. Converted to yen, the time 1 expected after-tax operating cash flow is $\$1,400,000(96 \text{ ¥/\$}) = ¥134,400,000$. (This conversion assumes the independence condition discussed in footnote 9.) The present value of the expected base currency operating cash flows, given a cost of capital of 9% and a perpetual growth rate of -4%, is $V = ¥134,400,000/[0.09 - (-0.04)] = ¥134,000,000/[0.13] = ¥1034$ million. This amount represents the total economic value of the subsidiary, if it is established. The total outlay in yen at time 0 is $\$12,000,000(100 \text{ ¥/\$}) = ¥1200$ million. The project's NPV is thus ¥1034 million minus ¥1200 million, which is −¥166 million. Since the proposed plant purchase has a *negative* NPV, the proposal should be *rejected*.

change rate. The reason, explained in full shortly, is that the use of the current spot exchange rate to convert expected future cash flows dictates the implicit assumption that the interest rates in the two currencies are equal, regardless of the risk involved.

To see this point, consider a mark-denominated cash flow stream of DM2000 per year forever. Assume that the mark payoffs are certain and that the mark riskless rate is 8%. The present value of the cash flow stream is thus DM2000/0.08 = DM25,000. If the spot exchange rate is currently 2 DM/$, then the asset's value in dollars at time 0 is clearly DM25,000/(2 DM/$) = $12,500. Now let us compare this assumed-to-be-correct value in dollars with a value computed from a present value analysis using the current spot exchange rate as the "best guess" of the future exchange rate. If we convert the foreign currency cash flow stream of DM2000 per year into dollars at the current exchange rate of 2 DM/$, we get a "best guess" base currency cash flow stream of $1000 per year. Then, knowing that the dollar value of the asset is $12,500 by assumption, the capitalization rate for the asset's converted stream of $1000 per year is implied to be 8%.

Although 8% is the assumed correct discount rate for a certain mark-denominated cash flow stream, there is simply no justification for assuming that 8% is the correct discount rate for the converted, and *risky*, dollar cash flow stream of the same asset. This is particularly true if the riskless interest rates in the two currencies were different, as is generally the case. (This point was also made in Chapter 11.)

Given that a capitalization rate other than 8% is generally appropriate for the risky dollar expected cash flow stream of the asset, and given that the correct time 0 value of the asset in dollars is known by assumption to be $12,500, the expected dollar cash flow stream to be capitalized thus cannot be $1000. Thus, the current spot exchange rate *cannot* be a valid forecast of future exchange rates, since the use of the spot exchange rate for forecasting implies a model where the interest rates in both currencies are the same, which is generally invalid.

A subtle assumption underlying the reasoning here, and the similar points made in Chapter 11, is that to value a pound-denominated expected operating cash flow stream of a British subsidiary, a British parent company would apply the same pound-denominated capitalization rate as a U.S. parent would. In other words, this assumption requires that an asset's value be the same to both domestic and foreign investors and that there are no "arbitrage or quasi-arbitrage opportunities" in time 0 present values of assets across international borders, considering the known time 0 spot exchange rate. While this assumption is abstract, it is a standard underlying premise in valuation models. For example, the assumption is implicit in the GAPM of equation (11-4) and equation (12-3) in this chapter.

Thus, the procedure of converting expected *future* foreign currency cash flow streams using the currently observed spot exchange rate is a generally incorrect procedure. If a capital budgeting analysis of assets that generate foreign currency cash flows is to be conducted in a base currency framework, one must really *forecast* exchange rates.

Summary

When one wishes to perform capital budgeting analyses in a base currency framework, when foreign projects and subsidiaries are involved, exchange rate forecasting is a necessary task.

This chapter reviewed factors and methods of exchange rate forecasting. The global asset pricing model provides a formula for the expected change in currency value and does not have the logical deficiencies of the interest parity condition. The formula for forecasting exchange rates with the GAPM is given in equation (12-3). Whether this model has empirical support will be seen in future academic research, but remember that an equilibrium model will not always apply in a world characterized by disequilibrium.

The chapter concluded the topic of global capital budgeting analysis with a discussion of converting foreign currency cash flows to base currency cash flows. In cases where streams of expected future foreign currency cash flows are level perpetuities, it was shown how to employ the constant growth formula for the valuation of the equivalent base currency stream.

Glossary

Peso Problem: A condition where forward exchange rates reflect proper expectations of random events, but where the events do not happen, and therefore retrospective empirical analyses will observe and report that the forward exchange rates appear biased even when they are not.

Siegel's Paradox: Under conditions of uncertainty, if the forward exchange rate is equal to the expected spot exchange rate, for a given direction in expressing the currency exchange, then it is mathematically impossible for the equality to hold for the other direction of currency exchange.

Discussion Questions

1. Pick two currencies. Try to make a forecast for the future exchange rate. Do you think that the currencies are misvalued at present? If so, what role does this misvaluation play in your forecast?

2. Discuss reasons why the uncovered interest parity condition may not hold, and therefore why the forward exchange rate may not be an accurate way to forecast the future spot exchange rate.

3. In what ways can the GAPM model improve on forecasts made by the forward exchange rate? What limitations of the forward exchange rate approach to forecasting are *not* eliminated by the GAPM approach?

Problems

1. Assume that the spot exchange rate for pounds and dollars is 1.00 $/£ at time 0 and will be either 1.25 $/£ or 0.80 $/£ at time 1, with equal probabilities. Demonstrate that the value of the pound and the value of the dollar are *both* expected to appreciate by the same amount. Also demonstrate that while a forward exchange rate of 1.025 $/£ is equal to the expected exchange rate in $/£, the reciprocal forward exchange rate of 1/(1.025 $/£) = 0.9756 £/$ is not equal to the expected exchange rate in $/£.

---

1. The pound and the dollar are both expected to appreciate by 2.5%. The forward exchange rate of 0.9756 £/$ does not equal the expected value of the pound.

2. Assume that the expected dollar rate of return on the global market portfolio, k_G, is 0.14 and the expected rate of change in the dollar value of the index of currencies, k_Q, is -0.03. Assume that the 1-year dollar LIBOR is the riskless rate in the base currency, dollars, and is 4%. Let the 1-year nominally riskless pound interest rate be 6%. Assume that the bivariate regression betas of percentage changes in the $/£ spot exchange rate on the dollar-denominated global market portfolio and the wealth-weighted index of the dollar value of foreign currencies are 1.30 and −0.70, respectively. What is the predicted time 1 exchange rate for the pound, given a time 0 spot exchange rate of 1.40 $/£? Compare your answer to the ad hoc predicted time 1 exchange rate that would be forecasted by the forward exchange rate, assuming that the uncovered interest parity condition holds.

3. Assume that a U.S. firm with a base currency of dollars is considering buying a plant in England and establishing a subsidiary. The subsidiary is expected to generate operating cash flows perpetually in the amount of £2,000,000 per year (after consideration of all taxes). If the pound is expected to appreciate by 5% per year against the dollar, find the expected operating cash flows of the subsidiary converted to base currency, for times 1 through 4, assuming no correlation between the foreign currency cash flows and the exchange rate. Assume $X^0_{\$/£} = 1.50$ $/£.

4. Consider an Italian company that generates U.S. dollar cash flows and expects the dollar cash flows to be a level perpetuity. Assume that the expected base currency equivalent of the time 1 foreign currency cash flow is $E_0(O^1) =$ L11,000,000. If the discount rate is 11%, what is the present value of the Italian lira cash flow stream if the lira is expected to appreciate by 5% per year against the dollar?

5. Assume that a U.S. firm with a base currency of dollars is considering buying a plant in England and establishing a subsidiary. Assume that the U.S. parent has a cost of capital of 11% and a tax rate of 20%. Assume that the plant in England would cost £30,000,000, which the U.S. parent can finance in part by borrowing £20,000,000 in the subsidiary's name. The rest of the outlay for the plant must be supplied by the U.S. parent (£10,000,000). The time 0 exchange rate is 1.50 $/£, and the pound is expected to appreciate by 5% per year; the English plant is expected to generate a level operating cash flow stream (before taxes) of £2,000,000 per year into perpetuity. Assume the credit method of taxation. Find the NPV of the project from the U.S. parent's point of view.

---

2. $E(x_£)$ = 15.9%. The predicted time 1 value of the pound is 1.6226 $/£. $F_{\$/£}$ = 1.374 $/£.

3. $E_0(O^1)$ = $3,150,000, $E_0(O^2)$ = $3,308,000, $E_0(O^3)$ = $3,472,000, and $E_0(O^4)$ = $3,646,000.

4. L69,796,954.

5. The project's NPV is −$3 million.

The following problem and answer relate to material presented in the appendix.

A-1. Assume a base currency of dollars. Let the expected time 1 foreign currency operating cash flow be FF5,000,000 and let the expected time 1 exchange rate between French francs and dollars be $E_0(X^1_{FF/\$})$ = 5.00 FF/$. Assume that the standard deviation of the French franc–denominated cash flows is FF1,250,000 and that the standard deviation of the $/FF exchange rate is 0.05 $/FF. (a) Consider the case of conversion exposure and assume that the French franc cash flows are not correlated with the exchange rate. What is the expected dollar cash flow? (b) Consider the case of competitive economic exposure and assume that the French franc cash flow decreases when the dollar value of the French franc increases. Assume that –0.60 is the correlation coefficient between the French franc cash flow and the dollar value of the French franc. What is the expected dollar cash flow?

A-1.   (a) $E_0(O^1)$ = $1,000,000. (b) $E_0(O^1)$ = $962,500.

THE CORRELATION ISSUE

In this appendix we confront an issue that may occur when converting expected foreign currency cash flows into expected base currency cash flows. The problem occurs when the foreign currency cash flows and the future exchange rates are correlated, as would be the case if there were some economic exposure effects of the competitive or demand variety.

To see the problem, consider a foreign currency cash flow at time 1 in the future, assumed to be a random variable. Let O_C^1 denote a realized time 1 cash flow denominated in foreign currency C, with the time 0 expectation of that cash flow denoted as $E_0(O_C^1)$. Next consider the future exchange rate in direct terms from the base currency point of view. The time 1 exchange rate is assumed to be a random variable, denoted X^1, with expectation (at time 0) of $E_0(X^1)$.

Then the problem is that although the time 1 *base currency* cash flow that actually occurs, denoted O^1, is equal to the product of the *actual* time 1 foreign currency cash flow and the *actual* time 1 exchange rate, $O_C^1 X^1$, the *expected* base currency cash flow, $E_0(O^1)$, is *not* necessarily equal to the product of the *expected* foreign currency cash flow and the *expected* exchange rate.

Only if the time 1 foreign currency cash flow and the time 1 exchange rate are uncorrelated will the expected base currency cash flow be equal to the product of the expectations of the future foreign currency cash flow and the future exchange rate. This situation may be relatively common, since it holds for cases of pure conversion exposure. However, it may also be relatively common for the condition to *not* hold, since there are many scenarios of economic exposure where the foreign currency cash flows are correlated with the exchange rate. In that case, the expected base currency cash flow $E_0(O^1)$ is equal to $E_0(O_C^1) * E_0(X^1)$ plus the covariance between the future foreign currency cash flow and the future exchange rate, which we'll denote $\text{cov}(O_C^1, X^1)$.

Since the covariance between two random variables (*x* and *y*) is equal to the three-way product of (1) the correlation between the two variables, denoted $\rho(x,y)$; (2) the standard deviation *x*, denoted Std(x); and (3) the standard deviation of *y*, denoted Std(*y*), we have equation (12A-1):

$$E_0(O^1) = E_0(O_C^1) * E_0(X^1) + \text{cov}(O_C^1, X^1)$$
$$= E_0(O_C^1) * E_0(X^1) + \rho(O_C^1, X^1) * \text{Std}(O_C^1) * \text{Std}(X^1) \quad (12A\text{-}1)$$

To demonstrate, assume a base currency of dollars. Let the expected time 1 foreign currency operating cash flow be $E_0(O_{DM}^1)$ = DM200,000, and let the expected time 1 exchange rate between marks and dollars be $E_0(X_{\$/DM}^1)$ = 0.50 \$/DM. Assume that the standard deviation of the mark-denominated cash flows, $\text{Std}(O_{DM}^1)$, is DM40,000 and that the standard deviation of the \$/DM exchange rate, $\text{Std}(X_{\$/DM}^1)$, is 0.15. Consider a situation of competitive economic exposure and assume that the mark cash flow decreases when the dollar value of the mark increases (since more U.S. competitors are assumed to try to capture German market share). Assume that the correlation coefficient between the time 1 mark cash flow and the time 1 dollar value of the mark, $\rho(O_{DM}^1, X_{\$/DM}^1)$, is −0.25.

In this case, the mark cash flow and the exchange rate are not independent. The covariance between them is the correlation coefficient times the product of the two standard deviations = −0.25(DM40,000)(0.15 \$/DM) = −\$1500. Using equation (12A-1), the expected dollar cash flow is $E_0(O^1)$ = DM200,000(0.50 \$/DM) + (−\$1500) = \$100,000 − \$1500 = \$98,500.

EXAMPLE 12-A1

Assume a base currency of dollars. Let the expected time 1 foreign currency operating cash flow be £1,200,000 and let the expected time 1 exchange rate between pounds and dollars be 1.50 \$/£. Assume a standard deviation of the pound-denominated cash flows of £300,000 and a standard deviation of the \$/£ exchange rate of 0.30. (1) Consider the case of conversion exposure and assume that the pound cash flows are not correlated with the exchange rate. What is the expected dollar cash flow? (2) Consider the case of competitive economic exposure and assume that the pound cash flow decreases when the dollar value of the pound increases. Assume that −0.50 is the correlation coefficient between the pound cash flow and the dollar value of the pound. What is the expected time 1 dollar cash flow?

Solution 12-A1   (1) Since the pound cash flow and the exchange rate are assumed to be independent, the expected dollar cash flow is equal to the expected pound cash flow times the expected \$/£ exchange rate. Thus, $E_0(O^1) = E_0(O_£^1)$ * $E_0(X_{\$/£}^1)$ = £1,200,000(1.50 \$/£) = \$1,800,000.

(2) In this case, the pound cash flow and the exchange rate are not independent. The covariance between them is the correlation coefficient times the product of the two standard deviations, $\rho(O_£^1, X_{\$/£}^1)$ * $\text{Std}(O_£^1)$ * $\text{Std}(X_{\$/£}^1)$, is −0.50(£300,000) (0.30 \$/£) = −\$45,000. Using equation (12A-1), the expected time 1 dollar cash flow is $E_0(O^1)$ = £1,200,000(1.50 \$/£) + (−\$45,000) = \$1,800,000 − \$45,000 = \$1,755,000.

chapter 13

MULTICURRENCY EXPOSURE ISSUES

This chapter contains a number of complex and related topics, oriented around issues in multicurrency exposure. In many cases, multicurrency exposure is linear, in which case the exposure may be estimated by multiple regression analysis. A form of nonlinear multicurrency exposure, *compound exposure*, is also identified and discussed in the chapter. The chapter concludes with some coverage of multicurrency equity ownership and the topic of *universal hedging*.

Linear Multicurrency Exposure

CURRENCY EXPOSURE AND REGRESSION ANALYSIS

Assuming that changes in operating cash flows are linearly related to changes in exchange rates, one approach to estimating a firm's operating exposure is by a simple regression of percentage changes in operating cash flows on percentage changes in exchange rates, in direct terms from the base currency point of view. The fact that regression coefficients are often symbolized by "betas" or "β's" is the reason that "B's" were used in prior chapters to denote currency exposures.

For example, if one uses a time series of percentage changes in a firm's operating cash flows as observations of the dependent variable, and regresses these observations against the percentage changes in direct terms exchange rates as the independent variables, the regression coefficients would be estimates of the exposures with respect to the exchange rates. While the regression coefficients estimate the exposures, the regression "errors" measure the influence of other factors on changes in operating cash flows.

Let us see how we would apply the results of such a regression analysis. Assume that your company's base currency is the dollar and that you run a time-series multiple regression of percentage changes in your firm's base currency operating cash flows on the percentage exchange rate changes between the dollar and three other currencies: the pound, the yen, and the mark. Assume that the regression analysis results in the following estimated model for the percentage change in the base currency operating cash flows:

$$\%\Delta O = 2.8(\%\Delta X_{\$/£}) - 0.48(\%\Delta X_{\$/¥}) - 0.60(\%\Delta X_{\$/DM}) + e \qquad (13\text{-}1)$$

where e is a random "error" term that captures the influence of other variables on operating cash flows. The coefficient 2.8 is the estimate of the operating cash flow exposure to the pound. Notationally, we must add a superscript so that we can keep straight the operating exposures to the different currencies. Let $\beta_O^£$ represent the operating cash flow exposure to the pound. The operating cash flow exposure to the yen and the mark, denoted $\beta_O^¥$ and β_O^{DM}, have been estimated by the analysis to be -0.48 and -0.60, respectively.

Given the estimated exposures, that is, the regression coefficients, one may assess the impact of potential exchange rate changes. For example, what would happen to the firm's expected base currency operating cash flows if in one period the pound depreciates by 5% relative to the dollar, the yen appreciates by 15% relative to the dollar, and the mark depreciates by 10% relative to the dollar? Ignore other potential influences that are not predicted (e).

The percentage change in the base currency operating cash flows would be

$$2.8(-0.05) - 0.48(0.15) - 0.60(-0.10) = -0.152, \text{ or } -15.2\%$$

Thus, the level of the firm's base currency operating cash flows would decline by 15.2%.

Some caution must be taken in the application of linear regression analyses, because not all underlying exposure relationships are inherently linear. Trying to estimate a nonlinear exposure with linear regression may not produce useful results. Exposures to single currencies may be nonlinear, due to nonlinearity in a firm's price elasticity of demand or other reasons. Later in the chapter, we introduce a case of multicurrency exposure that has compound effects, a nonlinearity that implies that the operating cash flow exposure cannot be properly estimated with multiple linear regression analysis.

A second potential problem with regression analysis is that exposures may not be constant over time, as was demonstrated in the appendices to Chapter 8 and 9. This situation could create some technical problems in estimation procedures that rely on simple ordinary least squares (OLS) regression analysis.

▣ EXAMPLE 13-1

XYZ Co. has a base currency of dollars. XYZ performs a multiple regression of its percentage changes in operating cash flows on the percentage changes in three exchange rates, from the point of view of the dollar as the base currency: (1) the pound, (2) the mark, and (3) the New Zealand dollar (NZ$), in that order. The regression output indicates that the first "beta" coefficient is −0.20, the second is 1.65, and the third is 0.86. If, relative to the U.S. dollar, the pound appreciates by 8%, the mark depreciates by 10%, and the New Zealand dollar appreciates by 4%, what does the model predict the percentage change in the firm's expected base currency operating cash flows to be?

Solution 13-1   The percentage change in firm's expected base currency operating cash flows would be $\%\Delta O = -0.20(0.08) + 1.65(-0.10) + 0.86(0.04) = -0.1466$, or −14.66%. The level of the firm's expected base currency operating cash flows would decline by 14.66%.

However, if the linearity and stability assumptions are reasonably valid, the use of regression analysis may be a useful method for estimating exposures. The reason is that it may be very difficult to *analytically* establish the exposure of operating cash flows to an exchange rate, especially given the potential multiplicity of possible effects (conversion, price, demand, competitive, and indirect).

Some early literature on the subject of measuring currency exposure via regression analysis did not perform the analyses with percentage changes, but rather with *levels*.[1] An orientation to the percentage change (i.e., elasticity) concept, instead of levels, avoids some empirical problems and has become a standard approach.

THE FUNDAMENTALS OF LINEAR MULTICURRENCY OPERATING EXPOSURE

In this section, we present the "theory" behind the regression model outlined in the prior section. The methodology used is to construct a hypothetical scenario of multicurrency exposure that is consistent with the estimated regression formula in equation (13-1).

Consider a hypothetical firm with a base currency of dollars. The company exports 70% of its products to England with the currency of determina-

---

[1]See Michael Adler and Bernard Dumas, "Exposure to Currency Risk: Definition and Measurement," *Financial Management*, Summer 1984, pp. 41–50, and C. Kent Garner and Alan C. Shapiro, "A Practical Method of Assessing Foreign Exchange Risk," *Midland Corporate Finance Journal*, Fall 1984, pp. 6–17.

tion being the pound. The other 30% of the products are shipped to Japan with currency of determination that is 60% the Japanese yen (see Chapter 8).

Assume that 40% of the company's operating costs have an exposure of 1 to the yen (due to some imported raw materials from Japan that have a yen currency of determination), while 20% of expected operating costs have an exposure of 1 to the mark (due to imported raw materials from Germany that have a mark currency of determination). Assume that at time 0, the expected stream of future base currency operating revenues are R^0 = $1,000,000 per year. Assume that at time 0 the future base currency operating cash flow margin is expected to be 25%. These assumptions are laid out down the left-hand side of Figure 13-1. What are the company's operating cash flow exposures?

Let us attack this complex situation by looking at each currency in turn, making use of equation (13-2), which is the same as equation (8-3).

$$\beta_O = \beta_R\left(\frac{R^0}{O^0}\right) - \beta_C\left(\frac{C^0}{O^0}\right) \tag{13-2}$$

Note that since the operating cash flow margin is assumed to be 25%, then R^0/O^0 = 4 and C^0/O^0 = 3. Because of the multiple currencies, we must superscript the operating revenue, cost, and cash flow exposures according to specific currencies, as was done previously in the chapter. For the pound, the firm's operating revenue exposure is $\beta_R^{£}$ = 0.70. Since there is no operating cost exposure to the pound, then equation (13-2) tells us that the operating cash flow exposure to the pound is

$$\beta_O^{£} = 0.70(4) - 0(3) = 2.8$$

For the yen, the firm's operating revenue exposure is $\beta_R^{¥}$ = 0.30(0.60) = 0.18, since 30% of the company's operating revenues come from Japan and since their exposure to the yen is 0.60. Since the imported raw materials from Japan constitute 40% of the expected base currency operating costs and have a conversion exposure to the yen, the firm's operating cost exposure to the yen is 0.40(1) = 0.40. Thus, equation (13-2) indicates that the firm's operating cash flow exposure to the yen is

$$\beta_O^{¥} = 0.18(4) - 0.40(3) = -0.48$$

Finally, since the imported raw materials from Germany constitute 20% of the expected base currency operating costs and have a conversion exposure to the mark, the firm's operating cost exposure to the mark is 0.20(1) = 0.20, and with no operating revenue exposure to the mark, the operating cash flow exposure to the mark is

$$\beta_O^{DM} = 0(4) - 0.20(3) = -0.60$$

Now note that the three operating cash flow exposures that we have computed, $\beta_O^{\pounds} = 2.8$, $\beta_O^{\yen} = -0.48$, and $\beta_O^{DM} = -0.60$, are precisely the same as the ones in the example regression equation discussed and applied earlier in the chapter. In other words, a company with the fundamental exposure characteristics described in the scenario would have an estimated regression equation for its overall multicurrency operating cash flow exposure expressed in equation (13-1). Let us "prove" this point by extending the numerical example further.

Given the exposure formula of equation (13-1), we found earlier that if in one period the pound depreciates by 5% relative to the dollar, the yen appreciates by 15% relative to the dollar, and the mark depreciates by 10% relative to the dollar, ignoring other potential influences that are not predicted (e), the percentage change in base currency operating cash flow stream would be $2.8(-0.05) - 0.48(0.15) - 0.60(-0.10) = -0.152$, or -15.2%. The level of the firm's expected operating cash flow stream would decline by 15.2%.

Let us verify this numerical finding using the firm's fundamental information. The 5% depreciation of the pound results in a decrease of the expected pound-based operating revenues by 5%, to $0.95(\$700,000) = \$665,000$ per year. (Alternatively, since $\beta_R^{\pounds} = 0.70$, we could say that the firm's initial expected base currency operating revenues of $1,000,000 per year decline by $0.70(0.05) = 0.035$, or by $35,000.) The 15% appreciation of the yen results in an increase of the expected yen-based operating revenues by $0.60(0.15) = 0.09$, or by 9%, to $1.09(\$300,000) = \$327,000$ per year. (Alternatively, since $\beta_R^{\yen} = 0.18$, the firm's initial expected base currency operating revenues of $1,000,000 per year increase by $0.18(0.15) = 0.027$, or by $27,000.) Thus, the firm's new expected base currency operating revenues are $R^1 = \$665,000 + \$327,000 = \$992,000$ per year (or, alternatively, $1,000,000 - \$35,000 + \$27,000 = \$992,000$ per year). Refer to the operating revenue section of Figure 13-1.

Since the time 0 expected operating cash flow margin was assumed to be 25%, the initially expected stream of future base currency operating costs, C^0, is $750,000 per year. Thus, the initially expected yen-based operating costs are 40% of $750,000, or $300,000 per year. Similarly, the initially expected mark-based operating costs are 20% of $750,000, or $150,000 per year. The remaining 40% of $750,000, or $300,000, are assumed to be dollar-based operating costs and are unexposed. The 15% appreciation of the yen results in new yen-based raw materials costs of $1.15(\$300,000) = \$345,000$. The 10% depreciation in the mark results in new mark-based raw materials costs of $0.90(\$150,000) = \$135,000$. Thus, the firm's new expected base currency operating costs are $C^1 = \$345,000 + \$135,000 + \$300,000 = \$780,000$ per year. Refer to the operating cost section of Figure 13-1.

The firm's new expected base currency operating cash flows are

$$O^1 = R^1 - C^1 = \$992,000 - \$780,000 = \$212,000$$

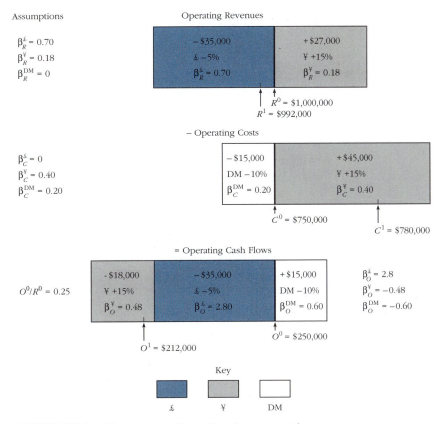

FIGURE 13-1   Multicurrency Operating Exposure—Linear

Since the expected stream of future base currency operating cash flows declines from $O^0 = \$250,000$ to $O^1 = \$212,000$, the percentage change is $(\$212,000/\$250,000 - 1) = -0.152$, or a decline of 15.2%, as indicated earlier using the regression equation. See Figure 13-1.

SIMULTANEOUS MULTICURRENCY EXPOSURE: THE CASE OF FINNING

The hypothetical example just given was a case of linear multicurrency exposure whose origins could be easily seen because of the distinct markets involved. A more subtle and complex form of linear multicurrency exposure is *simultaneous (linear) multicurrency exposure*, where a single operating revenue or cost stream is independently influenced by more than one currency at the same time. In simultaneous multicurrency exposure, at *most* one currency creates a conversion exposure. The others must be indirect or competitive exposures. Simultaneous multicurrency exposure is typified by the case of the Canadian distributor of heavy equipment, Finning Co.[2]

Recall from Chapter 8 that Finning's base currency (the Canadian dollar) operating revenues depended upon the C$/$ exchange rate (an indirect exposure) and simultaneously upon the C$/¥ exchange rate (a competitive exposure). This situation is different from the "divisional" scenario earlier in this chapter in that Finning does not have two markets, each with its own distinct exposure. Instead, the firm's single domestic operating revenue stream is subject to two simultaneous economic exposures.

For illustration purposes, let us hypothesize a similar firm whose expected future base currency operating revenue stream is assumed to simultaneously have an (indirect) operating revenue exposure of 0.80 to the U.S. dollar (denoted $\beta_R^\$$) and a (competitive) operating revenue exposure of 0.60 to the Japanese yen (denoted $\beta_R^\yen$). If the firm's operating cost exposure to the U.S. dollar is $\beta_C^\$ = 0.40$ and to the yen is $\beta_C^\yen = 0$, and if the firm's time 0 expectation for the future operating cash flow margin is 25%, then from equation (13-2), $\beta_O^\$ = 0.80(4) - 0.40(3) = 2$, and $\beta_O^\yen = 0.60(4) - 0(3) = 2.40$.

Since the multicurrency exposure is a simultaneous exposure, we will find it useful to first define the notion of a *unilateral change in the value of a currency,* where the currency changes in the same proportion relative to all foreign currencies and the rates between the other currencies stay the same. For example, if the U.S. dollar appreciates unilaterally relative to both the Canadian dollar and the yen, then the C$/¥ exchange rate does not change. In our illustration, since the firm's $\beta_O^\$$ is 2, the expected base currency operating cash flows increase by a percentage that is twice the percentage appreciation of the U.S. dollar.

If the yen appreciates unilaterally relative to both the Canadian dollar and the U.S. dollar, then the C$/$ exchange rate does not change. In this case, since $\beta_R^\yen$ is assumed to be 2.40, the firm's expected base currency operating cash flows change by 2.4 times the percentage change in the value of the yen relative to the Canadian dollar.

More generally, when there is neither a unilateral appreciation of the dollar nor the yen, both the C$/¥ exchange rate and the C$/$ exchange rate will change. In this case, the nature of the two exposures allow them to be considered in a linearly additive way. In other words, the combined effect on the firm's expected base currency operating cash flows is captured in the following expression

$$\%\Delta O = 2.00(\%\Delta X_{C\$/\$}) + 2.40(\%\Delta X_{C\$/\yen}) \tag{13-3}$$

---

[2]The Finning case is discussed in Gregory J. Millman, *The Floating Battlefield: Corporate Strategies in the Currency Wars* (New York: AMACOM, The American Management Association, 1990).

Companies like Finning Corp., the Canadian distributor of heavy equipment, have complex multicurrency exposures.

The fact that the percentage change in the expected base currency operating cash flows may be expressed in the preceding linear form implies that multiple linear regression analysis may be an appropriate means to estimate the exposures in this simultaneous exposure situation. The regression analysis would be a useful supplement to any theoretical reasoning.

Compound Multicurrency Exposure: Western Mining Company

The material in this section was developed from an exploration of the multicurrency exposure situation of Western Mining Co.[3] Recall (from Chapters 8 and 9) that Western Mining produces metals in Australia with Australian dollar (A$) operating costs, and Western Mining's equityholders have a base currency of Australian dollars. The firm sells its products in the United States, Canada, and Europe, and the currency of determination for the products is the U.S. dollar.

[3]See Peter J. Maloney, "Managing Foreign Exchange Exposure: The Case of Western Mining," *Journal of Applied Corporate Finance*, Winter 1990, pp. 29–34.

For many years, the management at Western Mining believed that the company's only operating exposure was the *conversion exposure* of its U.S. dollar–denominated operating revenues into base currency Australian dollars. However, during a period of a U.S. dollar appreciation relative to the Australian dollar, Western Mining did not experience the increase in base currency operating cash flows that it had expected. The reason, management discovered, was that the U.S. dollar had also appreciated relative to European currencies (represented here in general by the ECU), and as the metals prices increased in Europe in terms of ECUs, the demand for the products by the Europeans declined. Thus, Western Mining Co. became aware of a *demand exposure* within the *U.S. dollar–denominated* operating revenues to changes in the $/ECU exchange rate.

Let us illustrate this multicurrency exposure problem with an example of a hypothetical Australian mining company, called Koala Mining Company. To help clarify the exposition, assume that the hypothetical firm sells products with a U.S. dollar currency of determination and has sales *only* in Europe. Thus, we'll assume that 100% of the operating revenues are subject to demand exposure to the $/ECU exchange rate.

For purposes of simplicity, assume initially that the exchange rates are 1 $/A$ and 1 $/ECU. Thus, the initial exchange rate between Australian dollars and ECUs is 1 A$/ECU. Assume that under the initial exchange rate conditions, Koala Mining expects to ship 1000 tons of metals to Europe per year. Assume that the going-rate price for the metals in the international commodity markets, in the metals' U.S. dollar currency of determination, is $1000/ton. This U.S. dollar price means that the Europeans pay ECU1000/ton at the assumed time 0 exchange rate of $X^0_{\$/ECU} = 1$ $/ECU. Since Koala expects to receive $1000/ton, the time 0 expectation for the future foreign currency operating revenue stream (in U.S. dollars) is $R^0_\$ = \$1,000,000$ per year, and the expected base currency (Australian dollar) operating revenue stream is

$$R^0 = \$1,000,000/(1\ \$/A\$) = A\$1,000,000 \text{ per year}$$

UNILATERAL CHANGE IN THE VALUE OF THE AUSTRALIAN DOLLAR

Now consider the case where the currency markets experience a *unilateral change in the value of the Australian dollar*, relative to all other currencies, in the form of a 20% depreciation to 0.80 $/A$ and 1.25 A$/ECU, and thus, the $/ECU exchange rate remains at 1 $/ECU. This situation would imply a 25% appreciation of the ECU (and the U.S. dollar) relative to the Australian dollar. If this unilateral Australian dollar move occurred, the expected foreign currency operating revenues (in U.S. dollars) would be unchanged, since the stability of the $/ECU exchange rate would imply no demand changes by the Europeans. However, the conversion exposure to the A$/$ exchange rate would imply that the new expected base currency operating revenues would be $1,000,000/(0.80 \$/A\$) = A\$1,250,000$, an increase of 25%. This change is due entirely to the conversion exposure of the base currency operating revenues to changes in the A\$/\$ exchange rate. See panel A of Figure 13-2.

UNILATERAL CHANGE IN THE VALUE OF THE U.S. DOLLAR

Now suppose that instead of the unilateral move in the Australian dollar, both the ECU and the Australian dollar depreciate by 20% relative to the U.S. dollar, a *unilateral change in the value of the U.S. dollar* relative to the other currencies. The new exchange rates are $X^1_{\$/A\$} = 0.80\ \$/A\$$, $X^1_{\$/ECU} = 0.80\ \$/ECU$, and $X^1_{A\$/ECU}$ remains the same at 1 A\$/ECU. In this case, the A\$/\$ exchange

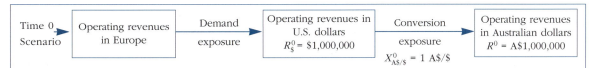

Time 0 Scenario → | Operating revenues in Europe | — Demand exposure → | Operating revenues in U.S. dollars $R^0_\$ = \$1,000,000$ | — Conversion exposure $X^0_{A\$/\$} = 1\ A\$/\$$ → | Operating revenues in Australian dollars $R^0 = A\$1,000,000$ |

A. Illustration of Unilateral Change in the Value of the Australian Dollar
 • Australian dollar depreciates by 20% relative to the U.S. dollar and the ECU.
 • The \$/ECU exchange rate does not change.
 • U.S. dollar appreciates by 25% relative to the Australian dollar (Siegel's paradox).

| Operating revenues in Europe | $\%\Delta X_{\$/ECU} = 0$ $\beta^{\$/ECU}_R = 0.60$ | $R^1_\$ = \$1,000,000$ | $\%\Delta X_{A\$/\$} = 0.25$ $\beta^\$_R = 1$ | $R^1 = A\$1,250,000$ |

$$\%\Delta R = [1 + 0.60(0)][1 + 1(0.25)] - 1 = 0.25$$

B. Illustration of Unilateral Change in the Value of the U.S. Dollar
 • U.S. dollar appreciates by 25% relative to the Australian dollar and the ECU.
 • ECU depreciates by 20% relative to the U.S. dollar (Siegel's paradox).

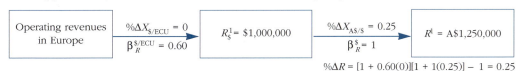

| Operating revenues in Europe | $\%\Delta X_{\$/ECU} = -0.20$ $\beta^{\$/ECU}_R = 0.60$ | $R^1_\$ = \$880,000$ | $\%\Delta X_{A\$/\$} = 0.25$ $\beta^\$_R = 1$ | $R^1 = A\$1,100,000$ |

$$\%\Delta R = [1 + 0.60(-0.20)][1 + 1(0.25)] - 1 = 0.10$$

C. Nonunilateral Currency Moves (Example 13-2)
 • ECU appreciates by 20% relative to the U.S. dollar.
 • U.S. dollar depreciates by 5% relative to the Australian dollar.

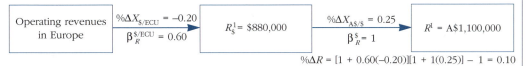
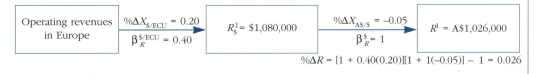

| Operating revenues in Europe | $\%\Delta X_{\$/ECU} = 0.20$ $\beta^{\$/ECU}_R = 0.40$ | $R^1_\$ = \$1,080,000$ | $\%\Delta X_{A\$/\$} = -0.05$ $\beta^\$_R = 1$ | $R^1 = A\$1,026,000$ |

$$\%\Delta R = [1 + 0.40(0.20)][1 + 1(-0.05)] - 1 = 0.026$$

FIGURE 13-2   Multicurrency Compound Exposure "Koala Mining Co." (Australia)

rate has taken the same time 1 value as it would in the case of the unilateral move in the Australian dollar. However, given a stable U.S. dollar price of $1000/ton, the new ECU sales price charged to the Europeans is ($1000/ton)/(0.80 $/ECU) = ECU1250/ton, as a result of the change in the $/ECU exchange rate.

Assume that the price increase in ECUs causes the expected European demand to fall to 880 tons. Thus, Koala's new expected foreign currency operating revenues (in U.S. dollars) are $R_\$^1$ = ($1000/ton)(880 tons) = $880,000 per year.

Since the expected U.S. dollar–denominated operating revenues drop by 12% in response to a 20% depreciation of the ECU relative to the dollar, the operating revenue exposure of the dollar-denominated operating revenues to the ECU is 0.12/0.20 = 0.60. We need a symbol for this exposure, and "β_R^{ECU}" will *not* work, since it would notationally represent, in our context here, the exposure of the expected base currency (i.e., Australian dollars) operating revenues to the A$/ECU exchange rate. Thus, instead we employ the notation $\beta_R^{\$/ECU}$ to represent the exposure of the U.S. dollar revenues to the $/ECU exchange rate.

The new expected base currency (Australian dollars) operating revenues are R^1 = $R_\$^1(X_{A\$/\$}^1)$ = $880,000/(0.80 $/A$) = A$1,100,000. The change in the expected base currency operating revenues, from R^0 = A$1,000,000, is due to two exposures: a demand exposure (to the $/ECU) exchange rate and a conversion exposure (to the A$/$ exchange rate.) See panel B of Figure 13-2.

Note, however, that Koala Mining's exposure *cannot* be measured simply in terms of changes in the A$/ECU exchange rate. In the case of a unilateral U.S. dollar move, we saw that the expected base currency operating revenues increase even though the A$/ECU exchange rate did not change. Thus, Koala's exposure problem cannot be described as an exposure of its base currency operating revenues to the A$/ECU exchange rate. Thus, Koala's exposure problem must be measured in terms of two exchange rates, the $/ECU exchange rate (for the demand exposure) and the A$/$ exchange rate (for the conversion exposure). However, the multicurrency exposure is not linearly additive.[4]

---

[4]To see that the exposure is not linearly additive, suppose we hypothesize a linear relationship, letting the expected base currency operating revenues have an exposure of 0.60 to changes in the $/ECU exchange rate and a conversion exposure of 1 to changes in the A$/$ exchange rate. Specifically, suppose we tried to employ these exposures by specifying %ΔR = 0.60(%Δ$X_{\$/ECU}$) + 1(%Δ$X_{A\$/\$}$). For the unilateral appreciation of the U.S. dollar by 25%, %Δ$X_{\$/ECU}$ = −0.20 and %Δ$X_{A\$/\$}$ = 0.25; thus, %ΔR would be calculated by the hypothesized linear relation as 0.60(−0.20) + 1(0.25) = −0.12 + 0.25 = 0.13. This result cannot correctly describe the situation here, since it does not reconcile with the 10% increase already found in the scenario for the unilateral U.S. dollar move.

COMPOUND EXPOSURE

The reason that the linear relationship does not apply to this currency exposure problem is that the situation is a *compound exposure*, where the U.S. dollar–denominated foreign currency operating revenues are exposed to changes in the $/ECU exchange rate, an exposure that is compounded into the conversion exposure of the base currency operating revenues to the A$/$ exchange rate.

It turns out that the percentage change in Koala's expected base currency operating revenues can be written in the following compound formulation as

$$\%\Delta R = [1 + \beta_R^{\$/\text{ECU}}(\%\Delta X_{\$/\text{ECU}})][1 + \beta_R^{\$}(\%\Delta X_{\text{A\$}/\$})] - 1 \qquad (13\text{-}4)$$

where $\beta_R^{\$/\text{ECU}}$ denotes the exposure of the U.S. dollar operating revenues to changes in the $/ECU exchange rate and $\beta_R^{\$}$ is the exposure of the base currency (Australian dollar) operating revenues to changes in the A$/$ exchange rate.

In the hypothetical Koala Mining example, $\beta_R^{\$/\text{ECU}}$ is 0.60 and $\beta_R^{\$}$ is 1. Thus, when the U.S. dollar move is unilateral, where the ECU depreciates by 20% relative to the U.S. dollar and the U.S. dollar appreciates by 25% relative to the Australian dollar, the percentage change in the expected base currency operating revenues is $\%\Delta R = [1 + 0.60(-0.20)][1 + 1(0.25)] - 1 = (0.88)(1.25) - 1 = 0.10$, or an increase of 10%, as was found earlier. See panel B of Figure 13-2.

When the Australian dollar move is unilateral, where the ECU is unchanged relative to the U.S. dollar and the U.S. dollar appreciates by 25% relative to the Australian dollar, the percentage change in the expected base currency operating revenues is $\%\Delta R = [1 + 0.60(0)][1 + 1(0.25)] - 1 = (1.00)(1.25) - 1 = 0.25$, or an increase of 25%, as was found earlier. See panel A of Figure 13-2. Thus, we see that the compound exposure measurement does describe the situation for the extreme cases involving unilateral currency changes. The following additional example addresses the case of nonunilateral currency moves and also provides some further analysis of the underlying fundamentals.

In the case of Western Mining Co., where all operating costs are denominated in the base currency and thus where $\beta_C = 0$, the percentage change in the expected operating cash flows is related to the percentage change in the operating revenues by the simple relationship $\%\Delta O = \%\Delta R(R^0/O^0)$. Thus, extending Example 13-2, if Koala's time 0 expected operating cash flow margin had been 25%, then the percentage change in the expected base currency operating cash flows in the scenario would have been $\%\Delta O = 0.026(1/0.25) = 1.04$, or 104%.

In reality, Western Mining Co. had sales elsewhere than in Europe. In particular, sales were also in the United States and Canada. Thus, a complete

EXAMPLE 13-2

Find the percentage change in Koala's expected base currency operating revenues, assuming that the U.S. dollar operating revenues have an exposure of 0.40 to the ECU, that the ECU appreciates by 20% relative to the U.S. dollar, and that the U.S. dollar depreciates by 5% relative to the Australian dollar. Given a time 0 exchange rate of 1 A$/$ and a time 0 expected future U.S. dollar operating revenues of $1,000,000 per year, find the time 0 expected base currency operating revenues and the time 1 expected base currency operating revenues. Show that the percentage change in the expected base currency operating revenues reconciles with the computed value for %ΔR from the application of equation (13-4).

Solution 13-2 Using the compound exposure measurement formulation, the computed %ΔR from equation (13-4) would be

$$\%\Delta R = [1 + 0.40(0.20)][1 + 1(-0.05)] - 1 = (1.08)(0.95) - 1 = 0.026$$

Thus, the percentage change in the expected base currency operating revenues should be 2.6%.

To see this result in the form of fundamental details, given time 0 expected future U.S. dollar operating revenues of $1,000,000 per year, note first that the time 1 expected future U.S. dollar operating revenues are 8% higher, given the exposure to the ECU of $\beta_R^{\$/ECU} = 0.40$ and the 20% appreciation of the ECU relative to the U.S. dollar. Thus, $R_\$^1 = \$1,080,000$ per year. Given a time 0 value for $X_{A\$/\$}^0$ of 1 A$/$ and a 5% depreciation of the U.S. dollar relative to the Australian dollar, the time 1 exchange rate is $X_{A\$/\$}^1 = 0.95$ A$/$, and the time 1 expected base currency operating revenues are $R^1 = \$1,080,000(0.95$ A$/$) = A\$1,026,000 per year, 2.6% higher than the time 0 expected base currency operating revenues of A$1,000,000.

analysis would have segmented the operating revenues by market currency. The U.S. operating revenues would be analyzed as having simple conversion exposure to the A$/$ exchange rate, while the European and Canadian portions would be analyzed with an equation for compound exposure, similar to the one just used, using the ECU and the Canadian dollar as the foreign currencies, respectively.

Equity Exposure and Universal Hedging

Often one will see regression analyses where realized stock returns are regressed against percentage changes in one or more exchange rates. Such procedures are similar to the ones discussed earlier, except that stock returns are used in lieu of percentage changes in operating cash flows. The resultant coefficients from the stock return regressions are estimates of a firm's *equity exposures* to exchange rate changes.

*T*HE COMPOUND EXPOSURE OF GEORGE WESTON, LTD. (CANADA)

Consider the compound exposure situation of George Weston Ltd., a Canadian firm that produces paper goods (among other products). The prices for paper products are known to be tied to the value of the Swedish krone, due to the preeminence of Swedish paper companies in the global marketplace. In other words, the Swedish krone is the predominant currency of determination for paper products. Consider George Weston's sale of paper products in the United States. From George Weston's viewpoint, the U.S. dollar revenue stream is a foreign currency revenue stream that is exposed to the \$/SKr exchange rate. The Canadian dollar revenues thus have a compound exposure to the \$/SKr exchange rate and the C\$/\$ exchange rate.

HEDGE RATIOS AND MANAGING MULTICURRENCY EQUITY EXPOSURE WITH DERIVATIVES

Consider a firm whose base currency equity exposure can be expressed in the following regression equation form:

$$\%\Delta S = \beta_S^{\mathrm{DM}}(\%\Delta X_{\$/\mathrm{DM}}) + \beta_S^{\yen}(\%\Delta X_{\$/\yen}) \qquad (13\text{-}5)$$

where β_S^{DM} and $\beta_S^{\yen}$ are the firm's equity exposures to the mark and the yen, respectively, and the base currency for the firm is U.S. dollars. Assume that $\beta_S^{\mathrm{DM}} = 1.80$ and $\beta_S^{\yen} = -0.40$, so that $\%\Delta S = 1.80(\%\Delta X_{\$/\mathrm{DM}}) - 0.40(\%\Delta X_{\$/\yen})$.

Assume that the market value of the firm's equity is currently $S^0 = $10,000,000$. A strategy that may be employed to eliminate the equity exposure is to go short $1.80(\$10,000,000) = \$18,000,000$ worth of dollar-denominated currency forwards or swaps on marks, and to go long $0.40(\$10,000,000) = \$4,000,000$ worth of dollar-denominated currency forwards or swaps on yen. The regression coefficients, interpreted as equity exposures, dictate the amount of hedging to do with derivatives, and are often referred to as *hedge ratios.*[5]

The use of derivatives to manage equity exposures, of course, requires a credit decision on the part of the derivative position counterparty, which in many cases is a financial institution. If a firm's equity exposure to a currency is relatively large, say, $\beta_S = 5$, implying the need for a short derivative position on the foreign currency of 5 times the amount of the company's equity,

---

[5]The interpretation of regression coefficients as hedge ratios has a significant body of pertinent literature that is beyond our scope here. One advanced issue is the uncertainty in future equity values for reasons other than uncertainty in exchange rates. For a discussion of ideas pertaining to this issue, see J. Kerkvliet and M. H. Moffett, "The Hedging of an Uncertain Future Foreign Currency Cash Flow," *Journal of Financial and Quantitative Analysis*, December 1991, pp. 565–577.

the firm may or may not be granted the credit to take such a position. Of course, the swap counterparty may be most concerned with whether the firm can meet difference check payments, which is easier than the full exchange of cash flows. From this perspective, a firm may be creditworthy enough to support the difference check payments on swaps with relatively large notional principals.

An important consideration in hedging stock values with derivatives is the timing of future cash flows. As we know, the basis for a firm's equity exposure is the exposure of its expected stream of future operating cash flows. If the uncertainty in the firm's time 1 equity value is hedged with a lone single-period forward contract, with the idea in mind of reestablishing a similar position in each period, the gains/losses on the forward may offset the gains/losses on equity.

However, we already know from Chapter 10 that a problem occurs in financial reporting because the profits/losses on the hedging derivatives will have to be reported in the firm's financial statements, whereas the gains/losses on equity values do not. This situation makes the firm's reported earnings more volatile, as covered in Chapter 10. This problem would be solved if the underlying operating cash flow exposure could be simultaneously matched, which would be better accomplished with a long-dated currency swap or a *strip* of forward exchange contracts whose total position value equals β_S times the company's equity value.

What should Western Mining have done, given the compound nature of its multicurrency exposure, if it had wished to eliminate its equity exposure? Should Western Mining's strategy have included the issuance of ECU-denominated debt or a "basket" of debt in various European currencies? The answer to this question is "No." Such a strategy, like a short position on ECUs in Australian dollar–denominated forwards/swaps, would have served to hedge an exposure to the A\$/ECU exchange rate. As discussed previously, exposure to the A\$/ECU exchange rate was not part of Western Mining's exposure problem. Since Western Mining reported that it did issue such debt (along with some U.S. dollar debt), it is not likely that this approach correctly solved the company's exposure problem.

In light of the compound nature of Western Mining's exposure problem, the best strategy may be to approach the problem in a compound fashion. Consider, for example, the strategy of first hedging the dollar-denominated operating revenue stream against changes in the \$/ECU exchange rate. If this exposure is $\beta_R^{\$/ECU} = 0.60$, then consider a dollar-denominated currency swap position to pay ECUs, with as long a horizon as available and with a contract size geared so that the swap's cash flows match 60% of the firm's expected U.S. dollar–denominated operating revenues. This swap position is intended to eliminate the uncertainty in the future U.S. dollar–denominated operating revenues due to the demand exposure to the \$/ECU exchange rate. (This strategy implicitly assumes that the demand exposure of the U.S. dollar–denominated operating revenues is linear in the \$/ECU exchange rate.)

Once the future U.S. dollar–denominated operating revenues are stabilized to the greatest extent possible with a $/ECU currency swap position, attention may be turned to the conversion exposure of the base currency operating revenues to changes in the A$/$ exchange rate. As known from Chapter 9, if the operating exposure is less than 1, this exposure may be handled by issuing U.S. dollar–denominated debt. However, because Western Mining's operating costs do not appear to be exposed (to the U.S. dollar), the company's operating exposure may well be greater that 1, perhaps significantly so, as we reasoned earlier. The U.S. dollar debt would certainly reduce the equity exposure (to the A$/$ exchange rate) relative to what it would be with the same level of Australian dollar debt. However, we know from Chapter 9 that the financial leverage effect of the debt would magnify the relatively high operating exposure.

The magnification effect would be even greater with the company's actual capital structure strategy of issuing European currency debt than it would have been if all the debt had been denominated in U.S. dollars, since the European currency debt has no currency hedging effect for the A$/$ exchange rate, but does have the same financial leverage effect as if Australian dollar debt had been used. Given the magnified level for β_S that follows from this reasoning, the company may have to turn to relatively large Australian dollar-denominated short derivative positions on the U.S. dollar, to hedge its residual exposure to the conversion effects caused by changes in the A$/$ exchange rate.

EQUITY EXPOSURE OF BASE CURRENCY OWNERS IN MULTICURRENCY EQUITY

Do base currency stockholders obtain some diversification benefits from the distribution of corporate ownership across national boundaries and currencies? The answer is that while such distribution may have some benefits, the reduction of base currency equity exposure is *not* one of them.

To see this point, consider XYZ Co., a U.S. dollar–based company that has *no debt.* Assume that at first XYZ's share ownership is 100% dollar-based investors. Assume total firm value of $100,000,000, which is also the equity value. Assume 1,000,000 shares, so that each share is initially worth $100.

Now suppose that XYZ buys back 40% of its shares using the proceeds of an equity issue of DM80,000,000 in Germany and that the capital raised is exchanged into $40,000,000 at the assumed current spot exchange rate of $X^0_{DM/\$}$ = 2 DM/$. To keep the number of shares the same, XYZ issues 400,000 "German" shares at DM200 per share. This transaction is assumed to be made at time 0. After the transaction, the base currency owners have 60% of the firm's equity with a current value of $60,000,000, while the German owners have 40% of the firm's equity with a current market value of DM80,000,000, which is equivalent to $40,000,000.

Assume that the firm has an operating exposure to the mark of 1.50. Thus, the total value of the firm, in dollars, rises by 15% (to $115,000,000 at time 1) with a 10% appreciation of the mark. Since the dollar-based owners have 60% of the equity, their time 1 wealth is 0.60($115,000,000) = $69,000,000.

The equity of the dollar-based owners has changed by $69,000,000/$60,000,000 −1 = 0.15, or 15%. Thus, their equity exposure is 0.15/0.10 = 1.50, unchanged from before, despite the "diversification" to some mark-based ownership. The original owners may have reduced the amount of their capital that is exposed, but have not changed the degree of exposure of their equity capital that remains.

Thus, we have demonstrated by example the following point: The equity exposure of a firm's base currency owners is the same regardless of whether some of the firm's equity is held by owners with a different currency base. See panel A of Figure 13-3.

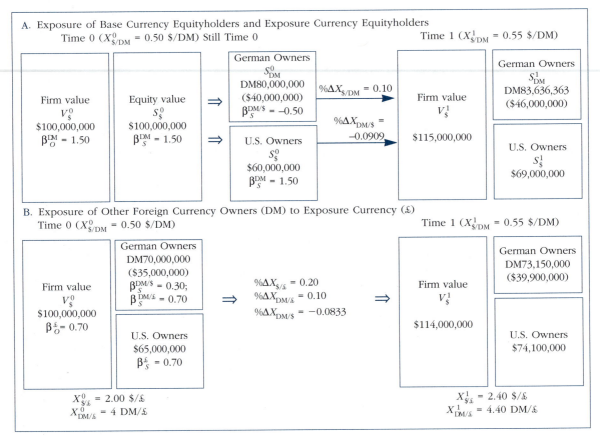

FIGURE 13-3 Exposures in Foreign Currency Equity Ownership

EXPOSURE OF FOREIGN CURRENCY EQUITY

The German shareholders start with a time 0 value of $40,000,000 or DM80,000,000. As the total value rises to $115,000,000 at time 1, their equity value rises (in dollars) to 0.40($115,000,000) = $46,000,000. Given the 10% appreciation of the mark, the time 1 exchange rate is $X^1_{DM/\$}$ = 1/{1.10[1/(2 DM/$)]} = 1/(0.55 $/DM) = 1.818 DM/$. Thus, the dollar value of the German holdings, $46,000,000, is worth in marks $46,000,000(1.818 DM/$) = DM83,636,363 (due to a rounding discrepancy here). Thus, the Germans gain DM363,636, or 4.545%, for a percentage change in the value of the dollar of (1.818 DM/$)/(2 DM/$) − 1 = −0.0909, or a 9.09% depreciation of the dollar. Thus, the Germans have experienced an equity exposure of $\beta^{DM/\$}_S$ = 4.545/(−9.09) = −0.50, where $\beta^{DM/\$}_S$ denotes the exposure of mark-based investors to changes in the value of the dollar. See panel A of Figure 13-3.

In both the text example for XYZ Co. and Example 13-3, the mark-based equity investors have an exposure of −0.50. This numerical result suggests that the percentage of ownership that is foreign has no bearing on the exposure of the foreign owners.

What does determine the exposure of the foreign owners, given the equity exposure of the base currency owners? In the case where the foreign owners' currency is the currency to which the base currency owners are exposed, it turns out that the exposures of the base currency owners and the foreign currency owners must sum to 1. Of course, the previous examples bear this point out, since 1.50 + (−0.50) = 1. Let's see if this works for another example.

Let $\beta^{\$/£}_S$ be notation for the equity exposure (the subscript S) of a dollar-

---

EXAMPLE 13-3

What if XYZ had sold only 30% of the shares. What would be the base currency shareholders' new equity exposure? Find the German investors' equity exposure assuming the mark appreciates by 20%.

Solution 13-3   The first question is sort of a trick question. The answer is 1.50, since we have already established that the base currency investors' equity exposure is the same regardless of the currency makeup of the other shareholders.

If the mark appreciates by 20%, the new exchange rate is 1.667 DM/$, and thus the dollar changes by (1.667 DM/$)/(2 DM/$) − 1 = −0.1667, or −16.67%. Since 30% of the equity is sold to Germans, they have 300 shares, worth an initial value of DM60,000,000. The time 1 dollar value of the German holdings would be $30,000,000(1.30) = $39,000,000, which in marks would be worth $39,000,000(1.667 DM/$) = DM65,000,000. Thus, the Germans' value would have increased by DM65,000,000/DM60,000,000 − 1 = 0.08333, or 8.333%. Since this change corresponds to a dollar depreciation of 16.67%, we again find that the Germans' equity exposure is −0.50.

EXAMPLE 13-4

ABC Co. is a dollar-based company, with time 0 equity of $S^0 = \$100{,}000{,}000$, that has an exposure to the British pound of $\beta_S^{\$/\pounds} = 0.70$. At time 0 ABC sells 35% of the equity to pound-based investors. What is the exposure of the British investors to the dollar?

Solution 13-4   If the exposure of the British investors is 1 minus the exposure of the base currency owners, then $\beta_S^{\pounds/\$} = 1 - 0.70 = 0.30$. Let's demonstrate this in detail. Consider an initial exchange rate of 2.00 \$/\pounds (= 0.50 \pounds/\$). Thus, the pound investors' initial investment is $0.35(\$100{,}000{,}000)(0.50 \text{ \pounds/\$}) = \pounds 17{,}500{,}000$. Assume that the pound appreciates by 20% to $X_{\$/\pounds}^1 = 2.40$ \$/\pounds (equivalent to 0.41667 \pounds/\$). Thus, the dollar changes by (0.41667 \pounds/\$)/(0.50 \pounds/\$) − 1 = −0.1667, a depreciation of 16.67%. The dollar equity value rises to $S^1 = \$100{,}000{,}000(1 + 0.70(0.20)) = \$114{,}000{,}000$, of which $0.35(\$114{,}000{,}000) = \$39{,}900{,}000$ belongs to pound-based owners and is worth $\$39{,}900{,}000(0.41667 \text{ \pounds/\$}) = \pounds 16{,}625{,}000$. The pound-based investors' value undergoes a percentage change of $\pounds 16{,}625{,}000/\pounds 17{,}500{,}000 - 1 = -0.05$. Thus, since we've found that the pound-based equity exposure at time 0 is $(-0.05)/(-0.1667) = 0.30$, it is indeed the case that the base currency exposure (0.70) and the pound-based exposure (0.30) sum to 1.

based investor to changes in the value of the pound from the viewpoint of the exchange rate in direct terms with the dollar as the base currency (i.e., \$/\pounds). Let $\beta_S^{\pounds/\$}$ be notation for the equity exposure of a sterling-based investor to changes in the value of the dollar from the viewpoint of the exchange rate in direct terms with the pound as the base currency (i.e., \pounds/\$).

In Example 13-4, where there has been exposure to only one exchange rate, and owners are from the only two countries involved in that exchange rate, we have the relatively simple relationship that $\beta_S^{\$/\pounds} = 1 - \beta_S^{\pounds/\$}$. However, this relationship is a special case of a more general one that we continue to develop.

EXPOSURE OF OTHER FOREIGN CURRENCY OWNERS TO EXPOSURE CURRENCY

What would be the currency exposure of ABC Co.'s foreign investors in Example 13-4 if at time 0 the 35% of its equity were sold instead to mark-based investors, even though ABC's base currency exposure is to the value of the pound relative to the dollar? On one hand, if the value of the pound rises relative to the dollar, and the DM/\$ exchange rate is unchanged, the mark-based investors benefit. But, on the other hand, if the dollar depreciates relative to the mark, this change works against the mark-based investors.

It turns out that the mark-based investors have a *multiple* equity exposure: (1) 0.30 to changes in the value of the dollar relative to the mark and (2) 0.70 to changes in the value of the pound relative to the mark. To see this result, let's work through an extended example. Assume that the DM/\$ exchange rate

Universal hedging is one of the many new developments that will continue to characterize the field of global financial management.

initially is $X^0_{DM/\$} = 2$ DM/\$, so that the initial DM/£ exchange rate is $X^0_{DM/£} =$ (2 DM/\$)(2 \$/£) = 4 DM/£. The initial *mark* value of the German investors' equity is 0.35(\$100,000,000)(2 DM/\$) = DM70,000,000.

If the pound appreciates by 20% relative to the dollar, the dollar value of the Germans' equity is \$39,900,000, as shown in Solution 13-4. If the value of the dollar stays the same relative to the mark, the Germans' equity is worth DM79,800,000. The time 1 DM/£ exchange rate is $X^1_{DM/£} = (2 \text{ DM/\$})(2.40 \text{ \$/£})$ = 4.8 DM/£, representing a 20% appreciation of the pound relative to the mark. And the equity exposure to the value of the pound in terms of the mark is thus 0.14/0.20 = 0.70.

What if the pound-mark exchange rate stays the same, such that $X^1_{DM/£} =$ 4 DM/£? Then, the time 1 DM/\$ exchange rate must be $X^1_{DM/\$} = (4 \text{ DM/£})/$ (2.40 \$/£) = 1.667 DM/\$, a 16.67% depreciation of the dollar relative to the mark. Thus, the \$39,900,000 equity value is worth only DM66,500,000, representing a loss of 5%. Thus, the time 0 exposure to the DM/\$ exchange rate is (−0.05)/(−0.1667) = 0.30.

If the pound appreciates by 20% relative to the dollar and by only 10% relative to the mark, is the percentage change in the mark-based equity consistent with the following linear model: $0.30(\%\Delta X_{DM/\$}) + 0.70(\%\Delta X_{DM/\pounds})$? Let's see. If the pound appreciates by 10% to the mark, the new DM/£ exchange rate is $X^1_{DM/\pounds} = 1.10(4\ DM/\pounds) = 4.40\ DM/\pounds$. Thus, the new DM/$ exchange rate is $X^1_{DM/\$} = (4.40\ DM/\pounds)/(2.40\ \$/\pounds) = 1.833\ DM/\$$, representing an 8.33% depreciation of the dollar relative to the mark.

If the linear formulation of the mark-based equity exposure is correct, then the equity value should change by $0.30(-0.0833) + 0.70(0.10) = 0.045$, or increase by 4.5%. Let's see. The dollar equity value is $39,900,000, which is worth $39,900,000(1.833 DM/$) = DM73,150,000 to the mark-based owners (due to rounding discrepancy here). The percentage change for the mark-based owners is indeed $DM73,150,000/DM70,000,000 - 1 = 0.045$, or 4.5%. This numerical example is depicted in panel B of Figure 13-3.

Thus, we see in this numerical example that if equity is owned by investors in foreign currencies other than the firm's equity exposure currency, those owners' exposure to the exposure currency is the same as that of the base currency owners. This exposure is 0.70 in our example. At the same time, their exposure to the base currency is the same as that of the exposure currency owners (if there are any). This exposure is 0.30 in our example.

GENERAL MULTICURRENCY EXPOSURE RELATIONSHIPS

The numerical findings are a special case of a more general specification, which we now state. To avoid too much symbolism, let us just express the generalization using four currencies, the dollar ($), the pound (£), the yen (¥), and the mark (DM). Assume that a stock's return, its percentage change in value ($\%\Delta S$), may be written in the following regression form from the point of view of the dollar as the base currency:

$$\%\Delta S_\$ = \beta_S^{\$/\pounds}(\%\Delta X_{\$/\pounds}) + \beta_S^{\$/¥}(\%\Delta X_{\$/¥}) + \beta_S^{\$/DM}(\%\Delta X_{\$/DM}) \quad (13\text{-}5)$$

Now consider an analogous regression from any foreign currency point of view. For example, a British investor's regression equation for the change in the value of his shares, incorporating the change in the $/£ exchange rate, is shown in equation (13-6).

$$\%\Delta S_\pounds = \beta_S^{\pounds/\$}(\%\Delta X_{\pounds/\$}) + \beta_S^{\pounds/¥}(\%\Delta X_{\pounds/¥}) + \beta_S^{\pounds/DM}(\%\Delta X_{\pounds/DM}) \quad (13\text{-}6)$$

Note that in equation (13-6) the exposures and the exchange rates are expressed from the point of view of the pound as the base currency. (The dollar is the base currency of the firm, but the pound is the base currency of the British owners.)

The relationship between the coefficients in the two regressions follow two key propositions:[6]

Proposition 1

In the foreign investors' regression model, for currencies that are also foreign to the base currency owners, the exposures are the same as those of the base currency owners.

Proposition 2

The exposure of the foreign investor to the base currency should be 1 minus the sum of the exposures in the base currency regression.

For example, assume that the dollar (base currency) owners of a firm face the following regression formulation

$$\%\Delta S_{\$} = 1.2(\%\Delta X_{\$/£}) - 0.30(\%\Delta X_{\$/¥}) + 0.45(\%\Delta X_{\$/DM})$$

This example formulation suggests that, after considering debt financing, especially foreign currency debt financing, the dollar-based owners have positive equity exposures to the pound and the mark and a negative equity exposure to the yen.

Then, for a British equityholder, Proposition 1 indicates that the corresponding regression would have $\beta_S^{£/¥} = -0.30$ and $\beta_S^{£/DM} = 0.45$. Proposition 2 indicates that $\beta_S^{£/\$} = 1 - (1.2 - 0.30 + 0.45) = 1 - 1.35 = -0.35$. Thus, the British owner's regression equation should be

$$\%\Delta S_{£} = -0.35(\%\Delta X_{£/\$}) - 0.30(\%\Delta X_{£/¥}) + 0.45(\%\Delta X_{£/DM})$$

Figure 13-4 summarizes this example and that of Example 13-5.

UNIVERSAL HEDGING

Because of the relationship between the exposures in the regressions from the viewpoints of the different foreign investors, there exists a result that allows a firm to hedge equity exposure in a manner that eliminates the exposure of all equityholders "universally," regardless of currency base.[7]

For example, reconsider the case discussed earlier where the dollar (base currency) owners of a firm face the following regression formulation $\%\Delta S_{\$} =$

---

[6]The results are adapted from in Michael Adler and Philippe Jorion, "Universal Currency Hedges for Global Portfolios," *Journal of Portfolio Management*, Summer 1992, pp. 28–35.

[7]The discussion in this section is based on results in Adler and Jorion, "Universal Currency Hedges for Global Portfolios."

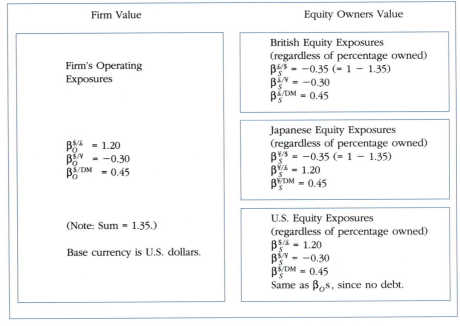

FIGURE 13-4 Example of General Multicurrency Exposure Relationships

$1.2(\%\Delta X_{\$/\pounds}) - 0.30(\%\Delta X_{\$/\yen}) + 0.45(\%\Delta X_{\$/DM})$. Assume that the company has $100,000,000 in total equity outstanding. To hedge the base currency equity values, the company takes the following positions in dollar-denominated forward or swap positions: go short pounds in the amount of $1.2(\$100,000,000)$ = $120,000,000, go long yen in the amount of $30,000,000, and go short marks in the amount of $45,000,000.

This strategy is "universal" in that it hedges sterling investors from any exposure to the yen and the mark, yen investors from any exposure to the pound and the mark, and mark investors from any exposure to the pound and

---

■ EXAMPLE 13-5

What would the regression equation for a Japanese owner of the example firm just discussed in the text?

Solution 13-5 Proposition 1 indicates that $\beta_S^{\yen/\pounds} = 1.20$ and $\beta_S^{\yen/DM} = 0.45$. Proposition 2 indicates that $\beta_S^{\yen/\$} = 1 - (1.2 - 0.30 + 0.45) = 1 - 1.35 = -0.35$. Thus, the Japanese owner's regression equation should be $\%\Delta S_\yen = -0.35(\%\Delta X_{\yen/\$}) + 1.20(\%\Delta X_{\yen/\pounds}) + 0.45(\%\Delta X_{\yen/DM})$.

> ### ☐ EXAMPLE 13-6
>
> If the 30% of the equity in Example 13-3 were owned by yen-based investors, instead of mark-based investors, even though the base currency owners have the exposure of 1.50 to the mark, what would be the currency exposure structure of the yen owners? Let the dollar appreciate by 20% to the mark and by 10% to the yen; what should be the percentage change in the yen owners' equity value? Assume that the ¥/$ exchange rate is initially $X^0_{¥/\$} = 100$ ¥/$, making the initial ¥/DM exchange rate equal to $X^0_{¥/DM} = (100$ ¥/$)/(2 DM/$) = 50 ¥/DM. The initial yen investment is $30,000,000(100 ¥/$) = ¥3,000,000,000.
>
> *Solution 13-6* The yen owners would have an exposure to the mark (valued in terms of the yen) of 1.50 and an exposure to the dollar (valued in terms of the yen) of −0.50. The new exchange rates are $X^1_{DM/\$} = 2.40$ DM/$, $X^1_{¥/\$} = 110$ ¥/$, and $X^1_{¥/DM} = (110$ ¥/$)/(2.40 DM/$) = 45.833 ¥/DM. The mark changes relative to the yen by (45.833 ¥/DM)/(50 ¥/DM) − 1 = −0.0833, or −8.33%. The percentage change in the yen owners' equity value should be 1.50(−0.0833) − 0.50(0.10) = −0.175, or −17.5%.
>
> Since the mark depreciates by 16.67% relative to the dollar, the dollar value of the yen ownership, given that the 1.50 exposure to the dollar value of the mark is $30,000,000(1 + 1.50(−0.1667)) = $22,500,000. The yen value at time 1 is $22,500,000(110 ¥/$) = ¥2,475,000,000. Thus, the change in the yen owners' equity value is ¥2,475,000,000/¥3,000,000,000 − 1 = −0.175, or −17.5%.

the yen. All that the foreign investors need to do is to cover their conversion exposure vis-à-vis the dollar. For example, if the British investors own 20% of the company's equity, $20,000,000, then the British investors can hedge this currency exposure, if they want to, by taking a pound-denominated short forward exchange position on dollars in the amount of their $20,000,000 investment.

▌ Summary

This chapter has introduced some topics in multicurrency exposure. The first part of the chapter shows how regression coefficients in multiple regression analyses relate to the currency exposure concept that was fundamentally developed in prior chapters. Compound exposure was also discussed and is another form of multicurrency exposure, but one that does not lend itself to regression analysis.

The use of regression coefficients in the management of equity exposure was covered. Also covered were some results on the equity currency exposure of foreign owners and the notion of universal hedging.

Glossary

Compound Exposure: A form of multicurrency exposure where the exposures affect the firm in a multiplicative, or compound, fashion, rather than in an additive, or linear, fashion.

Hedge Ratio: The percentage of an asset's value that should be hedged to minimize the exposure. The hedge ratio is equal to the asset's unhedged exposure, often measured as a regression coefficient.

Simultaneous Multicurrency Exposure: The case where a single operating revenue or cost stream is independently influenced by more than one currency at the same time.

Unilateral Change in the Value of a Currency: A situation where the value of a currency changes by the same percentage relative to all other currencies, leaving the exchange rates between the other currencies unchanged.

Universal Hedging: The property that the same exposure hedging strategy can be used to manage the currency exposure of all of a firm's equityholders, regardless of their currency base.

Discussion Questions

1. Can you think of any other examples of compound multicurrency exposure?

2. Try to explain in words the implications of universal hedging, without looking at the book.

Problems

1. Your firm is based in the United States and the base currency is U.S. dollars. Sales in the U.S. account for 60% of your expected annual operating cash flows; the U.S. operating revenues are subject to exposure of 0.35 to the yen, due to Japanese competition. Your firm also exports products to England, where the pound is 80% of the currency of determination and the other 20% is the dollar. There is no demand exposure for the sales in England. The expected operating cash flows from the exports to England account for the other

---

1. (a) $\%\Delta O = -0.06(\%\Delta X_{\$/\yen}) + 1.28(\%\Delta X_{\$/\pounds}) - 0.60(\%\Delta X_{\$/DM})$. (b) $\%\Delta O = 5.16\%$. (c) The new expected base currency operating cash flow stream is $262,900 per year.

40% of the firm's expected operating revenues. Assume an operating cash flow margin of 25%.

Assume that the company's raw materials are imported from Japan and Germany. The yen and the mark are the currencies of determination of the imported raw materials, respectively. The yen-based raw materials comprise 30% of the expected base currency operating costs, while the mark-based raw materials comprise 20% of the expected base currency operating costs. The rest of operating costs consist of labor costs, in U.S. dollars.

(a) Develop a multicurrency expression for the percentage change in the company's expected base currency operating cash flows. (b) If, relative to the dollar, the mark appreciates by 5%, the yen depreciates by 8%, and the pound appreciates by 6%, what is the net percentage effect on the company's expected base currency operating cash flows? (c) Assume that the time 0 expected future base currency operating revenues are $1,000,000 per year, find the firm's time 0 and time 1 expected future stream of operating cash flows and demonstrate that the percentage difference reconciles with your answer in (b).

2.   Consider the hypothetical assumptions for the Finning scenario in the text. Assume that the time 0 expected base currency operating revenues are C$1,000,000 per year. If the yen depreciates by 20% relative to the Canadian dollar, while the U.S. dollar appreciates by 10% relative to the Canadian dollar, what is the new expected base currency operating cash flow stream?

3.   Consider the hypothetical assumptions for the Koala Mining Co. scenario in the text. Recall that $\beta_R^{\$/\text{ECU}} = 0.60$ and $\beta_R^{\$} = 1$. For an expected operating cash flow margin of 12.5%, find the percentage change in the company's expected base currency operating cash flows if the ECU depreciates by 12% relative to the U.S. dollar and the U.S. dollar depreciates by 5% relative to the Australian dollar.

4.   Assume that ABC Co. is a U.S.-dollar based company that has an operating exposure of 2.80 to the German mark. Assume that ABC has issued foreign currency debt denominated in Japanese yen. The yen debt constitutes 30% of the firm's capital structure in market value terms. The rest of the firm's capital is base currency equity. Express the firm's equity exposure as a multicurrency regression relationship.

5.   A Japanese company has base currency equity exposure of 3 to the value of the mark in terms of the yen. The Japanese company sells 25% of its eq-

---

2.   The new expected future base currency operating cash flows would be C$180,000 per year.

3. $\%\Delta R = -0.1144$; The expected base currency operating cash flows would decrease by 91.52%, almost enough to put the company into the red.

4. $\%\Delta S = 4(\%\Delta X_{\$/\text{DM}}) - 0.43(\%\Delta X_{\$/\text{¥}}) + e.$

5.   3.

uity to mark-based investors. What is the new equity exposure of the remaining Japanese shares?

6. In the preceding problem, what is the exposure of the mark-based investors to the value of the yen in terms of the mark?

7. Assume that NOP Co. is a Swiss company with the majority of its ownership having base currency of Swiss francs. the base currency equity has an exposure of 1.25 to changes in the value of the dollar relative to the Swiss franc. If the company has Japanese investors, what is the currency exposure of the Japanese equity owners?

6. −2.

7. The yen owners should have an exposure to the dollar (valued in terms of the yen) of 1.25 and an exposure to the Swiss franc (valued in terms of the yen) of −0.25.

INDEX